THE ARAB-ISRAELI CONFLICT TRANSFORMED

SUNY SERIES IN GLOBAL POLITICS

James N. Rosenau
editor

THE ARAB-ISRAELI CONFLICT TRANSFORMED

Fifty Years of Interstate and Ethnic Crises

HEMDA BEN-YEHUDA

and

SHMUEL SANDLER

STATE UNIVERSITY OF NEW YORK PRESS

Published by

STATE UNIVERSITY OF NEW YORK PRESS, ALBANY

© 2002 State University of New York

All rights reserved

Printed in the United States of America

For information, address
State University of New York Press,
90 State Street, Suite 700, Albany, NY 12207

Production, Laurie Searl
Marketing, Patrick Durocher

Library of Congress Cataloging-in-Publication Data
Ben-Yehuda, Hemda, 1954,
    The Arab-Israeli conflict transformed : fifty years of interstate and ethnic crises /
Hemda Ben-Yehuda and Shmuel Sandler.
        p. cm.
    Includes bibliographical references and index.
    ISBN 0-7914-5245-X (alk. paper) — ISBN 0-7914-5246-8 (pb : alk. paper)
        1. Arab-Israeli conflict. 2. Ethnic conflict—Israel. 3. Israel—Ethnic relations. 4.
Jews—Israel—Identity. 5. Palestinian Arabs—Ethnic identity. I. Sandler, Shmuel. II. Title.

DS119.6 .B465 2002
956—dc21

                                                                                    2002017695

10   9   8   7   6   5   4   3   2   1

In loving memory of my parents
Dora and Ehud Ben-Yehuda,
and their devotion to the realization
of Eliezer Ben-Yehuda's dream:
The national revival of the Jewish people,
in their homeland, speaking their native tongue.

Hemda Ben-Yehuda

And to Sara Lainer,
a special lady
who also believed in the Jewish people and their language.

Shmuel Sandler

CONTENTS

LIST OF TABLES

PREFACE

As we write this in the winter of 2001, the Middle East is again suffering through a dangerous state of continued strife. It is our contention, however, that despite serious and sustained violent outbursts, the overall nature of the Arab-Israeli relationship has been changing over the last two decades. This study uses a theoretical framework and empirical evidence to support the perhaps surprising argument that the Arab-Israeli conflict has been winding down and changing from a predominantly interstate dispute into a Palestinian-Israeli ethnic-state struggle. Our theoretical analysis considers and then goes beyond the current debate within the International Relations (IR) field over the relative merits of the realist/neorealist versus the neoliberal-institutional approaches in explaining international order. In addition, we integrate the ethonational theoretical literature into our frame of analysis.

It is very difficult for two Israelis to write an objective book on the Middle East. Hence, we searched for what we believe is an unbiased source—the worldwide data-set drawn from Michael Brecher and Jonathan Wilkenfeld's International Crisis Behavior (ICB) project. Our contribution in identifying and explaining change in the Arab-Israeli conflict is the index of crisis magnitude (CMI), which measures the extent of change in crisis attributes. The CMI's three realms (context, process, and outcome) and its six indicators (gravity of threat; number of actors; superpower role; crisis management techniques; scope of violence; and termination) serve as our basis for illuminating change in crisis evolution and conflict dynamics, for a period of over fifty years.

Another theoretical contribution is the set of conditions that we suggest affect moderation in a protracted conflict. These conditions induce change from an anarchical system to one in which a security regime promotes order. We test these conditions along critical turning points in the evolution of the Arab-Israeli conflict. Subsequently, we analyze changes in the ethnic-state domain, the latter being the primary source for the continuing nontermination of the conflict.

The book is thematically divided into seven chapters. Chapter 1 presents the theoretical framework for all further analysis. Chapters 2–4 focus on the interstate dimension, while chapters 5 and 6 analyze the ethnic-state and interethnic dimensions of the conflict. Chapter 7 integrates the interstate and ethnic aspects and suggests directions for new research. To assist the reader we provide a glossary that outlines all the 26 crises in the Arab-Israeli conflict, at the end of the book.

It is never easy to write with certainty about a conflict as twisting and furious as the Arab-Israeli one. It is even more difficult to do so in the midst of milestone events, such as the Oslo peace process, on the one hand, or the Intifada 2000, on the other. Given that the Intifada 2000 is a prolonged crisis, we decided to end our analysis with the close of the century, on 31 December 2000. Without the benefit of hindsight, we can only strive to rationally understand the forces at work around us, and hope that the fruits of our work contribute to a better comprehension of this bitter dispute.

We thank our colleagues who responded to presentations of this work at different stages of completion at several International Studies Association annual conferences. Sustained contributions and assistance came from Michael Brecher, Jonathan Wilkenfeld, and Laura Zittrain Eisenberg, to whom we express our gratitude. The Sara and Simha Lainer Chair in Democracy and Civility provided material resources for which we thank the Lainer family. Despite this wise tutelage, however, the responsibility for any errors of fact or fancy lies with us alone.

Acronyms

CMI	Crisis Magnitude Index
CMT	Crisis Management Technique
CSBM	Confidence and Security Building Measures
CSCE	Conference on Security and Cooperation in Europe
DMZ	Demilitarized Military Zone
DOP	Declaration of Principles
EC	European Community
FLN	Front Liberation National
ICB	International Crisis Behavior
IDF	Israeli Defense Force
IR	International Relations
LIC	Low Intensity Conflict
MAC	Mixed Armistice Commission
NPT	Non-Proliferation Treaty
NRR	Normal Relations Range
NSA	Non-State Actor
PA	Palestinian Authority
PFLP	Popular Front for the Liberation of Palestine
PGM	Precise Guided Munitions
PLDC	Palestine Land Development Company
PLO	Palestine Liberation Organization
PNC	Palestine National Council
SLA	South Lebanese Army
UAR	United Arab Republic
UNEF	United Nations Emergency Force
UNIFIL	United Nations Interim Force in Lebanon

CHAPTER 1

THEORETICAL APPROACHES TO CONFLICT AND ORDER IN INTERNATIONAL POLITICS

Since the late 1970s, students of international relations have been caught up in the debate between the realist/neorealist schools, on the one hand, and the neoliberal-institutional approach on the other.[1] To some extent the roots of this debate can be traced back to the traditional contest between political idealism and realism, or between the role of norms and power in state behavior. The debate in the last quarter of the twentieth century has concentrated on the tension between the postures of anarchy and order, conflict and stability, in world politics. What is the dominant principle in international relations? Is it the anarchical nature of the international system predominant in many parts of the world, resulting, as the neorealists contend, in cycles of conflict and an ongoing search for security? Or is international institutionalism, currently prevailing in the more developed parts of the globe, the wave of the future, as the nonrealists assert? Can institutionalism common in international economics replace the security dilemma in international politics?[2]

The maxims of realism now face a challenge from another direction. Along with the growing order in relations between states, we are also witnessing the emergence of ethnic conflict on a global scale. A large share of contemporary violence and disintegration in the world stems from ethnic conflicts both intrastate, such as within Northern Ireland and Canada, or with an interstate link, as in the ethnic confrontations in Afghanistan, Cyprus, Iraq, Lebanon, Turkey and the Kurds, and former Yugoslavia. The shift of conflict from the interstate realm to the intrastate domain calls for some amendment in realist contentions, while also challenging the institutionalist precepts.

Thus, the task of explaining change from anarchy to order in international relations must also include an ethnic theory.[3]

The core of our study focuses on the Arab-Israeli conflict as reflected in twenty-six international crises over the 1947–2000 period. Our study explores the relative merits of realism and institutionalism in explaining international phenomena and remains open to evidence supporting each. A priori we admit to a predilection for the realist school because of the subject matter; the dynamics of the Arab-Israeli conflict are more compatible with power politics. Similarly, by adopting international crisis as our conceptual framework and as the basis for our empirical research, we are obviously choosing a conflict-oriented approach. We do hope to explain, however, the appearance of international order and some institutionalism in a conflict-ridden region. Our realist disposition will be modulated, as previously noted, by an appreciation for the worldwide phenomenon of ethnic conflict, which has dogged the Arab-Israeli conflict since its inception. This study thus supplements classical international politics theory with its attention to both institutional and ethnic elements.[4]

In pursuing the interstate dimension we integrate concepts from both the realist and institutional schools of international relations. From the realist school we draw concepts of international interactions such as conflict, international crisis, balance of power, and deterrence. From the institutional school we derive cooperative concepts such as rules, regulations, and regimes. When we turn to the ethnic dimension we use terms such as ethnonational aspirations, civil wars, and interethnic crises. In our application of these approaches we also intend to probe their validity. By taking such a comprehensive perspective, this inquiry will not only provide a better understanding of the Middle East conflict but will also produce theoretical insights useful for the study of other conflicts.

This study examines change in the Arab-Israeli conflict as reflected by the dynamics of international crises. Three questions arise in this context: Was there change in the attributes of international crises over time? If yes, in which dimensions and directions did change take place? Why did changes in conflict occur? In order to answer these questions we pursue five goals:

(1) to devise an index for detecting change in crisis;

(2) to identify the main trends and areas of change in crisis;

(3) to link these changes in crisis with trends in the conflict;

(4) to evaluate whether changes in crisis dynamics reflect upon trends in conflict; and

(5) to explain changes in conflict with international relations theories.

In this chapter, we start with a review of the main paradigmatic approaches and theories debated in the discipline. We suggest a set of conditions taken from the theoretical literature that explain change from conflict and confrontation to some form of accommodation and collaboration. Next, we offer a theoretical framework for the analysis of crisis magnitude designed to measure change from anarchy to some institutionalism. In doing so we apply concepts and data from Michael Brecher and Jonathan Wilkenfeld's International Crisis Behavior (ICB) project. We conclude our theoretical presentation by highlighting main concepts in ethnonational theory and its application to world politics. Special emphasis is devoted to the spillover of ethnic elements in interstate conflicts or vice versa. The conclusion of this chapter will extend our theoretical framework for the analysis of crisis magnitude to the ethnic domain.

ANARCHY AND ORDER IN WORLD POLITICS

The puzzle of anarchy and order is inherent in world politics; the mixture of disorder and organization preceded the inception of the international system and accompanied its evolution.[5] The coexistence of violent and amicable relations among political units has always been in the background of theory building in international politics. Anarchy and order as core foci of inquiry of international politics came to prominence following the establishment of an international system of states, and crystalized with the evolution of a global system that simultaneously includes nation-states, regional groupings of states, and international organizations devised to preserve world order.[6] The coexistence of immense violent conflict, actual and potential, alongside evidence of intensive cooperation demands scholarly inquiry as to the dominating principle of international relations.

Current international relations theory comprises four approaches regarding the role of international institutions in maintaining order: neorealists who perceive order as directly linked to structure; realists who see some role for institutions in promoting order; neoliberals who allow an independent role for institutions; and constructivists who totally reject structure and view cooperation as growing out of a reformed process of international relations. In the following pages we address some concerns of all four perspectives.

The neorealists provide an explanation of international behavior primarily at the international or world politics level. As Kenneth Waltz put it when responding to John Vasquez's attack on the realist paradigm, "Old realists see causes as running directly from states to the outcomes . . . New realists see states forming a structure by their interactions and then being strongly affected by the structure their interactions have formed."[7] Neorealists see the structure of the international system, as defined to a large extent by the distribution of power, as solely responsible for international order. In their eyes international regimes and international institutions play no role in promoting order at the international level.

Neorealists have difficulty with the concept of institutions because of their distinction between anarchy, which is the organizing principle in the international system, and hierarchy, which is the dominant principle in the domestic system. Their frame of reference makes it difficult to adopt concepts such as international regimes and institutions. As Helen Milner pointed out, anarchy implies not only the lack of order but also the lack of government.[8] Hence, international politics, from a neorealist perspective, may not sustain domestic concepts of order. By its very nature international politics constitutes the opposite model of domestic politics. Classical realists, however, have fewer inhibitions toward international institutions and differ here from their successors.[9]

When neorealists accept the existence of institutions in international politics, they do so in a particular way. When John Grieco, a realist, asserts that the most critical deficiency of structural realism is to explain the "tendency of states to undertake their cooperation through *institutionalized* arrangements,"[10] the neorealists' response would be that institutions reflect the realities of power of international politics. In John Mearsheimer's words, "[F]or realists, . . . institutions largely mirror the distribution of power in the system. In short, the balance of power is the independent variable that explains war."[11] At the same time that the neorealists "may disagree on the nature, extent, and causes of that order,"[12] they must concede that world politics is not just a permanent struggle for power. It does exhibit some order.

Neorealists and classical realists differ on the role of institutions or, alternatively, international regimes, but are not very far apart in their definitions. Mearsheimer defines institutions as "a set of rules that stipulate the ways in which states should cooperate and compete with each other. They prescribe acceptable forms of state behavior, and proscribe unacceptable kinds of behavior."[13] Krasner, writing a decade earlier, defines an international regime as a setting in which international actors accept "sets of implicit or explicit principles, norms, rules and decision making procedures around which actors' expectations converge in a given area of international relations."[14] Jervis describes security regimes as "principles, rules, and norms that permit nations to be restrained in their behavior in the belief that others will reciprocate."[15] Noticeably, Mearsheimer, who is the closest among the three to neorealism and to Waltz, does not include norms in his definition.

Indeed, most of the respondents to Vasquez's attack on the realist paradigm asserted that we must not cluster all realists together.[16] Despite the high regard for power in old realism, classical realists, as already pointed out above, did not totally disregard the role of institutions.[17] One example is Kaplan, who wrote his pioneering study on international systems at the time when political realism dominated the discipline of international relations. Krasner made a very definite distinction between the two realist approaches: "Waltz's conception of the balance of power, in which states are driven by systemic pressures to repetitive balancing behavior, is not a regime; Kaplan's conception, in which equilibrium requires commitment to rules that constrain immediate, short-term power maximization . . . is a regime."[18]

While realists, or as Krasner defined them "modified stutructuralists," perceive some role for regimes or institutions depending on the world in which they operate,[19] neoliberals, or those influenced by the Grotius tradition, go one step farther than the moderate realists and see regimes as independent variables influencing international order and cooperation.[20]

The international order in Europe during the last decade of the twentieth century serves as a case that supports the neoliberal approach. Grieco, on the basis of the European Community's (EC) renaissance in the wake of the Cold War, admits that realists must contend with the survival of international institutions despite structural changes.[21] The continuation of international institutions in Europe after the disintegration of the Soviet Union supported the neoliberal contention that international regimes and institutions survived a shift in the distribution of power, and eventually generate their own rationale and sustenance. Mearsheimer, who represents the doctrinaire neorealist approach, indeed expected European institutionalism to collapse following the end of the Cold War.[22]

Naturally, the neoliberal explanation for the survival of international institutions following the Cold War is that institutions have their own rationale of existence and independently support international order. Accordingly, if institutions serve the interests of the actors of the system they will persist even following structural changes. But the European case is limited in proving the neoliberal argument since it is possible to argue that the institutions did not fulfill any function in the transformation of the Cold War. The constitution of the Conference on Security and Cooperation in Europe (CSCE) accompanied the decline of the Cold War rather than contributed to its demise.

While neorealists have trouble explaining Europe in the wake of the Cold War, neoliberals have their own difficulties. Indeed, the main problem for non-realists is that the phenomenon of institutionalism so far has either been confined to a geographic area, such as Western Europe, or employed globally in functional areas such as international economics. A more rigorous test for the relevance of institutions in contributing to international order would come from an area experiencing some structural change and the inauguration of some institutionalism, but where violence is still a vivid option and hence the states' main concern is not international economy but security. The identification of a case study of intense conflict followed by some cooperation advances the study of the role of international institutions in promoting cooperation. In the Middle East the states' main concern is not international economy but security. It will be our task to detect whether the Arab-Israeli conflict serves as an empirical case that fulfills the requirements for advanced theoretical testing of realist and nonrealist claims. Does this rivalry exhibit the genesis of international institution building that fosters regional international order, and if so why?

The European phenomenon suggests the rationale that once institutions are in place, they create a new reality and are not easily abolished. This brings us to the impact of the praxis of cooperation via international institutions on the emergence of a new approach to international politics. Did the experience of the Western European states within the framework of international institutions mollify mutual fears of one another and increase confidence and interest among them in the benefits of cooperation? Alexander Wendt suggests that "four decades of cooperation may have transformed a positive interdependence of outcomes into a collective 'European identity' in terms of which states increasingly define their 'self' interest."[23]

Wendt's approach to institutionalism is influenced by constructivist theory, which grew out of critical theory. Constructivism focuses on the process of identity and interest formation, arguing that this was the most crucial factor in determining anarchy and international order. Unlike neoliberals, critical theorists, as represented by Wendt, state clearly that structure has no role in international politics "and that if today we find ourselves in a self-help world, this is due to process, not structure. . . . Structure has no existence or casual powers apart from process. . . . Anarchy is what states make of it."[24] Such an argument would be difficult for realists to accept in light of the practice of international politics.[25] Nevertheless, the role of process in explaining order in the midst of anarchy should not be disregarded, particularly in areas such as the Middle East where the norm has been violence and the discourse of cooperation is only slowly being inaugurated.

COLLABORATION IN CONFLICT:
TOWARD A THEORY OF CHANGE

Four schools have been identified in explaining international order. In accordance with the above analysis regarding the role of structure versus institutions in maintaining international order we present them as: neorealists, realists, neoliberals, and constructivists. Against this background of perspectives, we turn now to our main question—how to explain change from anarchy to international order?

As a departure point we pinpoint Krasner's theory of change: "When regimes are first created there is a high degree of congruity between power distribution and regime characteristics." But with time, he argued, since "power distributions are more dynamic [than regime characteristics]—they are constantly changing . . . thus, regimes and power distributions are not likely to change at the same rate." With time, if the incongruity between the two realms becomes too severe, "there is likely to be revolutionary change as those with the greatest power capabilities move to change underlying principles and norms."[26] Krasner departed from neorealism in that he also accepted that regimes once created assume lives of their own and influence international behavior and the creation of national interests. Arthur Stein articulates what could be considered a contribution to a realist-based theory of change affirming that interests determine regimes and that the distribution of power is one of the affecting factors. Distinguishing between "those who make a direct link between structure and regimes" (neorealists) and those who presume that interests intervene between structure and regimes, he asserts that shifts in patterns of interests would cause regime change.[27] Krasner provides an additional distinction between change of regimes and change within regimes. "Changes in rules and decision-making procedures are changes within regimes," while, "changes in principles and norms are changes of the regime itself."[28]

While these theorists rejuvenated realism, a profound look into classical realism would discover that it offers a variety of elements that today appear to belong to competing approaches. Almost two-thirds of Morgenthau's much celebrated *Politics among Nations* is dedicated to norms, principles, and international institutions and organizations that influence and limit the procession of violence in international politics.[29] Henry Kissinger's analysis of the emergence of the nineteenth-century institutional system similarly included both structure and institutions as pillars of international order.

Kissinger, a classical realist, articulated a theory of international order that included a composite of structure, international norms, and process in the promotion of change. In *A World Restored,* which deals with the emergence of the Concert System in Europe, Kissinger presents two main elements for the establishment of a stable international order in an environment of constant conflict: an equilibrium of forces and legitimizing principles. "The security of a domestic order resides in the preponderance power of authority, that of an international order in the balance of forces, and in its expression, the equilibrium. But . . . it is constructed in the name of a legitimizing principle."[30] The third element that coincides with stability is diplomacy, defined by Kissinger as "the adjustment of differences through negotiation . . . possible only in 'legitimate' international orders."[31] The last part of the sentence points to the subordination of practice to structure and a normative environment. Significantly, the practice of peace for almost a century caused the leaders of Europe to forget "that states could die, that upheavals could be irretrievable, that fear could become the means of social cohesion."[32]

A World Restored makes it clear that the stable system Kissinger was talking about was not the same as Karl Deutsch's concept of a war-free security community: "A legitimate order does not make conflicts impossible, but it limits their scope. Wars may occur, but they will be fought in the name of the existing structure."[33] The stable world (the Concert System) that Kissinger identified in the nineteenth century, could today be defined as a "security regime," namely, an international system managed by principles, rules, and norms accepted by all actors in the system regarding restraint on states' behavior. Despite the discrepancy between international order and war, evidence indicates that other cases of institutional behavior within areas of incessant conflict do exist. U.S.-Soviet relations during the Cold War, as delineated by Michael Mandelbaum, represented a "managed balance of power," a system comparable to the Concert System, a configuration that contained characteristics of institutionalism.[34] Charles Lipson defined even the East-West rivalry as a security regime. Jervis saw a security regime in the Concert of Europe system, in which the great powers did not maximize individual power positions and took each others' interests into account, despite the struggle for power.[35] In the words of Jervis, "Of course the Concert did not banish conflict. But it did regulate it."[36] The balance of power system, as long as we define a balance of power system by Kaplan's parameters, such as the one that existed during the ancien regime or during the Concert, would still fall within the regime category, even though exhibiting some conflict.[37]

On the basis of the above theories and case studies we devised a set of conditions that would explain change from a "revolutionary system," to use Kissinger's terminology, to a more stable one that accepts some minimum international order. Learning from the experiences of Europe during the last two centuries, we see the relevance of institutions alongside structure in establishing international order. Hence, we try to bridge the gaps among differing elements from the various institutional approaches, with an inclination toward realism as the perspective most appropriate in areas such as the Middle East. Realism as we see it does not ignore the impact of international institutions and diplomacy on international order.

We start from the premise that in a system of sovereign states, the distribution of power is the basic structure for providing security to actors whose main concern is to survive.[38] The emergence of a *balance of power* is thus our first condition for security in a self-help system. A framework of security is one in which a revisionist actor cannot achieve unilateral goals without drawing retaliation exceeding its potential gains. In the absence of deterrence, revisionists may attack other system members for opportunistic reasons[39]. In regional systems, such as the Middle East, and especially within the Arab-Israeli context, the distribution of power is complex since the number of actors is always shifting. It is further complicated by an extraregional great power balance.[40]

The emergence of a balance of power by itself is not sufficient, it must be accepted by the members of the system. Hence, the acceptance of the balance of power or, in other words, *legitimacy* is our second condition for change to a more stable system. States in a conflict situation face security dilemmas and hence they cannot permit relative gains by their potential rivals. Even liberals would agree that in a conflict-ridden system, when the actors' achievements are not necessarily at the expense of their competitors, they nevertheless cannot limit the scope of their interests to common gains.[41] In a world where states have huge incentives to take advantage of one another and no restraints to prohibit aggressive behavior, a state that ignores a rival's gains may create a power gap that could lead to an existential threat. According to the classical security dilemma, gains in one actor's security may pose existential threats to its rivals.[42] Hegemonic powers that seek absolute security thus constitute obstacles to stability. Acceptance of the balance of power is therefore linked to the acceptance of relative security, or to use Kissinger's words, "The foundation of a stable order is the relative security—and therefore the relative insecurity—of its members."[43] At various times in the Middle East, Egypt, Iraq, or Syria aspired to achieve hegemony, as most Arab states suspect of Israel as well. The removal of such ambitions is an integral part of the emergence of stability.

Legitimacy, according to Kissinger, necessitates the advent of common norms. Intense conflicts such as those of the European system during the Napoleonic wars, Europe under Hitler's reign, the Cold War during its early years, or the Arab-Israeli conflict at different times, constitute cases in which a balance of forces existed without the recognized legitimacy of some of the system's members. As a result these periods were ridden with continuous crises and wars. Without the abandonment of radical goals, which present an existential threat, there can be no chance for international institutions to have a lasting impact on international relations.[44] However, acceptance of the right to exist among parties to the conflict can come prior to the actual termination of conflict. Mutual acceptance, even if on a limited basis, constitutes a more advanced stage and as such a second condition for the emergence of collaboration in a system still experiencing persistent conflict.

How can parties to a conflict accept a balance of power when they do not share any common norms, even after an equilibrium of forces has been established? Why should antagonist states abandon total mutual denial and adopt compromise interactions reflective of a regime? Adversaries may have to espouse rules to coordinate their interaction, as Arthur Stein points out, not because of shared values but because of a shared stake in averting a certain course of action.[45] Process calculation, in addition to structure, affects behavior. Theorists call the acceptance of certain rules by actors lacking common norms in order to prevent an undesirable outcome "common aversions." As Stein states, "Anarchy in the international arena does not entail continual chaos."[46] The common enemy of the great powers in the post–Congress of Vienna system was social revolution; despite the rivalry that persisted between actors such as Russia and Britain, they adopted rules and procedures that regulated their competition.

Acceptance of the balance of power can be seen as the adoption of rules and norms of behavior within a conflict system, as Krasner interprets Kaplan's balance of power system theory. Paradoxically, but in accordance with the logic of common aversions, these rules and norms would be induced by a boost in the *cost of war,* our third condition for change. When the potential damage of war drastically exceeds any potential gain from war, states will strive to create security arrangements that diminish the chances of war. This is essentially the rationale of deterrence, particularly nuclear deterrence. On the modern battlefield, even conventional warfare may be so destructive as to make war unattractive, although there is no equal to a nuclear deterrent.[47] A major inducement to the acceptance of a regime to regulate conflict systems is its members' fear that crises will get out of control.

Mistrust is a basic impediment to the transformation from anarchy to a regime, even under conditions of common aversions or legitimacy. For instance, the rationale for the two strategic doctrines "preventive" and "preemptive" strikes assumes a complete lack of trust. The threat of such escalations provides the parties to the conflict with additional incentives to accept some rules and norms of behavior. Aversion to sudden changes in the balance of power is crucial especially in an international system in which the competing sides possess advanced military technologies. Both the ability of several states to form an alliance against one other actor, or one actor's breakthrough in the military domain that shatters the balance of power, can provoke a preventive war. The advantages of a first strike can also induce a preemptive attack. The negative alternative to a regime is often an intensive arms race that may ultimately escalate into war.[48]

In a self-help system the fear of such escalation in light of mistrust, or "defection," in the language of game theory, necessitates transparency and a mechanism for detection of alterations in the status quo. Regulatory practices guarding against cheating are often spelled out in international agreements. This kind of *institutionalism* is the fourth condition for the formation of international order in a conflict system. Measures designed to lead to the reduction of uncertainty on both sides with regard to unilateral strategic-military moves are known as Confidence and Security Building Measures (CSBM).[49] These measures cannot be established in a total conflict situation where there is not even the rationale of "common aversions." Similarly, their utility is modest when a full-fledged international security community has been established. It makes sense that this concept was first used in the context of the CSCE in Helsinki in 1976, when the East and the West agreed to adopt measures that would reduce the potential for a surprise attack. The form of CSBM in a subsystem such as the Middle East may differ from the European experience. Extraregional powers or superpowers could fulfill a prominent role in supporting the CSBM. The great powers may be useful in regulating the arms race and in providing reassurance to the parties in conflict, and thus reduce a rationale for prevention or preemption in order to maintain their security.[50]

Do we recognize an institutionalized international order when we see one? The answer is not clear. The conditions described above would be conducive to the transition from an anarchic international order to an institutional one, but in order to recognize a regime we must evaluate two patterns of interaction as indicated in the literature; one where order is administered purely via deterrence—and one in which order is maintained through the establishment of a regime. A system cannot be said to have achieved a regime if political actors are dissuaded from aggression simply because the potential gain of their act would be outweighed by the potential cost inflicted by other actors, even if this relationship is regulated by rules. The rationale of deterrence requires disproportion between the potential gain and retaliation in favor of the latter, and the need to demonstrate determination in order to gain credibility. A basic requirement for the formation of a security regime is "that major actors prefer the status quo—with the possibility of modification by uncoerced changes—to the world of possible gains and possible losses that they expect to flow from the individualistic pursuit of security policies."[51] In a deterrence relationship, security is not accomplished via a cooperative effort, it is an absolutely individualistic endeavor. An institutionalized international order could thus be defined as the abandonment of protecting the status quo via unilateral measurements to a collaborative effort.[52]

This distinction between a deterrence relationship and a security regime does not always exist in the real world of international politics. They are two ideal types of relations, which form a scale ranging from total anarchy on the one hand to a security community on the other. In reality a deterrence posture and a security regime are not always mutually exclusive: stable deterrence may provide an incentive for sustaining a security regime. Our examination of stability in conflict systems looks for a process of change from one disposition to another.

To describe and analyze a course of change and to detect nuances that come to characterize the dynamics of conflict over time, we adopt the concept of an international crisis and develop an operational index designed to measure changes in the magnitude of international crises.

INTERNATIONAL CRISIS AND CONFLICT
TRANSFORMATION

So far we have demarcated the boundaries of a conflict in both the realist and nonrealist viewpoints, and addressed the conditions for change from severe confrontation to gradual conflict regulation. Still missing is a unifying concept that embraces both structure and process and reflects the transition from stability to instability and back. We regard crisis as a concept that encompasses change from anarchy to order and vice versa.

The literature on international crisis is vast. It includes both theoretical studies and empirical research.[53] Perhaps most salient among them is the International Crisis Behavior (ICB) Project, which integrates theory and in-depth historical analysis of conflict, crisis, and war. The project explores 412 international crises that incorporate 895 foreign policy crises worldwide from 1918 to 1994. Its analysis focuses on crisis attributes, the participating state actors and their characteristics, the regional and international system(s) in which a crisis occurs, and the role of third parties, namely, major powers and international organizations, in crisis management. This study draws upon the core concepts developed by ICB as well as on the Middle East section of its data-set for the 1947–1994 period.[54]

According to Brecher and Ben-Yehuda an *international crisis* denotes: 1) an increase in intensity of disruptive interactions among system actors; and 2) incipient change within the structure of an international system, more precisely, in one or more structural attributes—power distribution, actors/regimes, rules, and alliance configuration.[55]

A central assumption of crisis theory is the existence of a link between the crisis and an "incipient change within the structure of an international system."[56] The evolution of a crisis can be conceived, as Brecher has done, as a process that will influence the structure of an international system, or, as postulated here, as an indicator of change. Like Brecher, we also look for structural changes that explain variations in crisis behavior. At the same time we focus on behavior in crisis that reflects change from anarchy to some degree of regime formation.

Our framework goes beyond Brecher and Wilkenfeld's ICB project. While we narrow the empirical focus to the analysis of the Arab-Israeli conflict, we expand its theoretical framework. Whereas the ICB's point of departure was the realist paradigm with international crisis as its core concept, we apply concepts from the neorealist-institutional schools, thus surveying not only power relationships but also the application of rules and regulations during the termination stage of crises and relate them to trends in conflict.

An international crisis among states is a critical stage in the transition from stability to the use of force in world politics. It is assumed that the reduction of such occurrences, or modifications in the mode of crisis behavior, would reflect both change in the pattern of relations among the involved actors as well as the introduction of rules and regulations. An international crisis can deteriorate to war but can also backslide to stability. Hence, we have chosen state behavior in international crises as an indicator of a potential transition from an anarchical to a more stable order. The duration of the crisis is the period in which the dynamics of transition from normal relations range to violent interactions and back are excessively at work.[57] On the basis of the above we assume that an international crisis—a microcosm of international politics and condensed change—will be an effective vehicle through which to evaluate the transition from a relationship of total conflict to a more regulated rivalry and, further, to some cooperation in a protracted conflict.[58]

All of the preceding inferences about the meaning of international crises in world politics depend upon a crucial assumption about how these observed events relate to unobserved processes. To be more precise, international crises are events that summon to mind images such as John F. Kennedy announcing the quarantine of Cuba (in essence, a blockade) to the world on television in October 1962 or troops moving around on trains throughout Europe in the summer of 1914. These things can be seen or at least imagined by the reader of a historical text. Thus, crises are part of human history and, in principle, can be measured in some way or another. The key point, then, is this one: a crisis is the observed manifestation, in a series of events, of some underlying and unobserved conflict. The conflict can be imagined, but it cannot be viewed on television, photographed, or experienced in any other sensory manner. Instead, conflict—the latent variable within this study—is understood to ebb and flow on the basis of its most intense and comprehensive visible referent: international crisis.[59] Thus, any number of variables that focus on the frequency and intensity (with the latter defined more specifically by the concept of magnitude throughout the remainder of the study) of crises as events may be developed in order to assess, on the basis of a time series, the direction in which some underlying conflict is moving.

We chose the ICB project as the empirical basis for our study because we require an objective data-set to provide us with a descriptive analysis of the Arab-Israeli conflict. The ICB, being a worldwide project, is as immune as possible to regional or state centric biases. Also attractive was its macro orientation, specifically its focus on international crisis within a protracted conflict, rather than on a foreign policy crisis. This allowed us to maintain an overall perspective in which the dangers of subjective analysis were relatively remote. For example, the definition of threat in a foreign policy crisis may vary from one state to another, depending on the perceptions of the decision makers. By contrast, in an international crisis gravity is evaluated from an overall-objective perspective, taking into account, the stakes over which the different adversaries contend and identifying the most salient threat in that particular confrontation. [60]

However, we depart from the ICB project in two major aspects: first, ICB focuses mainly on crisis while for us the study of crisis is a means for the study of conflict as a core subject matter in international politics. Accordingly, while ICB models analyze change within a single crisis, we identify and explain change in a series of crises that take place within a protracted conflict. Second, while ICB dissects a crisis and describes its stages of onset, escalation, and de-escalation, we take the crisis as an integral whole, identify its overall magnitude, and compare the magnitude of different crises over time. Variation in levels of crisis magnitude, indicating trends in conflict, is our research objective in this section of the study.

REALMS OF CRISIS AND THE CRISIS
MAGNITUDE INDEX (CMI)

The concept of *crisis magnitude* and its operational tool—the CMI—are designed to characterize changes that occur in interstate behavior during international crises. Crisis magnitude focuses on the entire crisis, embodying the extent of disruption that takes place during the crisis period and identifying three specific domains in which disruption occurs. Based upon the ICB definition of an international crisis presented above, crisis magnitude is a composite of three realms: context, process, and outcome. These realms describe the attributes of change in both the dynamic and static elements of crisis. The first and last realms—context and outcome—are the relatively static attributes, which characterize the slowly changing elements of disruption during a crisis, whereas the second realm—process—is the dynamic domain where more rapid transformation takes place.

Integrating these realms of crisis, we developed an index of crisis magnitude designed to measure the extent of change in crisis attributes. The CMI is composed of six indicators emanating from the above three distinct realms that serve as our basis for the illumination of change in crisis evolution and of the patterns of conflict escalation or de-escalation.

The first realm—CONTEXT—encompasses three attributes: (1) gravity of threat to values; (2) number of crisis actors defining the extent of distortion in behavioral regularities due to the conflicting issues between actors; and (3) the level of superpower involvement, indicating the severity of the crisis from a global perspective, as well as the potential for conflict escalation or regulation. In essence, this realm accounts for the structure of the regional system in which the crisis occurs and the threats that emanate from the distribution of forces and the objectives of the participating actors. But context also transcends structure since it also includes forms of institutionalism represented by superpower participation, which places constraints on the use of power in regional crises.

The first indicator—*gravity of threat*—is composed of seven categories: existence; grave damage; internal stability/political regime; territorial integrity; economic; influence; limited military damage.[61]

Gravity of the value threatened serves as an indicator of an actor's motivation for involvement in the crisis. States engage in conflict, crisis, and war in order to promote their foreign policy goals. Gravity encompasses both the interests at stake and the distribution of capabilities among the adversaries. Our postulate is that the higher the gravity of threats, the greater the magnitude of the crisis and the lower the prospects of conflict regulation following crisis termination. Compare, for example, threats to Israel in the 1947–1948 Arab-Israeli war and the 1973 war: In the first case, the threat was to Israel's very existence and accordingly crisis magnitude was high and intense conflict ensued. The threat during the October War was of grave damage to the Jewish state and its civilians, indicating some decline in magnitude.

The indicators of crisis magnitude, together with their values, expected levels of crisis magnitude and propositions linking each indicator to overall magnitude are presented in Table 1.1 which follows.

The next context indicator, *number of crisis actors* under threat, ranges from six, the highest number of actors in the Arab-Israeli conflict (involving Egypt, Iraq, Israel, Jordan, Lebanon, and Syria), to the lowest possible—one.[62] Number of crisis actors serves as an indicator of magnitude since the number of rivals in a dispute affects the distribution of power, state actor interests, issues at stake, as well as the extent of disruptive interaction among the competing parties. Hence, the larger the number of actors the greater the disturbance in the conflict system and, therefore, the smaller the prospects of conflict de-escalation. In the number of crisis actors we include both regional and global actors. Some crises involve only regional adversaries while others also include major powers and superpowers from the global system.

TABLE 1.1
The CMI—REALMS, INDICATORS, VALUES and POSTULATES

REALM	INDICATOR	VALUE	POSTULATE	CMI LEVEL
CONTEXT	Gravity of Threat	Limited military damage	Low threat - limited disturbance	Low
		Economic		
		Political		
		Influence		
		Territorial	High threat - substantial disturbance	High
		Grave damage		
		Existence		
	Number of Actors	Single actor	Few crisis actors - limited disturbance	Low
		Two actors		
		Three actors		
		Four actors	Many crisis actors - substantial disturbance	High
		Five actors		
		Six actors		
	Superpower Involvement	None	No/low superpower involvement - limited disturbance	Low
		Political		
		Semi-military	Semi-military/military superpower involvement - substantial disturbance	High
		Direct military		
PROCESS	Crisis Management Technique	Negotiation/ mediation nonmilitary pressure	Non-military/ nonviolent behavior - limited disturbance	Low
		Nonviolent military multiple including violence	Military nonviolent/ violent behavior - substantial disturbance	High
	Violence	None	No/low violence - limited disturbance	Low
		Minor clashes		
		Serious clashes	High violence/war - substantial disturbance	High
		Full-scale war		
OUTCOME	Termination	Formal agreement	Accommodative outcome - limited disturbance	Low
		Semi-formal agreement		
		Tacit understanding		
		Unilateral act	Non-accommodative outcome - substantial disturbance	High
		Imposed agreement		
		Faded/other- non-accommodative		

Within protracted conflicts one must differentiate between two major groups: global conflicts, where the superpowers are the core adversaries, and regional conflicts in which the superpowers may be involved but are not the primary actors. In the first category—global confrontations—such as in the 1962 Cuban Missile Crisis, U.S. and USSR activity is part of the process realm detailed below, since both states are the major participants in the confrontation and it is disagreement over their core values and goals that triggers the crisis. By contrast, in regional crises, as in the 1973 war, the principal clash of issues is among local rivals although the superpowers may have exacerbating or moderating effects on regional processes. Superpower activity in regional cases creates constraints for client states, forming a contextual realm for local adversaries. The Arab-Israeli conflict in the Middle East belongs to the second category—that of regional conflicts—and we therefore consider superpower activity in our study as part of context, reflecting the link between the global and regional dynamics.[63]

The third indicator, *superpower involvement,* ranges from military, semi-military, economic, or political to no involvement at all.[64] Superpower involvement serves as an indicator of magnitude since the extent of third party involvement leaves its trace on crisis dynamics. In evaluating the impact of external powers in an ongoing dispute we must distinguish between diplomatic and military involvement. Even though both represent the capabilities of the great powers, the latter is much closer to power politics, while diplomatic involvement carries the potential for accommodation and interstate institution building. We may assume that the higher the diplomatic involvement, the greater the chances of conflict regulation. By contrast, the higher the military involvement, the greater the likelihood of conflict escalation. On the whole, high levels in context indicators, namely grave threats to basic values, many crisis actors, and intensive superpower military rivalry, point to high crisis magnitude and vice versa.

The second realm—PROCESS—includes two behavioral attributes of the crisis: (1) type of management technique used by the actors in order to cope with the crisis and (2) level of violence throughout the event.

The first process indicator, *Crisis Management Technique (CMT),* differentiates among crises processed by means of violence, a mixture of violence and diplomacy, demonstration of force, and negotiations. CMT functions as an indicator of magnitude since it encompasses a wide range of interactions ranging from diplomacy to violence and the combination of both as means of bargaining in international interactions. As such, it defines boundaries of behavior among rivals and signals the transition points between "zero-sum" violent confrontations and negotiations representing mixed motive situations. Accordingly, CMT has an impact on conflict termination. Violence alone signals escalation, while negotiations reveal moderation and a trend toward reconciliation. When viewed together, both diplomacy and violence measure the extent of distortion during the crisis. The outbreak of hostilities, with no other management technique, represent the violent side of high crisis magnitude, and "coercive diplomacy," to use Shelling's term, whereas nonviolent measures coupled with negotiation techniques denote low magnitude.[65] Management of a crisis via negotiations also signals the introduction of institutional procedures into the relationship.

The next process indicator, level of interstate violence, explores the range of hostilities that occur during an international crisis. This indicator is divided into four subcategories: war, serious clashes, minor clashes, and no violence. Level of violence is a core aspect of international crisis escalation. The initial transformation from non-crisis to crisis situation is triggered by an increase in hostility and a rise in the prospects of violence. Moreover, international crises vary in levels of violence, some being intermediate changes from the normal relations range—such as insurgency actions and retaliations (e.g., 1953 Qibya, or 1968 Beirut airport), while others consist of a major shift in existing patterns—such as interstate wars (e.g., 1947–1948 war, 1956 Sinai campaign, 1967 Six Day War, 1973 October War).[66] On the whole, we propose that the level of violence reflects the severity of the conflict; the harsher the violence, the smaller the chances for resolution of the conflict. At the same time, we are aware that in severe cases only major confrontations induce attempts at conflict resolution. We refer to this phenomenon as the "violence-accommodation" relationship.

The third and last realm—OUTCOME—focuses on the winding down of crises: the content of crisis outcomes and the form they take. Crisis *termination* serves as the sixth indicator of crisis magnitude because the dynamics within protracted conflicts are shaped by the way each crisis ends. More specifically, a distinction is made between crises terminated by dictate—imposed or unilateral endings—and those concluded by compromise embodied in semiformal or formal agreements. Crises falling within the first group reflect failure to overcome via mutual agreement the disturbance that caused the crisis. The potential for institutional arrangement is dim with this type of termination. Events in which crisis is terminated by compromise reflect a higher potential for reduced rivalry. A crisis that ends in compromise epitomizes the wishes of the parties to conclude the conflict and their readiness to accept common rules of behavior. Our study anticipates that the conclusion will have an impact on future conflict dynamics. High magnitude exists in cases resolved by an imposed agreement, by a unilateral act or in cases that fade over time, since the conflicting stakes in these cases are not resolved among the crisis actors. By contrast, in a crisis terminated by tacit, semiformal, or formal agreement, crisis magnitude is low, reflecting the reduction of crisis-generated tensions among participants.

Since we do not want to introduce a priori assumptions regarding the relative importance of each indicator in the overall score of crisis magnitude, we assigned equal weight in the composite index to the indicators in all three realms. The overall CMI score was derived from the following formula: SUM of all indicators per case (with High = 1) + SUM of all indicators per case (with Low = 0). The possible range of overall magnitude is 0 to 6. The index serves our purpose of setting forth a defined set of indicators that enable us to compare crises in the Arab–Israeli protracted conflict over time. In the future it may lead to further comparisons of crises in other geographic areas or in diverse periods. The subdivision of all six indicators into the three realms of context, process, and outcome provides us with another means with which to compare change in crisis magnitude and conflict evolution. A comprehensive analysis of these crises and changes in crisis magnitude over time will be presented in chapters 2–4.

The CMI is a counterpart of an earlier Index of Severity formulated by the ICB project.[67] Both indexes attempt to characterize international crisis and to highlight the extent of disruption/change manifested in the crisis events. As such, both indexes relate to a time frame from the onset of the crisis to its outcome. However, the CMI identifies three realms and assigns equal weight to all indicators. By contrast, the ICB severity index specifies a deductively derived weight for each indicator. The indicators that appear in both indexes are number of actors, superpower involvement, and violence. The severity index indicators of geostrategic salience, heterogeneity, and issues are replaced in the CMI with gravity of threat, crisis management technique, and termination. The rationale behind this approach is that while the three variables that were dropped are valuable for a project that compares interregional behavior, they are superfluous for a comparative analysis within the same region.[68]

In summary, the CMI is built on key definitions of an international crisis that involves a change in the intensity of disruptive interaction and a challenge to the structure of the regional/international system. The assumption is that a reduction in threat, number of crisis actors, involvement of the superpowers, the role of violence in crisis management, the scope of violence and frequency of hostile interaction reflect changes in the magnitude of the crisis. The persistence of such a trend over time would indicate an elementary change in conflict dynamics.

Our assessment of conflict transformation is also based on an appraisal of crisis frequency over time affecting change in conflict dynamics. The rationale for measuring frequency of crises is that the higher the frequency, the greater the turbulence of conflict. It follows that the reoccurrence of crisis points to a profound dissension among the parties, and a decline in the reiteration of crisis must represent some basic changes in the judgments of the parties to the conflict regarding their interests. Conflict abatement is affected not only by the substance of crisis but also by the intensity of crisis occurrences within the conflict. The decline in the appearance of crisis indicates acceptance of some restraints on conflict procession. Moreover, we hold that a decline in the occurrence of interstate crisis indicates state awareness that hostile escalation may bring the parties to war without reciprocal gains from such violence.

One way to appraise frequency would be to divide the number of crises over the years and then distinguish between periods. But distribution of crises is not spread out evenly, that is, in several years more than one crisis erupted. We therefore gauge the evolution of the conflict according to years free from crises, years of middle-range crises (where violence was absent or only used in a limited form), and years of major crises (where the threshold of war was crossed, or at least massive military interaction took place). We consider a year in which more than one crisis took place according to the more severe crisis of that year. Similarly, if a crisis carried over from one year into a large part of the next, we also consider the second year as a year of crisis.

Having presented the concept of crisis magnitude, as well as the CMI—a tool designed to measure continuation and change in crisis attributes—we turn now to the ethnic elements in international crises. While recognizing the prominent role of the interstate dimension of the Arab-Israeli conflict we must also consider the centrality of the non-state level of interaction. We therefore supplement traditional crisis analysis with an ethnic dimension in order to improve our understanding of crisis magnitude and conflict dynamics.

ETHNICITY AND CHANGE IN A PROTRACTED CONFLICT

Despite attempts to search for similarities, some conflicts have their own character and rules of the game.[69] Our point of departure is that not all regions are alike in terms of violence; some international systems prohibit violence, while others permit it. Since the Arab-Israeli conflict belongs to the protracted conflicts category, we must take into account characteristics specific to this type of dispute, including the propensity to resort to interstate and sub-state violence. Edward Azar probed the theoretical attributes of protracted conflicts and introduced the term Normal Relations Range (NRR).[70] Within this framework he demonstrated how certain conflicts can be sustained for a long time following rules and procedures considered unbearable or system threatening in other systems. Such systems exhibit explicit or implicit rules of the game. They are unique in that an unusual cooperative event among some parties to the conflict will cause others to resist collaboration in favor of a return to some form of conflict within the borders of the NRR. Change is thus a deviation from, or an alternation of, an existing pattern of interaction in the direction of a new NRR, or a new equilibrium.[71]

Azar, Jureidini, and MacLaurin added an important insight to the explanation of protracted conflicts—the ethnic dimension. They attributed the persistence of most conflicts, including the Arab-Israeli conflict, to a mixture of communal and interstate disputes. Based on their typology distinguishing conflict as either " interstate," "inter-communal," or "mixed," they concluded that it was especially the ethnic dimension of the conflict that prohibited a solution. It was also the ethnic dimension, they argued, that kept a certain NRR.[72] At the same time, the Arab-Israeli experience suggests that the interstate component (including that of the great powers) also kept the ethnic dimension from disappearing. Azar thus introduced two ideas into the scholarly analysis of ethnic conflict: the linkage between the interstate and ethnic domains, and the prolonging effect of the ethnic element on the conflict.

On the relationship between the ethnic and the interstate domains Sandler proposed the concept of "compound conflict," which defines the Arab-Israeli conflict as "a structure composed of two bordering domains of violence, interstate and inter-communal."[73] Afflicted by both spheres since its inception, the Arab-Israeli conflict has become the prototype of a compound dispute, especially following the 1973 war and the increased salience of the ethnic dimension.[74]

Academic attention to the ethnic dimension of international conflict was scarce when the expectations of the modern state were high, but the literature on the ethnic variable has grown enormously in the last three decades.[75] In contrast to the earlier state centric model of international relations, students of world politics in recent years have included the intrastate scene and ethnic conflict in their terms of reference; appreciation for the ethnic factor in international relations has markedly increased.

Ted Robert Gurr's "Minority at Risk Project," a worldwide comprehensive empirical study of some fifty ethno-political conflicts is a key example of the rising relevance of ethnic conflicts. Gurr and Barbara Harff distinguish between two main kinds of ethnic groups and minorities in world politics: collectives that demand representation within the state they inhabit, and separatists who demand autonomy from the state that rules over them.[76] The ethnic minorities in America represent the first type whose conflicts, according to Gurr and Harff, are less severe and rarely spill over from the internal to the international domain. The Yugoslav civil war illustrates the second type, and demonstrates the severe international implications of this kind of ethnic conflict.

Minorities and national peoples are among the politicized communal groups Gurr defines in his comprehensive analysis of ethnicity and conflict dynamics. He defines ethno-national groups as: "relatively large regionally concentrated peoples who historically were autonomous and who actively seek to improve their status in the modern state system."[77] Among the ethnic groups Gurr identifies as ethno-nationalists are the Palestinians, the core ethnic group investigated in this study.

Gurr's main conclusions reflect the increasing salience of ethnic elements in politics and their impact on conflict : (1) Ethnic fragmentation had been generated already in the mid 1960s, much earlier than the end of the Cold War, when international relations theorists began to regard it as an important field of research; (2) The main issue characterizing current ethno-political conflicts is power contention among communal groups; (3) Unless associated with a fight for independence, struggles for indigenous rights are subsiding in world politics. In short, most ethnic conflicts, even if disguised as ideological or religious campaigns, are ultimately directed at achieving independence.[78]

These conclusions are in accord with Anthony Smith's observations that contemporary ethnic revival is related to nationalism. Walker Connor had already noticed in the early 1970s the rise of what he called "ethno-national-ism." Smith based his work on ethnic nationalism upon an observed cultural community, namely, one whose members believe that they deserve to be and can become a nation-state. But while Connor focused attention toward domestic pluralism in the constitution of the nation state, Smith pointed toward the international aspects of ethnic revival. Principles such as self-determination, cultural identity, and national sovereignty are the legitimate basis for an ethnic community's demand for a nation-state.[79] When these aspirations are translated into secessionism or irredentism, linkage with the international system forms.[80] In the Arab-Israeli context, for instance, the current struggle is over Palestinian secession, but the potential threat of a Palestinian state for both Israel and Jordan is that of Palestinian irredentism.[81]

Our book focuses on conflict dynamics. Although Azar's thesis regarding the impact of the ethnic component on prolonging conflicts implies continuity and our work encompasses change, we have in common a sensitivity to the intersection of interstate and ethnic conflicts. We ask, why in one period is the interstate domain predominant, and under other conditions does the ethnic element become salient? Even if we know why certain conflicts endure, we still need to explain why ethnic animosity situated in the international context of conflict persists, mounts, or declines. In other words, within the framework of compound conflicts, we are concerned with the impact of ethnicity on the regulation or stabilization of protracted conflicts. Moreover, the endurance and intensity of protracted conflicts do not always concur. A major task of this study is to distinguish between the endurance of the conflict in terms of time and changes in intensity of the conflict, especially as the interstate and ethnic levels are concerned.

Not all the work in the area of internal wars supports Azar's thesis on the endurance of civil wars. Roy Licklider's comprehensive study of civil wars concludes that the patterns of identity-based civil wars are not different from those political/economic wars and "identity wars do not last longer" than non-identity wars. Where identity civil wars differ is in termination. Licklider's data support Robert Wagner's hypothesis that "negotiated settlements of civil wars are more likely to break down than settlements based on military victories."[82] This finding, that a resolution based on power relationships supports stability in ethno-national conflicts goes against the very essence of institutionalism and regime formation. The latter assume that in the interstate realm negotiated settlements indicate stability, while dictates usually break down and continued struggle prevails. In realist terms, this insight would imply that preponderance is more conducive to international stability than a balance of power.[83]

William Zartman, a collaborator in Licklider's research enterprise, raises another germane insight along the lines of both Gurr's findings and Smith's contention: "A likely outcome of internal wars is de facto secession, where each side has effective, unchallenged control of a territory and population."[84] This observation is further supported by other studies that assert that separation of groups is the key to ending ethnic civil wars.[85] Partition in effect transforms the interethnic conflict into an international one. Power-sharing arrangements, though to a lesser degree, can also be associated with separation.[86] The preference for partition over other solutions by students of interethnic conflict corresponds with the preference for decisive outcomes. More subdued ethnonational conflicts in which leaders failed to reach decisive conclusions such as partition would support Azar's findings of endurance and protractedness. But not all partitions imply an end to the conflict, as the Indo-Pakistani experience has demonstrated time and again.

Against this background our study is of relevance. First, we will examine whether Azar's thesis on endurance indeed holds in the Arab-Israeli case. Did the Palestinian factor prolong the conflict in the Middle East? Second, we explore whether these links between the interstate and the ethnic realms of conflict affect the transition of the Arab-Israeli conflict from pure confrontation to some form of institutionalism. Of interest are the bearings of international arrangements on ethnonational conflict, and vice versa. Accordingly we explore the impact of conflict resolution or regulation at the interstate level on the ethnonational conflict, that is, the impact of behavioral patterns and balance of power at the interstate level on conflict regulation at the ethnonational level.

In our analysis of the interstate and ethnic components of a protracted conflict, we use the ICB data-set in which both settings of conflict exist. The concept of crisis magnitude and its operational counterpart—the CMI—are useful and appropriate for measuring patterns of escalation or cooperation in both interstate and ethnic-state type international crises, defined below.[87] Approaching the Arab-Israeli conflict from a compound perspective, namely an ethno-national as well as an interstate one, produces a more accurate picture of overall change in the conflict. The Arab-Israeli conflict provides an empirical basis for testing international relations theories. Our findings will thus be relevant to analysts examining the transformation of a protracted-compound conflict from anarchy to some international order elsewhere in the world.[88]

In their original work, Brecher and Wilkenfeld, the authors of the ICB project, were state centric in their orientation. They fused the ethnic dimension into the statist framework or excluded from the project cases, where the ethnic dimension was predominant and did not seem to have a direct interstate axis of interaction (such as the 1987 Palestinian uprising known as the Intifada). Nevertheless, in their comprehensive book *A Study of Crisis* Brecher and Wilkenfeld ascertain that "35% of all international crises from the end of World War I through 1994 had an ethno political dimension."[89] Recognizing the salience of the ethnic element in conflict, crisis, and war, they investigated at length the relationship between ethnic and state behavior in crisis.[90] In doing so, ICB distinguishes between two ethnicity variables: "ethnic related" and "ethnic driven". The first, ethnic related, describes a crisis as ethnic if ethnicity was a factor in the behavior of one or more adversaries in an interstate crises. Ethnic driven focuses on ethnicity as a preeminent causal factor, affecting the behavior of states and the configuration of the international crisis.[91] The ethnic related variable, championed by David Carment, corrects the earlier deficiency by incorporating a broad range of ethnic phenomena into the study of crisis.[92] But one should not automatically assume a causal relationship between the existence of some ethnic attributes and the outbreak of interstate confrontations. Brecher and Wilkenfeld introduce the ethnic–driven variable in order to supplement their earlier state centric viewpoint, distinguishing between domestic ethnic elements that have some effects on interstate relations, and ethnic factors that are preeminent throughout an interstate rivalry.[93]

Brecher and Wilkenfeld also accept the common distinction between two types of ethnic conflict: secessionist and irredentist, but choose to combine them "into a single measure of interstate ethnic conflict."[94] By contrast, Carment maintains the distinction between the two, and he also suggests a typology of ethnic cases and anticipates that the effects of ethnicity will be most pronounced in irredentist cases.[95]

The ICB's approach suits our purpose, since in the Arab-Israeli conflict it is difficult to differentiate between the two types of ethnic conflict. The tension between the Palestinian demands for an independent state to replace the state of Israel and more recent proposals for a two state solution demonstrates that it would be simplistic to classify the Middle Eastern dispute either as solely a secessionist or an irredentist conflict.[96] Similarly, we do not find the differentiation between ethnicity related and ethnicity driven typology useful for our analysis since almost every crisis in the Arab-Israeli conflict identified by the ICB project was to some extent related to the Palestinian problem and hence can be categorized as ethnic related.

On the whole, ICB's approach to ethnicity as a contextual attribute of international crisis behavior does not fully overcome the realist barriers. Its analysis of ethnic elements is based on states' concerns, namely on national interests that unfold into interstate confrontations, and on the military-security issues that develop as a consequence of ethnic unrest. Since ethnic minorities can operate within a state or at times increase tensions between states, ethnicity is a constraint characterizing interstate conflicts and affecting international crises. ICB does not consider ethnic groups as major independent actors, thereby overlooking their role in crisis and their impact on crisis escalation and de-escalation.

Recognizing that ethnic groups constitute meaningful political actors, we move away from the discussion on whether ethnicity is a minor or salient element in escalating interstate confrontation and outline a threefold classification of crises in world politics: (1) *Interstate crises* are events involving at least two states in which the ethnic factor does not play any role in the international crisis. For instance, the 1973 war fits this category of cases in the Arab-Israeli conflict. (2) *Ethnic-state crises* are incidents in which an ethnic Non-State Actor (NSA) is preeminent in either triggering a crisis between or among states, defining the issues at stake, or participating in its procession. For example, the 1982 Lebanon war, in which three states—Syria, Lebanon, and Israel—participated and where the PLO played a central role in the onset as well as during the crisis and its termination, falls in this category. (3) *Interethnic crises* are hostile encounters between or among ethnic groups within one polity that do not involve an interstate confrontation. The three waves of ethnic rivalry between the Jewish and Arab communities in Palestine in the pre-1948 period are typical examples of this group.

These three types of crises will serve as our departure point for a comparison of crisis attributes and trends in conflict dynamics over time. Hence we have organized this book according to these three categories of crisis. Chapters 2–4 analyze international crises focusing on the interstate domain while ethnic-state and interethnic crises are the topics of chapter 5 and part of chapter 6. We are interested in three perspectives. First, we describe the distinct profiles of interstate, ethnic-state, and interethnic crises, specifically looking for differences in their core crisis attributes. Second, we address the question of the relative salience of each type of crisis over time, indicated by the frequency of crisis occurence. Third, we probe the linkage, if any, between the trends of crisis in the interstate and ethnic domains. We ask: does the decline or rise of crisis in one domain influence similar occurrences in the other, and vice versa.

The first query—a comparison among the three types of crisis—is conducted along the six CMI indicators, namely: gravity of threat, number of actors, the role of the superpowers, CMT, the level of violence, and termination. The aggregate testimony of these indicators provides us with significant insights regarding the disposition of the conflict. Evidence as to the frequency of each mode of conflict facilitates a significant insight into both interstate and the ethnic-state type crises. While measurements help us understand the relationship between the two modes of conflict, the findings here cannot be exclusvely quantitative. Because of the dearth of ethnic variables in the ICB project, a qualitative perspective is imperative. The qualitative mode of analysis is also indispensable to the third question, regarding the relationship between the interstate and the ethnic-state dimensions of conflict.

In conclusion, our theoretical framework for the analysis of crisis magnitude and conflict dynamics is based on a core contention: the realist paradigm of international politics must be complemented by both institutional and ethnic dimensions. In our search for transformation within the Arab-Israeli conflict, we stipulate that international crises should reflect trends of change, if indeed they exist, and that they will relate to all three approaches. Within this framework we probe the links between low/high levels of international crisis magnitude, the evolution of institutions in the interstate domain, and the evolution of an ethnic dimension. We postulate that the higher the magnitude of crisis, the more intense the conflict; conversely, the lower the magnitude of crisis, the greater the extent of regime/institutions building. Hence, a persistent decline in magnitude of crisis indicates the metamorphosis of the conflict from extreme hostility to inceptive cooperation. A special variant of international conflict are protracted-compound conflicts that contain ethnic elements. The double capacity of an international crisis—to reflect both the ethnic and interstate dimensions of conflict—serves as an integral part of this book. We demonstrate that the interstate and the ethnic domains interact with each other and influence the institutions that regulate international interaction among the political units.

Crisis frequency, changes in crisis magnitude—reflected through variations in the realms of context, process, and outcome—and the linkage between statist and ethnic elements, describe the overall state of conflict. The statist outlook prevails when we concentrate on context in chapter 2, on process and outcome in chapter 3, and on overall magnitude in chapter 4. The analysis of crisis magnitude identifies trends and turning points. A shift in outlook in chapters 5 and 6 puts the ethnic domain at the core of our analysis, in search of a better understanding of the Arab-Israeli conflict as a whole. Chapter 7 integrates the interstate and ethnic aspects and suggests new directions for additional research.

CHAPTER 2

CONTEXT, CRISIS MAGNITUDE, AND CHANGE

In chapter 1 we presented a theoretical framework for the analysis of crisis magnitude, change, and conflict transformation. Before we apply this framework to the twenty-six international crises in the Arab-Israeli conflict, we must identify turning points in the conflict, by appraising crisis frequency over time.[1] Subsequently, we will assess the findings through the prism of crisis magnitude. The concept of crisis magnitude is an analytical tool that helps identify and assess changes taking place within three realms: context, process, and termination. For each realm, specific indicators measure the extent of crisis magnitude. Context includes three indicators: gravity of threat, number of state actors in crisis, and level of superpower involvement. We begin by highlighting ongoing tendencies and locating turning points.[2]

CRISIS FREQUENCY AND CONFLICT TRANSFORMATION

In order to assess the state of an international conflict, we need to appraise the frequency of crisis over time. The rationale for measuring frequency of crises is the assumption that the higher the frequency, the greater the severity of conflict. The reoccurrence of crisis reflects a profound dissension between the parties, and a decline in the reiteration of crisis must represent some basic changes in the judgments of the parties regarding their interests. Conflict abatement is affected not only by the substance of crisis but also by the intensity of crisis occurrences within the conflict. Less frequent crisis commencement must indicate acceptance of some restraints on conflict procession. On the whole, we supplement crisis frequency with changes in magnitude that are reflected

27

through variations in context, process, and termination. Together they reflect the overall state of the conflict.

Our point of departure is that the year 1973 makes a useful demarcation line, since it constitutes the last interstate war over territorial-interstate issues, marking a shift in state behavior from violence to more peaceful modes of conflict management and resolution. From 1974 on, the ethnic elements in international crises gained prominence, reflecting the gradual transformation of the conflict.[3] Does the frequency measure confirm this assertion?

One way to appraise frequency is to divide the number of crises over the years. The span of the first period was twenty-five years, beginning with the first crisis, Palestine partition—Israel independence, on 29 November 1947, and ending with the termination of the Yom Kippur War in May of 1974.[4] With a record of seventeen events during this period, a crisis erupted on average at intervals of a year and a half. In comparison, during the twenty-seven years of the second period, from 1974 to 2000, nine crises took place at intervals of about three years, though crises occurred more often in the early part of this second period than in its later part. In real life, however, the distribution of crises was not spread out evenly, and several crises erupted in one year. The uneven time gaps between crises, especially at the end of the twentieth century, led us to gauge each period according to years free from crises, years of middle-range crises, and years of major crises defined as events involving ponderous military interactions. If a crisis carried over from one year into a large part of another year, then the second was also considered as a year of crisis. A year in which more than one crisis took place was considered one of at least mid-range severity.

The two periods under study are similar in length but the distribution of crisis cases in each is not equal. Twelve out of twenty-five years of the first period (48 percent) were free of international crisis, and another five years (20 percent) of the period endured one or more middle-range crises.[5] Nine years (33.3 percent) witnessed the initiation or the continuation of major crises.[6] During the second period, seventeen out of twenty-seven years (63 percent) were free of crises.[7] The other years were divided equally between middle and major crises, four years (15 percent) for each category.[8] With seventeen cases in the first period and only nine in the second, the average of crises per year is 0.68 and 0.33 respectively. The drop in crisis occurrence is especially true after 1985, with only two crises erupting since.[9] At first glance, then, it would appear that the second period reflects a meaningful trend of conflict moderation. These findings on the frequency of international crises point to a gradual winding down of the Arab-Israeli conflict.[10]

However, our observation of frequency cannot and should not sidestep regional developments that were not considered by ICB as belonging to the protracted Arab-Israeli conflict and were therefore not included in the figures presented thus far. To supplement our analysis we suggest a wider view that integrates the 1987 Intifada years and the 1990–1991 Gulf war during which Israel was threatened and eventually attacked by Iraq. With this outlook in mind, four of our crisis-free years were not totally free of conflict. If these years are taken into account, then only 48 percent of the years in the second period were crisis free, and another 52 percent qualify for either middle or major crises. These proportions are similar to those of the first era, and lead to the conclusion that in some aspects the situation did not improve or may even have worsened.

And yet, even this mode of analysis reveals that the conflict has been transformed in its nature: in the interstate domain there was a shift in location—from the core to the periphery with the new focus on the Israel-Iraq rivalry—and in the central issues of contention—that is, from conventional to nonconventional ones concerning subconventional warfare or weapons of mass destruction. Alongside the moderation in the interstate domain, the ethnic sphere was also showing some signs of toning down. In the late 1990s, incidents in the Lebanese security zone did take place, but these events did not transcend the normal relations range or trigger new international crises. The withdrawal of the Israeli Defense Force (IDF) from southern Lebanon in May 2000 without the outbreak of a major international crisis also sustains our thesis regarding moderation. The events of Intifada 2000 and their impact on the protracted conflict are analyzed in chapter 6. This outbreak of violence also supports our conclusion that conflict transformation has occurred, both in the specifics of the CMI that characterize international crises and in the relative salience of interstate and ethnic-state aspects of the compound conflict.

CONTEXT AND CHANGE IN INTERNATIONAL CRISES

This chapter looks at the twenty-six crises in the protracted conflict and explores their specifics by focusing on three core questions related to context and change: 1. When do contextual changes occur? 2. In which contextual attribute is it manifested? and 3. Can distinguishable periods be identified in terms of a rise or decline in context-derived crisis magnitude?

Having established a noticeable turning point in patterns of crises, based upon the frequency of such events, we now focus on changes in the contextual attributes of crisis as outlined in our theoretical framework. As we shall see, change in context can be detected over time: most cases of high level crisis magnitude occurred during the 1947–1973 period, whereas the post-1973 period witnessed a notable decline in magnitude. More specifically, the conflict, which at its inception was characterized by high gravity, intensive major/superpower involvement, and a large number of adversaries, underwent drastic change, involving low gravity, few adversaries, and minimal superpower involvement.

GRAVITY OF THREAT AND CRISIS MAGNITUDE

The first contextual indicator associated with crisis magnitude is gravity of threat. It denotes the content and importance of the fundamental stakes over which states compete. In the Arab-Israeli conflict, gravity ranges from threats to existence (the highest degree), through grave damage, threats to the political regime, threats to a state's territorial integrity or its influence, and, at the lowest range, economic threats or those of limited military damage.[11] The gravity of an international crisis is evaluated from a system level perspective, that is, each case is assigned a characteristic threat level based upon the essential issues involved in the confrontation and their centrality to the crisis as a whole. This holistic approach sidesteps the definition of threat in a foreign policy crisis, which may vary from one state to another depending upon the perceptions of the decision makers. By contrast, gravity in an international crisis, our focus of analysis, is evaluated from an overall-objective perspective. It takes into account the stakes over which the different adversaries contend and identifies the most salient threat in any particular confrontation.

In general, one can identify specific threats and describe changes in the content of threat in different crises, or over time. Alternatively, one can concentrate on several categories denoting levels of threat, and then compare two categories of high and low threat. In this chapter, we combine both approaches, paying special attention to changes in the levels of threat over time, from the high level threat characterizing the first period, and low level threats that gained prominence in the post-1973 years. However, within the categories of low and high level threats, we also examine the specific content of threat. Table 2.1 presents a summary of context attributes for the twenty-six international crises in the Arab-Israeli conflict. We begin with an analysis of high gravity crises.

High gravity crises

High gravity involves threats to existence, to military-related grave damage and to territorial integrity. First among these, threats to existence, the peak level issue at stake, were evident in three of the twenty-six cases under study, two of them in the pre-1973 period and only one in the post-1973 years. All three cases highlight the destabilizing effects of high threat and all of these cases focused on the issue of Israeli survival in the region, surrounded by Arab states who refused to accept its right to exist. In the 1947 Palestine partition—Israel independence crisis the existence of Israel as a sovereign state was the central issue at stake.[12] The United Nations General Assembly resolution 181 of 27 November 1947 marked the onset of this crisis. Its call for the establishment of two independent states, Palestine and Israel, was unacceptable to Egypt, Iraq, Jordan, Lebanon, and Syria, who totally rejected the idea of an independent Israeli state in the midst of the Arab world. Consequently, on 8 December 1947, the League of Arab States reaffirmed its determination to preserve Arab Palestine as an integral and indivisible entity, and announced plans to recruit an

TABLE 2.1
CONTEXT ATTRIBUTES OF CRISES IN THE ARAB-ISRAELI CONFLICT

CRISES IN THE FIRST PERIOD	DATE	ACTORS	GRAVITY	SUPERPOWERS	
				USA	USSR
Palestine partition/Israel independence	Nov.1947	Egypt, Jordan Iraq, Israel, Lebanon, Syria	Existence	Political	Political
Sinai incursion	Dec.1948	Egypt, Israel, UK	Territory	Political	None
Hula drainage	Feb.1951	Israel, Syria	Territory	Political	Political
Qilya	Oct.1953	Jordan	Political regime	Political	None
Gaza raid	Feb.1955	Egypt, Israel	Political regime	Political	Semi-military
Suez war	July 1956	Egypt, France, Israel, UK, USA, USSR	Grave damage	Political	Semi-military
Qalqilya	Sept.1956	Israel, Jordan	Territory	Political	None
Rottem	Feb.1960	Egypt, Israel	Influence	None	Political
Jordan waters	Dec. 1963	Egypt, Israel, Jordan, Lebanon, Syria	Economic	Political	Political
El Samu	Nov. 1966	Israel, Jordan	Grave damage	Political	None
Six Day war	May 1967	Egypt, Israel, Jordan, Syria, USA, USSR	Existence	Political	Political
Karameh	Mar. 1968	Israel, Jordan	Grave damage	Political	Political
Beirut airport	Dec. 1968	Lebanon	Political regime	Political	Political
War of attrition	Mar. 1969	Egypt, Israel, USSR	Grave damage	Political	Direct military
Libyan plane	Feb. 1973	Israel	Grave damage	None	None
Israel mobilization	April 1973	Israel	Grave damage	None	None
Yom Kippur war	Oct. 1973	Egypt, Israel, Syria, USA, USSR	Grave damage	Semi-military	Semi-military

TABLE 2.1 *(continued)*
CONTEXT ATTRIBUTES OF CRISES IN THE ARAB-ISRAELI CONFLICT

CRISIS IN THE SECOND PERIOD	DATE	ACTORS	GRAVITY	SUPERPOWERS	
				USA	USSR
Entebbe raid	June 1976	Israel, Uganda	Grave damage	None	None
Syria mobilization	Nov. 1976	Israel	Influence	Political	None
Litani operation	Mar. 1978	Lebanon	Territory	Political	Political
Iraq nuclear reactor	Jan. 1981	Iraq, Israel	Existence	Political	Political
Al-Biqa missiles I	April 1981	Israel, Syria	Influence	Political	Political
War in Lebanon	June 1982	Israel, Lebanon, Syria	Influence	Political	Semi-military
Al-Biqa missiles II	Nov. 1985	Israel, Syria	Influence	Political	Political
Operation Accountability	July 1993	Israel, Lebanon	Limited military damage	Political	None
Operation Grapes of Wrath	April 1996	Israel, Lebanon	Limited military damage	Political	None

Arab volunteer army, to prevent the emergence of the Jewish state. With the declaration of Israeli independence on 14–15 May 1948, Arab fear became a reality. On 15 May, five Arab states invaded Israel and presented an imminent threat to the existence of the newly established state, but ultimately failed to destroy it.

Israel's existence was again at stake twenty years later, during the 1967 Six Day War crisis. The crisis began on 17 May, with an Egyptian military aircraft flight over Israel's nuclear research center at Dimona and the dispatch of Egyptian divisions into the Sinai desert.[13] Additional escalation occurred on the eighteenth when the United Nations Emergency Force (UNEF), stationed in the Sinai since the 1956 Suez nationalization-war crisis, was withdrawn at the demand of Egyptian president Nasser. Israel had long warned that it would consider this Egyptian act, in violation of international law, as a *casus belli*. Egypt upped the ante with a blockade of the Israeli port of Eilat by closing the Straits of Tiran to Israeli shipping. Confronted with the danger of being choked within its small frontiers, Israeli existence was once again put to the test of Middle Eastern power politics. Although intensive international diplomacy tried to restore the status quo ante, it was only the Israeli surprise military attack on 5 June that removed the immediate threat to Israel's existence.

The only existence case in the post-1973 period occurred during the 1981 Iraq nuclear reactor crisis. This crisis was not a conventional military threat to the state of Israel, as in the former cases, but rather the threat of a nuclear strike in the Middle East and an end to the Israeli nonconventional strategic advantage. With a somewhat diminished nuclear option, Israel worried about its ability to deter a conventional Arab attack aimed at its destruction. Nuclear capability in the hands of a ruthless leader such as Saddam Hussein constituted an even more critical existential threat for Israel.[14]

Ongoing Arab efforts to refute Israeli nuclear supremacy climaxed with the building of the Osirak project. The French-supported Iraqi nuclear research site near Baghdad, begun in 1975. All Israeli diplomatic efforts to persuade France to halt its participation in the project failed, and on 28 October 1980 the Israeli government decided to attack the Iraqi reactor. France's announcement in January 1981 that the Osirak reactor would be fully operational by 14 July presented Israel with a clear deadline and marked the crisis trigger. Delay beyond that date would make the military option virtually impossible due to the extremely costly consequences of bombing a live reactor. Israel's surgical air attack on Iraq's nuclear installations on 7 June successfully removed the threat to its existence and re-established its nuclear deterrence within the Arab-Israeli conflict system.

In addition to these three crises of peak magnitude, eight of the twenty-six Arab-Israeli crises included a threat of military-related grave damage to some or all of the participating adversaries. Belonging to the high crisis magnitude range, seven of these cases took place during the 1947–1973 years and only one in the second period under study. As with the existence factor, high gravity characterizes the first period and rarely appears in the second period.

The 1956 Suez nationalization–war was the first in a series of crises involving grave damage. The Egyptian nationalization of the Suez Canal on 26 July 1956 precipitated a crisis for England and France. Both extraregional powers had been increasingly alarmed by the growing radicalization of Colonel Gamal Abdel Nasser's regime and its close association with the USSR. Both European nations foresaw threats to their economic interests and severe military-related consequences. Among these were Nasser's continued support to the Front Liberation National (FLN)—resisting French control in Algeria. Israel felt threatened by the continuous cross-border infiltrations of Palestinian Fedayeen from the Egyptian-controlled Gaza Strip and Sinai Peninsula, and by the expanding flow of Soviet arms supplies to Egypt since the September 1955 Czech–Egyptian arms deal.[15] The Israeli invasion into the Sinai on 29 October 1956 drew the USSR into the crisis. Egypt now faced the grave consequences of war, which also threatened the USSR by challenging the internal stability of its Middle Eastern client. The prospects of grave damage reached peak level when the USSR warned that it would use force if the situation was not rectified immediately. Sent in the midst of the Cold War, the Soviet warning introduced an acute element of nuclear threat to the urban centers of England, France, and Israel.

The 1966 El Samu crisis provides the next case in which grave damage was the highest threat on the agenda, focusing this time on Jordan. Though a much less severe crisis than the 1956 Suez case, El Samu is nonetheless regarded as a prelude to the 1967 Six Day War. The situation on the Israeli-Jordanian border had been deteriorating rapidly due to repetitive attacks by Palestinian infiltrators carrying out acts of sabotage within Israel. There was the potential of returning to the unstable situation of the 1950s when such attacks made daily life on the Israeli side unbearable. On 12 November, a land mine destroyed an Israeli army command car near the border, leaving three soldiers dead and six wounded. The next day, Israel carried out a reprisal commando raid on the village of El Samu, designed to warn Jordan that continued support for the Palestinians carried with it the consequences of grave IDF counterattacks. The situation escalated to an interstate confrontation and heavy fighting took place between the IDF and the Jordanian army.

A very similar incident occurred between Israel and Jordan in Karameh. On 18 March 1968, an Israeli school bus hit a mine near the Jordanian border. Two children died and twenty-eight were wounded. Israeli defense minister Moshe Dayan warned Jordan again that its continued support for the Palestinian Fedayeen would provoke grave consequences. Accordingly, Israeli forces attacked the village of Karameh, site of a Fedayeen base, on 21 March. Jordan dispatched its army to the area and massive fighting ensued, involving both Jordanian and Palestinian forces. The fact that the IDF launched both El Samu and Karameh retaliations in broad daylight and did not shy from engaging the Arab Legion signaled a major threat to Jordan, but the heavy casualties entailed a grave damage threat to Israel and the Palestinians as well.

The 1969 War of Attrition between Israel and Egypt, like the 1956 Suez case, entailed not only a threat of war but also grave domestic costs for both adversaries. The short-term period of tranquility between Israel and Egypt, which followed the 1967 Six Day War, ended abruptly on 8 March 1969. Egyptian forces directed severe artillery fire against Israeli fortifications along the Suez Canal. Continuous Egyptian shelling occurred throughout the next three months, inflicting heavy Israeli casualties. But this grave reality was not confined to the Israeli side alone. On 20 July, introducing a step level change in the confrontation, Israel launched an aerial bombing campaign inside Egypt. Hostilities escalated farther as Israel initiated deeper penetration attacks into Egypt. Israel hoped this acceleration in violence would make the price of war unbearable for Egypt by amplifying unrest. As in the 1956 Suez crisis, the stability of President Nasser's regime was again at stake. The USSR reacted by introducing Soviet military personnel in Egypt to operate the newly installed missile batteries in the canal zone, a step level increase in military dangers. Threats of escalation reached a peak on 18 April 1970, when Israeli pilots clashed with a Soviet-piloted aircraft.

In contrast to the prolonged threat of grave damage present throughout the year and a half of the Egyptian-Israeli War of Attrition, a more acute threat of this sort occurred in 1973 during a thirty-minute Libyan plane crisis. The Israeli cabinet received information regarding Palestinian intentions to hijack an airplane and blow it up over a major Israel population center. On 21 February 1973, Israeli radar spotted a Libyan Boeing 727 heading toward Israel's nuclear plant in Dimona. Coupled with earlier threats, the presence of a hostile airliner presented Israel with a threat of grave damage to its military sites and urban centers. Twenty minutes of sustained warnings and repeated demands that it identify itself were to no avail. The increased sense of grave damage led to an order by the Israeli chief of staff, Lieutenant-General David Elazar, to shoot down the plane.[16]

The 1973 Israeli mobilization case, a prelude to the 1973 October War, involved a grave damage threat to Israel that did not materialize into actual fighting. At the beginning of April, Egypt's president Anwar al-Sadat publicly stated that his country was preparing for war with Israel and announced a large-scale Egyptian army military exercise. Similarly, Israeli intelligence reports on 10 April warned that an Egyptian attack had been planned for 15 May. In response, Israel, too, began to prepare for war, placed its army on alert, and called reserve units into service. Apparently neither side wanted to cross the brink. To prevent the high costs of war, Israel and Egypt confined themselves this time to a contest of wits as opposed to a real collision of armies. Although a military encounter was aborted, this crisis proved a crucial precedent for the October War six months later, at which time, once again, Israel had to weigh the costs of mobilizing its army in response to intelligence estimates regarding a pending Arab attack. Our research suggests that Israel's timely mobilization deterred the Egyptian attack early in 1973. Deterrence rather than international mediation prevented the escalation to war. Tragically for Israel, it chose early mobilization for the aborted crisis and opted to postpone mobilization in the October case, where the real Egyptian-Syrian surprise attack was implemented.

In contrast to the May 1973 episode, above, the October-Yom Kippur War crisis involved not only threats but also actual grave military damage for Israel and all its Arab adversaries. On 5 October, the change in Egyptian army posture from defensive to offensive, coupled with movement of its forces toward the Suez Canal, triggered a crisis for Israel. War, which had been averted earlier in April, now seemed inescapable. The careful balance of power maneuvers that had characterized the former crisis were missing this time and escalation was rapid. Hostilities broke out the next day and lasted until 26 October. Swift Egyptian and Syrian military advances in the south and in the north introduced an increased Israeli sense of grave damage, and led to the implementation of the "Samson Option"—the visible preparation of Israel's nuclear weapons for immediate use, in order to deter conventional Arab military escalation. Israeli forces managed to reverse the military situation in the Golan Heights by 10 October and in the Sinai on 14 October. With the military threat reversed, Israel returned its nuclear weapons to storage.

The only case in the second period in which the ICB project acknowledged grave damage, occurred in the 1976 Entebbe raid. This time however, ICB analysis focused on a much narrower topic, the fate of the hijacked aircraft's passengers, and not on a war involving the Israeli or Arab population. On 27 June an Air France plane en route from Tel-Aviv to Paris was hijacked after a stopover in Athens. This act, carried out by the Popular Front for the Liberation of Palestine (PFLP), with the support and participation of terrorists from Germany's Bader-Meinhof group presented Israeli leaders with a grave threat to the lives of Jewish and Israeli passengers alike. After landing in Libya, the plane was forced to fly to Entebbe, Uganda. Once the hostages of other nationalities were separated from the Jewish and Israeli ones, indicating a grave situation for the latter, Israel opted for a military rescue operation.

A close examination of Arab-Israeli crises shows that a threat of the loss of territory rarely served as the most salient stake for any of the adversaries. Only four of the twenty-six Arab-Israeli crises involved a threat to territorial integrity, and each time the vulnerable party was Arab, namely, Egypt in 1948, Syria in 1951, Jordan in 1956, and Lebanon in 1978. Three of these cases occurred in the 1947–1973 period and only one in the post-1973 years, thus denoting higher magnitude in the former and lower magnitude in the latter.

The 1948 Sinai incursion case, which occurred during the first Arab-Israeli war, was the first crisis in which a threat to territorial integrity was present in and of itself, to both Israel and Egypt. When Egypt invaded parts of the Negev and its forces reached the Hebron area, Israel's territorial integrity was at stake. By mid-October, the IDF had expelled the Egyptian army from the latter region and encircled the Egyptian army in the Negev, exposing Egypt to a similar threat. On 25 December, Israeli forces crossed into the Egypt's Sinai Peninsula, confronting Egypt with the prospective loss of territory should the areas under Israeli de facto military control be recognized as part of a future Israeli sovereignty.

Territorial quarrels persisted after the end of the 1948–1949 hostilities. The 1949 armistice agreement between Israel and Syria demarcated a temporary boundary between them, but differing interpretations produced the 1951 Hula drainage crisis. On 12 February 1951, the Israeli Palestine Land Development Company (PLDC) began work on the Hula drainage project in the Demilitarized Military Zone (DMZ) between Israel and Syria, north of the Sea of Galilee. Syria regarded Israeli work in the area as a violation of the armistice, which designed the DMZ as a "no man's land." Israel's goal was to eliminate malaria in the swamps surrounding Hula Lake and to use the reclaimed area and its water for agriculture and irrigation. Syrian diplomatic efforts to bring the project to a halt ultimately failed. On 15 March, Syria opened fire at an Israeli bulldozer working in the Hula area and escalated the crisis. This resort to violence indicated the Syrian perception that Israeli territorial ambitions would be realized at Syria's expense.

A third case of territorial threat was the 1956 Qalqilya raid in which Jordan found itself in a crisis situation following a series of Palestinian attacks from across its borders into Israel. The crisis erupted following an Israeli attack on a Jordanian police station near Garandal on 13 September 1956. Unable to curb Fedayeen activity and fearful of Israeli retaliation, the Hashemite Kingdom tightened its bonds with Iraq, which promised to make its forces available to Jordan upon request. Further incidents brought additional Israeli raids. After guerillas striking from Jordan ambushed an Israeli bus, the IDF launched a particularly harsh retaliatory raid against Qalqilya. In response, Iraq declared a willingness to send troops to Jordan immediately. Alarmed by the prospect of Iraqi soldiers on its border and realizing that the core issue of the crisis had been sliding from a low level ethnic threat to a balance of power issue, Israeli foreign minister Golda Meir announced that Israel would consider such an Iraqi move a threat to Israeli territorial integrity.[17] Qalqilya proved that tension along the Israeli-Jordanian border could lead to unpredicted escalation and that an ethnic-related incident could materialize into a full-fledged international crisis over realist issues. At the time the Qalqilya raid took place, plans to end the hostile and unstable Israel-Fedayeen situation via an attack on Egypt , the core supporter of Palestinian irregulars at that time, were already almost completed.[18]

The only case in the post-1973 period involving territorial threat occurred during the 1978 Litani operation. As in the earlier case of Qalqilya, a deteriorating situation on Israel's border, with frequent violent attacks by Palestinian elements, caused an interstate confrontation. On 11 March, a seaborne attack originating from PLO bases in Lebanon, was launched on the major coastal highway north of Tel-Aviv. Thirty-five Israelis were killed and another seventy wounded before some of the terrorists were killed and others were captured. In reprisal, the IDF struck PLO strongholds in the southern part of Lebanon. The territorial threat to Lebanon became actual when it realized that the Israeli units would remain stationed in those areas until an acceptable political solution for the region were negotiated.

The threats described thus far, to existence, of grave damage, and to territory, were major contributors to high gravity and therefore to high crisis magnitude. Other threats, to a political regime, to influence, to economic interests, or of limited military damage, led to lower levels of gravity and thereby to low crisis magnitude.

Low gravity crises

In three of the twenty-six crises in the Arab–Israeli conflict a threat to the domestic stability of a political regime was the main issue at stake.[19] All these cases, in the 1947–1973 period, were triggered by Israeli military reprisal attacks, in response to continuous Fedayeen infiltrations from the neighboring Arab states. Israel's policy was to hold any Arab regime that permitted its territory to function as a staging area for acts of sabotage against Israel responsible for the consequences of an Israeli counterattack. Consequently, threats to the domestic stability of neighboring Arab regimes was a byproduct of Israel's war against the Palestinian ethnic elements operating from their territory against Israeli targets.[20] Israel calculated that the prospects of domestic unrest and instability, resulting from Israeli raids, would compel the Arab states to restrain Fedayeen activity. This logic became part of Israel's deterrence policy.[21] However, Israeli retaliation was intended to be limited in scope and fell short of presenting a real existential threat to any Arab regime.[22]

Israel exercised this deterrent reprisal policy against the Hashemite regime in the Qibya crisis of 1953. As early as 1951, Palestinian infiltrations from Jordan were common. In October 1953 the situation escalated after an Israeli woman and her two children were murdered by infiltrators from Jordan. The international crisis started on 14 October, when the IDF, in a reprisal raid, killed sixty-nine civilians and destroyed forty-five houses in the Jordanian village of Qibya. The scale of the Israeli attack endangered the domestic stability in Jordan and put pressure on the Hashemite regime to resist the inter-Arab approach, which advocated a permissive hand toward the Palestinian Fedayeen campaign.

Egypt also experienced the threat of internal instability during the 1955 Gaza raid crisis. As in the former case, the Israeli reprisal policy aimed to halt ongoing Fedayeen attacks that originated in the early 1950s from the Egyptian-controlled Gaza region. Egyptian support for these Palestinian activities were part of President Nasser's pan-Arab ambitions. The Israeli raid on Gaza, on 28 February 1955, resulted in thirty-eight Arab deaths and thirty-two others injured. The attack constituted an element in Israel's emerging deterrence policy and signaled Egypt and the Arab world that no regime that supported the Palestinian guerillas would be immune from Israeli counterattack. President Nasser perceived this reprisal action as directed against his regime and according to his evidence, it prompted him to turn farther toward Moscow.[23]

The last threat to domestic stability occurred during the 1968 Beirut airport raid. Lebanon was the target of an Israeli reprisal since it too, like Jordan and Egypt, allowed the Palestinian Fedayeen to use Lebanese territory as their recruiting and training ground and outpost for cross-border raids into Israel. As in the earlier cases, Israeli reprisal came in response to an escalation in Palestinian military activity. Israel struck shortly after members of the PFLP attacked an Israeli civilian plane at the Athens International Airport. On 28 December, an Israeli raid on the Beirut International Airport destroyed thirteen jetliners belonging to Middle East Airlines, along with other Lebanese-owned planes. The message was clear: if Israeli aviation was unsafe, the same rule applied to all Arab airlines. Due to the fragile political situation in Lebanon, this raid brought about not only physical damage, but also an internal Lebanese political crisis and increased domestic unrest.

Five of the twenty-six crises in the Arab-Israeli conflict involved a low magnitude threat to influence. Only one of them occurred in the first period, with the remaining four in the post-1973 years. Since a threat to influence is lower than the threats to existence, of grave damage, or to territory described earlier, these findings indicate a relative decline in levels of threat in crises and a winding down trend in the conflict in the second period.

Of the five influence cases treated here, the 1960 Rottem crisis between Israel and Egypt was the single case recorded by ICB in the first period. Following the 1956 Suez war, Israel's border with Egypt was relatively calm, but this was not the case along its northern border with Syria.[24] Violent escalation involved repeated Fedayeen infiltrations from Syria into Israel and Israeli reprisals, but none of them reached the level of crisis. Coinciding with this escalating sub-state and interstate tension, the United Arab Republic (UAR)—a unification of Egypt and Syria—also confronted Israel with the threat of a new hostile political entity.

The crisis commenced on 15 February 1960, when Egyptian president Nasser obtained information from the USSR regarding an Israeli troop concentration along its northern border, apparently to attack Syria. Faced with a threat to its influence in the young UAR union, Egypt reacted promptly. On 23 February, Israeli intelligence informed Israel's defense and prime minister, David Ben Gurion, that the Egyptian army had crossed the Suez Canal and stood poised at the southern border with Israel. Challenged by these military deployments, Israel ordered the Rottem maneuver and consequently moved its forces southward to face the Egyptians. Evidently, the bilateral Egyptian-Israeli struggle for influence rapidly shifted from words to restrained military deeds. Yet crisis magnitude remained low and the two states did not actually cross the threshold of violence, indicating the stabilizing role of the balance of power that deterred both sides from escalation. Consequently, when threat remains low, and gravity does not exceed the specific issues of confrontation, hostilities may be restrained.[25]

All four threat to influence crises in the second period involved confrontations between Israel and Syria. First among them was the Syria mobilization crisis of 1976. Within the context of its participation in the Lebanese civil war, which erupted in 1975, Syria moved to consolidate its presence and influence in Lebanon. At the same time, Israel regarded south Lebanon as a security zone providing additional protection for Israel's northern border, and was determined to deter Syria from advancing toward the Israel-Lebanon border. Neither Syria nor Israel wanted a war with each other, so both states tacitly accepted the Litani River as a "red line" that separated their respective zones of influence and established a delicate balance between the two states within Lebanon. Challenges to this tacit understanding ignited threats to influence crises several times, starting with the 1976 case. On 21 November, Syrian troops in Lebanon launched a military drive toward the south. Fearing that Syria might disregard their understanding and cross the Litani River, Israel saw the Syrian move as a direct threat to its influence in Lebanon. Diplomatic channels in Washington were successfully activated to assure that the Litani line understanding would prevail, averting military confrontation and a change in the balance of power between the Syria and Israel in Lebanon.

The 1981 Al Biqa I crisis constituted the second case of a threat to influence between Israel and Syria in the post-1973 years. The crisis was again part of the tacit Israeli-Syrian "red line" Litani understanding.

On 28 April, Israeli planes shot down two Syrian helicopters carrying supplies to Syrian forces on Mount Sanin, overlooking the city of Zahle. Zahle is situated in a strategic location controlling the Beirut - Damascus highway and in the spring of 1981 was a stronghold of the Lebanese Christian militia. Syria responded to the Israeli assault by attacking the Christian militia in Zahle, and moved to deter Israeli air power by introducing SAM-3 ground-to-air missiles in the Lebanon battle zone. Those missiles threatened Israel with the prospects of change in the balance of power and influence in Lebanon, to Syria's advantage. To preserve Israeli dominance of Lebanese air space, Israeli planes destroyed the Syrian missile bases on 28 May.

Third among the post-1973 international crisis that ICB classified as a threat to influence was the 1982 Lebanon war.[26] Unlike the previous cases where violence was only threatened or minimal, struggles over influence in June 1982 ignited full-scale war, engulfing Israeli, Lebanese, and Syrian forces in a dangerous confrontation. This escalation followed a period of PLO hostilities against Israel in the form of Katyusha rocket shelling from southern Lebanon into the upper Galilee, and an assassination attempt against the Israeli ambassador in London, Shlommo Argov. On 5 June, Israeli forces invaded Lebanon, ostensibly to destroy the PLO infrastructure in that country. In an effort to preserve the Israeli-Syrian balance of influence, Israel indicated to Syria, via Washington, that it would not cross into Syrian-controlled areas unless its forces were attacked by Syrian troops. However, Israel's military advances led, on 7 June, to a confrontation with Syrian forces in the Biqa—the valley of Lebanon—a Syrian-controlled region.

The fourth and last Israel-Syria threat to influence case was the 1985 Al Biqa II crisis. As in the previous Al Biqa case, an Israeli attack on Syrian aircraft in Lebanon marked the onset of the crisis, indicating Israeli determination to maintain free skies over Lebanon for its own air force. On 19 November, Israel shot down the Syrian planes after they interfered with Israeli planes on a reconnaissance mission over Lebanon. Syria replied by setting up SAM-6 missiles in the Biqa region along the Beirut-Damascus highway, and in locations close to the Israeli-Lebanon border. On 27 December, Israeli defense minister Yitzhak Rabin warned Damascus that Israel would act to remove the missiles, irrespective of the cost involved. Again, both states had to calculate the price of upsetting their delicate balance of power in Lebanon.

Given the salience of military-security issues in international crises, it is not surprising that throughout the protracted Arab-Israeli conflict, the ICB data-set contains only one case where the highest threat was economic.[27] This was the 1963 Jordan waters crisis, in which the sphere of contention was confined to the economic domain. The question of Arab and Israeli use of water from the Jordan River, which was an unresolved issue of the first Arab-Israeli war, broke open once again in this low magnitude international crisis. With no agreement to coordinate the water projects of the different states, each went ahead with its own plan.[28] Jordan launched its water program in 1958 and Israel followed in 1959 with the National Water Carrier project. Arab opposition to the Israeli water diversion plan intensified in December 1963 as the Israeli project came close to its completion. A conference of Arab chiefs of staff met in Cairo to discuss a joint plan of action. Only one day after the Arab conference ended, Yigal Allon, the Israeli minister of labor, declared that Israel would unilaterally and fully operate its National Water Carrier as per its original implementation plan. Syria upped the ante with threats of war, although Egyptian president Nasser preferred to curb escalation at a time when Egypt was not yet ready for war.

The relative absence of other economic threat crises indicated how far the region was then and still is now from topics of integration and interdependence in comparison to the frequent security and ethnic related challenges that occurred even in the second period.

The lowest type of threat evident in the Arab-Israeli conflict is one of limited military damage. This threat was present only twice, in the post-1973 period, during the 1993 Operation Accountability crisis and the 1996 Operation Grapes of Wrath case, which was in many respects a continuation of the 1993 confrontation. The absence of other low level military threat in Arab-Israeli crises points to the relatively high levels of threat characterizing international crises in this protracted conflict. However, the presence of these crises also indicates that in the second period, the protagonists could weigh military action separately from political interests, leading to a more controlled environment during crisis, even when violence did occur.

The 1993 crisis began with a 10 July Hizbullah attack in the Israeli security zone in southern Lebanon, killing five Israeli soldiers and wounding others. Yizhak Rabin, Israel's prime minister, called on Syria to restrain Hizbullah. After several additional attacks, the IDF launched "Operation Accountability," heavy artillery and air raids against Hizbullah bases and south Lebanon villages, designed to create a massive flow of civilians northward toward Beirut. Israel hoped the crush of refugees would compel Lebanon and Syria to act decisively against Hizbullah and prevent additional attacks against Israel. Hizbullah strikes and Israel's retaliation caused Israel and Lebanon, respectively, a threat of limited military damage. However, both sides viewed this as a relatively confined episode of neither grave magnitude nor the prospect of spillover implications for other national interests.

Quite similarly, during the 1996 crisis, tensions between the South Lebanese Army, Hizbullah, and Israel escalated into an Israeli reprisal operation aimed to break Hizbullah's ability to undertake military attacks within southern

Lebanon and into northern Israel by destroying Hizbullah camps, supply lines, arms depots, and fighters. The Israeli limited military damage threat became coupled with a similar one to Lebanon when a flood of refugees began its way north toward the capital and Israeli attacks against targets in Beirut intensified. As in 1993, Israel hoped that suffering civilians in the south would blame the Hizbullah elements in their midst for provoking Israel's wrath, but no issues of long-term Israeli territorial conquest or of Lebanese existence were involved. Even the domestic stability of the regime in Beirut was not impinged upon since those Lebanese with little sympathy for Hizbullah's wider aspirations (such as creating an Islamic state) rallied behind the refugees and against Israel.

Returning to the questions we raised at the onset of this chapter, several conclusions regarding the gravity of threat in crises appear in this analysis. First, the gravity of threats found in the 1947–1973 period tend to be higher in magnitude (existence, grave damage and territorial threat cases) than those characterizing the 1974–2000 years (mainly influence and threats of limited military damage). Change in gravity is therefore found not only between different crises, but also over time.

Second, some low gravity cases do appear in the first period, indicating that the possibility of less severe confrontations is not altogether ruled out, even in the midst of an intense protracted conflict.

Third, the intertwining of the interstate and ethnic dimensions is an important contributor to lower gravity cases. Crises that escalate from the substate domain to the interstate arena remain relatively low in terms of their gravity. The second part of this study—chapters 5 and 6—will further illuminate this critical relationship between the interstate and ethnic domains of crises in the Arab-Israeli conflict.

Gravity of threat is a core indicator of crisis magnitude, but as suggested in the theoretical framework of this study, other contextual elements also denote extent of magnitude. Among these are the number of actors and the extent of superpower involvement in crises. These aspects are addressed in our analysis of crisis actors and crisis magnitude.

CRISIS ACTORS AND CRISIS MAGNITUDE

The second context indicator of international crisis is the number of adversaries considered to be crisis actors. This indicator is based on the ICB distinction, presented in the theoretical framework, between *actors in crisis,* that is, states that are involved in the crisis in some form or another, and those that are *crisis actors,* namely, states that encounter the three conditions of a foreign policy crisis: threat to basic values, finite time for response, and a perceived prospect of future hostilities between the adversaries in crisis.[29] Crisis actors are the more important participants in any encounter and they are the states that create the basic agenda for the confrontation and its resolution. Similarly, our concept of crisis magnitude is measured by the number of crisis actors, since it is their power, interests, and type of activity that are crucial during the crisis. The larger the number of crisis actors, the larger the span of interests involved and, consequently, the more complex the diplomatic struggle over stakes, with a finite time for response, thereby making it harder to resolve the confrontation without resort to violence. Many crisis actors participating in an international crisis indicate severe turmoil.

In multi-actor hostile environments, regardless of the distribution of power, an early resort to military options as a way to protect the vital goals of each side is more likely than in a crisis with a lower number of participants. Therefore, the participation of a larger number of Arab states marks escalation and severe crisis while a decline in the number of adversaries indicates crisis moderation.

Our analysis differentiates between two levels of participation in crisis: high and low. Four and more crisis actors denote a high participation level and therefore high magnitude, while cases with one to three crisis actors are considered as a low participation level, indicating low crisis magnitude. The unique nature of the Arab-Israeli conflict—with a single Jewish state and multiple Arab adversaries—frequently escalates beyond the bilateral-type confrontations. Accordingly, any case with only three actors or fewer is regarded as a low magnitude crisis. Moreover, given the importance of nonregional actors who also took part in this protracted conflict, many crises display multiple participants from outside the region and a wide range of conflicting interests. One or more Arab states allied against Israel was the characteristic pattern in the conflict, but some cases of higher magnitude such as the 1956 Suez nationalization-war saw Israeli major power allies, namely, Great Britain and France, fight alongside Israel and against Egypt, or the superpowers at the brink of confrontation alongside their regional proxies in the 1973 October War.

High crisis actor participation

Crises in the Arab-Israeli conflict vary in their number of participants, ranging from high levels, which most often characterize the 1947–1973 years, to a low number of adversaries involved in the cases that occur mostly in the post-1973 period. These findings accord with the trend described earlier regarding the decline in the gravity of threat over time.

Starting with the peak number of participants, there were three crises with six crisis actors, all of them in the first period. In the 1947–1948 Palestine partition-first Arab-Israeli war, Egypt, Iraq, Jordan, Lebanon, Syria, and Israel were all crisis actors.[30] Notably, this was the only multiple actor case where no major power from outside the region participated as a crisis actor. As such, this case represents the highest number of local adversaries involved in any confrontation throughout the entire conflict. Significantly, the crisis was not triggered by any of its participants, but rather by an institutional decision—resolution 181 passed by the UN General Assembly on 29 November 1947, supporting the establishment of two independent states, Arab and Jewish, in Palestine.

The high number of actors involved in this case, with all the Arab countries from the core and the periphery, also added to the scope of issues at stake, prolonged its duration, shaped the extent of violence, and left its imprint on the nature of crisis termination. As will be seen in chapter 3, the process of managing the complex and diverse issues at stake made it necessary to conclude bilateral agreements between Israel and the Arab states that dealt with specific topics relevant to each pair in the conflict.

The second case involving six states was the Suez nationalization-war of 1956. France, the UK, Egypt, the USSR, the United States, and Israel were its crisis actors. In contrast to the Palestine partition case, states from outside the region outnumbered the regional actors and considerably escalated the crisis, indicating for the first time the dangers of spillover from regional to global conflict. Moreover, both major and superpowers participated in the confrontation, marking the transformation of the Arab-Israeli conflict from a zone of colonial struggle for influence to an area of intense superpower competition and containment.

Unlike most international crises, which are triggered by one state initiating a direct hostile act against its adversaries, this crisis began with an internal political change that was regarded as a hostile move by other states. On 26 July 1956, Egypt's president Nasser announced the nationalization of the Suez Canal, thereby abrogating the ninety-nine-year lease of the Anglo-French Suez Canal Corporation, which was due to expire in 1968. Alarmed, the UK and France first pursued a diplomatic resolution via multilateral talks including the United States and Australia. Additional escalation took place at Sevres, on 22–25 October, when the UK joined France and Israel in their plans for a joint attack. The Israeli invasion of the Sinai Peninsula on 29 October was followed, two days later, by a British and French landing of forces in the canal zone. The active participation of major powers in military action raised the stakes in this confrontation and increased its magnitude.

The United States and USSR were also involved as crisis actors whose role in the confrontation was not confined to escalation and brinkmanship. They also served as a restraining factor that led to its termination and to the establishment of an agreed upon institutional mechanism that enhanced regional stability.[31]

The participation of the major and superpowers escalated the crisis and prolonged its duration. Rather than remaining a bilateral clash between Israel and Egypt on the issue of cross-border infiltrations, the confrontation broadened into a power struggle between the former colonial powers and Egypt, together with a regional test of wits for the superpowers, who were at that point consolidating their respective spheres of influence in the Middle East and Western/Eastern Europe. As such, this case reflects not only a large number of crisis actors, but also the widest range of actors present—regional and global—in a single crisis throughout the Arab-Israeli conflict. Turmoil was also enhanced by the actual use of direct military means by nonregional powers, an outstandingly rare event in the Arab-Israeli conflict that had occurred only once earlier, during the 1948 Sinai incursion case, and was repeated in only one additional case—the 1969 War of Attrition—which involved high salience active participation but on a very limited scope.[32]

The 1956 crisis marked the end of the intercolonial struggles in the Middle East.[33] Instead, a period of intense and prolonged superpower rivalry commenced in the region, a struggle that lasted until the collapse of the USSR. The rise of a bipolar global deterrence system, in place of the old colonial competition in the Middle East, came into full play in the next multiple actor crisis: the 1967 Six Day War. Israel, Jordan, Egypt, the United States, Syria, and the USSR were crisis actors in this case where, as in 1947, regional states constituted the core adversaries, namely, all the Arab confrontation states except Lebanon and Iraq. It also furthered the dangerous prospects of direct superpower confrontation triggered by their client states, mentioned earlier in our analysis of the 1956 Suez nationalization case. It is, however, interesting to note that both the regional states and the superpowers added to crisis escalation while only the superpowers were actively involved in crisis abatement. After an Israeli surprise attack on 5 June, and an Arab refusal to accept a UN-sponsored ceasefire that would have left Israeli forces in control of large Arab territories, both superpowers entered into a brinkmanship process, threatening intervention if their regional client states refused to end hostilities immediately. De-escalation was facilitated once the USSR and the United States shifted their role from crisis escalators to managers, pressuring their client states to accept UN Security Council ceasefire resolution 242.[34]

In addition to the three high magnitude cases described above, with six crisis actors in each, two cases in the Arab-Israeli conflict involved five crisis actors, and these also occurred in the first period. During the 1963 Jordan waters crisis, only the regional powers Jordan, Lebanon, Syria, Egypt, and Israel took part. Israel triggered this crisis with its announcement that, despite Arab disapproval, it would continue construction of a national water carrier according to original plans. The crisis escalated due to the coordinated action of the four Arab protagonists, but Israel completed its water project on 5 May 1964, uneventfully, making this the only case with a high number of crisis actors where escalation was confined and violence was averted. However, the importance of this multi-actor crisis was in the formation of an Arab coalition, which convened periodic inter-Arab summits, and ultimately participated three years later in the 1967 Six Day War.

By contrast, the second five actors case of the October-Yom Kippur War of 1973 involved both superpowers and three local adversaries: Israel, Egypt, and Syria. As in the 1956 Suez case, the United States and the USSR were not only mediators and crisis managers who offered their good offices to the contending parties, but rather crisis actors, themselves threatened by the sequence of crisis escalation, and thereby adding to the overall magnitude of the case. Turmoil and confrontation that began with a joint Egyptian-Syrian surprise attack on 6 October 1973 along the Suez Canal and the Golan Heights, rapidly developed into a superpower show of force. Aware of the grave consequences of nuclear escalation, the United States and the USSR also exercised their efforts to enforce the ceasefire agreement that in effect ended the crisis, though its final resolution was postponed to the formal acceptance of U.S.-mediated Israeli-

Egyptian and Israeli-Syrian disengagement agreements signed on 18 January and 31 May 1974, respectively.

On the whole, the examination of crises with a large number of adversaries points to a clear tendency: these cases occur in the 1947–1973 period, they involve core interstate issues in the military-security sphere, and more often than not they overlap with full scale violence crises. In these cases, not only regional states but also major and super powers as well participated in the course of events. But the involvement of the latter, who were active in political as well as in military domains, has a significance of its own, shaping the core attributes of the confrontation from its onset, via its escalation and concluding with the modes of crisis abatement. Hence, it is crucial to take a close look at the role of superpower participation and its contribution to crisis magnitude, a topic we will explore after our review of crises with a small number of actors.

Low crisis actor participation

Crises with a small number of participants indicate low crisis magnitude. We anticipate that they are usually less complex, cover less central issues, which matter to a few states only, and the adversaries frequently find escalation easier to control. Core among these confrontations were crises involving ethnic strife and escalations over cross-border infiltrations and reprisals. Consequently, alongside the ethnic elements who incited tension, these cases tended to involve only regional states, thereby adding a restraining element. Indeed, if violence occurred it was limited in scope and remained confined to a small—usually bilateral—number of contending state adversaries.[35]

Some crises of this type occurred in the first period, but such cases became more frequent in the post-1973 years, signaling two noteworthy tendencies: first, a relative decline in crisis magnitude derived from the number of actors contextual component, indicating a slow winding down process in the Arab-Israeli conflict; second, the occurrence of crises with only a few adversarial actors demonstrates that some of the state actors—weary of the prolonged duration of the conflict—were opting to leave the cycle of violence and leave it to the sides involved directly.[36] This decline in confrontations and crisis magnitude, reflected in the number of actors, possibly suggests a winding down period preceding the full resolution of the conflict.

Only three Arab-Israeli cases involved three crisis actors. Two of them took place in the first period, and only one in the post-1973 years. All three actor cases included major powers from outside the region, but escalation was confined since only one major power was active, thereby ruling out the danger of a global confrontation.

The first of those cases was the 1948 Sinai incursion, in which Egypt, the UK, and Israel participated. The crisis occurred as an escalation in the first Arab-Israeli war. After Israeli forces invaded the Sinai Peninsula on 25 December and threatened Egyptian territory, Egypt requested help from the UK, its former colonial patron, based upon their former—though expired—military treaty of

1936. The UK responded diplomatically, with an ultimatum to Israel calling for the immediate withdrawal of its forces from the Sinai. This move was coupled with military measures: British planes engaged in military action, and the Israeli air force shot five of them down. These intense pressures, combined with a UN Security Council call for a ceasefire, eventually led to an Israeli withdrawal, which was completed by 10 January 1949, signaling the termination of this crisis. The relatively small number of actors reduced the salience of major power participation and made compromise possible.

The next three actor case was the 1969 War of Attrition. The participants were again Israel, Egypt, and a major power from outside, but this time it was the USSR and not the UK who sided with Egypt. Moreover, turmoil in this crisis was longer in duration, though, once again, the role of outside intervention was limited and focused on a single event. Hostilities between Israel and Egypt, which began on 8 March 1969, rapidly escalated into a lengthy war of attrition, with two significant turning points, on 20 July 1969 and 7 January 1970, when Israel introduced step-level increases in its use of air power in an effort to end the war. In the course of the second deep penetration bombing phase of the war, Israeli planes confronted Soviet-piloted aircraft in a single military encounter on 18 April. It was later confirmed that four Soviet pilots were shot down.

The 1982 Lebanon war, last among the three actor crises, occurred in the post–1973 period. Escalating from protracted Palestinian low level military hostility directed against Israel, which the Lebanese government was unable to prevent, this international crisis involved Lebanon, Syria, and Israel. Unlike the two previous cases all of the participants in this crisis were regional actors and ethnic actors. The Palestinians and internal Lebanese factions played an active role exacerbating this crisis. The unique attributes of this case represented the transformation of the conflict from a bilateral or multistate confrontation to complex and overlapping interstate and interethnic rivalry. The new realities were also reflected in the prolonged duration of this case, from 5 June 1982, when the IDF invaded Lebanon, until 17 May 1983, when the short-lived Israeli-Lebanese peace agreement was signed. Though this crisis represented a territorial breach of Lebanese sovereignty, its major topics were the PLO presence in the country, particularly in the Beirut area, and the Israel-Syria influence struggle dating to their protracted involvement in the Lebanese civil war. Noticeable, too, was the absence of traditional crisis actors such as Egypt, Jordan, and the USSR, confirming the emergence of new conflict attributes.

The most common type of crisis contributing to low crisis magnitude is the two actor case. Twelve crises of this type occurred, with an equal distribution of six cases in each of the two periods discussed throughout this study. While this low magnitude, bilateral type confrontation persisted over time, the adversarial sides in these events did change. Israel and Jordan and Israel and Egypt were the most common dyads in the earlier period, whereas Israel and Syria and Israel and Lebanon dominated the later years.

Early cases involving Israel and Jordan as crisis actors were the 1956

Qalqilya, 1966 El Samu, and 1968 Karameh episodes. All three cases illustrated how a low magnitude confrontation could escalate to violence as a consequence of sub-state ethnic provocations. The core issue in these cases was one of defining state policy toward the Palestinian Fedayeen, operating within the territorial sovereignty of Jordan. Before the crisis began, a relatively long period of cross-border infiltrations occured, with Palestinian fighters penetrating Israel from Jordan and carrying out sabotage against both army and civilian targets. In order to induce a severe anti-Fedayeen reaction by Jordan to these incidents, Israel implemented a policy of harsh reprisals.

Notably, in all three dyadic cases, interstate confrontation resulted from sub-state ethnic provocations, and though violence did take place, its duration and magnitude were defined by the small number of crisis actors, making it easier for them to control levels of escalation and to limit the potentially costly consequences.

Two bilateral cases involved Egypt and Israel, and both occurred in the early years of the Arab-Israeli conflict: the 1955 Gaza raid and Rottem in 1960. The first case followed the pattern of crises generated as a result of sub-state activity, mentioned above in the Jordanian context, while the second case constituted a clear interstate power confrontation. The halting 1955 Gaza crisis was the largest in a sequence of Israeli raids aimed at a raising tide of Palestinian Fedayeen infiltrations from the Egyptian-held Gaza Strip into Israeli territory. The deteriorating situation added uncertainty to the delicate balance of power between Israel and Egypt. Unlike the Jordanian situation, in which both sides attempted to avert conflict, this Israeli reprisal caused an escalation in the regional arms race, evidenced when Egypt signed an extensive arms deal with Czechoslovakia and Israel concluded a counter deal with France.[37]

The 1960 Rottem case, also reflected a test of the regional balance of power between Egypt and Israel, but in a direct interstate encounter. Egypt undertook extensive troop maneuvers across the Suez Canal, causing a change in the existing status quo, an unacceptable contingency for Israel. Nevertheless, both sides succeeded in limiting the crisis to its initial dyadic level with no resort to violence, illustrating the significance of limiting the number of crisis actors. The pre-crisis balance of power was restored and the conflict was maintained at a low magnitude level. In contrast, during the 1967 Six Day War, when the number of actors had increased, Egypt and Israel did not manage to defuse their crisis peacefully.

Common to the three Israel-Jordan and two Israel-Egypt bilateral cases in the early years, as well as to the Israel-Syria cases described below, is their limited duration, relatively controlled escalation process, and low political impact. A small number of adversaries provoked relatively low turmoil and consequently limited crisis magnitude. This manifestation confirms our expectation regarding the winding down of the Arab-Israeli conflict, which has a numerical dimension. In the second period, the most common type of crisis was the two actor confrontation.

Between 1951 and 1985 Israel and Syria confronted one another in three bilateral crises. The Hula drainage case in 1951 concerned a territorial dispute, while the two latter cases of Al Biqa I in 1981 and Al Biqa II in 1985 focused on the establishment of respective influence zones in Lebanon as part of Israeli and Syrian involvement in the prolonged Lebanese civil war.

Additional low magnitude bilateral cases involved Israel and Uganda in 1976, Israel and Iraq in 1980–1981, with one case each, and Israel and Lebanon with two crises in 1993 and 1996. All of these crises occurred in the post-1973 years, indicating the trend of lower magnitude, as expressed also by the number of crisis actors, during this second period. All these cases represented sub-state/ethnonational and nuclear-nonconventional issues of contention between Israel and an Arab state adversary, which escalated to violence.

In the 1976 Entebbe hostage crisis, Israel acted against the Ugandan army after President Idi Amin allowed the PFLP and the German Bader-Meinhof gang to bring a hijacked Air France plane to the Entebbe airport. After negotiations failed on 3 June 1976, the IDF carried out a military rescue mission, with only minor clashes taking place between the Israeli commando forces and the Ugandan soldiers stationed in the airport. The main targets of the Israeli attack were the terrorists.

Anti-Israeli activity by irregular forces operating in Israel's self-declared south Lebanon "security zone" similarly provoked Operation Accountability in July 1993 and Operation Grapes of Wrath, which escalated into violence that lasted much longer. These two crises with common attributes were separated by a three-year period during which low level hostilities persisted without crossing the threshold of crisis. In July 1993, following repeated Hizbullah attacks against the IDF and its ally, the South Lebanese Army (SLA), the Israeli military initiated a large scale air and artillery raid against Hizbullah bases and the towns that supported them. The crisis ended on 31 July, through intensive U.S. mediation, which established a tacit agreement between Israel and Hizbullah. Though the international crisis ended, low level sub-state hostilities endured. Violence escalated once again in 1996 during the Operation Grapes of Wrath crisis when continued Hizbullah attacks provoked a campaign similar to the 1993 one. However, in 1996 the Israeli–Hizbullah agreement clarified the terms established in 1993: both sides would seek to avoid striking civilians and would limit their conflict to the Security Zone. The significant feature in this case was that despite the involvement of Syria and Iran, who supported the Hizbullah, and Lebanon, who was powerless to control Hizbullah activities in and from its territory, the crisis did not expand. The Syrian and Lebanese armies were hardly involved in the crisis.

In another two party crisis, Israel and Iraq confronted one another in the June 1981 Iraqi nuclear reactor case. Determined to deny Iraq the option of becoming a nuclear power, Israel destroyed the nuclear facility in Osirak, just as it was on the verge of becoming operational. Though the crisis touched upon nuclear proliferation, a topic of highest magnitude for Israel and the other Arab states, who feared Israel's nuclear option, the dyadic nature of the confrontation prevailed and despite Iraqi outrage and international indignation the crisis failed to escalate. The dangerous potential for all-out hostilities during this crisis only emerged several years later during the 1990–1991 Gulf crisis, when Iraq did bomb Israel with conventional Scud missiles. The fact that violence remained under control in both crises and did not spread into the usual Israeli–Arab confrontation indicated that a contextual change was taking place.[38]

The last category of low magnitude international crises involves the smallest possible level of participants: one. In all but one case, these confrontations were the outcome of Palestinian activity that triggered an Israeli reprisal and created a limited crisis environment for the state whose sovereignty and regime stability were at risk. These crises illuminate the high price paid by the Arab states hosting non-state actors within their sovereign territory, an activity that, left unchecked, can develop into a "state within a state." Such was the case of the PLO and Jordan in the late 1960s and in Lebanon thereafter.[39]

There were six single actor crises throughout the 1947–2000 period, four in the first period and two after 1973. In all but two of these international confrontations, escalation followed actions by Palestinian non-state elements that brought about Israeli reprisals. Israel was a crisis actor in one rare case of these sub-state triggered confrontations, and in all other cases it initiated the international crisis, deliberately raising the threshold of violence from the sub-state to the international level.[40]

Jordan was the first target for a sequence of limited Israeli reprisals, but in the 1953 Qibya operation hostilities expanded into an international crisis, with only Jordan as a crisis actor. Similar to many Israeli military operations against Fedayeen activity, Israel was careful not to allow the crisis to expand beyond its single actor scope. Israel confined its activity to the Jordanian outpost from which the irregulars came, triggering an international confrontation. Like many other cases of the same type, this crisis ended with an Israeli withdrawal, and brought about only a short period of calm.

The 1968 Beirut airport crisis made Lebanon the only crisis actor for the first time and signaled a shift in the territorial domain of ethnic activity from Jordan and the Egyptian-controlled Gaza strip to Lebanon. Following an escalation in Palestinian strikes against Israeli targets and a PFLP attack on an Israeli plane in Athens, Israeli commandos raided Beirut as punishment for allowing the Palestinians to use Lebanon as a base. Violence in this case was restrained in that despite the destruction of more than a dozen Lebanese planes, there was no loss of life during the operation. The lesson was lost on Lebanon, however, which remained unable to effectively enforce its full control over the Palestinian elements operating there, paving the road for more international crises on Lebanese territory.

In the 1978 Litani operation, Lebanon again was the only actor, but the scope of violence was more severe. After a Palestinian attack against a civilian bus within Israel, the IDF undertook a massive invasion into Lebanon, aimed at PLO bases in the south. Despite pitched Israeli–PLO battles indicating a high level of violence, the crisis remained a one actor case and, most important, did not harm the newly developing Israel-Egypt peace process. The Israeli army withdrew from Lebanon only after UN troops came to replace it.

But Israel was not only an initiator of crisis. It also found itself in the threatened position during three single actor cases. The first of these occurred in 1973 as a result of Israeli intelligence regarding an impending operation in which terrorists would blow up a civilian plane over Israel. On 21 February of that year, Israel intercepted a stray Libyan plane. The IDF shot the plane down, killing almost all the passengers aboard, only then learning that it had made the crucial mistake of attacking a civilian plane.

Two additional Israeli single actor cases were triggered by a change in the posture of an Arab adversary's army—the 1973 Israeli mobilization crisis and the 1976 Syrian mobilization crisis. Unlike the other single actor cases, in which the Arab states involved were less powerful than Israel, these crises involved Arab actors of similar power rank to that of Israel, making these cases balance of power confrontations, testing the resolve and determination of both parties. Egypt provoked the Israel mobilization crisis of May 1973, while the Syrian mobilization crisis of 1976 was a consequence of Syrian military advances toward southern Lebanon.

In all these single actor cases, high levels of crisis-generated stress were confined to one state, thereby reducing the overall magnitude of the confrontation. Consequently, hostilities remained relatively limited in scope and the impact of these events on the protracted conflict as a whole was minimal.

Cases with a small number of adversaries occurred frequently in the 1947–1973 period, involved sub-state and interstate violence, and more often than not did not escalate to the full use of violence. Moreover, only regional states tended to participate in these events, with the superpowers, namely the United States, playing an active political mediation role.

When the first and second periods are compared for both small and large number of adversaries, the findings point to similar conclusions as those on gravity: First, multi-adversary cases dominate the first period, whereas the number of states in crisis becomes much smaller in the second period. Change in magnitude due to the number of participating adversaries therefore exists, not only between different crises, but also over time.

Second, some low magnitude cases, especially one actor cases and dyadic confrontations, did also occur in the first period, indicating the possibility of less severe disputes even during these years of intense conflict.

Third, the main source of lower magnitude crises are cases with mixed elements: interstate and ethnic. Chapter 5 presents an in-depth analysis of the relationship between these two domains of crises in the Arab-Israeli conflict.

SUPERPOWER INVOLVEMENT IN CRISES

We have so far analyzed two context attributes of crisis magnitude: gravity of threat and number of crisis actors. The third and last indicator of context, super-power involvement, focuses on the extent of United States and USSR involvement in crises. In contrast to the previous category where we measured the complexity and magnitude of crises by the number of all crisis actors, here we consider the pivotal role of the United States and USSR in crisis escalation or abatement. We use four categories of involvement: direct military, semi-military, political, and no involvement at all.[41] The first two categories mark high magnitude while the last two indicate low magnitude. To explore the particulars of superpower role we raise several questions: Does change occur in the type and level of superpower activity in different crises or over time? Is the 1947–1973 period, associated, as we have observed earlier in this chapter, with high gravity and a large number of protagonists, also characterized by intense superpower involvement? And, does the post-1973 era likewise show a decline in magnitude due to less superpower involvement?

Superpower participation in regional conflicts denotes the extent of global influence on local confrontations. As such, it is a relatively slow changing-context attribute of crisis, rather than a dynamic-process element. Moreover, when we analyze superpower role in crisis, we do not assume that the United States or USSR are always crisis actors. That is, each superpower may experience, but most frequently does not, the three ICB crisis conditions of threat, time pressure, and likelihood of war. Hence, superpower involvement reflects a broader spectrum of cases than those mentioned previously as crises where the United States or USSR or both were among the crisis actors.[42] In other words, while one or both were crisis actors in only four crises (1956, 1967, 1969, and 1973), all occurring in the first period, high levels of superpower role were detected in five cases (1955, 1956, 1969, 1973, and 1982), one of them in the post–1973 period.[43]

High superpower involvement

A clash of peak magnitude, namely, dyadic U.S.-USSR direct military con-frontation, never occurred in the Arab-Israeli conflict system. During the 1956 Suez war, France and the UK, two major (but not super) powers, engaged in active fighting with a local actor but halted their operations when the Soviets threatened escalation with a major warning that French and British cities were located within the range of Soviet missiles. The one exception in which a super-power engaged in active fighting was the 1969 War of Attrition crisis in which Israeli pilots participated in an air battle against Russians piloting Egyptian planes. This extreme level of superpower involvement exacerbated the crisis and led to intense U.S. efforts toward crisis abatement, which finally bore fruit with the signing of the Rogers B plan. But even in this case, only one superpower pursued military confrontation, not both, and its activity was limited to a single air incident. The dynamics of superpower involvement in crises, unlike their prolonged activity in the conflict as a whole, illustrate that both the United States and the USSR were aware of the dangers of uncontrolled escalation, and therefore confined their participation in crises to the semi-military or political domains, contributing to a rather low and relatively constant level of crisis magnitude. Prolonged U.S. and Soviet involvement in the Middle East was manifested mostly in processes such as arms races, diplomatic initiatives, and mediation efforts, such as the Camp David deliberations, during non-crisis periods.

The United States never resorted to direct military engagement in crises.[44] However, it too, like the USSR, used semi-military involvement, but less frequently than did the USSR: only during the 1973 October crisis, whereas the USSR did so in 1973 and three additional cases: 1955, 1956, and 1982.[45]

The 1973 October War illustrates both the grave potential of superpower competition in regional confrontations as well as the benefits of responsible crisis management. The exacerbating role was evident during the first part of the crisis, while the moderating effects of superpower attention became evident during the prolonged negotiations designed to stabilize the ceasefire and reach separation of forces agreements between Israel and Egypt and between Israel and Syria. Superpower brinkmanship included movement of ships stationed in the region, massive air and sea rearrangement of the adversaries, and a clear Soviet threat to intervene unilaterally if Israeli advances on the west bank of the Suez continued. The United States counteracted by pressuring Israel to allow nonmilitary supplies to reach the encircled Third Egyptian Army, but also by placing its Strategic Air Command and other armed forces on high alert. Both superpowers played the nuclear card: while the U.S. alert included forces with nuclear capabilities, the USSR sent a freighter to Alexandria reported to be carrying nuclear weapons. At this point the crisis reached its peak magnitude.

As mediators the superpowers pressed the local adversaries to solve their differences in a nonmilitary manner. The crisis de-escalated once Israel, Egypt, and Syria accepted the UN Security Council ceasefire resolution, sponsored by both the United States and USSR. The superpowers also co-sponsored the Geneva Conference of December 1973.

The 1973 case was not the first time the USSR used semi-military involvement as its major role in crisis. Earlier, during the 1955 Gaza raid crisis, it offered military support to back up Egyptian president Nasser's stance against continued Israeli raids into Egyptian-held Gaza, but this role contributed to a more rapid crisis abatement. However, when viewed in a longer range perspective, this Russian military resupply of Egypt escalated the general situation on the Israel-Egypt front and led to the Suez campaign the following year. Though the crisis between Israel and Egypt began as an Israeli reprisal against Palestinian irregulars in Gaza, the Soviet role marked the transformation of the crisis into a power struggle between the two state actors, with each side, particularly Egypt, searching for new sources of weapons. The introduction of massive arms shipments from Czechoslovakia helped reduce Egyptian threat perceptions, but inspired Israel to restore the military balance, which it did via an arms deal with France. This French-Israeli arms transfer served as a prelude to the 1956 anti-Egyptian alliance between the two countries.

Similarly, but with a global hue, during the 1956 Suez war the USSR again chose the path of semi-military involvement with a veiled Soviet threat to use its missiles to restore the balance of forces between Israel and Egypt and bring about an early withdrawal of all foreign troops, Israeli, British, and French, from Egyptian territory. The USSR further increased its involvement and influence when, on the diplomatic front, Soviet premier Bulganin proposed a joint intervention against France, Britain, and Israel. Though the United States strongly rejected such a move, the stern USSR warning, coupled with political pressure from the United States on its allies, ultimately brought an end to the crisis and the establishment of a special UNEF to act as a buffer between Israel and Egypt.

The last case of semi-military USSR involvement occurred in the post-1973 period, during the 1982 Lebanon war. As in the earlier crises, Soviet involvement included emergency shipments of military aid to its Arab clients, in this case the Syrian forces in Lebanon, which received supplies to replace their war losses. This role in crisis coincided with a political posture supportive of the PLO-Syrian positions and thereby contributed to crisis management and conflict abatement.

The lower level of USSR involvement in other cases during the second period reflected its decline as a superpower during the late 1980s as well as its preoccupation with the Afghan war and its severe domestic problems. This decline fits the trend of a general winding down of the Arab-Israeli conflict. Again in line with this post-1973 tendency, the low magnitude political role of the United States—as will be analyzed in the next section of this chapter—proved more meaningful than the role of the USSR in crisis abatement.

The analysis of all five crises with high levels of U.S./USSR involvement —1955, 1956, 1969, 1973, and 1982—enables us to answer the queries posed at the beginning of this section and highlights several conclusions. First, change did occur in the type and level of superpower activity both in different crises and over time. The fact that only five cases represent intense superpower participation also suggests that their role in crises is much less salient than the popular impression of critical superpower involvement in the protracted Arab-Israeli conflict.

Second, and most important for this book's thesis, all but one of these high level superpower involvement crises occurred in the pre-1973 period, reinforcing the findings on frequency, gravity, and number of crisis actors, all of which indicate the high magnitude of crises in that early stage of the conflict.

Third, superpower contribution to high crisis magnitude derived mainly from Soviet activity, and much less so from U.S. behavior. Though both superpowers actively engaged in the long-running conflict by assisting their regional clients, we found that the United States was more cautious in its resort to high level crisis involvement.

Fourth, most cases of high level U.S. and USSR participation were crises of long duration, involving severe violence and usually crossing the threshold of full-scale war between or among regional adversaries.

For a more complete answer to the last question—was the post-1973 period represented by a decline in superpower activity and thereby characterized by lower magnitude of international crises?—we turn to an analysis of crises with low levels of superpower participation. In these cases, the United States and/or the USSR played a political role, often by assisting the conflicting parties in reaching compromise. But overall, it was the low rather than high level activity of the superpowers, indicating reduced magnitude, that helped bring about the winding down process of conflict in the region.

Low superpower involvement

Political involvement was the most common superpower role in crises, contributing to low crisis magnitude, but the extent of U.S. and USSR diplomatic activity and its impact on crisis outcomes varied. On the whole, the United States was the more politically active of the two and its involvement played a more meaningful part in conflict abatement.

Some degree of U.S. political activity existed in twenty-one of the twenty-six crises under review, in both the early and later periods. Interestingly, this positive U.S. contribution to crisis termination was linked not only to its rising status in the post-1973 period, and particularly after the 1991 collapse of the Soviet Union, but rather, it appears as a continuous attribute in most of the major Arab-Israeli confrontations. This finding contradicts the claim that the role of the United States grew significantly only after the disintegration of the Soviet Union, during the post–Cold War years.

Political efforts during crisis often took the form of diplomatic mediation, as in the 1969 War of Attrition. Another mode of U.S. involvement was to exercise political pressure on the protagonists, to persuade them to halt their violent engagement. American diplomacy was often coupled with military moves signaling a commitment to deter unilateral USSR actions in the Middle East, as in the 1973 October War. An early example of intensive U.S. mediation efforts leading to compromise and crisis accommodation occurred during the 1969 War of Attrition. However, U.S. mediation was more salient in the second period, throughout the 1976 Syria mobilization, Al Biqa missiles I and II (1981 and 1985), and the 1982 war in Lebanon.

A combination of diplomatic and limited semi-military acts on the part of the United States occurred during the 1956 Suez war and the 1967 June war. At times the political involvement was limited to exercising political pressures on Israel to withdraw from territory, as in the 1947 Sinai incursion case, or to refrain from executing its anti-Fedayeen reprisal policy, as in the 1956 Qalqilya crisis.

In ten of twenty-one cases exhibiting U.S. political involvement, however, its role contributed only marginally, if at all, to conflict resolution. These include the 1947 Palestine partition, 1955 Gaza raid, 1961 Hula drainage, 1963 Jordan

waters, 1966 El Samu, 1968 Karameh, 1968 Beirut airport, 1978 Litani operation, 1981 Iraq nuclear reactor, 1993 Operation Accountability, and 1996
Operation Grapes of Wrath. These cases share predominantly an overall low
level of crisis magnitude, and usually focused on ethnicity issues. Only three of
these crises constituted direct interstate cases with no ethnic elements: 1961,
1963, and 1981. By contrast, four crises, namely, those in 1947, 1955, 1968, and
1978, involved overall high magnitude.

In most of these cases with low level and relatively ineffective U.S. political involvement, as in the 1978 Litani operation and 1993 Operation
Accountability, the United States supported Israel's right to defend itself against
infiltrators, but criticized what it saw as Israeli excessive violence against its
adversaries' civilians. Following a similar policy, even when the issue of non-
proliferation was raised in the 1981 Iraqi nuclear reactor case, the United States
joined the rest of the world in condemning Israel's attack against the Iraqi
nuclear reactor and, for a short time, delayed routine military aid.

In only one case throughout the conflict, 1953 Qibya, did U.S. political
involvement exacerbate the crisis, according to the ICB data-set, and only to a
minimal extent. President Dwight Eisenhower sent Eric H. Johnson as his personal representative to the Arab states and Israel in an effort to reduce tensions
and restore interstate stability. The United States also joined France and the UK
in requesting that the UN Security Council discuss the matter. But there was
no serious effort to solve the core problem of cross-border infiltrations and
reprisal raids. In its resolution, the UN coupled its condemnation of the Israeli
raid on Qibya with a call for the strengthening of the UN truce supervision
machinery.[46]

The USSR's political involvement was less frequent and its contribution to
crisis abatement was usually negative, although it did occasionally help the
adversaries reach an acceptable compromise at the end of their crisis. For example, the USSR escalated the 1967 war by passing false information to the Arab
states indicating an Israeli plan to attack Syria. But after the IDF defeated the
Egyptian army the USSR played a more responsible and moderating role. On
the global level, Moscow used the hotline to agree with the United States that
both superpowers should not become involved in the war and initiated a UN
call for a nonconditional ceasefire. At the same time, the Soviets also expressed
concern over the defeat of their allies, accused Israel, of violating the ceasefire,
implied that they might employ military measures against Israel, and warned
that a "grave catastrophe" would occur unless Israel unconditionally halted its
operations within a few hours.[47]

In most cases, USSR political involvement had marginal or no impact on
the way crises were concluded. The Soviet modus operandi in times of crisis
generally consisted of political warnings, coupled with condemnation of
Israeli aggression, often followed by some military assistance to the Arabs or
even the implied threat of acting unilaterally itself. To illustrate, the 1963
Jordan waters, 1968 Beirut airport, 1978 Litani operation, and the 1981 Iraq

nuclear reactor crises all involved this type of behavior pattern. Similarly, but with a slightly more meaningful political participation in crisis was its involvement in the 1951 Hula drainage, the 1968 Karameh, and the 1985 Al Biqa II cases. In other confrontations, the USSR combined criticism of Israel with a military response, as in the 1947 Palestine partition, 1981 Al Biqa missiles I, and 1982 war in Lebanon cases. The 1947 Palestine partition episode, however, stands out as the only case in which Soviet arms supplies, in the form of military supplies from Czechoslovakia, went to support the newly established IDF. Subsequently, the Soviets consistently supported the Arab side of the conflict.

The escalating impact of USSR policy in crisis was evident in the 1960 Rottem case when USSR diplomatic activity alone, devoid of military aspects, exacerbated the crisis. As in 1967, so too in this case did the Soviet embassy in Cairo pass on fabricated information to Egyptian president Nasser indicating an Israeli plan to attack Syria. This marked the onset of the international crisis. Soviet political support to Egypt continued throughout the crisis. But as a consequence of careful and controlled military moves by the adversaries designed to prevent war, the crisis dissolved without the resort to violence.

In the 1981 Al Biqa I crisis the USSR reinforced its political support of the Syrian regime by conducting joint landing maneuvers with Syrian forces. Similarly, in the 1982 Lebanon war the Soviets granted political support to the PLO and Syrians and also rushed them supplies designed to replace their war losses; condemnation was directed toward Israel alone.

As noted in our theoretical introduction, we have deliniated the role of superpowers in crises to the realm of context, since their role in regional conflicts indicates attributes of bipolarity and of global settings for the Arab-Israeli protracted conflict. Even though the United States and USSR were crisis actors in some of the cases, they were never the primary protagonists and therefore do not count as full participants to be addressed in the process realm (analyzed in chapter 3). Moreover, even as crisis actors, neither of the superpowers experienced the three ICB crisis conditions of threat, time pressure, and likelihood of war in anywhere near as high levels as did the local participants.[48]

When the extent of low level superpower participation is viewed in a comparative way, several trends emerge. First, in most crises involving many regional actors and high stakes, both the United States and the USSR became involved politically and contributed to both high crisis magnitude and to crisis termination. Only in three rare cases were neither of the two superpowers involved: the 1973 Libyan plane incident, the 1973 Israel mobilization case, and the 1976 Entebbe event. These exceptions, all dyadic cases of relatively short duration and limited issue complexity, illustrate the norm.

Second, with the exception of the 1982 Lebanon war, all the crises in the post-1973 years involved low superpower political activity and that primarily by the United States acting to preserve the status quo. This pattern supports our earlier findings on gravity and the number of crisis actors, leading us to the conclusion that the second period enjoyed lower crisis magnitude, and hence a relative winding down of conflict over time.

Third, many crises in the 1947–1973 period involved only low level U.S. or USSR political involvement, signaling that externally induced escalation, political pressure, and imposed agreements need not be the rule in local conflicts where the superpowers were involved, even in the more tense years. In the severe crises that occurred, spillover from political to military superpower participation was confined to a few exceptional cases. This finding confirms that regional actors were ultimately the main contributors to escalation as well as to the winding down of the conflict over time.

Fourth, the United States participated politically in more crises and played a more meaningful role than did the USSR. This U.S. activity had a mainly moderating effect on the course of international crises and their outcomes.

CONTEXT AND CONFLICT TRANSFORMATION

In this chapter we have presented a comparative analysis of the attributes characterizing the context realm in twenty-six international crises in the Arab-Israeli conflict. We found that comparative patterns and converging trends existed regarding all contextual factors.

Based on the frequency of international crises, we established the year 1973 as a basic divide between two distinct periods: 1947–1973 and 1974–2000. Our findings reveal that gravity of threat, number of participating actors, and superpower involvement in crisis all fit a common pattern: crises in the first period consisted mainly of threats to existence and grave damage, encompassing between four and six adversaries and including military or semi-military superpower involvement. Crises in the second period consisted primarily of low gravity threats, few adversaries and a political-moderating superpower role.

The decline in magnitude indicates that the possibility of less severe confrontations exists, even in an intense protracted conflict. This convergence on all three contextual attributes of crisis magnitude leads to a core question concerning conflict termination: Why is it that the first period is characterized mainly by high magnitude while the reverse is true for the second period? In other words: Why did the levels of conflict rise during the early years and what brought about their relative decline in the more recent period?[49]

But contextual attributes represent only a portion of crisis magnitude. The full picture requires an analysis of crisis escalation, violence, crisis management, and the modes of crisis termination, which is forthcoming in chapter 3.

CHAPTER 3

PROCESS, OUTCOMES, OVERALL
CRISIS MAGNITUDE, AND CHANGE

In addition to context, the CMI considers two realms: process and outcome. In the analysis of process we describe two interactive patterns that characterize international crisis: crisis management and level of violence between adversaries. The third CMI realm is outcomes. It encompasses the modes of crisis termination, marking the extent of accommodation and conflict moderation or of nonaccommodation and conflict escalation. In this chapter we identify and evaluate changes in process operating in tandem with the context realm, discussed earlier in chapter 2. A basic assumption underlying our study is that changes in context alone are not sufficient in measuring crisis dynamics or levels of conflict. Nor can contextual changes alone explain areas of change and conflict moderation. A full understanding of trends in the Arab-Israeli conflict ultimately requires an analysis of all three magnitude realms, the examination of links between them, and the evaluation of spillover effects between the three CMI realms of context process and termination.[1]

THE CMI - PROCESS DIMENSIONS

Among the primary factors affecting the course of an international crisis is states' behavior, that is, the type of Crisis Management Techniques (CMTs) to which they resort. Table 3.1 presents a summary of process (and outcome) attributes for twenty-six international crises in the Arab-Israeli conflict.

As noted in Table 3.1, violence was a prominent device of crisis management. States quickly climbed the escalation ladder and crossed the threshold from diplomacy to military hostilities. But alongside this hostile

59

TABLE 3.1
PROCESS AND OUTCOME ATTRIBUTES OF CRISES IN THE ARAB-ISRAELI CONFLICT
First period: 1947-1973

CASE	DATE	ACTORS	CRISIS MANAGEMENT TECHNIQUE (CMT)	VIOLENCE	OUTCOME
Palestine partition	Nov. 1947	Egypt, Jordan, Iraq, Israel, Lebanon, Syria	Violence	War	Formal agreement
Sinai incursion	Dec. 1948	Egypt, Israel, UK	Multiple with violence	Serious clashes	Unilateral – Israeli compliance
Hula drainage	Feb. 1951	Israel, Syria	Multiple with violence	Serious clashes	Formal agreement
Qibya	Oct. 1953	Jordan	Negotiation	Serious clashes	Unilateral – Israel
Gaza raid	Feb. 1955	Egypt, Israel	Non-violent military	Serious clashes	Other – ally
Suez war	July 1956	Egypt, France, Israel, UK, USA, USSR	Multiple with violence	War	Unilateral – Israeli compliance
Qalqilya	Sept. 1956	Israel, Jordan	Multiple with violence	Serious clashes	Unilateral – ally
Rottem	Feb. 1960	Egypt, Israel	Non-violent military	None	Tacit agreement
Jordan waters	Dec. 1963	Egypt, Israel, Jordan, Lebanon, Syria	Non-violent military	None	Unilateral – Israel, Lebanon, Syria
El Samu	Nov. 1966	Israel, Jordan	Violence	Serious clashes	Unilateral – Jordan
Six Day war	May 1967	Egypt, Israel, Jordan, Syria, USA, USSR	Violence	War	Imposed agreement
Karameh	March 1968	Israel, Jordan	Violence	Serious clashes	Unilateral – Jordan
Beirut airport	Dec. 1968	Lebanon	Mediation	Minor clashes	Other – faded
War of attrition	March 1969	Egypt, Israel, USSR	Multiple with violence	War	Formal agreement

TABLE 3.1 (*continued*)

CASE	DATE	ACTORS	CRISIS MANAGEMENT TECHNIQUE (CMT)	VIOLENCE	OUTCOME
Libyan plane	Feb. 1973	Israel	Violence	Serious clashes	Unilateral – Israel
Israel mobilization	April 1973	Israel	Non-violent military	None	Unilateral – Israel
Yom Kippur war	Oct. 1973	Egypt, Israel, Syria, USA, USSR	Multiple with violence	War	Formal agreement

Second period: 1974–2000

CASE	DATE	ACTORS	CRISIS MANAGEMENT TECHNIQUE (CMT)	VIOLENCE	OUTCOME
Entebbe raid	June 1976	Israel, Uganda	Violence	Minor clashes	Unilateral – Israel
Syria mobilization	Nov. 1976	Israel	Non-violent military	None	Tacit agreement
Litani operation	March 1978	Lebanon	Negotiation	Serious clashes	Unilateral – Israel
Iraq nuclear reactor	Jan. 1981	Iraq, Israel	Multiple with violence	Minor clashes	Unilateral – Iraq
Al-Biqa missiles I	April 1981	Israel, Syria	Non-violent military	Minor clashes	Formal agreement
War in Lebanon	June 1982	Israel, Lebanon, Syria	Multiple with violence	War	Semi-formal agreement
Al-Biqa missiles II	Nov. 1985	Israel, Syria	Non-violent military	Minor clashes	Tacit agreement
Operation Accountability	July 1993	Israel, Lebanon	Multiple with violence	Minor clashes	Tacit agreement
Operation Grapes of Wrath	April 1996	Israel, Lebanon	Multiple with violence	Minor clashes	Tacit + semi-formal agreement

mode, some signs of conflict moderation are evident over time. In fact, in ten of the twenty-six Arab-Israeli crises, the protagonists did not resort to violence as a primary CMT.

When violence is used, its levels also vary, ranging from no violence to minor clashes to serious clashes to full-scale war. Why is it that some confrontations involve low levels of violence while others escalate? Are low levels the result of the winding down of the conflict identified earlier? The following analysis pays special attention to crises one would expect to have escalated into violence but did not, and those that seemingly promised nonviolent resolutions, only to see an outbreak of hostilities.

MODES OF CRISIS MANAGEMENT AND CRISIS MAGNITUDE

Based upon ICB definitions, four categories describe the types of primary management techniques employed during international crises: negotiations, nonviolent demonstrations of force, a mixture of political and violent CMTs, and violence alone. The use of diplomatic negotiations and other nonviolent means to resolve an international crisis indicates low crisis magnitude, while violence alone or mixed with other CMTs points to high crisis magnitude. During a crisis, adversaries often use one or more of the management techniques. ICB details the most important mode of adversarial behavior, and records instances of multiple and co-equal behavior.

What are the attributes of state behavior in crises and are there characteristic patterns in interstate interaction processes during crises? One can detect differences in the type of CMT used and varying levels of violence. But are there notable changes in the CMTs and scope of violence over time; that is, can we identify escalation patterns in the pre-1973 period, and moderation cycles in the post-1973 years? Such findings would accord well with the trends in context attributes previously detailed in chapter 2 regarding the gravity, the number of adversaries, and superpower involvement in crises.

To investigate how crises evolved and to assess their magnitude, we will start with the uncommon cases where violence was not used as a primary CMT and then elaborate on the more frequent cases where violence was present. Finally, we will observe the changes that exist in scope of violence used in the Arab-Israeli conflict and examine the links between violence and crisis outcomes.

The diplomatic process in crisis management

Of the twenty-six Arab-Israeli cases recorded by the ICB project, there were only three in which negotiations alone were the primary CMT. All three of these were cases with only one state experiencing a crisis situation: Qibya 1953 (Jordan), the 1968 Beirut airport crisis, and the 1978 Litani case (both Lebanon). Notably, all three cases also belong to the interstate-ethnic type confrontations. Unexpectedly, two of them happened in the pre-1973 years, generally associated with high context-derived crisis magnitude.

As noted in chapter 2, the first two cases were triggered by low level Fedayeen activity that provoked strong Israeli reprisals. Both times Israeli violence marked the onset of hostilities but was not matched by a similar Arab response. Instead, the Arab CMT was political-diplomatic in nature and led to nonviolent outcomes. In the Qibya 1953 case, the Hashemite Kingdom resorted to several diplomatic channels designed to forestall future Israeli raids, by making them more costly for Israel in political terms. More specifically, Jordan conferred with the UK and the United States, placed a complaint against Israel with the UN Security Council and also called for an Arab League meeting. Consequently, both organizations condemned Israel, whose own domestic constraints caused it to halt reprisals for a few months. This nonviolent response served short-term Jordanian interests well, and temporarily reduced the scope of escalation, but it did not solve the problem of cross-border infiltrations.

The Beirut airport case in 1968 displays Lebanon's application of the same pattern of diplomatic CMT. Israel intended its surgical retaliation attack against several Arab aircraft at Beirut International Airport as a warning to Lebanon to rein in the PLO. Unable to repress PLO activity in the country or to bring an end to Palestinian strikes against Israel, the Beirut government resorted to the only means possible: activating international political pressure designed to deter Israel. It placed a complaint against Israel with the UN Security Council, coupled with the mobilization of Lebanese reserve troops. Since Lebanon could not militarily compel Israel to drop its reprisal policy, this activity must be regarded as a token of protest and not as a meaningful resort to arms. This second nonviolent case, like its predecessor, does not represent moderating trends in crisis management because no compromise was reached and shortly after this case ended, international terror reasserted itself.

The Litani operation in 1978 was managed differently than the 1968 case, since the Lebanese diplomatic deliberations led to some institutional arrangements. After a March attack on the Israeli coastal road, IDF troops crossed the border into Lebanon in a major assault against PLO strongholds. Lebanon requested that the UN Security Council handle the case, but this time more effective measures led to the establishment of a UN peacekeeping force—the United Nations Interim Force in Lebanon (UNIFIL)—designed to prevent further cycles of terror and reprisals across the Israel-Lebanon border. Israel had defined the establishment of UNIFIL troops as a precondition for its withdrawal from Lebanon, but the institutionalization of UNIFIL forces as a barrier between the PLO and Israel was not adequate to prevent further Israeli-PLO clashes. Despite its limitations, UNIFIL became part of the regulative measures in the protracted Arab-Israeli conflict.[2]

Unfortunately, the limited scope of violence and low crisis magnitude in these cases involved no adaptation or learning processes between the Palestinian elements and the state adversaries, and no progress was made toward the resolution of core issues. In the pre-1973 period, Jordanian and Lebanese appeals to the UN did not mark the introduction of new resolution mechanisms into the conflict. Even after UNIFIL was established, in the second period, it was not coupled with broader measures designed to bring an end to the Lebanese civil war and its collateral conflicts ensued. As a result, sub-state violence against Israel continued to linger even after the interstate confrontation ended.

Still in the domain of nonviolent CMTs, seven cases involved the demonstration of force. Four of them occurred in the first period and three in the post-1973 years. This near-equal distribution of crises in the two periods does not accord with the findings on context, which would lead one to expect fewer crises managed by nonviolent CMTs in the first period and more in the second.

As in the diplomatic-negotiation cases discussed above, the 1955 Gaza raid too was triggered by an Israeli reprisal raid, this time against Egypt. Israel again played the role of crisis initiator. As long as Israel was meeting the menace of Fedayeen activity without triggering a crisis for Egypt, the impact of its activity on regional stability was minor. With the spread of tension to the interstate domain and the confrontation of two major states, however, escalation was rapid. Unlike the muted responses of Jordan in 1953 and Lebanon in 1968, this crisis resulted in an arms race when Egypt signed an arms deal with Czechoslovakia, a Soviet proxy. A threatened shift in the regional military balance of power saw Israel sign two agreements with France for combat planes and ammunition. Though violence did not occur, process alone was evidently not enough to mellow the Arab-Israeli conflict.

The remaining six "demonstration of force" cases, were lower in overall magnitude than the 1955 Gaza raid, yet they too were not entirely benign. This frequent use of flexing military power illustrates the rapidity with which states in the Arab-Israeli conflict system resorted to arms and hostility. In some of these cases, actors refrained from crossing the threshold of violence. Characteristic of such processes was the Rottem case where Israel reacted to Egyptian military movements in the Sinai with a show of force designed to signal Egypt that the IDF was ready to meet any military challenge. The crisis was resolved without resort to violence, but tacit understanding regarding the restoration of the status quo ante was not supported by the establishment of mechanisms designed to prevent future miscalculations and costly escalations. Consequently, seven years later, a quite similar escalation process resulted in the 1967 war.

The third low magnitude crisis that involved no violence was the 1963 Jordan waters case. Israeli determination to implement its water carrier project and repeated Arab threats to disrupt it put the protagonists on the slippery road to escalation. Egyptian president Nasser demonstrated Arab political unity with a symbolic show of force but without incurring the costs of an actual war. At a time when pan-Arab ideology was at its height, this crisis indicates that confrontations could, at times, be contained. However, this relatively moderate action-reaction process was not coupled with a structural-institutional change or with a learning process by which states might internalize the merits of compromise. Consequently, change in the dynamics of the protracted conflict did not occur in this period.

The 1973 Israel mobilization crisis was a nonviolent demonstration of force case that, again, did not lead to the outbreak of hostilities and war. Intelligence about a pending Egyptian attack led Israel to place its army on alert, call up reserve units, and begin war preparations. Though war was prevented in May, a similar situation emerged early October of the same year, but Israel refrained from mobilizing its army. The subsequent Arab surprise attack caught Israel unprepared, destabilized the regional scene, led to superpower brinkmanship, and contributed to the high magnitude of the October War. Hence, the early Israeli mobilization crisis in which no violence occurred actually fostered future destabilizing conditions.

Syria and Israel, shared three "nonviolent" cases focused on the situation in Lebanon, with both regional powers making shows of force against each other. All these crises took place in the second period: the 1976 Syria mobilization crisis, and the 1981 and 1985 Al Biqa I and II cases, respectively. In 1976, an Israeli concentration of infantry and tanks along its border with Lebanon sent a signal strong enough to halt Syrian advances in southern Lebanon. The 1981 and 1985 crises began with Israeli air attacks, which destroyed Syrian planes. Each time Syria responded with the deployment of missiles in the confrontation zone. Significantly, both states were as quick to use caution and U.S. good offices in conveying their respective intentions to avoid war as they were to flex their military muscles. Thus, despite the initial air clash, violence was not regarded as their major CMT. The complexity of the Lebanese quagmire required more than positive motivation and skillful crisis management to prevent an undesirable escalation and war. The impact of U.S. mediation was helpful, but it was secondary to the tacit understanding that emerged between Israel and Syria. This code of restraint was put to the test during massive Israeli military action in Lebanon in the 1982 Lebanese war and in 1993's Operation Accountability and 1996's Operation Grapes of Wrath.[3]

Although, as noted in chapter 2, the second period was characterized by overall lower contextual-derived magnitude, both periods exhibit cases that were managed through negotiations and others that only involved nonviolent confrontations. If so, why was the first period associated in the contextual realm with crises of high magnitude and the second with low magnitude? Schelling's term " diplomacy of violence" and his observation on the linkage between the use of diplomatic measures and those of violence, explain this apparent discrepancy between context and process attributes. In the Arab-Israeli conflict, negotiations and nonviolent CMTs are part of an overall strategy combining diplomacy and force.

Crisis management via coercive diplomacy and violence

The combined use of diplomacy and force was the most common form of crisis regulation in the Arab-Israeli conflict.[4] Six such cases developed in the 1947–1973 period and an additional four cases occurred in the post-1973 years.

By this process indicator, the division between the two periods confirms our stipulation: a decline in violence occurred after 1973.

The 1948 Sinai incursion was the first case where diplomacy and violence were of co-equal importance in crisis management. The crisis escalated during the first Arab-Israeli war, after the IDF had crossed into the Sinai Peninsula and threatened Egyptian control in the area. Cairo's first response to the Israeli offensive was a request that the UK side with Egypt, as per their (unrenewed) 1936 treaty. Accordingly, London demanded an Israeli troop withdrawal. The crisis was not over before Israel shot down five British planes observing its withdrawal. As with many cases of great power involvement, British activity exacerbated the struggle but also had a moderating effect, bringing about Israeli withdrawal without widening the scope of violence.

The 1951 Hula crisis began as a diplomatic–economic dispute and was rapidly transformed into a military confrontation, but remained confined to regional actors. The Israeli–Syrian rivalry over the drainage project and the status of the demilitarized zone between the two parties touched upon their respective interpretations of their 1949 armistice agreement. A Syrian request that the UN Security Council stop the Israeli project was followed by discussions within the UN Mixed Armistice Commission (MAC). Unsatisfied with the diplomatic outcome, the adversaries resorted to increasingly hostile measures, and serious clashes ensued. Institutionalization in the form of the MAC created as a consequence of the first Arab-Israeli war was helpful during this confrontation, but not effective enough to prevent escalation.

Regional and nonregional states chose violence combined with diplomacy as the primary CMT at the outset of the 1956 Suez crisis. The three invading parties—Israel, France, and the UK—all expected the coordinated attack to bring about high payoffs, such as a period of tranquility in Fedayeen cross-border activity, a decline in Egyptian support for the FLN in Algeria, and perhaps even the downfall of Nasser's regime in Egypt.

Besides military assistance against the invaders, Egypt requested military and diplomatic aid from Moscow. The projection of Soviet military power forced all parties, once again, to reassess the effectiveness of using violence in their confrontation. Coercive diplomacy soon appeared but this time at the superpower level with the USSR and U.S. warnings to the adversaries (case 6 in Glossary). Intense diplomatic negotiations between the great powers led to a UN General Assembly decision to send an emergency force to the Sinai and Gaza regions to replace the British, French, and Israeli troops.[5]

During the 1969 War of Attrition, the resort to violence by Israel, Egypt, and the USSR was also accompanied by intensive U.S. mediation designed to prevent further escalation. But moderation gained salience only after Israel decided not to confine its air raids to the canal zone and implemented a bombing campaign deep into Egyptian territory. The USSR reacted by installing sophisticated missile air defense systems along the Suez Canal. An Israeli-Soviet air battle also reflected this willingness to escalate in order to gain advantage, and served as a signal to the regional adversaries, as well as to the superpowers, that the situation was extremely volatile. American diplomacy expressed via a series of "Big Four" talks (the United States, USSR, UK, and France), turned into "Big Two" talks (the United States and USSR) and succeeded in containing the war along the canal.[6]

The 1973 war, unlike the 1967 war, involved coercive diplomacy combining severe violence and intense bilateral negotiations mediated by the United States. The accompanying nuclear level standoff that took place between the superpowers, each siding with its regional proxy and risking global confrontation, was also of extreme importance. Unlike the 1956 Suez crisis, where the USSR exercised the highest resort to military threats, in 1973 the United States placed most of its armed forces on alert, including the Strategic Air Command with its nuclear capability. Another manifestation of the nuclear element occurred when rumors surfaced that a Soviet vessel had arrived in Alexandria with nuclear weapons on board. In a supreme effort to avoid a catastrophe, both superpowers drafted a UN Security Council ceasefire resolution accepted by the regional parties. U.S.-mediated negotiations finally resulted in agreements on the separation of forces between Israel and its Arab adversaries.

The 1981 Iraqi reactor case represented a confrontation between Israel and a distant Arab rival potentially threatening Israel's existence. Before the 1981 crisis and at its early phase, Israel tried to resolve the nuclear spread issue via diplomatic channels, and had attempted to halt French participation in the Iraqi nuclear project at Osirak. Unable to restrict French assistance or curb the pace of Iraqi nuclear development, Israel resorted to the use of force. The only immediate option Iraq had was the implementation of a diplomatic campaign against Israel, criticizing it for its blunt violation of international laws and Iraqi sovereignty.[7]

Alongside the emergence of the nuclear issue since the 1973 war, marking a shift from territorial to nonconventional struggle in the region, an additional change appeared—a rise in the centrality of Palestinian elements in crises. As mentioned earlier, some expressions of these Palestinian inputs into interstate crises already existed in the first period, but they clearly dominated the post-1973 period.[8]

The 1956 Qalqilya case evinced crucial Palestinian elements in the form of frequent Fedayeen infiltrations, causing, in this instance, an Israeli–Jordanian escalation where diplomacy and violence were also coupled. In order to deter future Israeli violence, Jordan chose to strengthen its alliance with Iraq. The threat that Iraqi forces would be stationed in Jordan upon request was an unacceptable contingency for Israel. Had the Iraqi commitment been fulfilled, the Israeli reprisal policy would have led to a unwanted shift in the local balance of power. But diplomatic means prevented further escalation and the situation stabilized .

The three cases where violence and diplomacy coincided in the post-1973 period were the 1982 war in Lebanon, the 1993 Operation Accountability, and the 1996 Operation Grapes of Wrath. Israeli reprisals were geared to stop Palestinian attacks (in the former event) and Hizbullah assaults (in the latter two) from Lebanon. Yet diplomacy, not military moves alone, helped reach partial agreements, a gradual reduction in tensions, and a temporary halt in hostilities. In June 1982, one of several Israeli invasions of Lebanon ended in a two-phased arrangement. First, intensive diplomatic mediation carried out by U.S. ambassador Philip Habib accompanied military engagements between Israel and Syria. Syrian disengagement was followed by the evacuation of PLO units from Lebanon and an IDF pullback from Beirut. Consequently, the PLO military presence in the country was reduced to a minimum. But the Lebanese crisis continued long after the PLO had withdrawn, and ended only when the short-lived Israel-Lebanon peace agreement, mediated by the U.S. secretary of state George Shultz, was reached on 17 May 1983.

This abortive peace treaty did not solve the issue of hostile activity directed from Lebanon against Israel. After 1982, Hizbullah replaced the PLO as Israel's main opponent in Lebanon and conflict continued in the border region, supported by Syria and Iran. These sub-state level hostilities resulted in two additional interstate crises in 1993 and 1996 (cases 25 and 26 in the Glossary). Though the source of violence this time was Hizbullah, not the PLO, the problem for Israel was an old one—how to deter hostile elements from using Lebanon as a base for assaults against Israel. Operation Accountability and Operation Grapes of Wrath were designed to stabilize the situation in northern Israel by implementing a harsh military strike against Hizbullah bases and its infrastructure. The domestic pressure of the flood of Lebanese civilians escaping toward Beirut away from the battle-torn regions in the south was supposed to bring about, according to Israeli planning, a stricter Lebanese policy toward Israel's Islamic fundamentalist foes. Instead, Lebanese across the board rallied behind Hizbullah and against Israel. In both cases a ceasefire between Israel and the Hizbullah was reached only after intensive U.S. mediation. The IDF accepted limitations on its military activity in areas beyond Israel's security zone in southern Lebanon and Hizbullah accepted a commitment not to fire missiles on Israeli villages in northern Israel. But the major issue of Israel-Syria relations was not settled in either of the crises and Hizbullah violence persisted along Israel's northern border. In May 2000, Israel pulled out of Lebanon unilaterally, and UN efforts were carried out to restore Lebanese control over southern Lebanon.

To sum up, high magnitude cases that combined the use of diplomacy and violence were more frequent in the 1947–1973 period, when interstate confrontations usually ended in war. In the second period, change occurred in issues of conflict and in the frequency of confrontations. One severe interstate crisis was related to the topic of nuclear proliferation in the Middle East, but other cases consisted of clashes between Israel, an Arab adversary, and Palestinian-Islamic elements, which were halted short of full-scale war.

Violence alone, as the only primary mode of crisis management, appeared in six crises, with only one of these pure violence cases occurring in the post-

1973 period. Two of these crises were full-scale war cases—1947–1949 first Arab-Israeli war and the 1967 war—while three confrontations involved serious clashes—1966 El Samu, 1968 Karameh, and the 1973 Libyan plane case; only the 1976 Entebbe crisis manifested minor clashes between adversaries. The concentration of the straight violent cases in the pre-1973 period was also accompanied by a higher scope of violence.

VIOLENCE AND CRISIS MAGNITUDE

The resort to violence, especially war, is the most critical means in interstate relations. As such, its employment or non-use, as well as its level of operation is a central indicator of crisis magnitude. Resort to violence should be viewed not merely through the existence of hostilities, but also with respect to varying levels of the use of force. The extent of violence wielded in a crisis was described, in ICB terms, along four categories: war, serious clashes, minor clashes, and no violence. The first two categories indicate high crisis magnitude while the last two characterize low magnitude cases.

So far, we have identified cases where violence was absent, pointing to low magnitude, and others where violence was present, indicating higher crisis magnitude. But sometimes, high magnitude derived from severe violence and war was constructive as far as crisis termination and overall magnitude were concerned. How does the scope of violence shape crisis accommodation? Clearly, high violence escalates tensions and threat while limited hostilities do not. But when extreme violence is present, outcomes tend to be formal and accommodative, while lower levels of violence frequently end with nonaccommodative terminations. To explore the links between violence and outcomes in the Arab-Israeli conflict, we start with the high magnitude cases and then descend in magnitude to the cases with less violence.

High magnitude war crises

Six crises in the Arab-Israeli conflict escalated to full-scale war, five of them in the 1947–1973 period and only one in the post-1973 years. Wars in this conflict were rather similar in their attributes, and all but one case—the 1982 Lebanon war—resulted in overall high crisis magnitude.[9] Moreover, war usually capped interstate confrontations, whereas crises involving Palestinian elements rarely led to full-scale war. The 1947 Palestine partition-Israeli independence crisis serves as an example. It involved six crisis actors, and lasted more than a year, from 14 May 1948 until 20 July 1949, with short periods of temporary ceasefire. In the middle of the war the crisis escalated with the 1948 Israeli incursion into the Egyptian Sinai (case 2 in the Glossary). Though this intrawar crisis involved only three crisis actors it was severe because the UK, a great power, participated in the hostilities as a full-fledged crisis actor. Formal agreement and some accommodation followed the first Arab-Israeli war, supporting the link between full-scale war and compromise as a crisis outcome.

During the 1956 Suez war between Israel and Egypt, almost a decade later, escalation to war was not sudden, but rather followed a tense pre-crisis period of infiltrations and reprisals. The Israeli military assault against Egypt was coordinated with joint action by France and the UK. When the United States and USSR weighed in with threats to act unilaterally in support of their regional clients, this episode exhibited the highest level of external major power participation in a local Arab-Israeli rivalry. War-related hostilities were short but intensive, lasting from 29 October to 8 November.[10]

Yet, the resolution of the case did introduce some institutionalization—by establishing the UN peacekeeping forces, which replaced the withdrawing forces. Consequently, both Egypt and Israel were able to enjoy relative interstate stability for almost a decade, though Egypt maintained its grievances and resorted to extreme rhetoric promising another war that would end in a striking Arab victory. President Nasser was careful not to let his propaganda campaign slide out of control or provoke actual fighting.

Three other wars ensued after 1956 in an unhappy cycle: the 1967 June War, the 1969 War of Attrition, and the 1973 October War. The first and last of these wars followed the pattern of the 1947 Palestine partition-Israel independence war in that they involved a large number of participants, and repeated the 1956 Suez war in that they drew great-power activity from outside the region. Unlike the 1947 war, these three were relatively short in duration, but the cumulative high cost of three wars in six years slowly entered into the parties' long-term considerations, especially in Egypt and Israel. The 1967 war ended with a ceasefire imposed from outside. Together with UN Resolution 242, these attempts to reach some agreement between the parties was not translated into a peaceful reality. The next two wars were concluded through negotiated formal agreements, however, thus signaling that some change took place. In accordance with the high violence-accommodative outcomes link described earlier some institutionalism was slowly developing. UN 242's formula set forth a principle that was gradually accepted by Israel and the Arab states. "Land for Peace" emerged as a joint compromise goal that would provide all the parties to the conflict with better security and well-being. Conditions for significant change were not yet ripe in the post-1967 period, and it was only after two additional showdowns in 1969 and 1973 that diplomacy took over as the prominent mode of conflict resolution in the Arab-Israeli conflict.[11]

In the 1967 war, four local powers engaged in hostilities, while both superpowers were primarily involved politically. The United States also resorted to a show of force, when President Johnson ordered the Sixth Fleet to move closer to Syrian territorial waters—in order to signal Moscow that its threat to intervene would be met with US counteraction. Although the war was short in duration, the adversaries used almost all of their conventional capabilities. The tank battles were among the largest since World War II and Israel's preemptive air attack was one of the most comprehensive and destructive in the annuals of modern warfare. Though Israel's military victory was its most decisive since its establishment, it was neither a solid basis for the creation of a balance of power deterrent nor a guarantee of future military superiority. The 1969 War of Attrition and the Arab-Israeli confrontation of 1973 demonstrated the quick recovery of the Egyptian and Syrian armies, indicating the crucial role the superpowers' arms shipments played during non-crisis periods. Another lesson to be learned was the limits of reaching a decisive military victory in the dispute with no followup in the diplomatic arena. In the absence of compromise, the war results were translated into an unstable reality that later triggered additional confrontations.

In the 1969 War of Attrition crisis, from 8 March 1969 to 7 August 1970, the Egyptians initiated a war they hoped would meet their goal of reclaiming their land without recognizing Israel's demand for peace and legitimacy. Having learned the lessons of the rapid 1956 and 1967 events, they chose a prolonged though limited war to maximize their capabilities while depriving Israel of its military doctrine of rapid and decisive victory, and leaning on its sensitivity to casualties. The Egyptians conducted primarily artillery bombardments while Israel responded with air raids, which included civil and economic targets. As a result, the stability of the regime in Cairo deteriorated and the role of the USSR became critical. Moscow, whose status had been damaged in 1967, was careful not to draw the United States into a direct confrontation, but nevertheless was determined not to allow another humiliating Egyptian defeat. Though only two local adversaries, Egypt and Israel, were involved at the outset, their confrontation rapidly introduced an external power, the USSR. Soviet pilots charged with deterring Israel from continuing its air attacks found themselves, on one occasion, in an actual air battle with Israeli aircraft. Aware of the explosive possible consequences, both Jerusalem and Moscow kept the air battle secret and limited all further confrontations to hostilities between Israeli and Egyptian forces, with the USSR providing its ally with substantive military aid. In order to counter Israel's air advantage without using their own pilots, the Soviets introduced SAM-2 batteries and a sophisticated missile air defense system in the Suez battle zone, operated jointly by Egyptian and Soviet personnel. This led to a counter supply of sophisticated U.S. weapon systems to Israel.[12]

Despite its prolonged duration, the scope of violence in this case was lower than that of 1967 or 1973. But the war and the U.S.-mediated Rogers B plan that concluded the crisis failed to reduce the Egyptian grievances or its drive for a major victory that would erase the trauma of the 1967 defeat. Relative stability was therefore short lived. Even though the war ended without any territorial changes, and Egyptian violence could not compel Israel to withdraw, the Egyptians nonetheless learned that controlled violence dictated by them could work in their favor. They were to try this formula again three years later, during the October War.

In some respects the 1973 war closed a cycle that had been inaugurated in 1948. The Arab surprise attack on 6 October found Israel unprepared, profoundly influencing subsequent Israeli military planning and Israelis' sense of security. Though the tide of battle shifted during the crisis from an initial Arab advantage to an Israeli military victory, this war constituted a trauma for Israel. During the first few days of battle, Israel was in despair and, fearing a conventional defeat, moved to operationalize its nuclear deterrence option. Even the Israeli advances in the latter phase of the war were unable to erase the shock of the disastrous opening stage.

The Egyptian-Syrian initiation of war was an attempt to dictate the terms of battle to their advantage. Actual fighting among Israel, Egypt, and Syria lasted from 6 October to 26 October when all parties accepted the UN ceasefire resolution. The war goals this time were more limited: to force Israel to withdraw from territories conquered in 1967 rather than to destroy the Jewish state.

In the post-1973 period, we find only one war but of a very different nature: a war related to ethnic-state issues and activity. Besides its sub-state component, the 1982 Lebanon war also contained an Israeli-Syrian confrontation. However, even between these two regional major powers the core issue of contention was the presence of PLO forces in Lebanon, and the demarcation of Israeli-Syrian spheres of influence in a country torn apart by a prolonged civil war. Hostilities began on 5 June when IDF troops invaded Lebanon, but the war was not limited to a battle against the PLO. It spread immediately to clashes in the Biqa region between Israeli and Syrian troops. Further escalation ensued on 8 June, when Israeli war planes downed sixty Syrian planes. Israel ultimately defeated the Syrian forces by cutting the strategic Beirut-Damascus highway. Additional Syrian-Israeli combat was averted when U.S. president Ronald Reagan sent envoy Philip Habib to delineate new spheres of influence between the major powers in Lebanon. In July the IDF laid siege to Beirut and both Syrian and PLO forces were caught in the city. On August 21, the Syrian forces were allowed to evacuate the Lebanese capital.

As the only full-scale war case in the post-1973 years, it marks the change in rivals and the decline in levels of violence during this period, pointing to a lower overall magnitude in crises during this stage. The participation of only the PLO, Lebanon, Syria, and Israel indicated that an Arab-Israeli war could indeed be confined to a few adversaries. The fact that peace between Israel and Egypt survived, and Cairo did nothing while Israel went to war with two other Arab states, reflected the changing Israeli-Arab equation.

Highlighting the violent side of crisis behavior, the Arab-Israeli wars discussed above were severe enough in the first period to involve not only regional escalation but also major/super power brinkmanship. At the same time, diplomacy and negotiations were also present and some compromise between adversaries was usually reached. Even in those cases where crisis termination was imposed (1967), some crisis regulation measures were established. In the post-1973 period, war became rare and when it occurred the combatants exhibited limitations on their use of violence. Was a similar pattern of conflict escalation and accommodation also apparent in crises with less extreme levels of violence?

Crises with severe violence

Nine crises, all but one in the 1947–1973 period, involved serious clashes that still fell short of all-out war. These cases pointed to the high levels of hostility in the first period, but unlike the trend toward negotiated termination noted in the war category, only one crisis led to some compromise and partial accommodative measures. In all other cases, severe violence was not followed by regulative outcomes.

First in this was the 1948 Sinai incursion. As noted earlier, after the IDF had crossed into the Sinai Peninsula, it confronted not only Egypt but also the UK, who had sided with Egypt. Israel shot down five British planes that had been sent to observe the Israeli withdrawal. This crisis led to a British ultimatum that induced Israeli withdrawal with no real compromise reached between Egypt and Israel. The fact that this intrawar crisis merged into the 1947–1949 case reduced its overall imprint on the conflict as a whole because the 1948 war ended through formal bilateral agreements.

The cycle of violence during the 1951 Hula drainage crisis was initiated by a Syrian attack against Israeli workers in the area. Later, Syrian soldiers killed seven Israeli policemen near al-Hama, triggering an Israeli air raid on a Syrian outpost. Syria responded with an attack on the Israeli post at Tel-al-Mutillah. Fighting was coupled in this case with intensive diplomatic activity that finally led to de-escalation and crisis abatement. As such this case was an exception in its category, supporting the violence-accommodation phenomenon.

The other cases where serious clashes occurred focused on a mixture of interstate and Palestinian elements rather than pure territorial issues between states. Four of these crises involved Israel and Jordan, with the Palestinians escalating tensions.[13] In the 1953 Qibya crisis, an Israeli raid into Jordan resulted in the deaths of sixty-nine civilians and the destruction of forty-five houses. More severe and with a growing role played by Palestinian elements, the 1956 Qalqilya, 1966 El Samu, and 1968 Karameh cases also involved large-scale fighting between the IDF and Jordanian/Palestinian units. In all these cases, Israeli retaliation was not intended to provoke serious clashes, but escalated into such. A similar crisis along the Egypt-Israel border occurred during the 1955 Gaza raid.

Miscalculation played a large part in the 1973 Libyan plane crisis. This odd event involved an Israeli military attack against a civilian Libyan plane mistaken for a hostile aircraft controlled by Palestinian terrorists, and turned into a heavy casualties case. Due to the very short time Israel had for response, and because of the pilot's refusal to comply with international aviation identification codes and protocol, Israel assumed hostile intentions and therefore shot the plane out of the sky. Only after the plane crashed did Israel discover its mistake. Misperception of an impending grave military damage provoked the use of violence with severe implications—the death of innocent civilian passengers.

In the post-1973 period Israel employed wide-scale violence only during the 1978 Litani operation when, as noted earlier, Israeli forces invaded southern

Lebanon in an effort to destroy PLO strongholds in the area. Interstate violence resulting from cases with sub-state violence and terror were usually somewhat more restrained in scope than interstate confrontations and rarely escalated beyond serious clashes.

Crises with minimal violence

The observation of violence also reveals cases where hostilities occurred on a relatively limited scale. These cases serve our dual purpose of testing trends in conflict dynamics and of illuminating the violence-accommodation link. Supporting the trend of a decline in crisis magnitude over time, only one incident with minor clashes occurred in the 1947–1973 period and six in the post-1973 years. Moreover, while war often led to institutional arrangements, minimal violence did not.

Two of the cases involving minor clashes were characterized by a unilateral Israeli act that led to the termination of hostilities. These were the 1976 Entebbe hijacking crisis and the 1981 Iraqi nuclear reactor case. The former ended after Israeli troops released the hostages and landed safely in Israel, while the latter was terminated by Israel's *fait accompli* destruction of the reactor, for which it was widely condemned. An additional case where a nonaccommodative ending followed the use of minimal violence was the 1968 Beirut airport crisis, which slowly faded after Israeli forces blew up thirteen Arab jetliners and returned to Israel.

Four additional crises of minimal violence occurred between Israel and Syria in Lebanon, escalating as a result of that country's civil war and domestic instability: the Al Biqa I and II cases in 1981 and 1985 respectively, as well as the nearly identical twin crises of 1993 Operation Accountability and 1996 Operation Grapes of Wrath. In the first two cases Israel and Syria tested each other's control over their spheres of influence with limited violence and a semiformal, tacit agreement ending the confrontations. Evidently, accommodation was possible following controlled escalation between the two regional adversaries. During the last two cases, in 1993 and 1996, the Islamic fundamentalist Hizbullah movement escalated hostilities in the Israeli controlled security zone in southern Lebanon, thereby leading to Israeli counterattacks, which resulted in the shelling of Israeli settlements in the northern Galilee. Though the duration of these hostilities was relatively longer than the use of violence in the two Al-Biqa cases, Lebanon, Israel, and Hizbullah eventually reached tacit understandings as before.[14]

Throughout the 1947–2000 period, in only four of the Arab-Israeli crises was no violence employed, and all were cases, as noted earlier, in which at least one adversary made a show of force: 1960 Rottem, 1963 Jordan waters, 1973 Israel mobilization, and 1976 Syria mobilization. Yet the diversity in their issues, actors and time frames points to the fact that even during an intense conflict, the use of violence could be averted. The first case was a test of the existing balance of power between Israel and Egypt, during the early years of pan-Arab extremism. The Jordan waters case focused on the lack of regional agreement regarding the use of scarce water resources. Violence was averted though the number of actors (five) was high and the situation could have easily escalated out of control.

Last among these cases, the 1976 Syrian mobilization crisis focused on Syrian-Israeli influence zones in Lebanon. The Lebanese domain led to many interstate crises but this single case with no violence proves that even during confrontations where sub-state elements are active and the rules of the game are vague, escalation can still be controlled.

And yet, in general crises did involve violence. When interstate territorial crises involved violence, it usually escalated to serious clashes or even full-scale war. The single exception to this rule focused on the issue of nuclear proliferation in the Middle East and was triggered by Iraqi attempts to break Israeli hegemony in this respect. During the 1981 Iraqi reactor crisis, hostilities were limited to the Israeli surprise attack of 7 June. Faced with an Israeli *fait accompli*, Iraq refrained from reacting militarily. Although the crisis involved a threat of existence, meaning peak level gravity, the actual level of violence was very limited. This crisis indicates that while gravity and mistrust were still high during the post-1973 years, the resort to severe violence was no longer an automatic response. On the contrary, it appears that both Israel and its Arab adversaries had learned to confine their use of hostilities and to climb the escalation ladder with greater caution than they had in the 1947–1973 years. Moreover, a shift in issues gradually appeared in the post-1973 period, with most cases belonging to the mixed interstate-ethnic domain. In these events it was much harder to reach accommodative outcomes and therefore the resolution of conflict was slower.[15]

CRISIS OUTCOMES AND CRISIS MAGNITUDE

Crises rarely linger on or fade away over time; they usually end decisively. In most cases, the outcome of a crisis reflects many influences such as the distribution of power among adversaries, the availability of superpower support a state can rely on, the extent of the threat to core interests, and the types of conflict resolution techniques to which the parties resort. ICB recognizes six types of outcomes: formal, semiformal, tacit, unilateral, imposed, and faded. Our study anticipates that the type of outcome will have an impact on future conflict dynamics. High magnitude exists in cases that end by an imposed agreement, by a unilateral act or in cases that fade over time, since the conflicting issues in these cases are not resolved among the crisis actors. We refer to the first category of crises as nonaccommodative-type terminations. By contrast, in a crisis that ends with a tacit, semiformal or formal agreement, crisis magnitude is low, reflecting the reduction of crisis-generated tensions among participants. We call this second type-accommodative outcomes.

ICB data for the Arab-Israeli conflict reveals that out of the six possible crisis outcomes crises ended most frequently in one of two forms: formal/semi-formal agreement (six cases), which led to lower crisis magnitude; and unilateral outcome (twelve cases), which marked high crisis magnitude.[16] The former type of resolution indicates some accommodation among adversaries while the latter points to the implementation of self-help and power prevalence principles. Accommodating outcomes indicate lower crisis magnitude, while nonaccommodation signals a raise.[17]

When we address crisis outcomes, the study focuses on several more specific research questions: Does the characteristic profile of crisis termination change over time in a protracted conflict? In other words, can we compare trends over time and locate changes in modes of termination, from less to more accommodative types or vice versa? How important is the violence-accommodation thesis in describing the way crises end? Do other context and process elements yield specific terminations? The following analysis of outcomes will assess these questions in a qualitative mode, while a quantitative analysis of the findings will come in chapter 4 on CMI changes and conflict transformation.

ACCOMMODATIVE OUTCOMES AND CRISIS MAGNITUDE

Five crises in the Arab-Israeli conflict system ended with formal agreements. Among these were the three major war crises of 1947, 1969, and 1973. Two additional cases were of lower crisis magnitude: the 1951 Hula drainage case and the 1981 Al Biqa I crisis. In accordance with the high violence-accommodation linkage, the first three cases involved war and were concluded with formal/semiformal agreements ending hostilities.

Despite its complexity, involving the largest number of regional actors, and its high severity, the 1947 Palestine partition - Israel independence case ended in a series of bilateral armistice agreements between Israel and each of its contiguous Arab adversaries. The major contribution of these agreements was not the establishment of a non-war relationship between Israel and its Arab adversaries, but rather the demarcation of boundaries and the establishment of several mechanisms designed to secure the accords. Thus, the termination of the 1947–1949 crisis through the armistice agreements created some behavioral regulations and interaction rules in a region where no regulations had existed. These included the Mixed Armistice Commissions (MACs) chaired by United Nations representatives, which enabled the parties to exchange direct communications, thereby facilitating the settlement of their disputes. Most of the issues debated in these committees were related to the military situation along the borders, and particularly the rise in armed infiltration into Israel from Jordan and Egypt, which often triggered ethnic-related crises. The relative success of the MACs indicated that the conflict could be managed in nonviolent modes. In the absence of a full and formal peace agreement, these accords and the mechanisms that they created provided some controlled stability within the protracted conflict.

While the first accommodative outcome took place at the onset of the interstate conflict in 1947–1949, the two other war crises that ended with accommodative outcomes took place at the end of the first period analyzed in this book: in the 1969 War of Attrition and the 1973 October War. The acceptance of U.S. secretary of state Rogers's plan, on 19 June, led to a ceasefire and to a formal agreement between Israel and Egypt. Similarly, the 1973 war also ended after intensive U.S. mediation diplomacy between Israel and Egypt resulted in a separation of forces agreement between the two countries on 18 January 1974.

U.S. diplomacy, already evident in the Rogers Plan, became very intensive in the aftermath of the Yom Kippur War. In the course of U.S. secretary of state Henry Kissinger's continuous and prolonged shuttle diplomacy, Israeli and Egyptian representatives solved the problems of withdrawal to the post–June 1967 war boundaries, the state of the encircled Egyptian Third Army, and an exchange of prisoners. The Geneva Conference of December 1973 was also an outcome of the war. Negotiations between Israel and Syria lasted much longer. On this front, diplomacy and force remained linked. In February 1974, escalation recurred, dubbed by some as a new "war of attrition." But another month of U.S. shuttle diplomacy led to the conclusion of a formal separation of forces agreement between Syria and Israel, concluded on 31 May 1974. Both interim-agreement accords focused on military issues, not normalization, but they led to a prolonged period of relative interstate tranquility, and marked the de facto termination of direct interstate hostilities between Israel and its two major adversaries.

These two separate agreements ending the 1973 war were followed by two long-range spillover effects. Between Israel and Egypt a peace process began in 1977 and concluded with the 1979 peace treaty. As of the year 2000, no Syrian-Israeli peace had materialized, but the Israeli-Syrian border remains quiet. In May 2000 the IDF pulled out of Lebanon, unilaterally removing an arena of friction and instability between these two regional powers.

Similar to the 1947, 1969, and 1973 war crises, although full-scale war was avoided in the 1951 Hula drainage case, it involved serious clashes between the adversaries that were still under the influence of the first Arab-Israeli war. This confrontation illustrates how institutions created to deal with future disputes, such as the MACs, could help during intense territorial confrontations. Specifically, during the Hula crisis, a formal agreement was finally reached after a UN Security Council resolution called for a ceasefire.

The 1981 Al Biqa I crisis also involved a dispute between Israel and Syria, but this time it was not blunt interstate rivalry but rather related to non-state actor presence and activity. Immediately at stake were the operations of the Palestinians and Phalange militia in Lebanon, as well as the demarcation of the Litani River as a tacit red-line between the influence zones of Israel and Syria in Lebanon. Both states accused one another of red-line violation. Outside influence prompted the parties into a ceasefire, which ended the crisis. Formally involved in the agreement were the Lebanese government and Israel; informally the PLO accepted the ceasefire, as well. In retrospect, this agreement served as a preamble to the direct bargaining process between Israel, the PLO, Syria, and Lebanon.

Though still belonging to the accommodative outcome domain, but unlike the five cases detailed above, which were concluded by formal agreements, the 1982 Lebanon war was terminated by a semiformal agreement, indicating that formalizing the principles of accommodation between states and non-state actors involved in a prolonged civil war was harder than reaching an interstate accord. But semiformal and formal agreements alike belong to the group of accommodative crisis outcomes. As such, even the 1982 war sustains the violence-accommodation thesis.[18] As in the Al Biqa I crisis, U.S. envoy Philip Habib actively mediated a series of agreements among the adversaries operating in the Lebanese quagmire. Three months after the Israeli invasion, Israel and Syria agreed upon ending the crisis between them. The Lebanese war lingered on, even after PLO and Syrian forces withdrew from Beirut and its vicinity. The formal peace agreement between Israel and Lebanon, of 17 May, meant little since the Lebanese regime fell under Syrian control with Damascus demanding the accord's abrogation. Some IDF units remained in south Lebanon long after the major crisis had ended, facing a low intensity war there with Hizbullah. Nevertheless, the Lebanese "peace" agreement reflected the spirit of the post-1973 period. Israel insisted on a peace treaty but ultimately realized that a peace cannot be imposed and withdrew unilaterally on May 2000.

Tacit understandings, an additional form of accommodative outcome, concluded five post-1973 crises. Though terminations of this type were less tangible and more ambiguous, these agreements nevertheless helped in establishing behavioral rules and regulations that could not be openly endorsed. Tacit understandings also contributed to a less hostile exchange among rivals when confrontations did occur. As such, tacit agreements had a moderating impact on crisis magnitude and conflict dynamics.[19]

The first case that ended with a tacit understanding was the Rottem crisis in 1960 between Israel and Egypt. As noted earlier, this crisis involved a test of wits between Israel and Egypt, with each state flexing its muscles via military maneuvers. The crisis ended with an implicit understanding to maintain the status quo ante. An implied consensus regarding the status quo emerged without a formal/official document or a negotiated diplomatic exchange, and indeed, no violence occurred. This case is an outstanding example of an accommodative ending in the more severe and hostile first period. But it also points to the limits of compromise in the absence of supporting formal regulatory and institutional devices. Alas, a quite similar confrontation in 1967 led to war with a nonaccommodative-type conclusion terminating the exchange of violence. In contrast, the Israeli-Egyptian peace has so far lasted for more than twenty years.

The other four interstate crises that ended by unwritten understanding involved Israel and Syria in the post-1973 years. All of them focused on mixed interstate-ethnic issues related to the Lebanese civil war and its implications for regional power and stability: the 1976 Syria mobilization crisis, the 1985 Al Biqa II case, and the nearly identical-twin cases of Operation Accountability in 1993 and Operation Grapes of Wrath in 1996.

In 1976, diplomatic mediation by the United States led Syria and Lebanon to accept, informally, the Litani River as the demarcation line between their respective zones of influence in Lebanon. Despite the somewhat vague nature of tacit arrangements, the Litani understanding helped reduce uncertainty and therefore contributed to the emergence of some stability between Israel and Syria in Lebanon.

In 1985, the loss of two Syrian Mig planes to Israeli jets over Lebanon led Syria to reintroduce SAM missiles along the Lebanese border. Israel regarded this move as a violation of the Litani red-line agreement. U.S. mediation efforts led to the reestablishment of the tacit Litani agreement in Lebanon, the removal of the Syrian missiles, the restoration of the status quo ante, and the termination of this confrontation. As such this crisis marks the dual character of tacit understandings: because of its vagueness it cannot prevent the outbreak of crisis, but it helps curb escalation and hence contributes to the emergence of regional stability.

Similarly, Operation Accountability in 1993 and Operation Grapes of Wrath in 1996 ended in tacit/semiformal agreements between Israel, Syria, and Hizbullah, defining acceptable behavior patterns and spheres of influence in Lebanon for Syria and Israel. Intense U.S. mediation efforts were necessary in order to establish the unwritten understandings between Israel and the Hizbullah. But with the United States and Syria as the supporting parties to these agreements, some limits were set to the ongoing cycle of hostilities along the Israel-Lebanon border during the late 1990s. Hence, though tacit agreements were more sensitive to disruptions that tested their endurance, they still manifested some degree of understanding, limits, and compromise.

NONACCOMMODATIVE OUTCOMES AND CRISIS MAGNITUDE

In twelve of the Arab-Israeli crises, confrontations ended with no agreement. Rather than compromise or negotiate an agreement, one or more adversaries resorted to a unilateral act that in effect ended the crisis.[20] Such outcomes represent a nonaccommodative form of crisis termination since no accepted regulations appear between the rival states as a consequence of their confrontation. Therefore, nonaccommodation marks high crisis magnitude and reduces chances of conflict regulation. Moreover, since no mechanisms are created to deal with future tensions, crises that end unilaterally tend to result in renewed escalation on the same issue. The resort to some violence in dealing with these issues, as well as the choice of a unilateral act to terminate the crisis, usually reflects the distribution of power and the unresolved topics of contention among the adversaries.

Within this group of nonaccommodative endings, variations exist and change over time does appear. Supporting the findings reported earlier on the decline in crisis magnitude during the post-1973 years, most of these cases occurred in the first period under review. They were usually ended by an Israeli act. Two of them—in 1948 and in 1956—reflected the power structure of a regional crisis in which major powers from outside were involved and forced Israeli compliance.

During the 1948 Sinai incursion, Israel attempted to translate its military advantage into political gain by invading the Sinai Peninsula, thus changing the balance of military power between Israel and Egypt. When the United Kingdom threw its weight behind Egypt, Israel was forced to accept the UN ceasefire resolution and ended this international crisis by unilaterally withdrawing its forces from Egyptian territory.

Even more intense extraregional pressure forced Israel to give up its gains in the 1956 Suez crisis. The Soviet threat to use nonconventional weapons on Egypt's behalf and the lack of a reliable U.S. counterthreat greatly enhanced Egypt's position. The fact that France and Britain, Israel's ostensible allies in this war, backed down left Israel keenly vulnerable to international pressure. Eventually Israel withdraw unilaterally, thus terminating the Suez war crisis. The capitulation of France and Great Britain in this crisis marked the end of their great power influence in the Middle East. With the two colonial powers gone, and the Soviet Union supporting the Arab side, the Arab states had no incentive to enter negotiations with the Jewish state.[21]

Both cases of Israeli compliance demonstrated that victory on the battlefields or temporary power gaps in favor of one regional actor do not necessarily lead to formal and tangible political accomplishments.[22] However, relative interstate stability was achieved after these two crises ended. In each, some regulative mechanisms emerged at the end of the war; the former included the establishment of the MACs to settle border disputes, while the later saw the dispatch of a UN Emergency Force to act as a buffer in Sinai. Ironically, violence may have acted as the catalyst for the establishment of some conflict regulation institutions; and almost ten years passed after each of these crises ended, with no major interstate war. Yet, peace did not follow and the situation escalated to war again once the parties felt that their security interests were in danger. The lesson is that the impact of the mechanisms that emerge from unilateral acts are short lived. A supportive context accompanied by formal agreements is more likely to endure, as the 1979 peace treaty with Egypt indicates.

Eight other crises also ended with an Israeli unilateral act. Five of these were interstate crises which escalated from low-level Palestinian border infiltrations and Israeli reprisals. Only three crises qualify as confrontations on pure interstate issues. This trend, whereby more sub-state and fewer interstate crises are resolved by a unilateral act, indicates that crises mixing state and non-state adversaries are more difficult to resolve via compromise and formal outcomes. Such cases tend to linger with no sign of accommodation. Illustrative of crises in this category are the 1953 Qibya case, in which an Israeli force executing a reprisal against Palestinians in Jordan unilaterally withdraw, with no arrangements to prevent the ongoing cycle of Fedayeen-Israeli hostilities. The more intense confrontation in Karameh in 1968, was terminated by separate unilateral acts by Israel and Jordan: the former withdrew its forces and the latter reopened the Allenby Bridge, indicating the return to a non-crisis routine. The Libyan plane crisis of February 1973 ended after Israel shot down a misidentified civilian Libyan aircraft. Taking place in the first period, the abrupt ending indicates the low expectations from each other that dominated both sides to the conflict. The hijacking crisis in Entebbe in 1976 was also terminated by a successful unilateral Israeli rescue raid. However, no guidelines or devices for interstate cooperation—to reduce or cope with such events in the future—followed in its wake. Lastly, Israeli-PLO hostilities across the Israeli-Lebanese border reached a peak during the 1978 Litani crisis, which was terminated by a unilateral Israeli withdrawal. As in the 1956 Suez crisis, once again a UN force was established. UNIFIL was designed to enhance regional stability but in the absence of a compromise spelled out in formal or even tacit terms, the reduction of tensions was only temporary.

Two additional unilaterally terminated crises ended with a Jordanian act: 1956 Qalqilya and 1966 El Samu. In the 1956 case, Jordan, which alarmed Israel and escalated the Fedayeen-triggered case by calling on the Iraqi regime for help, also played a crucial role in crisis abatement when it clarified that Iraqi forces would not, in fact, enter Jordan. The return to the status quo ante ended the crisis. But the core problem of Fedayeen cross-border activity was not really handled or solved.

As in earlier cases, also in the 1966 El Samu crisis, Jordan was confronted with the consequences of Fedayeen activity and Israeli reprisals. Heavy fighting occurred, but this time the crisis was confined to the issue of cross-border infiltrations alone. Once Jordan ended its military state of emergency, tensions diminished and the crisis ended. A major war followed both cases, supporting the supposition that unilaterally terminated crises remain highly vulnerable to re-escalation.

Whereas mixed interstate-ethnic crises often ended with a unilateral act and no accommodation, interstate cases rarely ended in this manner. Only three such crises exist: the 1963 Jordan waters confrontation, the 1973 Israel mobilization crisis, and the 1981 Iraq nuclear reactor case. All three crises ended with an Israeli act, accompanied by Iraqi actions in the last instance. The fact that most interstate crises do not end unilaterally, though they involve high magnitude and fundamental stakes, indicates that these cases are affected not only by the attributes of the crisis situation, but rather by some inherent conditions in the conflict that require the combined use of violence and diplomacy to achieve compromise. [23]

Other types of nonaccommodative crisis termination are imposed agreements enforced upon both sides to the confrontation, of which there is only one

Arab-Israeli example, the 1967 June war. This type of outcome is scarce because the multipolar regional balance of power and the two international superpowers deeply involved in regional cases mitigated against the possibility of a dictate. This one exception points to the role the superpowers played in Arab-Israeli crises. Often one or both superpowers participated and even exerted influence in crisis exacerbation or abatement, but neither could impose an outcome on a crisis among the regional participants. The 1967 crisis was the only exception to this rule, in which both the United States and USSR compelled their regional allies to accept a ceasefire.

ICB data-set assigned an "other" type of outcome to two Arab-Israeli cases. The first was the 1955 Gaza raid and the second was the 1968 strike on the Beirut airport. Both belong to the nonaccommodative-type category of crisis termination. The 1955 Gaza raid crisis ended temporally with an arms race when each side to the confrontation—Egypt and Israel—resorted to the signing of an arms agreement with a nonregional supplier (Czechoslovakia and France). Reflecting the instability involved in cases that end with such terminations, the situation re-escalated a year later into the 1956 Suez war.

The 1968 Beirut airport crisis faded rather than ended, with no clear event marking its termination. Instead, the level of regional tension gradually abated, and within two weeks a non-crisis routine had returned. As with other nonaccommodative cases, this crisis neither contributed to conflict regulation nor established rules of behavior to facilitate coping with future crises.

So far we have observed the attributes of crisis outcomes, highlighted the differences in the way confrontations end, and explored the trends of outcome-related crisis magnitude during the pre and post-1973 periods. The winding down of the Arab-Israeli conflict, indicated by context and process CMI components is also marked by outcome characteristics.

CRISIS MAGNITUDE AND CONFLICT TRANSFORMATION

Though conflict and disorder characterize Arab-Israeli relationships from 1947 until the present date, some regularities appear. Moreover, crises do not always involve violence, and violence does not necessarily lead to nonaccommodative outcomes. Over time, some change in process does occur, and levels of violence are far from being identical in all crises. Yet this diversity does not unfold in neat patterns as far as the time dimension is concerned, and the role of violence seems independent of all other crisis attributes.

The decline in the use of violence and the outbreak of interstate war appears in the post-1973 period, but only when the scope of violence indicator is considered. When violence as a primary CMT is evaluated, change is less evident. Accordingly, the extent of crisis magnitude based on the CMT indicator alone did not drop in the second period. The winding down of the conflict between Israel and its Arab adversaries, as postulated and supported by this study, must be attributed to other indicators of magnitude, the elements of context, scope of violence, and the modes of crisis termination.

Turning to the spillover effects between CMI realms and to the links between the six CMI indicators, five lessons emerge. First, it is evident that neither context nor process alone can determine levels of crisis magnitude and conflict dynamics. Only their interplay gives the most accurate picture of trends in crises and conflict over time. Accordingly, profound variations occur in the process realm of crisis, especially with respect to the scope of violence. It is significant that the "use of diplomatic CMTs combined with violence" was the most common procedure of crisis regulation in the Arab-Israeli conflict. This mixture indicates that while the conflict is very harsh and the adversaries were prepared to advance political goals via the use of violence, they still used nonviolent channels as well. Six such cases existed in the 1947–1973 period and an additional five cases occurred post-1973. Notably, as with the context elements discussed in chapter 2, some change in process exists and the decline in magnitude occurs only after 1973, but findings show that the drop characterizes limitations on the scope of hostilities but not in the willingness to use violence as a CMT.

Second, violence alone as a primary CMT was used in six crises, only one of which occurred post-1973. The violence indicator reveals that six crises in the Arab-Israeli conflict system escalated to full-scale war and that five of them occurred in the 1947–1973 period. Similarly, eight crises in the 1947–1973 period involved serious clashes among adversaries, and only one in the more recent period. Again, the end of 1973 is the turning point in the evolution of the conflict.

Third, all six cases in which diplomacy was coupled with violence in the 1947–1973 period were interstate confrontations, linked to war. In the second period two out of four cases in which diplomacy was combined with force had a salient interstate component, such as the 1980–1981 Iraqi nuclear reactor crisis or the Israel-Syria confrontation during the 1982 Lebanon war. The inference is clearly that the combination of diplomacy and war is the characteristic mechanism of the interstate domain.

Fourth, in fifteen of the Arab-Israeli crises, confrontations ended with no agreement. Instead of some mutual understanding, one or more adversaries resorted to a unilateral act that terminated the crisis. Such outcomes represent a nonaccommodative interstate relationship, since no regulations appeared as a consequence of the confrontation. Moreover, without mechanisms to deal with future tension, crises that ended unilaterally tended to result later in new escalation on the same issue.

Fifth, besides confirming the shift that took place after 1973 and the distinction between interstate and ethnic crises, this chapter exposed the war-accommodation linkage that helps explain the extent of compromise and accommodation between adversaries, particularly in the interstate domain. During the 1947–2000 period, six major wars occurred, while only one of them developed in the post-1973 years. These major crises were interspersed with many other cases of lower magnitude, some of the cases involving violence and others not. Examination revealed that while a decline in crisis magnitude represented the winding down of the conflict, the major crises in the first phase ended mostly (except 1956 and 1967) with accommodative-type terminations. Accommodative endings rightfully appear at the outset and the conclusion of the first period. While indicating a period of instability, crisis is also a stimulant to the formation of regulative institutions and confidence-building measures. In a protracted conflict, crises may be considered as "warning signals" that the conflict is harsh, but can also serve as opportunities for establishing conflict regulation mechanisms.

Finally, the analysis of the indicators and realms of crisis by itself does not provide an explanation for the trend toward resolution in the Arab-Israeli conflict. The fact that some crisis outcomes reflect conflict regulation and the winding down of the conflict and others do not requires further analysis.

Accommodative outcomes, already present in the pre-1973 years, were not enough, in and of themselves, to prevent the outbreak of other confrontations with negative impacts on regional stability and conflict escalation. Neither were lower CMI indicators of context in some cases, or lower CMI indicators of process in others, enough to mark a clear transition toward reconciliation and conflict resolution. For a more complete picture we must return to the theoretical framework presented in chapter 1, and take a closer look at the conditions for change that are rooted in the major theories of international relations. In other words, gravity of threat, number of participating actors, and the superpower role in crisis, the contextual indicators discussed in chapter 2, were all found to be higher in the first period than in the second period. Similar patterns were revealed for process indicators. While CMT remained more or less identical, the scope of violence and its use as a sole CMT changed, marking the winding down of the conflict in the post-1973 years. To understand these trends and to explain conflict transformation, we must examine the conditions for change spelled out in chapter 1.

CHAPTER 4

CRISIS MAGNITUDE AND
CONFLICT TRANSFORMATION

Considering the particular context, process, and outcome attributes identified in the earlier chapters, it does not seem surprising that in a prolonged conflict such as the Arab-Israeli case in 1947–2000 many crises have occurred. In the course of these frequent confrontations and severe turmoil, patterns, regularities, and characteristic attributes exist, leading us to an in-depth observation of the CMI as an indicator of change in crisis and conflict dynamics. First we begin with a concise quantitative inquiry of the six CMI components: gravity, asctors, superpowers, Crisis Management Technique(CMT), violence, and outcome. Afterward, we will integrate the separate findings on each realm into a composite analysis of the CMI—an aggregate score that characterizes the crisis as a whole. In the last section of this chapter we shift in perspective from a descriptive orientation to an explanatory approach. The conditions outlined in our theoretical framework will then be applied to the realities of the Arab-Israeli conflict in order to reach a better understanding of continuity and transformation described in detail in chapters 2 and 3 and analyzed quantitatively in the first two sections of this chapter. Like the two previous chapters, we adopt here a straight statist orientation in the analysis of international crisis. The ethnic perspective will appear in chapters 5 and 6.

REALMS OF CRISIS MAGNITUDE IN THE
ARAB-ISRAELI CONFLICT

The data on 26 Arab-Israeli crises within the ongoing protracted conflict are analyzed according to the three CMI realms presented in chapter 1: context, process, and outcome.[1] The first among these is context, which encompasses gravity of threat, defining the core state interests in confrontation; number of crisis actors, denoting the distortion in behavioral regularities due to the conflicting stakes between actors; and the level of superpower involvement in the crisis, indicating superpower role and the potential for crisis escalation or regulation in regional and global terms.

Conventional wisdom has always considered the gravity of threat in the Arab-Israeli conflict as extreme because of the denial of Israel's right to exist by its neighbors. Despite this truism, the ICB project only identified 11.5 percent of the Arab-Israeli crises as existential. Though signs of moderation have appeared in other CMI indicators as well as in threat levels, it is interesting to note that existential threats did not disappear in the post-1973 years, and that a strikingly similar weight of these threats is found in the two periods under study (see data presented in Table 4.1). On the temporal axis, the 1967 war qualifies as the turning point in terms of existential threat. After 1967, only the 1980–1981 Iraq nuclear reactor crisis was regarded as existential, and it was distinctive because this case involved a preventive act against a future nuclear threat.

High magnitude threats involved not only those to existence, but also threats of military-related grave damage, as well' as threats to the territorial integrity of the adversarial states. Grouping both existential threat and grave damage together suggests the October 1973 crisis as the breaking point; nine out of eleven crises (82 percent) in these two categories occurred between 1947 and 1973. More specifically, five out of six crises (more than 80 percent) that occurred between the 1967 and the 1973 wars involved grave damage (see Table 2.1). In contrast, two-thirds of the crises that took place after 1974 involved struggles for influence and prospects of limited military damage, both of which constitute a lower gravity conflict. When the pre and post-1973 periods are compared, the findings indicate that crisis magnitude reflected by the gravity of threat was declining over time. A summary of findings on the gravity of Arab-Israeli crises is presented in Table 4.1.

Still in the high gravity domain we also find threats to territorial integrity, which also dropped after 1973: from 17.6 percent in the early years to 11.1 percent in the post-1973 period. However, given the centrality of the territorial element in the conflict, it is clear that most major confrontations were defined on other issues such as existence or grave damage, rather than being straight territorial crises.

Observing low magnitude gravity, we shift to threats to internal stability, to economic interests, to confrontations entailing limited military damage, and to cases where influence is at stake. Starting with crises with a political threat that impinged on domestic unrest, 17.6 percent of the cases raised such threats in the pre-1973 period and this type of threat disappears from crises after 1973. These findings mark the stabilization of political regimes in the Arab states. Regime legitimacy, nevertheless, was and remains important in Middle Eastern politics.

TABLE 4.1
GRAVITY OF ARAB-ISRAELI CRISES, 1947–2000

YEARS CMI ATTRIBUTE	1947–1973		1974–2000	
GRAVITY	no.	%	no.	%
Low Threats:				
limited military damage	—	—	2	22.2
economic	1	5.9	—	—
political	3	17.6	—	—
influence	1	5.9	4	44.4
High Threats:				
territorial	3	17.6	1	11.1
grave damage	7	41.2	1	11.1
existence	2	11.8	1	11.1
TOTAL *	17	100.0	9	100.0

* Percentages may not add-up to 100 due to rounding.

Two other types of low level threats—economic and limited military damage—are very difficult to measure in the Arab-Israeli context because they have accompanied the conflict throughout the entire period. Israel's retaliation strategy in the 1950s would fall within this category. The 1978 Litani operation, which implied limited military damage, fell into the territorial threat category since the Lebanese government feared Israeli territorial ambitions. By contrast, the 1993 Accountability operation fell within the limited military damage category since Israeli occupation was ruled out. The mere fact that they occurred fifteen years apart also reflects changes in the modus operandi of the conflict. Because of the ongoing Arab economic boycott, economic threats are very hard to measure. The one and only crisis focusing mainly on an economic threat recorded in the ICB is the 1963 Jordan waters crisis, on allocation of water resources between the contending parties. Interestingly, in the 1990s the salience of economic and natural resources, primarily that of water allocation, gained prominence. Given the transformation in the core attributes of the Arab-Israeli conflict, articulated in this chapter, it may serve as a potential issue for future collaboration in an interdependent "New Middle East." It might, however, also unfold into a new zone of turmoil and confrontation if the conditions for change discussed in the second part of this chapter fail to preserve the dynamics of moderation to which we point in this study.

When low and high gravity threats are compared over time a clear trend is evident: high magnitude threats are in decline and correspondingly low threats take a greater share. Accordingly, grave damage drops from 41.2 percent to 11.1

percent in the two periods respectively. Similarly, territorial threats decline from 17.6 percent to 11.1 percent. The most noticeable change in Table 4.1 is the increase in the share of influence as a core threat in crises, from a low of 5.9 percent in the first period to 44.4 percent in the second. Though intense competitions for influence are a core aspect of international relations, when viewed in the context of a protracted conflict, such threats are much lower relative to existence and grave damage ones. Hence, this increase sheds light on the relative moderation features that take place in the conflict during the post-1973 years.

When all categories of high threat are combined—territorial, grave damage, and existence—they amount to 70.6 percent while low threats account for 29.4 percent in the first period. During the second period the figures change drastically, reversing the former trend, with 33.3 percent for high gravity and 66.6 percent for low gravity. In sum, though a threat to existence still loomed over the Arab-Israeli arena, a clear drop is noticed over the years in levels of threat, indicating some mellowing of the conflict.

The number of crisis actors has varied greatly in the Middle East crises. The conflict commenced with six states participating in the 1948 war. Most of the crises that ensued thereafter featured two adversaries, of whom at least one felt threatened. In the crises that escalated to war, at least three actors, and usually more, participated, a fact that enables us to infer that there is a linkage between the number of actors and the occurrence of major war confrontations. A gradual decline occurred in the number of crisis actors from among the core countries over time, the first of which is Jordan. In retrospect, the detachment of Jordan from the cycle of war dates from the King's 1970–1971 Black September crackdown on the PLO and the ultimate expulsion of the PLO from the Hashemite Kingdom. The Camp David accords extricated Egypt in 1978, leaving only Israel, Syria, Lebanon, Iraq, and the Palestinians. In 1982 Iraq's involvement in a war with Iran left only Israel, Syria, Lebanon, and the PLO as combatants.[2]

A summary of findings on the number of actors in the Arab-Israeli crises appears in Table 4.2. A comparison of the two periods under study identifies no change in the one and three actor cases, amounting to some 23 percent, and 12 percent of the cases in each period, respectively. However, the high magnitude cases of five and six actors, involving 11.8 percent and 17.6 percent respectively, occur in the first period only. In the post-1973 years, only one crisis exceeded two actors and indeed it is the only case that escalated to war (1982). Evidently, as was the case with gravity of threat, a winding down trend is found in the crisis magnitude measured by the number of crisis actors.

Superpower participation in the Arab-Israeli crises also varies over the years, but to a much smaller extent than gravity and number of actors described above. Following ICB definitions we differentiate in our analysis among five role levels ranging from full military activity—the most acute type of intervention— via semi-military, economic, political involvement to no participation at all. This CMI category manifests an inversion, instead of a clear-cut decline. At the outset, the UK was militarily involved while the two superpowers only

TABLE 4.2
ACTORS IN ARAB-ISRAELI CRISES, 1947-2000

YEARS / CMI ATTRIBUTE	1947-1973		1974-2000	
NUMBER OF CRISIS ACTORS	no.	%	no.	%
single actor	4	23.5	2	22.2
two actors	6	35.3	6	66.6
three actors	2	11.8	1	11.1
four actors	—	—	—	—
five actors	2	11.8	—	—
six actors	3	17.6	—	—
TOTAL*	17	100.0	9	100.0

* Percentages may not add-up to 100 due to rounding.

intervened politically. In 1956, all four great powers participated, with the UK and France involved in full-scale regional war that also marked the end of their direct activity in Arab-Israeli crises. Thereafter, a shift in focus to the super-powers took place and the United States and USSR alternated between a political or a military related role. They also employed mutual threats and nuclear brinkmanship, culminating in the 1973 nuclear alert.

A summary of findings on superpower participation in the Arab-Israeli crises is presented in Table 4.3. U.S. involvement in international crises in the region was overwhelmingly confined to the political sphere, ranging between 76.5 percent in the first period and a high of 88.8 percent in the post-1973 years. At the same time, American supremacy in the Middle East was coupled with a more limited Soviet participation in most crises. The USSR abstained from any participation in more than one-third of the cases. Yet, between 1955, when Soviet penetration began, and 1973, when the Soviet Union reacted its peak during the war, Soviet activity exceeded that of the United States in type and in intensity. Accordingly, in those same years, the Soviet share in semi or direct military role involved 23.5 percent of the cases, while U.S. involvement of this level was limited to 5.9 percent only. After 1973, Moscow played a declining role in Arab-Israeli crises: it hardly reacted to the Israeli raid on the Iraqi nuclear reactor, did not match the U.S. semi-military involvement in Lebanon in 1982, and eventually totally vanished from third party crisis management in the 1990s.

This disappearance of the USSR corresponded with increased direct American involvement in Beirut (1982) and in the (1990–1991) Gulf crisis. The decline of Soviet influence both globally and regionally correlates with the readiness of the PLO and Syria to accept Israel's existence, resulting in lower crisis frequency. The ICB project does not record the Gulf war as an Arab-Israeli

TABLE 4.3

SUPERPOWER INVOLVEMENT IN ARAB-ISRAELI CRISES, 1947–2000

CMI ATTRIBUTE \ YEARS	1947–1973		1974–2000	
U.S. ROLE	no.	%	no.	%
none	3	17.6	1	11.1
low-political	13	76.5	8	88.8
semi-military -covert	1	5.9	—	—
TOTAL*	17	100.0	9	100.0
CMI ATTRIBUTE \ YEARS	1947–1973		1974–2000	
USSR ROLE	no.	%	no.	%
none	6	35.3	4	44.4
low-political	7	41.2	4	44.4
semi-military - covert	3	17.6	1	11.1
direct military	1	5.9	—	—
TOTAL*	17	100.0	9	100.0

* Percentages may not add-up to 100 due to rounding.

crisis because it was initiated by Iraq against Kuwait, with Israel abstaining from direct military participation. Accordingly, its major issue was defined as a Gulf area confrontation and not a topic related to the Arab-Israeli conflict. Notably, it was the only act of major violence that took place in the wake of the Soviet collapse, besides the twin crises with Hizbullah: Operation Accountability in 1993 and Operation Grapes of Wrath in 1996.[3]

To sum, the nonactivity as well as the low level political involvement categories characterize the majority of superpower involvement in crises, thereby indicating that this CMI component contributes mainly to low rather than to high overall crisis magnitude. This trend of superpower activity as regulative agents in regional confrontations is further supported when the impact of their mediating efforts (usually that of the United States alone) is taken into account, leading to compromise and accommodative crisis outcomes. And yet, the rare but extreme cases of semi-military nuclear alerts and active military participation should not be overlooked. In total, four such cases occurred, encompassing the perils of escalation and unstable arms races (1955 Gaza raid), the dangers of spillover from regional to global conflict (1969 War of Attrition and 1973 October-Yom Kippur War), as well as pressures by outside powers, which obliges the regional adversaries to terminate their use of violence (1956 Suez War, 1967 Six Day War) and to reach a compromise (1969 War of Attrition and 1973 October-Yom Kippur War).

Process, the second CMI realm, includes two behavioral attributes: the type of management techniques with which to cope with the crisis and the various levels of violence used throughout the event.

CMT represents the spectrum of diplomacy involving negotiation/mediation as well as nonviolent military means, ranging through coercive diplomacy, in which violence plays a role alongside other forms of bargaining, and climaxing with the use of violence alone to resolve the crisis. A summary of findings on crisis management techniques in the Arab-Israeli crises appears in Table 4.4.

TABLE 4.4

CRISIS MANAGEMENT TECHNIQUE IN ARAB-ISRAELI CRISES, 1947-2000

CMI ATTRIBUTE \ YEARS	1947-1973		1974-2000	
CRISIS MANAGEMENT TECHNIQUE	no.	%	no.	%
negotiation/ mediation	2	12.0	1	11.1
non-violent military	4	24.0	3	33.3
multiple including violence	6	35.0	4	44.4
violence	5	29.0	1	11.1
TOTAL*	17	100.0	9	100.0

* Percentages may not add-up to 100 due to rounding.

High magnitude is represented by the violence and multiple with violence categories while low magnitude is indicated by the negotiation/mediation and nonviolent military categories. Observing the use of CMT over time reveals both continuity and change. The share of coercive diplomacy, namely, the multiple including violence category, is the most frequent CMT used in the Arab-Israeli conflict and actually rises somewhat over time, with 35 percent of the cases in the first period and 44.4 percent in the post-1973 years. Though negotiation/mediation are the least frequently used CMT in the conflict they too hardly change in their relative weight with 12 percent and 11.1 percent in the two periods, respectively.

Alongside this trend of continuity, which highlights the dominance of the hostile aspects of the conflict and the limited role of pacific modes in resolving crises, change appears over the years with respect to the use of violent and nonviolent military means. A significant drop is evident in the use of violence alone as a primary CMT from 29 percent to 11.1 percent in the two periods. Corresponding with this decline, a rise is found with respect to nonviolent military means with 24 percent in the first period and 33.3 percent in the second.

Yet it should be noted that even this rise indicates some moderation since the shift is from violence—a high magnitude category—to nonviolent military—a low magnitude one.

Overall, the salience of violence as a mode of crisis management declined substantially corresponding with the trend mentioned earlier on gravity and number of actors. Transformation has appeared over the years in core crisis attributes, signaling lower degrees of confrontation among the contending parties.

Scope of violence also changes, shedding more light on the CMT dynamics analyzed in the previous section. Violence is measured following the four ICB categories of no violence, minor clashes, serious clashes, and full-scale war. The first two categories indicate low magnitude while the last two denote high magnitude.

A summary of findings on violence in the Arab-Israeli crises is presented in Table 4.5.

TABLE 4.5
VIOLENCE IN ARAB-ISRAELI CRISES, 1947-2000

YEARS CMI ATTRIBUTE	1947-1973		1974-2000	
LEVEL OF VIOLENCE	no.	%	no.	%
Low Level:				
none	3	18.0	1	11.1
minor clashes	1	6.0	6	66.6
High Level:				
serious clashes	8	47.0	1	11.1
war	5	29.0	1	11.1
TOTAL*	17	100.0	9	100.0

* Percentages may not add-up to 100 due to rounding.

During the first period, serious clashes, the largest category, involves 47 percent and another 29 percent of the cases are full-scale war confrontations. In total, the high magnitude category amounted to 76 percent of the crises. By contrast, only 18 percent of the cases in the first period were free of violence and in 6 percent some violence appeared, though on a minor scale.

Turning to the second period, change is noticeable in all four categories of violence, thereby pointing to a very different profile: low magnitude takes the lead, with minor clashes being the most frequent type of violence in 66.6 percent of the cases, and an additional 11.1 percent of the crises involve no violence at all. Parallel, serious clashes and war almost disappear, with a single case in each category amounting to a low of 11.1 percent of the cases each.

Considering the violence-accommodation linkage raised in chapter 3, the findings on the decline in the salience of violence in the Arab-Israeli conflict are also most likely to manifest themself in a change in the characteristic outcome profiles for the two periods.

Outcomes focus on the winding down of crises and highlights the level of conflict accommodation at the final stage of the crisis. Drawing upon ICB definitions, we divided crisis termination into five possible outcomes: imposed settlement, unilateral act, tacit understanding, semiformal and formal agreements. For the purposes of this study, these outcomes divide again into two categories reflecting more and less accommodation: tacit, semiformal, and formal agreements indicate a higher level of accommodation and thereby low crisis magnitude, while imposed agreements and unilateral acts point to enduring conflict and high magnitude.[4]

A summary of findings on outcomes that conclude crises in the Arab-Israeli conflict appears in Table 4.6.

TABLE 4.6
OUTCOMES IN ARAB-ISRAELI CRISES, 1947-2000

YEARS CMI ATTRIBUTE	1947-1973		1974-2000	
TYPE OF OUTCOME	no.	%	no.	%
Accomodative				
formal agreement	4	23.4	1	11.1
semiformal accords	—	—	1	11.1
tacit understanding	1	5.8	4	44.4
Nonaccommodative				
unilateral act	11	65.0	3	33.3
imposed agreement	1	5.8	—	—
TOTAL*	17	100.0	9	100.0

* Percentages may not add-up to 100 due to rounding.

Two main types of outcome characterize the 1947–1973 period: unilateral acts, which take place in 65 percent of the cases, and formal agreements, which are found in 23.4 percent of them. These two extreme types of nonaccommodative and accommodative endings, respectively, are not surprising. Given the hostile nature of the Arab-Israeli milieu, nonaccommodative outcomes seem the most reasonable way to conclude a confrontation, leading to a perpetual cycle of violence begets violence with short intervals of non-crisis periods between escalations. However, in the midst of such intense instability the appearance of formal agreement in one-fourth of the cases is not quite fitting. These accommodative events accord with the violence-accommodation thesis discussed in chapter 3: situations where war is coupled with compromise and crises are settled by a formal agreement.

Tacit understanding and imposed agreements representing accommodation and nonaccommodation respectively, appear in 5.8 percent of the cases in the first period, thereby not affecting the dominance of the nonaccommodation identified earlier for this period.

In the second period, accommodation gains prominence as a mode of concluding crises and findings reverse themselves compared to the 1947–2000 years, with 66.6 percent for accommodative outcomes and 33.3 percent for nonaccommodative outcomes respectively. These figures are especially interesting given the decline in the scope of violence mentioned in the previous section. Although violence drops, and the violence-accommodation link no longer affects the way crises end, accommodation still surfaces following crises with much less violence than before.

Prior to our search for explanations that would help us understand the trends mentioned thus far, we will conclude our analysis with an examination of overall crisis magnitude, designed to characterize the crisis as a whole and to denote the integrated picture of crisis and conflict dynamics over time, formed by all six indicators jointly.

OVERALL CRISIS MAGNITUDE

The findings on overall crisis magnitude scores regarding the twenty-six crises throughout the 1947–2000 period, as well as levels of the six indicators of the CMI, are summarized in table 4.7.

Since we do not want to introduce a priori assumptions regarding the relative importance of each indicator in the overall score of crisis magnitude, equal weight in the composite index is assigned to the indicators in all three realms. The overall CMI Score was derived from the following formula: SUM of all indicators per case (with High = 1) + SUM of all indicators per case (with Low = 0). The possible range of overall magnitude is 0 to 6. Overall score of one to three denotes low magnitude and overall score four to six denotes high magnitude.

Based upon the CMI several trends are evident. First, during the 1947–1973 period, the spread of the seventeen cases is mainly in the high magnitude domain: one case scores 6, two cases score 5, and six cases score 4, and the remaining eight cases score 3 or less, with only one case scoring 1. In other words, more than half of the crises in this period fall into the high magnitude category, indicating the relative instability of the region at that time. By contrast, in the 1974–2000 period, only one case scores 4 whereas the remaining eight cases score 3 or less, of which two cases score 1 and two cases score 0. Notably, a sharp decline in crisis magnitude compared to the previous period.

Second, the main contribution to high magnitude in the first period derives from high scores in all the indicators, especially gravity, violence, crisis management, and outcome indicators. The main contribution to high magnitude in the second period is confined to high scores in CMT.

Third, the contribution of superpower involvement to crisis magnitude in the Arab-Israeli cases is strikingly low: it effects only five cases (four of them in the first period and one in the second) where high Soviet involvement increased the magnitude score and only one case, the 1973 Yom Kippur War, where U.S. participation led to a rise in magnitude. Notable, too, is the fact that among these cases only one, the Lebanon war, occurred in the post-1973 period.

On the whole, almost all the magnitude indicators measured in this study for a period of over fifty years suggest that the Arab-Israeli conflict was winding down. The gravity of crises was reduced, the number of crisis actors was smaller, and the level of both military and political involvement by superpowers in the conflict was decreasing. This trend has been matched, albeit to a more limited extent, by a decline in the severity of violence in crisis and a move to more peaceful modes of crisis management. Similar symptoms were detected in the form and content of crisis outcomes.

UNDERSTANDING CHANGE: LINKAGES BETWEEN CMI REALMS

Before we turn to an explanation of changes in the conflict we suggest some interim conclusions on the question of correspondence between changes in the CMI indicators and realms, as well as the linkages between changes in different realms of the CMI. Findings from the present study point to a correspondence between changes in the Arab-Israeli milieu and a decline in the magnitude of crisis represented in each of its three realms. Moreover, linkages are evident between the occurrence of change in a particular realm and its manifestations in other realms. The data suggest a spillover process: change first appears in the context, shifts to the termination modes, and is finally evident in the process realm too.

More specifically, lower gravity in crisis and a move from a relative to a joint gain situation was reflected first in the context indicators of crisis magnitude. Total conflict is represented by high-existential threats and Cold War superpower rivalry, arms races, and regional confrontations including both clients and patrons. A move from total confrontation to conflict regulation requires not only a change in the definition of stakes by the contending parties, but also a decline in the number of crisis actors who feel threatened, along with a constructive mode of superpower involvement in the conflict. Therefore, temperance in context appears as a necessary stipulation for conflict stabilization.

Contextual changes are accompanied by modifications in the third realm—outcome. Modes of crisis termination may be the result of actor values or may

TABLE 4.7
CMI SCORES OF CRISES IN THE ARAB-ISRAELI CONFLICT 1947–2000

FIRST PERIOD

YEAR		CONTEXT			PROCESS		OUTCOMES	
		Gravity	Actors	U.S.	U S S R	CMT	Violence	Termination	Score *
1947-48	First Arab-Israeli War	H	H	L	L	H	H	L	4
1948	Sinai Incursion	H	L	L	L	H	H	H	4
1951	Hula Drainage	H	L	L	L	H	H	L	3
1953	Qibya	L	L	L	L	L	H	H	2
1955	Gaza Raid	L	L	L	H	L	H	H	3
1956	Suez War	H	H	L	H	H	H	H	6
1956	Qalqilya	H	L	L	L	H	H	H	4
1960	Rottem	L	L	L	L	L	L	L	0
1963	Jordan Waters	L	H	L	L	L	L	H	2
1966	El Samu	H	L	L	L	H	H	H	4
1967	Six Day war	H	H	L	L	H	H	H	5
1968	Karameh	H	L	L	L	H	H	H	4
1968	Beirut Airport	L	L	L	L	L	L	H	1
1969	War of Attrition	H	L	L	H	H	H	L	4
1973	Libyan Plane	H	L	L	L	H	H	H	4
1973	Israel Mobilization	H	L	L	L	L	L	H	2
1973	Oct. – Yom Kippur War	H	H	H	H	H	H	L	5

TABLE 4.7 (continued)

SECOND PERIOD

YEAR		CONTEXT			PROCESS		OUTCOMES	
		Gravity	Actors	U S	U S S R	CMT	Violence	Termination	Score ★
1976	Entebbe Raid	H	L	L	L	H	L	H	3
1976	Syria Mobilization	L	L	L	L	L	L	L	0
1978	Litani Operation	H	L	L	L	L	H	H	3
1981	Iraq Nuclear Reactor	H	L	L	L	H	L	H	3
1981	Al Biqa Missiles I	L	L	L	L	L	L	L	0
1982	Lebanon War	L	L	L	H	H	H	L	3
1985	Al Biqa Missiles II	L	L	L	L	L	L	L	0
1993	Operation Accountability	L	L	L	L	H	L	L	1
1996	Operation Grapes of Wrath	L	L	L	L	H	L	L	1

★ The magnitude score is the sum of each indicator when L=0, H=1. For superpowers, whether one or both score high, the magnitude score equals 1. Overall score of 1-3 denotes Overall Low Magnitude. Overall score of 4-6 denotes Overall High Magnitude.

occur due to outside assistance/pressure, that is, superpower involvement in crisis regulation. At the same time, crisis termination through mutual agreement—tacit, semiformal, or formal—promotes joint gains, helps increase the gap between the negative price of crisis initiation and the positive payoffs of cooperation, as well as influencing the recurrence of crisis in the future.

Do contextual changes correspond with a decline in the process realm, namely, in violence during the crisis itself? The evidence in this study is mixed. While in the post-1973 era severe violence or full-scale war were used in only two crises, threats of military confrontations and/or some use of violence were manifest in all nine crises. We may assume that due to the persistence of habits in state behavior, modifications in process require more time to take root than changes in context and termination. However, only a change in the process indicators points to an effective establishment and consolidation of regulated security regimes in a protracted conflict. As such, process, together with context and outcomes, appears to be a necessary step toward conflict resolution.

On the basis of these links between change that occurs in the three crisis realms, we must maintain that the mellowing down of the conflict does not imply an Arab-Israeli relationship that is elevated into what was termed by Karl Deutsch a "security community."[5] Whereas a definite decline in the level of violence took place in the latter period, the fact that some form of violence remained an integral part of crisis management excludes the region from becoming a security community. We must also recall that only one-quarter of the crises since 1974 were resolved through formal or semiformal agreements, 44.4 percent ended with a tacit understanding, and 33.3 percent were terminated by unilateral actions. Such a record is far from representing full institutionalism in the cooperative "liberal" sense; it corresponds more with a power politics–based rationale. At best, the state actors in the conflict grudgingly accepted the reality that the continuation of international crises and war is not in their best interests, but they do not rule out violence or threat of violence as a means to resolving differences. Therefore, it would be inappropriate to fully apply the cooperative-institutional frame of reference to the Arab-Israeli relationship.

Moreover, when turning to the frequency of crisis data, the rise in interstate "crisis free" years since 1974 is limited to the outbreak of international interstate crises.[6] There was hardly any decline, and possibly even escalation, in crisis occurrence if ethnic-intrastate interaction and the 1990–1991 Gulf confrontation are added. First, it may be articulated that the conflict has been moving from the interstate-conventional level to the intercommunal level, and second, from the conventional battlefield to the nonconventional arena. The outbreak of the two waves of Intifada (1987 and 2000) was the best proof of the first assertion. The second assertion was demonstrated by the Iraqi missile attack on Israel in the midst of the 1991 Gulf war. The latter might have also indicated a spatial move from the core of the Middle East to the periphery.

EXPLAINING INTERSTATE CONFLICT TRANSFORMATION

What explains changes toward a winding down of the Arab-Israeli conflict? In chapter 1 we outlined a set of conditions that favor moderation in a protracted interstate conflict: balance of power, legitimacy, unbearable cost of war, and institutional arrangements. In accord with both the realist and the institutional approaches, these conditions induce change from an anarchical system to one in which a security regime promotes order. Five critical turning points in the evolution of the Arab-Israeli conflict lend themselves to analysis along the lines of these potentially moderating factors, dating from the first war of 1948 through the war of 1973 and beyond. As will be illustrated below, between 1947 and 1973, only some conditions for change emerged and therefore the turning points during the first period were only potential ones. After 1973 all four conditions co-emerged, making it a real turning point for conflict transformation. Our intent to detect nuances of change and to outline trends leads us to address both potential and real turning points in our analysis and to examine the aspects of change in each one of them.

THE 1948-1973 ERA

Our first condition for change was structural, namely that if the Arab-Israeli arena is to see peace, a balance of power is basic to the organization of security. Here "balance of power" does not mean an equitable distribution of forces but rather a distribution of forces that makes aggression by any side a costly proposition that outweighs potential gains from this act.[7] But a balance of forces in itself is not sufficient for a stable equilibrium, and even has a troublesome record in promoting stability in the Arab-Israeli milieu.[8] At different times it has both prevented armed conflict and contributed to war. A proper balance of power is, nevertheless, an essential condition in the promotion of international order.

The lack of a balance of power, or rather the inability of the adversaries to gauge correctly the real distribution of forces among them, contributed to the outbreak of the first Arab-Israeli war in 1947–1949. The Yishuv (the pre-state Jewish community in Palestine) had never before seen action in a full-fledged military confrontation against the regular Arab armies, and seemed to be an easy target. Five states (31,500 troops), joined by the semi-regular Arab Liberation Army (ALA) under the command of Fawzi el Qawukji (5,500 troops) and the Arab Army of Salvation (5,000 troops) led by Abd-el Kader el Husseini, confronted a young Israeli force initially numbering 34,400 men in 1947. Along with a numerical advantage, the Arab states also enjoyed apparent superiority in that they possessed regular armies with a full complement of units, while the newly born Israeli army did not have an artillery, armored units, or an air force.[9] Despite a population ratio of 1:46 between Israelis and Arabs, the newly born Israel Defense Force (IDF) succeeded in mobilizing an army that almost equaled the Arabs' in manpower. By the end of the war the number of Israelis under arms overpassed 90,000, surpassing that of the combined Arab forces and including tanks, artillery, and an air force (see Table 4.8).[10] Israel translated its military success into geopolitical accomplishments in determining armistice lines that exceeded the 1947 boundaries designated for the Jewish state by the UN 181 resolution calling for the partition of Palestine. But the huge disproportion between a small resource-poor Jewish state and a phalanx of Arab states with tangible resources limited Israel's advantage on the regional level.

TABLE 4.8
THE 1948 WAR: OPPOSING FIELD FORCES*

FORCES	15 MAY 1948	OCTOBER 1948
ALA	5,500	3,000
Army of Salvation	5,000	5,000
Lebanon	2,000	2,000
Syria	5,000	5,000
Jordan	7,500	10,000
Egypt	7,000	20,000
Iraq	10,000	10,000
Arabs	42,000	55,000
Israel	34,400	45,000 (90,000 mobilized and under arms)

* Excluding Israeli and Palestinian Home Defense Forces.
Source: Adapted from Trevor N. Dupuy, *Elusive Victory*, p. 123.

The post-1949 balance of power was not a stable structure. Nor were other crucial conditions for an Arab-Israeli entente, such as legitimacy and unbearable cost of war, present in the ensuing years. Political legitimacy was wanting both in the domestic and international settings of the Middle East. The defeat in the war accelerated military revolutions in Egypt and Syria, followed later by other Arab countries. Many citizens viewed the monarchies as reactionary servants of the colonial powers. These domestically illegitimate regimes themselves fell victim to the process of decolonization which turned the Arab states into revolutionary actors. The Arab refusal to recognize Israel challenged the legitimacy of the regional order, which worsened with the penetration of the Cold War into the region, especially the involvement of the Soviet Union and third world countries that by definition rejected the existing international order.[11]

A prohibitive "high cost of war," which might have led to caution and restraint, was also absent. Despite the price paid by Israeli society, which lost almost one percent of its population (6,000 civilian and military fatalities), the reestablishment of a Jewish state after two thousand years seemed apparently worth the cost. By contrast, though they lost the war, the Arab states did not actually lose any territory, and in light of their large populations their heavy casualties were not staggering. With the balance of nuclear terror nonexistent yet, both sides could still consider war a rational means of accomplishing political goals.

And yet, the first Arab-Israeli war set some institutional arrangements in motion, with limited success. The UN issued several calls for ceasefires, and passed relevant resolutions such as 194 which suggested to the Arab Palestinian refugees the right to choose between returning to their homes or receiving reparations. The UN also established the Palestine Conciliation Commission, which convened several conferences in ultimately futile attempts to reconcile Arabs and Israelis. Furthermore, it was under the UN during 1949 that four Arab states (Egypt, Lebanon, Jordan, and Syria) signed armistice agreements with Israel.[12] Although not peace treaties these agreements produced bilateral institutional arrangements in the form of Mixed Armistice Commissions (MACs) on each front which served as points of contact through which the protagonists could reduce politically explosive border incidents. The armistice regime between Syria and Israel functioned between 1949 and 1955, playing an important role in containing the Hula drainage crisis.[13]

Jordan and Israel moved beyond the armistice and secretly negotiated a draft of a nonaggression pact but domestic constraints and pressure from the Arab League delayed its revelation. King Abdullah was assassinated before it could become a fact.[14] The armistice agreement itself was feeble in preventing Palestinian insurgency and Israeli retaliation back and forth across the border. Nor did the Israeli-Egyptian armistice prevent Palestinian infiltrations from Gaza into Israel and Israeli retaliation. Other hostile acts between the two countries included an Egyptian blockade of Israeli shipping in the Suez Canal and the Gulf of Aqaba.[15]

In the absence of a stable structure of power and legitimacy, these paltry institutional arrangements were inadequate in preventing frequent outbreaks of violence. By the mid-1950s, following political revolutions within many of the Arab states, a "second round" of Arab-Israeli warfare seemed likely.[16] A summary of the conditions for conflict transformation in 1948, as well as in the other potential and real turning points considered below, is presented in Table 4.9.

Rapid changes in the distribution of military power contributed to the Suez war of 1956, our second potential turning point in the conflict. As Table 4.10 indicates, the Soviet Czech-Egyptian arms deal of September 1955 alleged a major potential tilt of the Egyptian-Israeli balance of forces in favor of Egypt. The strongest Arab state was about to more than double its strength in almost all branches of its military. In addition, the quality of weaponry introduced a new era of military technology into the Middle East. The French countered the Soviet arms supply with a largescale arms sale to Israel, including seventy-two Mystere IVs and two hundred Amx-13 tanks. This infusion of military hardware

TABLE 4.9

CONDITIONS FOR CHANGE IN THE ARAB-ISRAELI CONFLICT

CONDITIONS	1948	1956
I BALANCE OF POWER STRUCTURE (resources and alliance configuration)	Pre & Post: imbalance – Establishment of a sover- eign Israeli state in the midst of a stronger and hostile Arab world	Pre: imbalance – from temporary Egyptian dominance to a temporary Israeli one Post: Israel as a status quo actor with military superiority
II LEGITIMACY (mutual acceptance and status quo orientation)	Non–acceptance of Israel and the legitimacy of the existing power structure by the Arab adversaries	Non–acceptance of Israel and the legitimacy of the existing power structure by the Arab adversaries
III HIGH COSTS OF WAR AND RISK AVERSION	Costs of war: acceptable	Costs of war: acceptable
IV INSTITUTIONALIZATION	Armistice agreements	Collapse of the armistice agree- ments, replaced by UN forces in the Gaza, partial demilitarization in the Sinai and free Israeli navigation in the Suez canal and Tiran straits
CONCLUSIONS	Only one condition *partly* present: institutions	Only two conditions *partly* present: balance of power and institutions
FREQUENCY AND MAGNITUDE OF INTERSTATE AND ETHNIC CRISIS	2 interstate crises: 1 high, 1 low magnitude. 3 ethnic-state crises: 1 high, 2 low magnitude	3 interstate crises: 2 high, 1 low magnitude. 2 ethnic-state: both high magnitude

somewhat restored the military balance of power, and thus should have acted to arrest the incentive for war. But instead of stabilizing the situation the arms race ultimately led to war.

Additional regional and global transitions aggravated the unstable military balance between Israel and Egypt. The evacuation of the British army (80,000 troops), in the fall of 1955, from its bases along the Suez, removed an important buffer between Egypt and Israel. On 12 September 1955, Egypt tightened its blockade of the Gulf of Aqaba against Israeli maritime traffic. In October Egypt and Syria signed a military pact; Jordan's membership a year later created a tri-partite Arab military command. The new alignment increased the power gap between Israel and its neighbors to the latter's advantage. Meanwhile, the Eisenhower administration declined Israel's requests for a U.S.-Israel alliance. Nasser's nationalization of the Suez Canal in July 1956 confirmed Egypt's anti-

TABLE 4.9 *(continued)*
CONDITIONS FOR CHANGE IN THE ARAB-ISRAELI CONFLICT

1967	1970	CHANGE: PRE-POST 1973
Pre & Post: imbalance– from a striking Arab coalition to a temporary Israeli dominance	Pre: from imbalance to an emerging balance of power in the post war period. Step level USSR military involvement	From emerging balance of power to a mutually recognized balance of power
Non-acceptance of Israel and the legitimacy of the existing power structure by the Arab adversaries	Gradual partial bilateral Egyptian-Israeli recognition of an existing balance of power & shift of orientation by Egypt from a revolutionary actor to a pro-Western status quo actor	Emergence of partial mutual legitimacy: from one sided (Egyptian) to bilateral (Egypt-Israel & Syria-Israel) mutual recognition of a balance of power
Costs of war: acceptable	Costs of war: acceptable	Beginning of a regional nuclear 'balance of terror'
Resolution 242: exchange of territories for legitimacy and security + special UN envoy Gunar Yarring diplomatic mission	From Rogers I to Rogers II plans	Israeli separation of forces agreements with Egypt and Syria leading later to formal peace with Egypt and Jordan and to gradual spill over to the ethnic-state sphere - the Oslo process
Only two conditions *partly* present: balance of power and institutions	Only 3 conditions *partly* present: balance of power, legitimacy and institutions	All four conditions *partly* present: balance of power, legitimacy, unbearable war costs and institutions
2 interstate crises: both high magnitude. 2 ethnic-state cases: 1 high, 1 low	2 interstate crises: 1 high, 1 low magnitude. 1 ethnic-state crisis: high magnitude	Only 1 interstate crisis of low magnitude 8 ethnic-state crises: all low magnitude

Western orientation. France's anger at Nasser's support for the Algerian rebellion against French colonial rule and the British anger at Nasser's nationalization of the Suez Canal, however, in confluence with Israel's own worries about Egypt led to classical tripartite alliance among them and to regional escalation.

The Treaty of Sevres was signed on 24 October. It provided for the coordinated French-Israeli-British attack against Egypt, launched on 29 October 1956. This collaboration resulted in a power gap to the detriment of Egypt, which was deserted by its Arab allies. A comparison of the forces on the battlefield, reveals that Israel not only enjoyed a qualitative advantage, but also almost closed the quantitative gap (see Tables 4.10 and 4.11).[17]

Explaining the onset of the 1956 war in balance of power terms suggests that Israel's actual military advantage prompted it to take advantage of its temporary superiority.[18] Stephan Walt's balance of threat theory can also explain

TABLE 4.10
ISRAEL AND EGYPT: THE DISTRIBUTION OF MILITARY POWER
AT THE END OF 1955

EQUIPMENT	ISRAEL	EGYPT	CZECHOSLOVAKIAN-EGYPTIAN ARMS DEAL
Formations	14 infantry + + 2 armored brigades	20 brigades (12 infantry + 3 armored)	
Medium and heavy tanks	200 Sherman M-3 & M-50	200 Sherman M-3 & AMX	230 T-34 & Stalin
Tank destroyers and light tanks	50	173	100
Jet fighters and jet bombers	48	80	125 (115 Mig-15 & 10 Mig-17) 40 Ilyushin-28
Destroyers			2
Frigates	3	6	
Torpedo boats	9	18	12
Artillery	230	375	500
Armored troop carriers	400	400	200
Additional			56 130 mm. Multiple rocket lanchers, 150 heavy vehicles, radar systems, 15 mine-sweepers, 2 submarines, 100 self pro pelled SU-100 tank destroyers and more light weapons

Source: Calculated on the basis of *Carta's Atlas of Israel, The First Years, 1948-1961*, (eds.) Yehuda Wallach and Moshe Lissak (Jerusalem: Carta, 1978), 124; and Yaniv, *Deterrence Without the Bomb*, p. 33.

Israel's behavior.[19] Walt's theory would hold that Israel's interest in forming an alliance with France and Britain did not stem from an immediate existential threat, but rather from fear that a potential imbalance of power might render a security threat somewhere down the road.[20] The unique constellation of international forces similarly interested in punishing Egypt seemed to provide Israel with a one-time opportunity to rectify the grim long-term trend facing it. Here we encounter the rationale of preventive war related to the balance of power. This kind of war cannot, in the short run, be regarded as strategy for stabilization. In initiating a preventive war a leader is expressing a preference for the manageable uncertainties of a war fought now rather than the more daunting uncertainties involved in future war under unknown circumstances.[21]

TABLE 4.11
THE 1956 WAR: DISTRIBUTION OF ISRAELI AND EGYPTIAN FORCES
ALONG THE SINAI FRONT★

EQUIPMENT	IDF SOUTHERN COMMAND	EGYPTIAN EASTERN FRONT
Formations	2 divisions	2 divisions
Infantry	5 brigades	6 brigades
Paratroopers	1 brigade	
Armor	3 brigades	1 regiment
National and border guard		2 brigades + 4 regiments
Tanks	250	58 + 55 tank destroyers
Airplanes	81 jet fighters and bombers	109 jet fighters and bombers

★In addition, the British assembled a force of around 50,000 soldiers and the French 30,000. Together they created a naval task force of 130 warships, hunderds of landing craft, 80 cargo boats, and hunderds of bombers and jet fighters.

Source: Adapted from *Carta's Atlas of Israel: The First Years, 1948-1961*, p. 126.

The 1956 war, in short, demonstrated the imperfection of the balance of power as a stabilizing device in the absence of other elements required for deterring adversaries from initiating war.

Legitimacy, the second condition for stability, was totally absent both prior to and following the 1956 hostilities. From the Egyptian perspective, the 1956 attack was a blunt aggression associated with neocolonial aspirations and was in no way considered as a defensive Israeli action to preserve the status quo, which Egypt perceived as oppressive. The influence of anti–status quo actors such as the Soviet Union in the region peaked as a result of the war. Within the Arab world conservative regimes such as the monarchy in Iraq were overthrown and replaced by revolutionary ones and the Hashemite rule in Jordan was threatened.

The third condition supporting stability, unbearable war costs, was also absent in the Suez case. Although it involved two great powers and the political involvement of two superpowers, the war was limited in scope, duration, and number of casualties. Moreover, the Soviet Union's threat to use missiles against the Western capitals and Tel-Aviv though severe never developed into a global confrontation.[22]

Several institutional arrangements, some tacit and some explicit, accompanied the 1956 crisis, thereby partly fulfilling the fourth condition for moderation. Formally, Egypt and Israel agreed to the stationing of a United Nations Emergency Force (UNEF) as a buffer between them in the Sinai. Future withdrawal of these forces required consent of Egypt, the UN secretary general, and the UN supervising committee. The UNEF's mission was to prevent cross-border infiltrations and to serve as an early detection device for an impending Egyptian attack on Israel. An additional institutional arrangement was a declaration by the United States, Britain, and France guaranteeing free Israeli passage in the Straits of Tiran. Tacitly, Egypt also agreed to limit the deployment of its forces in the western Sinai to two divisions and 250 tanks.[23]

All in all, the 1956 war occurred within the milieu of two partially stabilizing conditions: a partial balance of power and some institutional arrangements. Legitimacy was entirely lacking. Even though Israel achieved military success, the distribution of power did not decisively favor Israel, assisted as it was by the forces of two former colonial powers and by the failure of the other Arab states to act in concert with Egypt. Institutional arrangements were incomplete because they were accepted only tacitly by Egypt. As a result violence declined between Israel and Egypt from 1957 to 1967. But with the other two conditions (legitimacy and unbearable war costs) absent, international crises continued to erupt along the Egypt-Israel axis.

In the post-1957 years the balance of power seemed rather stable. As Nadav Safran concluded on the basis of a comprehensive study of defense expenditures and armed forces at the time: "Analysis of the balance of forces revealed a long range trend in favor of Israel in the capacity to sustain the arms race; however this trend was more a portent of diminishing than of increasing chances of war because Israel was the party content with *status quo*."[24] Stability was further bolstered by the de facto demilitarized zone in the Sinai, maintained by the UNEF and by Israel's freedom of navigation through the Straits of Tiran as assured by President Dwight Eisenhower on 3 March 1957. Apparently effective for more than a decade, the combination of a balance of power and institutions did not preclude the outbreak of another major war in 1967. In the post-Suez era several of the major actors were still unable to accept legitimacy of the system and none of them had yet calculated that the cost of war might be unbearable.

An unrefined distribution of forces analysis, as Table 4.12 indicates, cannot explain the Six Day War. From a military power perspective neither side had any incentive to initiate war. The Arab quantitative advantage in the tangible elements of military power was well balanced by Israel's qualitative advantage in the intangible dimensions, namely, military leadership, motivation, technical skills, and so on. The ratio in armed forces and military equipment was roughly 2.5:1 in favor of the Arab coalition (Egypt, Syria, Jordan, and Iraq).[25] But this ratio, without an Arab qualitative leap, was considered as balanced.[26] In light of Egypt's poor performance in 1956, Israel did not foresee the huge military-technological surge of Egypt before it could endanger Israel's existence. The same seemed true for the other Arab states. A profound change in the configuration of power required a broad Arab coalition coordinated under one command with Egyptian divisions stationed in the Sinai and other Arab armies stationed along Israel's narrow waist in the center of the country. Such a scenario seemed to develop in May 1967 when belligerent acts and statements by Nasser accompanied by an alliance of several Arab armies suggested that an Arab first strike was plausible and would pose an existential threat to Israel.[27]

TABLE 4.12

THE JUNE 1967 WAR: THE ARAB-ISRAELI MILITARY BALANCE

	EGYPT	JORDAN	SYRIA	IRAQ	TOTAL ARAB	ISRAEL	RATIO: ISRAEL–ARAB
Armed Forces	250,000	56,000	70,000	80,000	456,000	275,000	1:1.6
Tanks	1,300	275	550	630	2,755	1,093	1:2.5
Artillery	840	184	460	600	2,084	681	1:3
Fighter-Bombers	431	18	127	106	682	286	1:2.4

Source: Adapted from *Carta's Atlas of Israel, The Second Decade, 1961 - 1971,* Yehuda Wallach and Moshe Lissak (Jerusalem: Carta, 1978), p. 52 and Trevor N. Dupuy, Elusive Victory, p. 337.

The June 1967 war, our third potential turning point, broke out following the collapse of the institutional arrangements established at the close of the 1956 war. Egypt disregarded Israel's declared "red lines" (such as free navigation in the Straits of Tiran, stationing of UN forces in the Sinai), undermined Israel's deterrence credibility, and challenged the status quo.[28] Arab antagonists interpreted Prime Minister Levi Eshkol's reluctance to respond to the hostile Egyptian signals as a sign of weakness. President Nasser, who based his leadership on anti-Western and anti-Israeli sentiments soon maneuvered his country into a position such that a failure to press ahead with threats against Israel would constitute a major blow to Egypt's prestige in the Arab world. It was only a question of time as to who would strike first.[29] Israel's deterrence doctrine and the assumption that the state that struck first would enjoy an advantage convinced Israel to preempt.[30] Deterrence, an outgrowth of the balance of power inhibitor of war, actually induced war rather than prevented it.

Israel's victory in 1967 transformed some of the basic elements in the Arab-Israeli equation. This third consecutive Israeli military victory (after 1948 and 1956) unprecedented in its speed and decisiveness confirmed the IDF's advantage over its opponents. The balance of power was once again reestablished within the framework of Israeli superiority, but with overwhelming Arab grievances. Israel's territorial gains in 1967 improved its geostrategic position, but exacerbated Arab motivation to uproot the results of their defeat.[31] Consequently, the occurrence of crises did not diminish. On the contrary, the relative stability that had existed at the Israeli-Egyptian border following the 1956 war did not recur after 1967.

With the limits of the balance of power factor in stabilizing the Arab-Israeli conflict exposed, the 1967 war produced a new element that should have moderated the conflict. Israel, for the first time, had assets to exchange in return for legitimacy. Theoretically, the prospect of exchanging territories for peace should have strengthened the diplomatic process of conflict resolution and cultivated legitimacy. An institutional device in the form of UN Resolution 242 of 22 November 1967 further advanced the notion of Israel trading territories captured in the war for peace. The essence of the resolution was that in exchange for Israel's withdrawal from territories conquered in 1967 to secured borders, the Arab states would recognize Israel's legitimacy. All fifteen members of the Security Council supported the resolution's recommendations for negotiations toward peace treaties, an ending to the state of war, all states' right to secure borders, mutual recognition of the sovereignty of all states in the Middle East, unobstructed navigation, and a resolution of the Palestinian refugee problem. The appointment of special UN envoy Gunar Jarring represented the intention of the council to see its resolution implemented.[32] Almost immediately, however, the Arabs and Israel expressed conflicting interpretations as to how much land Israel could keep in order to enjoy secure borders and how to negotiate Israeli withdrawal. Israel insisted on direct negotiations and interpreted UN Resolution 242 as not demanding total withdrawal, while the Arabs rejected this interpretation.[33] In the absence of legitimacy and common perceptions regarding the prohibitive high costs of war, a balance of power favoring the status quo and institutional arrangements did not suffice for promoting stability.

The limits of the post-1967 balance of power and institutional factors in preventing war were manifest when, less than two years after Israel had destroyed its military, Egypt initiated the War of Attrition, the fourth potential turning point we address in this study. The resumption of hostilities by Egypt against a militarily superior enemy can be explained by the style of war. The Egyptians opted for a low level long-term static war, thereby depriving Israel of its technological advantage. Egypt intended that the long duration of the war and the slow but steady flow of casualties would cause excessive pain to Israel and thus compel a withdrawal from the territories captured in 1967.[34] Instead, Israel responded by constructing a series of defensive outposts known as the Bar-Lev line, and raised the ante with deep penetrations bombing Egyptian cities, designed to cause equivalent pain to Egypt. Yet another destabilizing element entered into this already grim situation: growing Soviet participation. During the War of Attrition, the Soviets provided Egypt with a complete air defense system manned by Soviet troops and pilots.[35] The one incident of an aerial dogfight in which Israeli planes shot down four Migs flown by Soviet pilots, on 30 July 1970, implied a new equation of power, and highlighted the dangers of spillover escalation from the regional to the global domain.[36]

The role of the great powers elevated the conflict to a higher level of confrontation and introduced the third condition for change, a growing potential cost of war transcending the parties' level of tolerance for violence. Further evidence of increased superpower activity was reflected in diplomatic interactions such as the "Two Powers Talks" starting in 1968 and a U.S.-USSR standoff in September 1970 over Syrian intervention in Jordan in favor of the PLO. This occurred in the ambiguous milieu of U.S.-USSR SALT negotiations limiting nuclear arms but also of superpower support for two opposing sides in Vietnam.[37] The conflict did not wind down early in the post-1970 era despite superpower involvement in rendering their services and the existing option of exchanging territories for peace.[38] The post-1967 institutional framework embodied in UN Resolution 242 and supported by both superpowers did not induce the parties to move toward a genuine peace process. Similarly, the Rogers Plan B for both a ceasefire and the resumption of negotiations, following the termination of the War of Attrition in July 1970 mediated by U.S. secretary of state William Rogers failed to start a peace process. UN representative Gunnar Jarring convened talks, but in September 1970 Israel withdrew from them citing Egyptian violations of the ceasefire agreements.[39]

Neither the stalemate that emerged after the War of Attrition nor the institutional framework of UN Resolution 242 and the Rogers Plan advanced a peace process or deterred war.[40] The 1973 war further invalidated the balance of power as a solely sufficient deterrent. Both the 1967 war and the War of Attrition could have been turning points to full conflict transformation, but instead failed to induce change in the levels of stability and conflict regulation.

How do we explain the weakness of the conditions one and four, balance of power and institutional arrangements, in promoting stability? Continued regional instability in the wake of the Six Day War and the War of Attrition strengthens the weight of the second condition: legitimacy, namely, acceptance of the existing structure of power. The origins of legitimacy, however, cannot be totally dissociated from 1967. Territorial assets ultimately provided an incentive for accommodation. UN Resolution 242 offered some framework for legitimacy, but the opposing interpretations of this resolution by Israel and the Arab states proved that the adversaries were not yet ready to recognize the newly emerging balance of power. Evidently, the balance of power cannot promote stability in itself when parties to the conflict are in a zero-sum situation.[41] As postulated by Janice Stein, "Where interests are wholly incompatible, where conflict is 'zero-sum,' . . . even the limited objective of the management of conflict may be impossible."[42] When politicide is the goal of struggle, as it was after 1948, then by definition state interaction cannot be considered a "mixed motive game." Until they resigned to Israel's existence among them the Arab states were unprepared to exchange territories for peace. Some ten years later, when other conditions loomed, Israel's acquisition of territorial assets of value to the Arab states did induce Egypt to sign a peace treaty with Israel.

After 1967, existential threat to Israel had subsided, a combination of a balance of power and some institutional arrangements had emerged, and some legitimacy to coexistence had appeared. Yet the early 1970s did not witness a shift in the frequency and magnitude of international crises in the Arab-Israeli arena. Still missing was a shared aversion to war on the grounds that the cost of further fighting would be unbearable.

THE POST-1973 ERA

The major turning point in the Arab-Israeli conflict according to the CMI empirical findings occurred in the aftermath of the 1973 October-Yom Kippur War. One outstanding feature of that war was that even though the Arab side opened hostilities, as in May 1948, its operational goal was not the destruction of the Jewish state. Accordingly, despite the severe setbacks Israel suffered and the initial panic of some Israeli leaders, ICB designated this crisis as one involving a threat of grave damage but not of existence, as was the case in both the 1948 and 1967. The abandonment of Israel's destruction as a war goal was related to the balance of power in the wake of the 1967 war. Preoccupied with their own territorial losses in June 1967 the Arab objective shifted to causing severe Israeli casualties thus forcing it to withdraw from those territories, preferably without direct negotiations.[43] The liberation of "Palestine," or in other words the territories conquered by Israel in 1948, was left for another time.

For Anwar al-Sadat, the principal initiator of the attack, the war aims were political, namely, the reclamation of Egyptian pride, honor, and territories if possible, so as to set the stage for negotiations between Israel and Egypt as equals.[44] As such he digressed from the traditional aim of politicide pursued by the Arab states until then. Another major participant in the previous war, Jordan, stayed out of the 1973 war thus restricting the fighting to the Egyptian-Israeli and Syrian-Israeli fronts. Despite the setbacks and intimidating moments for a surprised Israel, the latter also limited its goals. While employing almost all of its conventional capabilities Israel unveiled its nuclear option in a very limited and discrete manner. With its limited and diplomatic goals, the October War resembled wars elsewhere during the second half of the twentieth century.[45]

Although the post-1967 balance of power contributed to the change in Arab goals and strategy, it could not prevent the outbreak of the 1973 war. On the other hand, Sadat's moderate policies following 1973 cannot be attributed to changes in the balance of power alone. The Arab-Israeli military balance presented in Tables 4.12 and 4.13 shows that between 1967 and 1973 there was no distinctive gap that could have tempted Sadat to think that he could win the 1973 war. Assuming that the qualitative symmetry remained constant, there was no change in the quantitative ratio to the extent that the Egyptian president could assume an Israeli defeat. Indeed, following the early military successes of the Egyptian and the Syrian armies, the IDF managed to terminate the war with new territorial gains and with the Egyptian Third Army under siege, on the verge of destruction. While the Israeli victory was not as convincing as it had been in 1967, it had clearly taken the lead in the final battles of the war. Cumulatively, a stable equilibrium was slowly emerging in the Arab-Israeli arena, further affirmed by the 1973 war.

Legitimacy, in the form of mutual acceptance, cannot be attributed solely to the 1973 experience but rather reflects the result of accumulative Arab-Israeli interactions. The previous wars in which Israel displayed its prowess fostered a

TABLE 4.13

THE OCTOBER 1973 WAR: THE ARAB-ISRAELI MILITARY BALANCE

FORCES	EGYPT	JORDAN (committed)	SYRIA	IRAQ (committed)	OTHER ARAB FORCES	ARAB TOTAL	ISRAEL	RATIO: ISRAELI-ARAB
Ground Forces	315,000	5,000	140,000	20,000	25,000	505,000	310,000	1:1.6
Tanks	2,200	150	1820	300	371	4,841	2,000	1:2.4
Artillery	1,210	36	655	54	100	2,055	570	1:3.6
Air Force	750		327	73	104	1,254	476	1:2.5

Source: Adapted from Col. Trevor Dupuy, *Elusive Victory*, pp. 606–608.

grudging de facto acceptance of the Jewish state by the Arabs. While the Six Day War demonstrated the futility of the Arab hopes of destroying Israel, the War of Attrition both confirmed the limits of violence in expelling the IDF from the territories and manifested the advantages of fighting a limited war with political goals. Accordingly, some form of war limitation and readiness to negotiate with Israel had already appeared during the War of Attrition and especially following Nasser's death and Sadat's rise to power in 1970.

A major landmark signaling acceptance of the emerging status quo was Sadat's realignment within the global ideological struggle. From an alliance with the Soviet Union for almost two decades, the new president shifted Egypt toward a Western orientation and thereby converted his country to an actor supporting the existing international order. Sadat signaled the new Egyptian international orientation in August 1972 when he expelled the Soviet advisors from Egypt, but the complete turnabout came only in the context of the 1973 war.[46] By allowing U.S. secretary of state Henry Kissinger to play the major role in negotiating the ceasefire agreement with Israel, Egypt indicated readiness to break with its Soviet patron. Indeed, in the subsequent months Kissinger served as the principal negotiator of the entire postwar peace process. Disengagement negotiations between Israel and Egypt took place under U.S. guidance, and in early 1974 Egypt and the United States restored bilateral diplomatic relations. In the ensuing years, U.S. economic and military aid to Egypt replaced the extensive Soviet aid of the past.[47] Egypt's realignment with the status quo superpower naturally led to a more moderate foreign policy and acceptance of the existing regional/international order.[48]

Israel's growing dependence on U.S. diplomatic and military support concurred with Egypt's turn to the West. The dependence on Washington's support had constrained Israel's military options during the 1973 war, arresting a preemptive strike at the outset of the crisis as well as the destruction of the Egyptian Third Army at the end of the war. Virtually a paraiah state, internationally condemned and isolated, Israel's reliance on the United States only increased after 1973.[49] The pre-1967 offensive *casus belli* doctrine was based on massive retaliation against Arab threats. In contrast, after the 1973 war Israel adopted a mixed, defensive-offensive, strategy.[50] In the negotiations on the interim agreements, Israel insisted on strategic depth in the Sinai and the Golan. Demilitarization of the Sinai in the Camp David accords also reflected this defensive logic.

While Egypt was slowly moving toward acceptance of a status quo based on the pre-1967 boundaries, at least as far as Sinai was concerned, Israel was discovering that the post-1967 borders were not sufficient to deter aggression. The short interval between the 1967 and 1973 wars, as opposed to the decade between 1956 and 1967 wars, demonstrated the potency of the Arab states' outrage at the loss of territory. Arab frustration served as a catalyst to war even when the power gap was not in their favor and military action involved a high cost to the attacking states. While conserving the assumption that vulnerable borders invited aggression, Israel learned that control of additional territories did not automatically translate into reduced Arab motivation for war.[51] More Israelis saw territorial compromise as the way to peace and perceived the territories acquired in 1967 as a strategic asset to be exchanged for legitimacy. The status quo ante earned some legitimacy among those Israelis.[52]

Acceptance of the status quo was related to a growing recognition by both Israel and some Arab countries of the limits of the military option as a sole means for advancing political goals. For Israel, the fact that the Arabs could rebuild their armies quickly after the June 1967 defeat highlighted the ineffectiveness of war as a long-term solution. That the Arabs could lose a war militarily and still win it politically in 1973, also diminished Israel's expectations that the military option could achieve foreign policy goals. Israel's exhaustion after three wars within six years and the subsequent battle of attrition in the north with Syria in early 1974 contributed to a weakened willingness to use war as a means to a political end. The Arab states, especially Egypt, while perceiving themselves now as Israel's military equals also realized the limits of war and opted for a combination of military and political means to satisfy their larger goals.[53] A pro-Western strategy seemed a promising political move and the United States seemed receptive. The price for playing the American card was the abandonment of extremist goals, such as the destruction of the state of Israel.

If the Arab states could depart from their revolutionary stances and come to some acceptance of Israel as a reality, Israel had to relinquish territories occupied during the 1967 war in exchange for peace. To be sure, Israel demanded what the Arab states considered "a heavy price" for returning the territories. But in the post-1973 period Egypt, at least, was able to envision exchanging an intangible asset—peace—for tangible territory. When the leading Arab country no longer considered preservation of the existing interstate structure as oppressive, room for common interests appeared. UN resolution 242, the institutional arrangement that had emerged after the 1967 war, gave "land for peace" international legitimacy that was ultimately accepted by both Israel and Egypt the post-1973 years.

A third condition for promoting conflict transformation that was missing until the 1973 war was the awareness of the unbearable costs of further war. The Yom Kippur crisis had exposed the skyrocketing cost of conventional warfare; even more critical was the potential devastation posed by the nuclear option also revealed in this war.

Both sides suffered a very heavy rate of attrition during the October War. Israel suffered more heavily if the base of comparison is the ratio of casualties to its total population. In relative terms of casualties to size of armies, the Arabs paid a higher cost for a war in which they were relatively successful. Avi Kober, on the basis of a comparative analysis of several sources, reached the following rates of attrition: IDF lost 0.7 percent of its manpower in comparison to 3.12 percent for the Arab armies; Israel lost 25 percent of its tanks while the Arabs lost 40 percent; a similar ratio was determined in air power; fourteen Arab missile boats were sunk compared to no Israeli boats.[54] The cost for Israel was traumatic in an additional respect: its economy lost the equivalent of an entire year's GNP. For Israel and the Arabs the increasing cost of war as a political means demanded a reconsideration of policy.

The appearance of nuclear weapons also influenced the growing cost of war. Evidence has persuaded some scholars that the setting of the May 1967 crisis already had a nuclear dimension, namely, Egyptian convictions that Israel was on the threshold of a nuclear capability. But the critical point for the cost of war factor was that Israel then did not make deterrent use of its nuclear capabilities, if in fact, they existed.[55] Even during the 1973 war, Israel did not openly declare a nuclear capacity.[56] Rather, it conveyed a message to both the Soviets and to Egypt, with the deployment of nuclear armed Jericho missiles visible to Soviet satellites.[57]

Several other incidents converged to expose Israel's capability such that the Arab states could no longer ignore the nuclear issue. On 4 September 1974 the CIA published a report asserting that Israel possessed nuclear weapons. Three months later, President Efraim Katzir stated that Israel had a nuclear option. Although his spokesman denied the statement the next day, it could not be disregarded when coming from the Israeli president, who was also a Weitzman Institute scientist.[58] A *Time* magazine article in April 1976 also asserted that during the Yom Kippur War Israel had prepared thirteen nuclear bombs for loading on Jericho missiles. The nuclear debate that broke out in Israel after the apparent decline in Israeli conventional deterrence capability,[59] exhibited in 1973, confirmed that Israel possessed a nuclear option.[60]

As evidence of Israeli nuclear weapons surfaced throughout the 1970s, the Arab states could not ignore these developments. Significantly, the most vocal on the nuclear issue among the Arab states was also the first to make peace—Egypt. The Egyptian elite was divided between those who essentially conveyed a message to Israel not to use its nuclear capability explicitly, and those demanding an Egyptian nuclear program or nuclear parity with Israel.[61] But even without the Israeli nuclear capability, the Soviets' increasingly direct Middle East involvement in the early 1970s, countered by a U.S.

readiness to respond with a nuclear alert, amplified the theme that further war would come at a terrible cost.[62]

This common perception of excessive high military cost—shared aversion, in theoretical terms—coupled with restoration of Arab self-esteem in the battlefield, induced some new thinking and the willingness to reconsider exchanging territories for peace as a worthwhile option. Additional elements helped bring about a more pragmatic Arab and Israeli posture. First, in light of the Israeli settlement drive that was gaining some momentum, it also became apparent that the land for peace option would not be available forever.[63] Second, the rise of Islamic fundamentalism threatening to both Israel and the secular Arab states added another dimension for cooperation; the final stages of the Israeli-Egyptian peace treaty were negotiated against the backdrop of the fall of the Shah of Iran and the establishment of the revolutionary Islamic Republic under Ayatollah Khomeini. That several Arab states had oil revenues to lose created another disincentive for war.

A significant rise in the cost of war, and the growing legitimacy of the post-1973 existing international order, sustained by a balance of power structure reestablished in the wake of the Yom Kippur War, all combined to modify the conflict. In other words, the post-1973 era could be classified as one in which a balance of power was solidified, common interests between Israel and the Arab states became conceivable, and war became very costly. Still missing in this new configuration was the full emergence of our fourth condition for change: institutions, namely a regime to guide nonviolent international behavior on the part of the regional actors.

Significantly, the convention of international institutions was not inherently foreign to the Arab-Israeli conflict. But none of the institutional arrangements—the 1949 armistice regime, the UNEF in the wake of the 1956 hostilities, Resolution 242, the Jarring mission, and the Rogers B plan, all accepted by Israel and Egypt—matured into a peace treaty. The resolution of the 1973 war introduced several new elements of institutionalization such as the Kilometer 101 talks between Egypt and Israel, followed by Secretary of State Henry Kissinger's "step by step" diplomacy, and the ensuing 1974–1975 interim agreements.[64] On 1 September 1975, Egypt and Israel signed an agreement constructed around three principles: (1) non-use of force in resolving conflict between Israel and Egypt; (2) separation of forces, a UNEF buffer zone, and the establishment of force limitation zones; (3) a special role for the United States in monitoring and surveillance of the agreement.[65] The difference between this accord and the previous 1957 one between Egypt and Israel touched upon all aspects of an international regime: the normative level—non-use of force; rules of behavior—the specification of written separation lines; and decision making procedures—the U.S. role in determining compliance and noncompliance (defection) by the parties to the agreement.[66]

The ultimate success of the Egyptian-Israeli interim arrangements came with the conclusion of a formal peace agreement in 1978–1979. In the Syrian-Israeli case, the lack of a formal peace reflected in the lack of a broad regime. Nevertheless, the ceasefire lines along the Golan Heights remained quiet. Israelis and Syrians exercised their crisis management and diplomacy of violence after the mid-1970s via Lebanon. [67] This new arena of confrontation implied more than a geographic shift. The nature of Lebanon's civil war, which re-erupted in 1975, introduced an ethnic component into what had been an interstate engagement.

The success of an international institution requires a regime of shared interests that make a unilateral defection harmful to all of the participants. International institutionalism, in the liberal sense, exists when inhibitions on relative gains are on the increase, making it not worthwhile for states to endanger each other's security. Ultimately, the actors must aim for absolute gains rather than relative gains. In the Middle East, none of the major actors have yet reached that level; they are still primarily concerned with calculating who would lose or gain more than the other in any evolving relationship. The classical security dilemma, whereby cooperation would benefit all the participants but successful defection would give the rogue advantages over the others, remains a reality. With the actors on constant guard, not only the Israeli-Egyptian relationship but even the Israeli-Jordanian arrangements could at best be considered a case of limited instituionalism.

In sum, the emergence of four mutually supportive conditions—balance of power, legitimacy of the existing structure, unbearable costs of war, and institutional arrangements—facilitated the relative winding down of the Arab-Israeli conflict. Prior to 1973 the Arab-Israeli arena suffered from an emerging and relatively unstable balance of power that was not coupled with legitimacy or high war costs. As a result, and despite the presence of institutional arrangements, recurrent crises occurred, some of which escalated into war. The appearance of all four conditions, even if not in a full-fledged manner, in the post-1973 era, contributed to a decline in crisis frequency, to lower magnitude, and to the transformed nature of the conflict.

At first, this shift characterized the interstate but not the ethnic elements of the Arab-Israeli conflict. For more than two decades after transformation was recognized in the interstate domain, the Palestinian-Israeli dispute still belonged to the category of an existence conflict in which dual nonrecognition characterized the antagonists.[68] Paradoxically, the Arab states' official recognition in the 1974 Arab League Rabat summit of the PLO as the sole legitimate representative of the Palestinian people advanced the incipient movement toward reconciliation in the interstate domain but intensified confrontation in the ethnic sphere. The decoupling of the Palestinian issue from those of the Arab states infused flexibility into the interstate negotiations, evidenced by the interim agreements of 1974–1975 between Israel and Egypt and Israel and Syria. Tacit partial separation between interstate and ethnic issues also contributed to the signing of the 1979 peace treaty between Israel and Egypt. But Egyptian insistence on linking "A Framework for Peace in the Middle East" and the fate of the West Bank and Gaza regions along with the bilateral Egyptian-Israeli peace treaty pointed to the fact that full resolution of the Arab-Israeli conflict ultimately required the resolution of the Palestinian issue.

CHAPTER 5

ETHNIC CRISES IN A COMPOUND CONFLICT

A compound conflict exhibits violence on both the interstate and ethnic-state as well as the interethnic levels. Our analysis thus far has focused primarily on the former. But an assessment of the Palestinian-Israeli domain since the late 1960s undoubtedly requires the incorporation of ethnonational features, particularly since the interethnic conflict preceded the interstate one in Palestine.

Our framework distinguishes among interstate, ethnic-state, and interethnic crises. The state centric ICB data-set supports analysis of the ethnic-state episodes, but not of the interethnic incidents, which pre-date the establishment of the Israeli state. We shall consider these crises in a qualitative manner in accordance with CMI parameters.

Our interest in mapping the direction of the Arab-Israeli conflict as indicated by crisis behavior leads us to explore two interrelated questions: (1) Are there distinct profiles for interstate and ethnic-state type crises in terms of their core crisis attributes? and (2) What is the impact of the ethnic dimension on the conflict as a whole?

The chapter will advance along three distinctive periods: the interethnic period: 1917–1947, the interstate period: 1947–1973; and the ethnic-state period:1974–2000.

INTER-ETHNIC CRISES IN THE 1917-1947 PERIOD

The year 1917 serves an appropriate point of departure for the outset of the Jewish-Palestinian conflict.[1] The Balfour Declaration, making the establishment of a Jewish National Home in Palestine part of British policy, was followed by the British occupation of Palestine. The two events suggested to both Jews and Arabs that the Zionist agenda was not merely a vision but could become a reality in world politics. There is scholarly debate as to the birth of a Palestinian Arab communal identity, but Britain's mandate to prepare Palestine for statehood left no doubt but that a race for control of the new state had begun.[2] Both the Jewish and Arab communities harbored ethnonational aspirations. In the rivalry for political power that ensued, ethnic violence several times reached crisis level.

The interethnic interaction of the conflict was determined by the nonsovereign nature of the opposing parties. The characteristics of this indigenous communal conflict bear some similarity to the dynamics of international disputes. An interethnic crisis denotes, however, hostile interaction ranging through demonstrations, strikes, economic boycott, riots, terrorism, civil uprising, revolt, and ultimately interethnic war. The demise of the dual authority system was determined by the maldistribution of resources between Jews and Arabs, the equivalent of the distribution of power in international politics.[3]

The Arab community developed several national institutions, including the Arab Executive (later replaced by the Arab Higher Committee) and the Supreme Muslim Council, the latter founded in 1922.[4] The Jewish national institutions included two branches: the World Zionist Organization and also the Jewish Agency, since 1929, on the one hand, and Knesset Israel and its affiliated organizations on the other hand. Each community founded its own political parties, trade unions, and illegal paramilitary organizations.[5] Structurally, Jews and Arabs functioned equally as "Palestinians" within the British Mandate Palestine but they were separated from each other by social, linguistic, and religious barriers.

The 1917–1947 period witnessed three consecutive waves of interethnic crisis involving Jewish and Arab-Palestinian non-state actors. According to the definition provided in chapter 1, an international crisis required two conditions: increase in disruptive interactions and the threat of an incipient structural change in the regional or global system. The first of these interethnic crises involved three zones of Arab–Jewish confrontations between 1919 and 1921. The separation of Palestine from the French Syria mandate in the summer of 1919 provoked violent Arab–Jewish skirmishes in northern Palestine. The crowning of the Emir Faisal as king of Syria in April of 1920 prompted a second Arab–Jewish outbust in Jerusalem. The third incident occurred in Jaffa in May 1921, triggered by Winston Churchill's confirmation of the British commitment to the Balfour Declaration.[6]

In total, the 1919–1921 wave of ethnic disturbances qualified as a crisis due to the sudden increase in the use of organized and severe violence.[7] Moreover, the Arab goal of abolishing the Balfour Declaration implied an existential threat for the Zionist side, hence implying an incipient structural change in the region. The involvement of Britain as the Mandatory power provided a change in the interethnic conflict: convergence with great power politics. The events in

Syria and Iraq manifested the first signs of linkage between Palestine affairs and inter-Arab politics.

The crisis was expressed via both interethnic and antigovernment violence. Violence between the two communities occurred primarily in the bi-ethnic cities where Jews and Arabs lived together, such as Jaffa and Jerusalem, but also included Arab attacks on small Jewish settlements. Violence was accompanied by direct negotiations between Zionist and Syrian leaders in the years 1921–1922 and indirect talks between Zionist and Palestinian Arab leaders. In these talks the British played an intermediary role.

The crisis subsided when the British propagated a series of unilateral acts including penalties and military actions against participants in the disturbances, and some formal concessions to each side. The Arabs won a temporary halt of Jewish immigration, land rights in the Beit Shan Valley, and the establishment of the Higher Moslem Council, presided over by Haj Amin Al-Husseini, the Mufti of Jerusalem known for his ethnonationalist, anti-Zionist attitudes. Compensation to the Zionists included a League of Nations council resolution in July 1922 confirming the legitimacy of a national home for the Jews in Palestine. The termination of the crisis without formal or semiformal agreement between the Zionists and the Arabs but rather an imposed solution from abroad was an omen for the future.[8]

A note of caution should be made with regard to the nonparticipation of the Arab states at this point in time. This Arab states' absenteeism could not be appreciated fully since besides Egypt all the other forthcoming Arab states were still in the process of becoming independent.[9]

The next wave of interethnic violence that ascended to the level of crisis occurred in 1929. Its genesis was in an Arab-Jewish scuffle on Yom Kippur— the Jewish day of atonement—of 1928, when the Jews coming to pray at the Western Wall brought benches and put up a wall to separate the men and women. Exaggerated rumors that the Jews were structurally altering the Wall below the Muslim Mosque Haram al-Sharif brought thousands of Muslims running to defend their holy site. Massive violence, however, broke out the next year in the wake of a Jewish demonstration at the same location along the Western Wall. The Jews were commemorating the both the Ninth of Av, a Jewish mourning day for the ancient destruction of the Temple, and their losses a year earlier at the same spot. The Arab reaction occurred that Friday, and took the form of riots that spread from the Dome of the Rock Mosque in Jerusalem to almost all of the Jewish neighborhoods, where Jews were attacked. The Arab riots again demanded the abolishment of the Balfour Declaration and a reversal in the League of Nations to endorsement of a Jewish homeland in Palestine. The Arab position constituted a severe threat to the Zionists' future plans, and a harsh direct threat to the Jewish victims of the riot.

That the crisis occurred at sites of worship and on religiously significant days contributed an important attribute in the context of this crisis. The ethno-religious character of the violence foreshadowed the nascent character of the emerging nations in the Middle East. The religious motif promised broader external support from other Muslim states for the Palestinian national movement. This was significant in that Arab states were just becoming independent at this time, and were not prepared to militarily support the Palestinian Arabs. The development of an interreligious aspect to the violence had the potential of broadening the conflict from a local ethnic dispute to a transnational religious confrontation, thereby altering the structure of the conflict and its balance of power. In December 1931 the Mufti convened an Islamic conference in Jerusalem with representatives from twenty-two countries and called upon Muslims elsewhere in the British Empire to agitate for a change in Britain's Palestine policy. The only tangible outcome was the mobilization of the Muslims of India behind the Palestinian cause, a factor important to the British government in its attitude toward the Palestine interethnic conflict.[10]

Turning from context to process, the clashes highlighted the potential for collective action by the two organized communities. Riots in mixed towns where Jews and Arabs had long coexisted, and the massacre of the ancient Jewish community in Hebron reinforced the interethnic nature of the disturbances. At the same time, the country-wide confrontation between Jews and Arabs in both urban and rural settings and the organized Muslim and Jewish response demonstrated that both communities were capable of mobilizing their respective masses behind a "national" cause. Both sides, non-state actors each, were preparing for the equivalent of civil war.

In managing the crisis, the British government did not limit its role to crushing violence and restoring order but also tried to promote negotiations. The high commissioner and the British government, especially the Colonial Office, became the main channels for diplomatic activity on both the Arab and the Jewish sides. Hoping to promote institutional arrangements between two completely mistrustful parties, London appointed government commissions to study Arab and Jewish grievances. The Shaw (1929) and the John Hope-Simpson commissions (1930) produced reports with recommendations on how to solve the intercommunal friction in Palestine. The 1930 Passfield White Paper, which came out of the two commissions' work in Palestine, responded to the main Arab complaint by endorsing restrictions on the two most significant aspects of the Zionist enterprise—Jewish immigration and land sales to Jews. Prime Minister Ramsay MacDonald responded to political pressures in London, however, and countered the Passfield White Paper with a 1931 official letter from the prime minister to Chaim Weizmann that reaffirmed Britain's Zionist commitments.[11]

The 1929 crisis, like the 1919–1921 crisis, ended without any formal or even semiformal agreement, again indicating the pattern of noncooperative crisis behavior and the lack of victory by one of the ethnic groups over the other that would become the hallmark of the struggle over Palestine.[12] In terms of magnitude, this crisis was even more severe than the previous one. Combining wide violence, especially the eradication of the Jewish inhabitants of Hebron, with the failure to engage in any direct negotiations represented deterioration in relations between the two ethnic communities.

With neither a decisive termination nor a tacit understanding between the two sides the eruption of another crisis was only a question of time. Contextual changes between the two rival communities caused the outbreak of a new wave of hostilities and a third interethnic crisis. The Arab strike and rebellion of 1936–1939 was the most severe of the three interethnic cases in terms of crisis magnitude. A change in the balance of resources, the interethnic equivalent of a balance of power among states, caused by the rise in Jewish immigration levels from 5,000 a year in 1929–1930 to more than 37,000 in 1933 and more than 66,000 in 1935, as well as increased Jewish land purchases during that period, activated the 1936 crisis.[13] The background to this massive migration was the rise to power of Hitler in Germany, and the growth of antisemitism in Poland and other East European states. Arabs in Palestine and their brethren in the region were alarmed by the sudden flood of European Jews into Palestine and the rapid disappearance of land from Arab control. Bands of Arab irregulars formed to battle the Jewish settlers, provoking the rise of armed Jewish forces in return. The discovery of smuggled weapons in the hands of the Jews and the slaying by the Mandate police of Az-a-Din al-Kasam, a popular Palestinian commander, triggered the mass mobilization of the Arab community behind its national leadership. Arab demands included the cessation of Jewish migration and land purchases, and the establishment of a representative legislative council reflecting the Arabs' majority status. Demonstrations and riots by Egyptians and Syrians against the European Mandate powers also encouraged the Arabs in Palestine. The broad support expressed for their strike and the generation of collective action exhibited the capability of the Arab leadership to mobilize the Arab masses in support of advancing Palestinian national goals.[14]

The gravity of threat to both sides was existential. For the Arabs, continued Jewish migration and land acquisition implied their transformation from a majority to a minority in Palestine. For the Jews, the Arab demands to halt Jewish immigration and land purchase meant the failure to achieve a Jewish National Home. With this power to affect immigration rates and land transfers within Palestine, the position of Great Britain in the role of great power was critical. In light of the Arab failure, in 1929, to procure gains by developing a religious element to the conflict, the Palestine Arab leadership now attempted to attract the surrounding Arab states and regimes into the ethnonational struggle for Palestine. This time, as we shall see, almost all the Arab states played a role in the management of the crisis.

As to process, the Arab-Palesinians hoped to influence the British position with a general strike, demonstrations, and the boycott of Jewish products. At the onset, the use of force was limited. Violent confrontation with the Mandatory government and the Jewish community ensued only after the Arab leadership realized that their boycott had failed and had even strengthened the Jewish side by forcing the Yishuv to become self-sufficient. Within the Jewish community debate raged regarding the use of force in response to the revolt. Not wanting to anger the British who were still technically committed to facilitating the Zionist operation in Palestine, the Jewish leadership chose a self-imposed policy of restraint *(Havlaga)*.[15]

The process and magnitude of the third interethnic crisis become clear if one breaks down the wave of hostilities into sub-phases. The first phase of the crisis took place between April and October 1936, which witnessed an unprecedented 305 deaths, including 197 Arabs, 80 Jews, and 28 British personnel.[16] The violence prompted negotiations between the Supreme Arab Committee and the British government, with third party participation at various times by the Arab states, especially Saudi Arabia, Trans-Jordan, Iraq, and Yemen. The main outcome of this combined process of violence and negotiations was the establishment of a royal commission headed by Lord Robert Peel to investigate Arab complaints. The Peel Commission produced a plan to partition Palestine into two states—Arab and Jewish—thus highlighting the interethnic dimension of the struggle. The Arab side totally rejected this proposal while the Zionists accepted it, with qualifications.[17] This attempt to terminate the crisis (and possibly the conflict) through a formal agreement failed.

In the fall of 1937, following the rejection of the Peel proposal, the second phase of the crisis began. The most dramatic act was the October 1937 assassination of the district commissioner of the Galilee, Lewis Andrews, a clear statement of Arab rebellion against the Mandatory government. Arab violence against the Yishuv intensified as well, as did violence against other Arabs suspected of collaboration with the Zionists. Compared to the two previous waves of interethnic hostility, the 1936–1939 Arab uprising, particularly in its latter phase, produced the highest level of violence. The Jewish and British responses were also unprecedented. In 1938 alone, close to 1,700 British, Arabs, and Jews were killed, clearly indicating an escalation in violence.[18]

Attempts to end the crisis via negotiations continued. But while the Peel Commission partition plan was at least partially accepted by the Zionist side, the Woodhead Commission report of November 1938, which came in the wake of the Peel Commission, was completely rejected by both Jews and Arabs.[19]

In February–March 1939 the British convened the St. James Palace Conference in London. Besides representatives of the Jewish and Arab communities of Palestine, delegates from Saudi Arabia, Iraq, Trans-Jordan, Egypt, and Yemen also participated. During the conference the Arab representatives refused to meet their Jewish counterparts and the deliberations ended without any agreement. Lacking formal or semiformal accords, the British government issued in May 1939 a new White Paper, essentially a unilateral act to be imposed on the parties. In this White Paper, the British government promised an independent Palestine within ten years, clarified that it did not see itself committed to the building of a Jewish state in Palestine, restricted Jewish land purchases, and limited Jewish immigration to 75,000 over the next five years.[20] Ironically, each side rejected the White Paper for being too conciliatory to the other.[21]

Ultimately the British military actions and internal Palestinian rivalries put an end to the Arab rebellion. The policy implications of the White Paper were circumscribed, however, by the outbreak of World War II in the fall of 1939. In short, the 1936–1939 crisis faded away, overwhelmed by political realities rather than settled by diplomacy.

In accordance with our basic assumption that a crisis reflects the essence of a conflict, the three interethnic crises described here portended future characteristics of the mature Arab-Israeli conflict quite accurately. Contextually, the struggle over Palestine, from its outset, manifested a battle over ethnic legitimacy whereby each side perceived the other as presenting an existential or grave damage threat thereby implying an incipient structural change in the conflict. From the Jewish perspective, the community was surrounded by a larger Arab community bolstered by neighboring Arab entities. The Arabs of Palestine saw the Jews as a settler movement dedicated to their eradication, and a foreign implant in their midst. As the Jewish population increased and its share in ownership of the land grew, time seemed to be on the Zionist side. The religious factor intensified mutual threat perceptions. The religious gambit was especially instrumental in a traditional society such as the Palestine Arab one, led by the Mufti of Jerusalem, a religious functionary.

Great power participation in the conflict occurred from the outset. All three crises involved Great Britain directly, with other great powers watching it closely. In the two early crises the League of Nations also responded, as did the French via their role in Syria and Lebanon. In the mid-1930s, the rise of the Axis powers also influenced the conflict. This implied involvement of both international institutions and international politics in the Palestine conflict. The role of Great Britain, however, went beyond mediation; in the 1936–1939 crisis British soldiers participated massively in the fighting.

The Arab states were similarly drawn into the fray, thus compounding the context of the conflict. Hardly involved in the 1919–1921 crisis, they expanded their role in the 1929 crisis, due to the religious factor, and became pivotal in the 1938 St. James Conference. In the 1947–1948 crisis, several of the Arab states participated directly in both war and diplomacy to the extent that interstate attributes overtook interethnic elements. Thus, the Arab-Jewish struggle in Palestine, during its early interethnic period, already adjoined the international domain. The expanding role of the international factor from crisis to crisis became a central feature in the evolving conflict in Palestine.

The process indicators of the crises also reflected violent features, marked by a steady escalation in the use of force. All three waves in interethnic confrontation involved serious antigovernment demonstrations, ethnic clashes, and deteriorating relations between the rival communities, with the last crisis reaching the level of a civil war. Direct negotiations between the sides to the dispute did not take place in any of the crises. Nor did nonviolent demonstrations of force. All mediation took place between Britain and the rival ethnic groups. It seems that the British Mandatory power did not put enough effort at the early stages of the rivalry into forcing face to face negotiations, because of its own interests. At the same time the government prevented a decisive outcome in the crisis. These processes of crisis management did not produce lasting institutional arrangements via tacit, semiformal, or formal agreements. All three crises' outcomes were instead a mixture of an imposed dictate and unilateral acts by the parties and the sovereign outside power. This new reality, however, of a decisive outcome in Israel's 1948 establishment did not end the conflict. The internationalization of the original interethnic conflict also did not decimate totally the ethnonational dimension of the conflict, but only postponed it temporarily.

In terms of crisis magnitude, qualitative analysis of these three Mandate-era interethnic crises suggests a trend of conflict expansion. The level of mutual threat grew from crisis to crisis as did the level of international involvement. The 1919–1921, 1929 and 1936–1939 crises moved from ethnic skirmishes to civil war. Casualties increased from the tens to hundreds and thousands. What started as a geographically limited ethnic contention evolved into a regional conflict involving the Arab states. By the third crisis, with violence at an apex and a virtual lack of direct diplomatic contact between Jews and Arabs, the British offered a venue and framework for a negotiated resolution. But it was too little, too late. The 1947–1948 interethnic confrontation was the most complex yet, evolving as it did into a full-fledged interstate war.

ETHNIC - STATE CRISES IN THE 1947-1973 PERIOD

ICB analysis of the Arab-Israeli conflict begins with the Palestine partition-Israel independence crisis, an event with immediate origins in the UN General Assembly Resolution of 29 November 1947 calling for the establishment of two states in Palestine. The Arab states entered the war only five months later, with the May 1948 proclamation of the Jewish state. The 1947 crisis marked the transition from the interethnic to the interstate conflict and contained the main components characteristic of the forthcoming protracted Arab-Israeli dispute—a mixture of interethnic and interstate violence.

This transformation was accelerated by the transition of the region into an interstate system. By the end of 1946, all of the countries surrounding Palestine had achieved sovereignty. In the ensuing years the new states' protection of their national independence and the Palestinians' struggle for the same were the central features of Middle Eastern politics. The fact that only one ethnic community achieved statehood while the other remained an ethnic Non-State Actor (NSA) sustained the ethnic component of the conflict.

The interstate aspect which had been at the background throughout the Zionist-Arab struggle moved forward with the affirmation of a statist goal by the Zionist Biltmore conference of 1942. The goal of establishing a Jewish state in Palestine was henceforth expressed explicitly and received immense momentum after the European Holocaust of World War II. The Arabs of Palestine demanded that Palestine be declared an Arab state. On behalf of their Palestinian Arab brethren the Arab states declared their intention to use force to thwart any plan for Jewish statehood anywhere in Palestine.[22] Despite the failure of the Palestinian Arabs in achieving their national goal they continued to play a role in the outbreak of ethnic-state crises in the Middle East. During the 1947–1973 period the ethnic factor played some role. Seventeen crises occurred during that period; eight of them were ethnic-state crises (Table 5.1) and nine were interstate ones (Table 5.2). The former category includes the 1947–1949 Palestine partition-Israel independence crisis, the 1953 Qibya case, the 1955 Gaza raid, the 1956 Qalqilia crisis, the 1966 El-Samu case, the 1968 Karameh crisis, the March 1968 attack on Beirut airport, and the 1973 Libyan plane crisis. The ethnic-state crises differed from the interstate ones by the participation of a nonstate actor with ethnonational aspirations.

CONTEXT ATTRIBUTES AND CRISIS MAGNITUDE

Starting with the gravity of the crisis, in accordance with the CMI framework, the period opened and closed with international crises posing acute threats to existence or threats of grave damage. It was also characteristic that at the onset of the Palestine partition crisis ethnonational threats (Arab-Zionist) were raised and were later transformed into an interstate issue with the establishment of the state of Israel and the formal entrance of the Arab states into the war. Although the *Hagana* turned from a Jewish militia to the IDF,[23] the presence of Palestinian forces among the Arab armies reflected the ongoing ethnic element within this interstate war.

In the period prior to May 1948 there were violent clashes between the Jewish militia—the *Haganah* and the *Irgun* underground—and the Palestinian-Arab irregular forces. Clashes and atrocities took place primarily in the major Arab-Jewish cities as well as in the north. In essence a civil war, more severe than that of 1936–1939, was being waged between the Arab and the Jewish districts of Jerusalem, Jaffa-Tel-Aviv, Haifa, Safed, and Acre. Another area of fighting in the civil war was the struggle over the major roads, and the defense of settlements against Arab attacks, and Arab villages from Jewish reprisals.[24] The Arab exodus served as further evidence of the interethnic existential threat. What started as an elite phenomenon—the middle and upper classes leaving the big towns and their immediate environs—spread to the countryside. Together with those Arabs forced off their land by the IDF, these refugees became the substance symbol of the Palestinian problem.[25]

In the midst of this crisis, the Arab states superseded the Palestinians in the struggle against the Jewish state and tried to resolve the conflict on the interstate level. Because of its transformed nature—from interethnic to interstate—this crisis differs from all other ethnic-state crises. In the subsequent ethnic-state crises no existential threat existed. In the years following the establishment of the Jewish state, only the Arab states (as opposed to the Palestinian guerilla groups) could conceivably constitute an existential threat to Israel.

Findings on the gravity of threat, as well as of other CMI components in ethnic-state and interstate crisis, are presented in Tables 5.1 and 5.2 respectively. Turning to nonexistential but harsh threats, a comparison of interstate and ethnic-state crises reveals that ethnic-state crises more often will involve a smaller spectrum of threats, while interstate crises run the gamut from severe threats (grave damage) to mild ones (influence and economic). Moreover, excluding the Palestine partition crisis that occurred during the unique transition phase of the 1947 interethnic conflict into the interstate type in May 1948, ethnic-state crises do not involve threats to existence. Seven out of eight ethnic-state crises in the 1947–1973 period ranged from political threat to grave damage threats. However, although the existential threats threshold was rarely crossed, both ethnic-state crises and the interstate ones in this period were characterized mostly with high magnitude threats (five out of eight and seven of nine respectively). Thus, the compound nature of the conflict is represented well in the gravity of threat CMI component: all crises in the first period, involving major confrontations or limited incidents, were associated with high stakes.

Findings on the second feature in our CMI framework, the number of crisis actors, demonstrate a clear distinction between interstate and ethnic-state conflicts. Half of the eight ethnic-state crises were limited to two adversaries and another three cases (Qibya, Beirut, and Libyan plane) even to one crisis actor. The 1947 partition crisis involved six crisis actors, but only after the crisis turned into an interstate case (May 1948). As with gravity, so too with the participants: the first interethnic period of this case corresponded with the ethnic-state pattern of limited participants (Jewish and Palestinian) while the post–May 1948 era accorded with the interstate pattern. This phenomenon of a limited number of crisis actors in ethnic state cases, once again portrays the superior strength of state interests, which in general did not easily allow the Palestinian insurgency to draw them into crisis situations. As Table 5.1 indicates, ethnic-state crisis participation was limited to Israel and the country from which Palestinian guerrillas launched their attacks.

The identity of actors can also help explain the low magnitude in terms of actor participation in ethnic-state crises. In the interstate dominant period (1948–1973), Egypt played a preeminent role in the crises that opened and closed the era. At that time, a wave of pan-Arabism spread throughout the Arab world, originating in Egypt and led by Gamal Abdel Nasser. Pan-Arabism superseded and even downgraded the Palestinian identity. Israel's illegitimacy served as a rallying point for Arab unity and its destruction was a maxim of pan-Arab identity. Accordingly, Palestinian initiated crises declined in the post–Suez war years, when Egyptian-oriented pan-Arabism was at its peak. The Cold War also eclipsed the Palestinian cause. The USSR and the United States replaced the old colonial powers and further overwhelmed non-state actors such as the Palestinians.[26]

TABLE 5.1
ETHNIC-STATE CRISES IN THE ARAB ISRAELI CONFLICT: 1947-1973

CASE	DATE	GRAVITY	SUPERPOWERS	STATE CRISIS ACTORS	ETHNIC ELEMENTS	CMT	VIOLENCE	OUTCOME
Palestine partition	Nov. 1947	Existence	Both - political	Egypt, Iraq, Israel, Jordan, Lebanon, Syria	Palestinian Arabs	Violence	War	Formal agreement
Qibya	Oct. 1953	Political regime	USA only - political	Jordan	Palestinian Fedayeen	Negotiation	Serious clashes	Unilateral - Israel
Gaza raid	Feb. 1955	Political regime	USA - political USSR - semi-military	Egypt, Israel	Palestinian Fedayeen	Non-violent military	Serious clashes	Other - ally
Qalqilia	Sept. 1956	Territory	USA only - political	Jordan, Israel	Palestinian Fedayeen	Multiple with violence	Serious clashes	Unilateral - ally
El Samu	Nov. 1966	Grave damage	USA only - political	Israel, Jordan	Palestinian Fedayeen	Violence	Serious clashes	Unilateral - Jordan
Karameh	March 1968	Grave damage	Both - political	Israel, Jordan	PLO	Violence	Serious clashes	Unilateral - Jordan
Beirut airport	Dec. 1968	Political regime	Both - political	Lebanon	PFLP	Mediation	Minor clashes	Other - faded
Libyan plane	Feb. 1973	Grave damage	Both - none	Israel	Palestinian terror	Violence	Serious clashes	Unilateral - Israel

TABLE 5.2

INTERSTATE CRISES IN THE ARAB ISRAELI CONFLICT: 1947– 1973

CASE	DATE	GRAVITY	SUPERPOWERS	STATE CRISIS ACTORS	CMT	VIOLENCE	OUTCOME
Sinai incursion	Dec. 1948	Territory	USA only – political	Egypt, UK, Israel	Multiple with violence	Serious clashes	Unilateral – Israeli compliance
Hula drainage	Feb. 1951	Territory	Both – political	Israel, Syria	Multiple with violence	Serious clashes	Formal agreement
Suez war	July 1956	Grave damage	USA – political, USSR – semi-military	Egypt, France, UK, Israel, USA, USSR	Multiple with violence	War	Unilateral– Israeli compliance
Rottem	Feb. 1960	Influence	USSR only – political	Egypt, Israel	Non-violent military	None	Tacit agreement
Jordan waters	Dec. 1963	Economic	Both – political	Egypt, Israel, Jordan, Lebanon, Syria	Non-violent military	None	Unilateral – Israel
Six Day war	May 1967	Existence	Both – political	Egypt, Israel, Jordan, Syria, USA, USSR	Violence	War	Imposed agreement
War of attrition	March 1969	Grave damage	USA – political, USSR – direct military	Egypt, Israel, USSR	Multiple with violence	War	Formal agreement
Israel mobilization	April 1973	Grave damage	Both – none	Israel	Non-violent military	None	Unilateral – Israel
Yom Kippur war	Oct. 1973	Grave damage	Both – semi-military	Egypt, Israel, Syria, USA, USSR	Multiple with violence	War	Formal agreement

In 1947–1973, four out of the five ethnic-state crises with two or more participants involved Israel and Jordan. The primacy of Jordan was obviously related to the demographic strength of the Palestinians in the Hashemite Kingdom. But the Hashemites also exhibited a less ardent pan-Arabism, a fact that made them suspect among Palestinian nationalists who then identified their cause with that of pan-Arabism and Egypt.[27] Despite the tacit relationship between the Hashemite regime and the Israeli Labor elite, the weight of the Palestinians in Jordan and the weakness of the regime following the 1951 assassination of King Abdullah allowed for Palestinian activity from Jordan against Israel.

Because of its common interest with the Hashemites in containing the Palestinians, Israel was selective in its retaliations for insurgency activity originating in Jordan, and tried to avoid direct confrontations with the Arab Legion. Both the Qibya and Qalquilya operations escalated beyond the original plans into international crises. Significantly, neither Israel nor Jordan allowed the crisis to escalate into a war. Indeed, for the next decade no crisis erupted between the two neighbors. In 1958, Israel allowed British troops to fly over its territory into Jordan in an operation aimed at bolstering the Hashemite regime against domestic pro-Nasserite and Palestinian radical forces.

But despite these strong interstate interests, two ethnic-state crises did serve as preludes to war. The 1955 Gaza raid and the 1966 El Samu crisis, both Israeli retaliations for Palestinian guerrilla acts, were followed by major interstate crises that ultimately led to war—the 1956 Suez campaign and the 1967 Six Day war, respectively. In both cases Israel chose to escalate the crises by initiating particularly strong reprisals; the 1955 Gaza raid caused a large number of Arab casualties and a 1966 El-Samua operation sent the IDF into the West Bank during daylight.[28]

In the wake of the Six Day War, Israeli-Jordanian tacit cooperation resumed, although in March 1968 the IDF attacked PLO bases on Jordanian territory in Karameh and ended up clashing with Jordanian forces. In September 1970, the two countries cooperated militarily when Israel, upon an American request, put its forces on alert to deter a Syrian attack against Jordan. "Black September" marked the beginning of Jordan's withdrawal from the Arab-Israeli conflict and later from the Israeli-Palestinian ethnonational struggle, as well.[29]

The super and great powers played a low-key role in ethnic- state crises. During the 1947–1948 partition crisis great power involvement was present but only during the second, interstate part of the crisis. The great and super powers tended to intervene in the crises that deteriorated into wars. Ethnic-state events, as discussed above, usually evolved into prolonged but not existential threat confrontations. The lesser role of the great powers in the purely interethnic crises also indicates the limits of the Palestinian ethnic factor during those years of statism in world politics.

PROCESS ATTRIBUTES AND CRISIS MAGNITUDE

The second realm of crisis is process, in which a correspondence between the high but not extreme level threats in ethnic-state crises and their level of violence emerged. Almost all of the ethnic-state crises (six out of eight) escalated into serious clashes but stopped short of war. The scope of violence in the interstate crises during those years was broader and so too was its spectrum: of nine interstate crises, four ended in war, the peak level of interstate hostility, two in serious clashes, while three did not breed violence at all (see Table 5.2). To be sure, the level of violence in the 1947–1973 period, in comparison to the next period (see below) was high in both interstate and ethnic-state crises because of the intensity of the conflict during those years. But, as with threat in the context realm, violence in the interstate crises covered the entire spectrum, whereas the ethnic-state crises always exhibited violence and mostly in a uniform level of serious clashes short of war.

In the CMT category, the pattern of the ethnic-state crisis is somewhat more complex. While the technique includes a range of options, from negotiation, nonviolent military demonstrations of power, to violence alone, more than half of these events were managed via diplomacy accompanied by violence or by violence alone. In four cases violence alone was the core mode of handling the confrontation (see Table 5.1). By contrast, though the interstate crises also revealed a similar range of crisis management methods and were also concentrated mostly in multiple with violence (five out of nine), the violence alone mode appeared in only one case (see Table 5.2). One can explain this variation thus: although the ethnic NSA was prepared to use violence in initiating crisis, the states on whose territory the NSA operated were not necessarily ready for war. Therefore, their attempts to manage the crisis included negotiation and mediation foremost, and limited violence only as a last resort. Jordan in 1953, Egypt in 1955, and Lebanon in 1968, did not want the Palestinians guerrillas to drag them into war and hence were ready to use alternative procedures to resolve crisis. Nevertheless, in some instances they were simply not capable of avoiding violence altogether. As we shall see, these characteristic profile of CMT changes profoundly in the second period.

OUTCOME ATTRIBUTES AND CRISIS MAGNITUDE

Findings on the way crises end reveal distinct profiles for ethnic-state and interstate crises (see Tables 5.1 and 5.2 respectively). Ethnic crises tended to end via unilateral and other acts (seven out of eight). Termination types in the interstate-type covered a broader range and proved to be more accommodative in nature, though even in the interstate-type cases more than half of the crises ended in unilateral moves (four out of nine) or an imposed agreement (one). The explanation is rooted in the dominance of the rigid makeup of the conflict during those years. One-third of the interstate crises, however, ended in formal agreements, as opposed to only one of the eight ethnic-state crises. And even the only ethnic case that ended in a formal agreement in 1949 was of mixed character-istics in its essence, as we noted earlier, and the negotiated outcome did not belong to its ethnic phase but rather to its interstate one. One can conclude that it is easier for states to reach formal agreements when they are totally involved and working with other states than when they have to deal with non-state part-ners. Timing was also important in determining how crises ended. The 1947–1973 era both opened and closed with crises terminated by formal agree-ments, as did two interim crises (Hula and Attrition). The 1947 and 1973 crises were all-out wars, while the 1951 Hula crisis and the 1970 War of Attrition occured within two and three years of them, respectively. Full-scale war appears to produce formal conclusions. In the interim period, the conflict deteriorated and bounced between ethnic and interstate crises without a diplomatic or an institutional outcome.

Overall, almost half of the crises that occurred during the 1947–1973 peri-od were ethnic-state crises. These cases differed somewhat from interstate crises in the degree of threat presented. The interstate crises tended to vary in terms of the threat, from existential (high) to economic (low); the ethnic-state cases all exhibited a more consistent mid-range level of threat. This quality was also evident in the number of participating actors, the involvement of superpowers, and the level of violence. Ethnic-state crises were more homogenous, with lim-ited actors, a confined superpower role, and involving a rather stable level of violence—serious clashes short of war. Interstate crises were more heteroge-neous, involving multiple actors, more intense superpower role, and a wider scope of hostility ranging from no violence to full war.

These findings lead to the conclusion that the ethnic element contributed to the endurance of the conflict during its first period, but that the interstate domain dominated the magnitude of the Arab-Israeli conflict. Constraints set forth by the superpowers and global milieu, the strength of pan-Arabism for the promotion of state interests, the strong statism predominant in the Israeli political system, and the reality of the newly established Arab states all overpowered sub-state and eth-nonational aspirations and trends.[30] The ethnic factor was strong enough to arrest tendencies toward conflict resolution, but not powerful enough to totally control the conflict's procession. Outcomes of ethnic-state crises were nonaccommoda-tive in nature while interstate cases revealed an opposite trend. And yet, through-out the 1947–1973 years, formal agreements were present only at the outset (1948–1951) and conclusion (1969, 1973) of that period. Otherwise, termination by unilateral action predominated. In the 1950s and early 1960s the zero-sum nature of the conflict originating from the proclaimed goals of the participating nation-states, the undercurrents of the Palestinian aspirations, namely, the destruc-tion of the Zionist state, and the rigid global confrontation prohibited the Middle East subsystem from institutional crisis outcomes.[31] The situation started chang-ing, as we have already illustrated in the previous chapter, in the mid-1970s with the winding down of the interstate conflict.

ETHNIC-STATE CRISES IN THE 1974-2000 PERIOD

The period since 1973 experienced nine Arab-Israeli crises of which only one—Israel's 1981 attack on the Iraqi nuclear reactor—was restricted to the interstate domain. This ratio of crises in itself testifies to the transformation of the conflict and its propensity during these years toward ethnicity. The prominence of ethnicity in crises was not limited to the Palestinian issue. The decline of the interstate dimension accelerated due to the intertwining of the Lebanese interethnic conflict with the Arab-Israeli one. In addition, Israel and the Palestinians plunged into a civil war in December 1987 that stretched out to the early 1990s without formal termination.[32] The main Palestinian actor in these cases was almost always the PLO, a non-state entity with aspirations for Palestinian statehood on territory that the Palestinians consider as their habitat.[33] These characteristics qualified it as an ethnic NSA.

The post-1973 war era marked the ascendance of ethno-nationalism within both the Israeli and Palestinian communities and, not coincidentally, the reduction of crisis magnitude in the Arab-Israeli conflict. To be sure, the period between 1967 and 1973 constituted a "twilight zone" between the interstate dominant and the ethnic-state dominant eras. Two ethnic-state crises occurred in the post-1967 period—Karameh and the Israeli raid on the Beirut airport. The 1970s witnessed the emergence of the PLO as the representative of the Palestinians in the West Bank and the Gaza Strip.[34]

The ascendance of the PLO in Jordan and its plans to fight a "war of liberation" against Israel from across the Jordan River eventually posed a political threat to the Hashemite regime. In September 1970, following a hijacking of three commercial airliners by the PFLP a radical group within the PLO, King Hussein decided to crush the armed Palestinian groups within his country. Hussein's decision on 15 September to put Jordan under martial law triggered threats from Syria and Iraq to intervene on behalf of the Palestinians. The crisis, primarily an inter-Arab one, both involved a civil war (Jordanian-Palestinian) and threatened a potential interstate crisis, should the neighboring Arab states invade. The crisis grew even more complicated when the Syrian and Iraqi threats drew the two superpowers into the struggle.[35]

The confrontation escalated after Hussein's crackdown on the PLO. Syrian tanks moved closer to the Jordanian border, crossing it on 18 September. Jordan turned to the United States, and agreed that the Americans would ask Israel to try and deter the Syrian invasion via a mobilization of its forces and, if needed, to intervene against the Syrian invasion. Washington in turn promised to deter both an Egyptian or Soviet retaliation against Israel. In face of the combined strength of the Jordanian army, Israel's movement of forces, and American maneuvers, Syria pulled out of Jordan on 22 September. Left to its own devices, the Hashemite regime destroyed the PLO infrastructure over the next ten months. PLO forces and their families fled Jordan for a new sanctuary in Lebanon, whose central government was too weak to resist their presence.

Lebanon bordered Israel and hence conformed with the guerrilla warfare strategy by which the PLO could continue its fight against the Jewish state. The PLO presence in Lebanon later triggered an interethnic conflict within Lebanon, with enormous consequences for the state of Israel.

Following the 1973 war the Arab states gathered at the 1974 Rabat conference and officially recognized the PLO as the sole representative of the Palestinian people. Most affected by this development was the Hashemite Kingdom of Jordan, which had ruled the West Bank from 1948 to 1967 and aspired to reclaim it. In 1974 the PLO gained observer status at the UN and the General Assembly received a speech by Arafat warmly. The PLO was further empowered by the landslide victory of PLO-affiliated candidates a year later in the West Bank municipal elections. Only in 1988 did Jordan bow to the PLO competition and totally disclaim its links with the West Bank. In the interim, the area of ethno-natinal confrontation moved to Lebanon, where the PLO stationed its headquarters after the expulsion from Jordan in 1970.

The most profound development during these years was the rise of ethnonational aspirations among both Palestinians and Israelis. The separation of the West Bank and the Gaza Strip from Jordan and Egypt in 1967 had helped to crystalize an ethnonational Palestinian identity. Initially the PLO had demanded the total replacement of Israel by a Palestinian state. With time, the object of PLO attention became more congruent with the West Bank and the Gaza Strip.[36] Access to the historic sites of the West Bank (called Judea and Samaria according to their Biblical Jewish names by Israeli religio-nationalists) activated an ethnonational momentum for Israel to keep the territory. The traumatic experience of the 1973 war, specifically disappointment with the failure of the international community to reward Israel's abstinence from preempting, which caused it heavy casualties, fanned the flames of Jewish ethno-nationalism further. The reaction within the Israeli body politic was the emergence of the Gush Emunim settler movement in 1974, the victory of the nationalist Likud in 1977, and the big settlement drive of 1979.[37] With the PLO located in Lebanon and its territorial constituency in the West Bank and Gaza the ensuing ethnic-state crises occurred in these arenas.

Out of the nine crises occurring in between 1973 and 2000 only one case was interstate: the 1980–1981 Iraq nuclear reactor. The PLO or other Palestinian organizations were actively involved in six, and five of these were indirectly related to the civil war that re-erupted in Lebanon in 1975. Two crises of the 1990s were directly associated with the internal Lebanese struggle and the rise of Hizbullah (Party of God), a Shia organization bolstered by Syria and Iran.[38] The relocation of PLO headquarters from Jordan to Beirut had upset the precarious balance of power in Lebanon between Christians and Muslims, which helped trigger the Lebanese civil war. In 1982 Israel invaded Lebanon, destroying the PLO infrastructure and forcing the organization's dislocation from the core conflict area to Tunis and Yemen. This allowed for the forceful emergence of militant Shia Islamic movements which had begun to develop during the previous decade. Since the mid–1980s, Israel had faced two ethnic enemies; one the Palestinian in the territories, and the second the Shia Hizbullah in Lebanon.[39]

CONTEXT ATTRIBUTES AND CRISIS MAGNITUDE

The ascendance of the ethnonational factor in the Arab-Israeli conflict occurred when the gravity of threat in all of the ethnic-state crises, including the 1982 war in Lebanon, was in decline. It should be noted that the destruction of any Arab state was never a realistic goal for Israel, given the immense territorial and population imbalance. By definition, existential threats within the Arab-Israeli conflict have always been directed at Israel by its Arab enemies. The only existential threat crisis was also the only interstate crisis in the period and Israel removed that threat with its June 1981 attack on the Iraqi nuclear reactor. The PLO did not present an existential threat to Israel but Israel's power severely threatened the PLO, as was demonstrated during the 1982 crisis. This reality created a more symmetrical equation.

The departure of Egypt from the confrontation cycle, starting with the interim agreements negotiated by Kissinger and concluding with the signing of the Camp David accords, reduced the gravity of threat level from two perspectives. First, the largest Arab army ceased from directly threatening Israel and second, it removed the need of the IDF to fight on two fronts. Even though Egypt did not abdicate its strategic role in the Middle East its direct threat to Israel diminished to a significant extent. Egypt's defection left Syria as the main opponent of Israel, but the demise of the Soviet Union thwarted Syrian aspirations to achieve strategic parity with Israel. The Iraq-Iran war in the 1980s reduced even further, in the short run, the military threat on the Eastern front for Israel. With a lower level of threat to Israel and the lack of an Israeli goal of dissolving any Arab state, the level of threat in international crises declined significantly.

With the Arab states' menace on the decline, the Palestinian demand for total replacement of the Jewish state by a Palestinian one and the growing stature of the PLO on the international scene posed a threat to Israel's legitimacy, which the Jewish state took soberly. The threat to Israel's legitimacy, rather than its physical existence expressed the ethnonational dimension of the conflict.

A summary of findings on the gravity of threat in ethnic-state and interstate crises, as well as of other CMI attributes in the second period is found in Tables 5.3 and 5.4 respectively.

A parallel trend also transpired in other indicators of crisis context, such as the dwindling of crisis participants. Ethnic-state crises in the previous period drew relatively fewer participants than interstate crises. With almost all of the crises being ethnic-state in the second period, in comparison to fewer than half previously, this trend continued. In addition, Syria and Lebanon replaced Egypt

TABLE 5.3

ETHNIC-STATE CRISES IN THE ARAB ISRAELI CONFLICT: 1974 – 2000

CASE	DATE	GRAVITY	SUPERPOWERS	STATE CRISIS ACTORS	ETHNIC ELEMENTS	CMT	VIOLENCE	OUTCOME
Entebbe raid	June 1976	Grave damage	Both – none	Israel, Uganda	PFLP	Violence	Minor clashes	Unilateral – Israel
Syria mobilization	Nov. 1976	Influence	USA only – political	Israel	Lebanese and Palestinian civil war factions	Non-violent military	None	Tacit agreement
Litani operation	March 1978	Territory	Both – political	Lebanon	Lebanese and Palestinian civil war factions	Negotiation	Serious clashe	Unilateral – Israel
Al-Biqa missiles I	April 1981	Influence	Both – political	Israel, Syria	Lebanese and Palestinian civil war factions	Non-violent military	Minor clashes	Formal agreement

TABLE 5.3 *(continued)*

ETHNIC–STATE CRISES IN THE ARAB ISRAELI CONFLICT: 1974 – 2000

CASE	DATE	GRAVITY	SUPERPOWERS	STATE CRISIS ACTORS	ETHNIC ELEMENTS	CMT	VIOLENCE	OUTCOME
War in Lebanon	June 1982	Influence	USA - political, USSR - semi-military	Israel, Lebanon, Syria	Lebanese and Palestinian civil war factions	Multiple with violence	War	Semi-formal agreement
Al-Biqa missiles II	Nov. 1985	Influence	Both - political	Israel, Syria	Lebanese and Palestinian civil war factions	Non-violent military	Minor clashes	Tacit agreement
Operation Accountability	July 1993	Limited military damage	USA only - political	Israel, Lebanon	Hizbullah	Multiple with violence	Minor clashes	Tacit agreement
Operation Grapes of Wrath	April 1996	Limited military damage	USA only - political	Israel, Lebanon	Hizbullah	Multiple with violence	Minor clashes	Semi-formal agreement

TABLE 5.4

INTERSTATE CRISES IN THE ARAB ISRAELI CONFLICT: 1974 – 2000

CASE	DATE	GRAVITY	SUPERPOWERS	STATE ACTORS	CMT	VIOLENCE	OUTCOME
Iraq nuclear reactor	Jan. 1981	Existence	Both - political	Iraq, Israel	Multiple with violence	Minor clashes	Unilateral - Iraq

and Jordan as crisis actors. This change held qualitative implications in terms of the balance of power as these two actors were weaker than their predecessors. The ascendance of Palestinian and ethnic Lebanese forces post-1973 also reduced the level of actor participation, since the non-state ethnic forces could carry much of the burden of ethnic-state crises with minimal state participation.

This new pattern of reduced state participation was especially visible in terms of superpower role in crisis. Both the U.S. and Soviet patterns of involvement in the post-1973 period continued to be low in magnitude (i.e., no intervention or only a low political one). Soviet abstention was not originally the result of its dwindling power, which ultimately resulted in its disintegration, or conected to its involvement during the late 1970s and early 1980s in the tribal war in Afghanistan. Following the loss of Egypt, the Soviets focused additional attention on Syria and other radical states, such as Libya, and the ethnic war in Chad, the Ethiopian Eritrean ethnonational struggle, as well as the South African internal war. The Soviets during that period consistently supported the PLO in international forums by providing both political and military means. This relatively limited role was similar to the reality observed during the previous period. Evidently the superpowers were more cautious in entering ethnic-state crises than interstate ones. Moreover, this pattern corresponded with the overall winding down of the Arab-Israeli conflict in the post-1973 period and the growing risks involved for those who would perpetuate it. In the Lebanon war of 1982 the United States did send in its marines, but this mission seems to be the exception rather than the rule. The lower overall Soviet involvement matched that of the United States. The two superpowers almost totally curtailed their high involvement in ethnic-state Arab-Israeli crises, even more so after the disintegration of the USSR.[40]

PROCESS, OUTCOMES AND OVERALL CRISIS MAGNITUDE

The level of violence in the post-1973 period dropped in comparison to the 1947–1973 years. From an international perspective, this trend was also influenced by the fact that the Arab-Israeli conflict acquired an ethnic flavor. Even the Litani operation and the 1982 Lebanon war, considered by the ICB to have involved "serious clashes," were primarily local confrontations fought between Israel and the Palestinians. This was a far cry from the previous era, which had witnessed four full-blown interstate wars (1947–1949, 1956, 1967, 1973) and one more limited interstate war (1969).

Change was also evident in a comparison of the level of violence among the ethnic-state crises in both periods. From 1947 to 1973, the ICB coded seven of eight ethnic-state crises as either war (1947–1948) or serious clashes. The second period saw only serious clashes in Lebanon (1978 and 1982 respectively) while five out of eight ethnic-state crises were classified by ICB as involving minor clashes, and one case (Syria mobilization, 1976) even ended without any violence. A comparison of Tables 5.3 and 5.4 demonstrates that in the second period along with the rise in the ratio of ethnic-state crises to interstate crises, ethnic-state crises also enjoyed a decline in terms of violence.

Another change from the pre to post-1973 eras was that apart from some isolated activity by Syrian soldiers in Lebanon during the Israeli invasion, in the twenty-seven years since 1973 Arab state armies were hardly involved in active combat against Israel. The main combatants were Israelis and Palestinians. Many of the new casualties in these clashes were civilians, especially Lebanese. The Palestinian guerilla groups replaced the Arab armies in the warfare with Israel.

Modification was also apparent in the Crisis Management Techniques in all the ethnic-state crises during the latter era. Since 1974, the violence alone category, which demarcated half of the ethnic cases in the first period, disappeared, signaling transformation in the mode by which ethnic-state crises were handled. Instead, violent interactions were accompanied by negotiations or were confined to the demonstration of force without violence. Negotiations were processed either via the United States or at the UN Security Council (e.g., the 1978 Litani and 1982 Lebanon war crises). President Ronald Reagen dispatched Philip Habib, a U.S. special envoy, to defuse crisis situations. Habib's mediation proved crucial in the adoption of an Israeli-PLO ceasefire in July 1982 and again two months later with an agreement for the evacuation of the PLO from Lebanon.[41] The United States played a similar role in limited IDF/Hizbullah confrontations in Lebanon. Already in Operation Accountability (1993), negotiations to end the crisis were processed by the United States and involved Israel, Hizbullah, Lebanon, and Syria. Indirect negotiations through the United States and the establishment of joint mechanisms of arbitration and negotiations between Israel and Lebanon were even more salient during and following Operation Grapes of Wrath in April 1996.[42]

Changes in the process of crisis evolution post-1973 were particularly felt in the outcome of crises. Only two out of eight ethnic-state crises (Entebbe and Litani) were terminated via unilateral actions, as was the Iraq nuclear interstate crisis. Ethnic-state crises in the second period, on the whole, ended in more stable finales. Two crises—Al-Biqa I and Grapes of Wrath—ended with formal agreements, one—Lebanon war—in a semiformal agreement, and the other three in tacit understandings. In comparison, almost all the ethnic-state crises in the previous period ended via unilateral action. Overall, the post-1973 ethnic-state crises ended with more accommodative outcomes than similar crises in the earlier era, marking the newly transformed nature of the Arab-Israeli conflict.

The dwindling of the state component and its displacement by the ethnic was not a seamless, smooth process. The Arab states continued to play a role in the conflict. At the Baghdad Conference of 1979, for instance, the Arab states imposed a boycott on Egypt for having signed a separate peace treaty with Israel. The compound interstate and ethnic nature of the conflict was reflected by the conference decision to establish a "steadfastness fund" to support the Palestinian struggle both on the international scene and in the occupied territories.[43] Another indication of this compound nature and of the difficulty in resolving the ethnic dimension of the struggle was similarly apparent in the Camp David accords, which included both elements: the bilateral Israel–Egypt peace (interstate) and Palestinian autonomy (ethnonational).[44] Significantly, the interstate element of the accords was implemented successfully while the ethnic-state negotiations repeatedly faltered and ultimately broke down. The Begin government's accelerated settlement drive in the West Bank and Gaza Strip, motivated by a historical ethnonational impulse on the one hand and the veto declared by the PLO on autonomy, accompanied by the assassinations of "Palestinian collaborators," closed the road for negotiations on this track.[45] The PLO-Israel struggle thus occupied a growing share in the confrontation when the Arab–Israeli interstate conflict began to decline. Explaining this coincidence needs some elaboration.

TOWARD TRANSFORMATION IN ETHNIC-STATE CRISES

Our framework, as presented in chapter 1, focused on three types of crises: interstate, ethnic-state, and interethnic. The progression of the Arab–Israeli conflict went through a cycle in accordance with these three types: it started as an interethnic rivalry, in the pre-1948 years, evolved into a dominant interstate conflict throughout the 1948–1973 period, containing an ethnic-state element, transposed into an ethnic-state dominant strife during the 1974–2000 years, and slid back into an interethnic contest (see next chapter).[46] The crises in the Arab–Israeli relationship mirrored this pattern.

In mapping the direction of the conflict, this chapter has also revealed an additional phenomenon: while a process of moderation commenced on the interstate level since the mid-1970s the Palestinian-Israel axis became more salient and signaled some escalation in its renewed ethnic fervor. Even though the ethnic confrontation involved lower levels of crisis magnitude, mutation into ethnic dominant prevented overall conflict resolution.

Crosscutting trends and spillover effects were present throughout the 1974–2000 years. Compromise and accommodation in the interstate domain forced the PLO to step in and take responsibility over Palestinian fate. The ascendance of the ethnic dimension in the Middle East also supported this trend; it promoted the PLO to the status of a separate official representative of the Palestinians. This process, in turn, reinforced the winding down of the interstate conflict by reducing Egyptian president Anwar Sadat's responsibility for the Palestinian cause. Egypt could then concentrate on regaining the Sinai through diplomatic means, leaving the fate of the Gaza Strip and the West Bank for resolution by Israel and the Palestinians. Similarly, the exit of Jordan from the West Bank put the burden on the Palestinians while the PLO's new status reduced the incentive for King Hussein to be active on the Israeli front. The departure of Egypt and the de facto Jordanian withdrawal from the military equation reduced the salience of Arab threats to Israel, thus allowing the Jewish state to reciprocate with moderation in its policy toward the Arab world and eventually the PLO.

On the whole it was the interstate confrontations that produced the more intense crises that led to war. The decline in interstate rivalry required adjustments in the ethnic milieu and put the Arab-Israeli conflict system into a state of temporary disequilibrium, to use Brecher and Ben-Yehuda's terminology.[47] Eventually, an ethnic salient equilibrium emerged in the late 1970s and persisted through the 1990s. The ethnic-state crises that did occur within this newly established Normal Relations Range (NRR) were less threatening. The conflict system thus re-stabilized around a less severe point of violence and involved lower overall crisis magnitude.

On the whole, two trends characterize the latter period : (1) moderation of the interstate rivalry spilled over into the ethnic confrontation, but (2) the ethnic dimension prevented the conflict from resolution. Put vice versa, while the return of the ethnonational rivalry to prominence sustained the conflict , the new equation ultimately moderated the overall conflict and also influenced the ethnonational forces to submit to some degree of accommodation.

How do we explain the phenomenon of the winding down of the overall conflict despite the infusion and convergence of the ethnonational dimension, especially when ethnic conflicts are generally loaded with even more animosity than interstate ones ? The answer lies in the predominance of the interstate dimension over the interethnic one. Once conditions for accommodation emerged on the interstate level, as we have demonstrated in chapter 4, the ethnonational component could prolong the conflict but not with the same temper as before. Some institutionalism slowly also began filtering into the Jewish-Palestinian level.

To understand the nature of conflict transformation, a distinction must be made between intensity and duration. To be sure, the gradual moderation in the goal of some of the Arab states modified their crisis behavior, but this new pattern of restraint was accompanied by the surge of the ethnic factor. While contracting in terms of overall magnitude and frequency of crisis the Arab-Israeli conflict did not disappear, but rather it expressed itself through its ethnic domain. Lack of resolution of the Palestinian problem evidently prolonged the conflict. Alas, despite the the dual nature of the Camp David accords—which placed a link between its interstate and ethnic frameworks—the Israeli-Palestinian rivalry lacked significant institutional accommodation for another decade and a half.

Final conclusions require an assessment of two additional events not included by ICB researchers in the Arab-Israeli protracted conflict: the Intifada and the 1991 Gulf war.

CHAPTER 6

NEW DIMENSIONS
IN THE ARAB-ISRAELI CONFLICT:
FROM THE INTIFADA 1987
TO INTIFADA 2000

We now turn our attention to crises waived by the ICB in its survey of the protracted Arab-Israeli conflict—the 1987 Intifada, belonging to the ethnic category, and the 1990–1991 Gulf crisis, an interstate-type crisis. The ICB project
excluded the Intifada because of its intrastate character and omitted the Gulf
crisis on the grounds that as an interstate conflict between Iraq and Kuwait, it
did not belong in the Arab-Israeli cluster of cases despite the thirty-nine missiles that struck Israel. The second Intifada, which began in the fall of 2000,
occurred subsequent to the publication of the ICB project's data-set, but would
have no doubt been excluded anyway for the same reason as the first.
Nevertheless, both types of crisis are major events in the evolution of the Arab-
Israeli conflict and no study of conflict transformation can be complete without them. It is conceivable that these forms of violent civil conflict and missile
wars will dominate future Arab-Israeli contentions and overshadow the trends
in conflict transformation identified in this book.

The original Intifada constituted a somewhat new form of interethnic crisis between Israel and the Palestinians, namely, a process of violent interactions
within one polity, involving ethnic elements and virtually no Arab state
involvement. While reminiscent of Jewish-Arab clashes in Mandate Palestine,
neither of the protagonists in the pre-1948 interethnic crisis enjoyed sovereignty. During the Intifada, the Palestinians remained a non-state actor pitted against
the Jewish state. During the September 2000 Intifada the Palestinians were
already a semi-state, awaiting formal declaration and recognition by the inter-

national community and Israel. The Gulf war of 1991, though an interstate event, revealed new forms of hostile crisis interactions that evolved into a series of one sided missile attacks by Iraq against Israel, with no counterreaction.

We start with an analysis of the Intifada I and the Gulf crises and continue with the diplomatic negotiations that followed these events in the early 1990s. The chapter concludes with analyses of the ethnic–state encounters involving Israel and Hizbullah in Lebanon (Grapes of Wrath) and the October 2000 Intifada, both crises that took place after the closing of the ICB project.

THE INTIFADA: AN INTER-ETHNIC CRISIS

The trigger for the Intifada was an 8 December 1987 road accident between an Israeli truck and a car carrying Palestinian laborers. As the word of the death of four Palestinian passengers spread, Gazans gathered for spontaneous and violent demonstrations. While these events clearly marked the onset of the Intifada, its exact termination date is much harder to determine. Interestingly, neither adversary regarded this violent outburst as a crisis at its outset. In Israel, the general at the head of the Southern Command, Yitzhak Mordechai, was initially not even informed about the accident that marked the opening of this crisis. Minister of Defense Yitzhak Rabin did not cancel his December 10 trip to the United States, where he was to meet his American counterpart. Similarly, the Pentagon chief did not raise the issue of violence in the territories in his 14 December meeting with Rabin. In fact, Rabin was absent from Israel for the first two weeks of the Intifada.[1]

In retrospect, early indications of increasing tension during the preceding year signaled that a crisis was developing. In both the Gaza Strip and the West Bank the number of violent incidents and disturbances more than doubled from 1986 to 1987. Almost every indicator of violence, such as the number of incidents, scope of disturbances, and casualties on both sides, increased by more than 100 percent throughout the months preceding the Intifada, in comparison to the previous year.[2] Post factum, this rise in violence created the step-level change in the salience of interethnic clashes between Israelis and Palestinians.

CONTEXT ATTRIBUTES AND CRISIS MAGNITUDE

The distribution of forces between the two sides contributed to the level of threats involved during the early stages of the Intifada. Relative to the military forces of the Arab states and following the 1982 expulsion of the PLO from Lebanon and the destruction of its military infrastructure there, the Palestinian threat to Israel did not constitute a credible menace. Nor did the Palestinians see an Israeli response such as the eradication of the Palestinians from the territory as feasible. After twenty years of low level disturbances, the events of December 1987 seemed like just another expression of Palestinian dissatisfaction with the occupation. A month of sustained rioting, unprecedented in its twenty year control of the territories, led Israel to change the procedural response from "standard security," to a "hard fist" policy. The duration of the demonstrations, the participation of women and youth, and their geographical spread across the territory finally convinced the Israeli leadership, particularly Minister of Defense Rabin, that the riots comprised a political threat to Israeli control of the territories that had prevailed since 1967.[3]

But even the Palestinians did not anticipate that Israel would relinquish the territories because of the Intifada. The strategists among them surely thought that at the most, it might generate a political process that would ultimately change the existing modes of control.[4] In Israel this threat resulted in the establishment in 1988 of a National Unity Government that collapsed in March 1990 precisely over the issue of policy toward the Palestinian problem.[5]

In the wake of the PLO's defeat in Lebanon, the continuation of the status quo presented a threat of grave damage to the Palestinians. Because of the distribution of forces between a government controlling a standing army and a civilian population, the Palestinians could also fear a massive Israeli crackdown, just short of expulsions. Paradoxically, an uncontrolled Intifada did not serve the PLO interest. Neither the PLO nor Arafat had anticipated the uprising, or its strength, persistence, and violence. In the past, the Palestinians inside the territories (the insiders) had never sought to usurp the mantle of leadership held by the PLO. The Intifada constituted a structural change within the Palestinian community in that the inside segment emerged as the vanguard of the Palestinian revolution, thereby threatening the PLO.[6]

The weakness of the PLO after its expulsion from Lebanon to Tunis and the resulting despair of the inhabitants of the West Bank and Gaza convinced the Palestinians of the interior that they must lead the struggle against Israel. Another core threat to the Palestinians was the Likud's 1979 settlement drive, which ushered thousands of new Israelis into the territories and instilled urgency among the Palestinians. Israel's appointment of pro-Jordanian mayors in the territories following the PLO's exit from Lebanon signaled a renewed partnership between Israel and the Hashemites, an alliance that posed yet another threat to the Palestinian cause. The PLO tried to squelch the Jordanian-inclined Palestinian leadership via assassinations of "collaborators" with Jordan and Israel. One of the goals of the Intifada was to obstruct a Jordanian-Israeli regime in the territories.

The interethnic Intifada crisis exhibited the limited actor phenomenon common to most ethnic-state crises: no other actors besides the Israelis and the Palestinians participated directly in the violence, although the Arab states all expressed their customary verbal support. The first Gulf war, then going on between Iraq and Iran, contributed to the minimal attention and lack of involvement on the part of the Arab states toward the Palestinian uprising. In addition to supporting Iran in that war, Syria was also expending considerable resources in Lebanon, where it supported factions in the PLO contesting

Arafat's leadership. Egypt used the crisis to restore its leading role in the Arab world and return to the Arab League, a task accomplished in March 1989. At the same time, Cairo was careful not to escalate the confrontation between the Palestinians and Israel so that it might be drawn into the confrontation.

Most unprecedented, however, was King Hussein's declaration of 31 July 1988, in which he severed administrative and legal relations between Jordan and the West Bank. Fearing the spread of the Intifada to his kingdom, and realizing that the London Agreement of 1987 negotiated between himself and Israeli foreign minister Shimon Peres would never materialize, King Hussein decided to cut his loses and bless the PLO's role as the sole representative of the territories, as recommended by the 1974 Rabat conference.[7] It was in the wake of this proclamation that the Palestine National Council (PNC) on 14 November 1988 declared an independent Palestinian state in exile, an act recognized by Jordan the next day.[8]

Once the PLO realized the opportunity that the Intifada presented, it moved in to take control of the revolt. A diffused alliance of local chapters of the uprising had formed a "united national command," but conceded leadership to the external PLO. Palestinian actors of the late 1980s inclined to challenge the PLO's authority in the territories included Hamas, the Islamic fundamentalist organization, and the smaller but even more extreme splinter group, the Islamic Jihad. The latter perceived itself as the match that had ignited the Intifada. On the other end of the spectrum, the Israeli Arabs represented a more moderate Palestinian stance. Israeli Arabs identified openly with their Palestinian brothers but were careful for the most part not to join in the violence of the Intifada. They did not hesitate, however, to express their sympathies through sporadic demonstrations, the collection of supplies for the rebellious Palestinians, and via their vote for Arab lists to the Knesset where they raised the issue of the Intifada.[9] These were the main forces that composed the Palestinian actor in the crisis.

In short, the crisis actors during the Intifada remained limited to Israel and the Palestinians of the West Bank and Gaza Strip, although the latter were represented on the international scene by the PLO. With the Arab states supporting the struggle politically but not militarily and the great powers merely watching the uprising via the media, the struggle to a large extent focused on public opinion. In terms of the distribution of power, the Palestinians had no chance of defeating the state of Israel and its army. In terms of the public relations battle, however, the Palestinian side confronted Israel with a formidable rival. Enjoying the advantage of being the underdog and the visual impact of children facing soldiers was bound to make Israel look bad. The Intifada did not directly involve any Arab state, it occurred in a territory controlled entirely by Israel, and thus constituted a direct confrontation between Jews and Palestinians, continuing the ethnic dimension left unresolved by the 1982 war. As an interethnic-type crisis, the Intifada resembled the great Arab revolt of fifty years earlier, but this time one of the rival communities, the Jewish one, enjoyed state status.

PROCESS AND CRISIS MAGNITUDE

The Intifada signaled a strategic change in the interaction pattern between the Palestinians and Israel. Immediately after the 1967 war, the PLO had tried to promote a popular armed struggle in the territories against Israel.[10] Following its expulsion from the territories in 1968–1969, the PLO called for *sumud*, meaning a "steadfastness" strategy. This approach assigned to the Palestinians inside the territories passive resistance and daily noncooperation with the Israeli authorities. There was no expectation that the insiders would launch an independent revolt or collective action. This was part of the PLO's strategy to keep its own leading political role in the Palestinian struggle.[11] In the mid-1980s, intellectuals and activists within the territories began to challenge the *sumud* doctrine on the ground that it had not advanced Palestinian statehood.[12]

The scope of violence

The prolonged Palestinian-Israeli struggle falls within the category of a Low Intensity Conflict (LIC), implying limits on the use of violence. Nevertheless, the use of violence in the Intifada differed from previous outbursts in several respects. First, it was a territory-wide revolt. It started in a Gaza refugee camp but within a day had spread to the cities, towns, and villages of the West Bank. The Palestinian residents of East Jerusalem, annexed officially by Israel, also joined the revolt. Previously, demonstrations were limited to one locale. The second variation was in the duration of the revolt. While violence in the territories had occurred often since their occupation by Israel in 1967, it was sporadic in nature. The sustained violence that began in December 1987 stretched successively through the PLO's recognition of UN Resolution 242 and of Israel on 15 December 1988, until the outbreak of the 1990–1991 Gulf crisis, when the PLO sided with Saddam Hussein.[13]

The third distinction of the Intifada involved the targets of violence, namely, Israeli soldiers and civilians and Arab collaborators. To be sure, Palestinian violence claimed victims in all three groups. In the Intifada, the ratio among the three victims changed, with civilians bearing the greater brunt of the violence. Terror against settlers and assassinations of collaborators reflected Palestinian attempts to differentiate between different segments in Israeli society and legitimize its terror.[14]

The fourth new characteristic of the Intifada was in the means applied, a composite of civil disobedience and subconventional forms of force. Standard weapons were stones, knives, and petrol bombs, with firearms and explosives used only sporadically. The absence of standard weapons reflected not their inaccessibility but rather a conscious decision by the commanders of the Intifada to preserve the populist character of the uprising. Supporting factors were Palestinian awareness of Israel's military superiority and the belief that a David versus Goliath uprising would be more effective in attracting the attention of the international media.

Precedents for Palestinian protest were civil disobedience and nonviolent resistance campaigns as practiced in India against British rule before 1947, and their own 1936–1939 revolt against British control of Palestine, discussed in the previous chapter. Accordingly, the Intifada included public demonstrations, strikes, boycotts of Israeli goods, the resignation of Palestinian policemen and tax collectors, refusal to pay taxes, and a general reduction of cooperation with the Israeli civil administration. But the greater dependence of the Palestinians on the Israeli economy than vice versa diminished the punitive impact of these activities on Israel. Therefore, civil disobedience was also accompanied by more violent actions.

Palestinian youth took to the streets, pelting similarly aged Israeli soldiers with stones, rocks, bricks, and petrol bombs. Slingshots were cheap, accessible, and effective. In addition, protesters spread nails and oil on the roads, and set tire roadblocks alight. Over time, Israel tailored its response to the particular features of the Intifada. In the absence of antiriot troops, crack IDF units and the Border Police were equipped with helmets to protect them from stones; plastic and rubber bullets for their guns; and batons and gas canisters. Israel even invented a gravel-throwing vehicle with which to disperse rock-throwing mobs. In a region that had seen thousands of lives lost to terrorism and conventional warfare, the use of discriminate firepower was novel.

Also unprecedented was the sheer number of Palestinian participants. Most civil uprisings fail to inspire the spread of violence among broad segments of the population, defined in the literature of revolt as "collective political violence."[15] Violent actions had been limited to small numbers of participants, in this case a small core of Palestinian nationalists. Passive resistance to Israel's rule in accord with the 1969 *samud* doctrine rarely resulted in disturbances in which more than several dozen people participated. The Intifada brought thousands of ordinary people out into the streets.[16]

One way of measuring the extent of popular involvement is to look for trends among detainees and casualties. Indeed, the number of Palestinian prisoners was unprecedented, running for the first few months of the uprising at around 1,500 per month, and declining to roughly 700 people per month after the first four months. At the height of the Intifada, between thirty and fifty thousand Palestinians were detained in Israeli prisons.

During the opening years of the Intifada Palestinian casualties were between 300 and 500 per year, then dropped in the early 1990s to between 100 and 200 per annum. Although the numbers are smaller, the Israeli civilian casualty rate showed the opposite trend, with steadily increasing losses for each year of the Intifada. The number of IDF troops killed also grew each year.[17]

A comparison of the level of violence during the Intifada to that of the previous twenty years suggests a meaningful escalation. Despite the Palestinian decision not to use firearms during most of the uprising, over time the scope in terms of geography, time, targets of violence, and variety of weapons rose to the level of open warfare.

Crisis management technique

From an early point in the crisis, both sides used a mixture of violence and diplomacy in their efforts to manage the conflict, a relatively new combination of crisis coping modes that appeared only in the post-1973 years. On the Palestinian side, the internal command of the Intifada designated the PLO its official representative, even though the initiative for the uprising originated from within the territories. In allowing the PLO to speak for them, the inside Palestinians indicated that they contemplated a political solution to their plight. The shift toward assimilating negotiations with violence was not a sudden event: the PLO had already begun moderating its strategy in the mid-1970s.[18]

On 15 November 1988, one year after the eruption of the Intifada, the nineteenth session of the PNC declared the establishment of a Palestinian state, called explicitly for the settlement of the Arab-Israeli conflict and endorsed an international peace conference. The PNC also echoed the internationally heralded campaign to eliminate nuclear arms and settle regional conflicts by peaceful means, without giving up its claim that the crux of the Middle Eastern conflict was the Palestinian question. At the end of a long paragraph listing all the Palestinian rights, invoking the appropriate UN resolutions, and announcing the establishment of a Palestinian state, the declaration also stated that the desired political settlement would provide "security and peace arrangements for all the countries in the region." In order to attain these goals, the PNC emphasized the need to convene an effective international conference under UN supervision with the participation of the UN Security Council permanent members. The conference, with the Palestinian cause as its essence, would include all the parties to the conflict in the region and its basis would be the PLO's acceptance of Security Council Resolutions 242 and 338.[19] While the resolution stated that the PNC rejects all forms of terrorism, it also demanded a ban on institutional terrorism hinting here at Israeli retaliation against PLO terror.[20]

On the Israeli side, Minister of Defense Rabin and his chief of staff Dan Shomron also signaled that Israel did not envisage a pure military solution to the Intifada. Each defined the IDF's goal as providing the political echelon with the best position from which to negotiate a political solution. Although some ministers demanded a military solution, Rabin's view, supported by all of the Labor ministers and some of the more moderate Likud ministers, prevailed.[21]

Just as the PLO had to respond to the will of the Palestinian "insiders," Israeli leaders had to consider public opinion. A majority of Israelis rejected harsh military measures against the Palestinians during the Intifada. Typical were the results of a poll that showed that the Israeli public preferred a "very limited use of force" in the context of the Intifada, whereas a majority supported harsh counteraction against terrorism.[22] This position may explain the hawkishness of Israeli public opinion as a result of the Intifada that we find in another poll.[23]

The eventual use of rifles and bombs confirmed an early Palestinian strategy of crisis management by way of a mixture of violence and political means. The initial Palestinian decision to refrain from the use of firearms reflected

Palestinian calculations that the image of unarmed civilians resisting the mighty Israeli army would bolster world opinion in their favor and also deny the IDF its advantage as a regular army. It was this tactic that qualified the disturbances as a civil uprising rather than terrorism, an incriminating characterization from which Palestinian actions had long suffered, and not without cause. Despite the militant rhetoric of the United National Command of the Uprising in its many communiques, the goal was to change the existing Israeli–Palestinian relationship structure by forcing Israel to the negotiating table.[24]

The mixture of violence and political means in resolving the Intifada crisis was constrained by the lack of mutual legitimacy between the two parties. The majority of Israeli decision makers, parties, and public opinion agreed that the PLO was not a legitimate partner for negotiations. Knesset legislation forbade any Israeli to have contact or interaction with the PLO, characterized as a terrorist organization. However, the Labor Party amended its 1988 election platform to allow negotiations with "Jordan and Palestinians."[25] In the wake of Hussein's disengagement from the West Bank, growing domestic support for a political solution to the Intifada, accompanied by American pressures to settle the uprising by diplomatic means, Israel modified further its taboo on negotiations with the PLO. Significantly, the PLO also changed its position on contact with Israeli leaders. By agreeing to direct negotiations, the PLO went a long way from its policy of assassinating Palestinian proponents, such as Issam Sartawi, for negotiating with Zionist leaders.[26]

Despite the friendly U.S -Israel relations during the Reagan presidency, during the Intifada U.S. policy moved from rejection of an international conference to cautious support. Prior to the Intifada, Washington did not want to share its new predominancy in the region with the Soviet Union and the Europeans. But the improvement in U.S.-USSR relations in the Gorbachev era, pressures from the Arab states friendly to the West, and a personal campaign in favor of a multilateral conference by Israel's foreign minister Peres modified Washington's position on this issue.[27] Secretary of State George Shultz went so far as to suggest that should the PLO accept Israel's legitimacy and renounce terror, the United States would open a direct dialogue with the PLO.

The leadership in the territories realized that it could not achieve Palestinian goals by violence alone and pressured Arafat to undertake political initiatives. When Washington insisted that neither the 1988 PNC declarations nor Arafat's address to the UN General Assembly that same year fulfilled U.S. conditions for opening a dialogue with the PLO, the latter launched a multifaceted initiative. On 15 December 1988, Arafat convened a press conference and read a statement accepting the right of all parties to the conflict, including Israel, to exist; formally accepting resolutions 242 and 338 as a basis for negotiations; and renouncing terrorism. This time he used the exact language dictated to him by Secretary Shultz and was rewarded the same day with an announcement by Shultz that "the United States is prepared for a substantive dialogue with PLO representatives."[28]

The United States–PLO dialogue influenced domestic politics in Israel. Although Yitzhak Shamir won the 1988 national elections and enjoyed a comfortable majority in the Knesset, he nevertheless opted to form a national unity government with the Labor Party. Shamir chose to share power with his main opposition based on his desire to solidify a broad Israeli consensus in the forthcoming negotiations.[29]

Soon after the entrance of new administrations both in Israel and the United States, in 1989, Defense Minister Rabin had floated the idea of elections in the territories in order to promote a local Palestinian leadership with whom Israel could negotiate. On 30 January 1989, Rabin formally presented his proposal before the Labor Knesset faction. In response to the Intifada, he stated, Israel must teach the Palestinians that by violence they would not achieve any of their goals, but that a peacefully negotiated solution could be possible. Stating explicitly that the rationale behind his plan was to strengthen the local Palestinians at the expense of the hated PLO, he proposed a four-stage plan: contraction of the uprising, holding elections in the territories for a political representation to negotiate with Israel, a transition period, and multilateral negotiations on the final status of the territories. Rabin indicated that his plan was in accordance with the autonomy portion of the Camp David agreement and thus could be also supported by the Likud. Three months later Prime Minister Shamir presented a plan to the new administration of President George Bush, of which the most novel point was a proposal to hold elections in the territories for the purpose of negotiating a Palestinian self-governing administration. Shamir, by this suggestion, indicated that he was also looking for a political solution to the crisis, although he still insisted that in the final negotiations Israel would demand sovereignty over Judea and Samaria.[30]

In the absence of direct Palestinian–Israeli negotiations, the Egyptians responded to this initiative in September 1989. President Mubarak's ten point plan included three principles that worried the Israeli government: that Israel must accept the principle of "territories for peace," halt further settlement establishment, and allow the participation of East Jerusalem residents in the West Bank elections.[31] What emerged in the wake of this proposal was a cross-cutting coalition, or, to use Keohane and Nye's language, a "transgovernmental" coalition that included Egypt, the Bush administration, and the Labor leadership.[32] This coalition resulted from the domestic split in the Israeli body politic between Labor, which supported a territorial compromise, and Likud, which objected to any partition of the land of Israel. Both the Mubarak proposal and an October 1989 Baker more limited five points plan were accepted by the Labor ministers, including Rabin, the hardliner among them.[33]

In the following months intensive negotiations ensued among Israel, the United States, and Egypt. While the PLO was pressing via the Egyptians to enter the negotiations, Baker was pressuring Shamir to let the Palestinians in.

Eventually, the disagreement between Israel and the United States narrowed down to two points: PLO participation in the negotiations, and the participation of East Jerusalem Arabs in the elections.[34]

In March 1990, the Israeli national unity government collapsed over Shamir's refusal to accede to Secretary Baker's proposals and the acceptance of the Baker plan by ministers Peres and Rabin. Peres failed to put together a majority in Parliament, but in June Shamir succeeded in doing so. The new government was composed of the right-wing nationalist and religious members of the Knesset.

OUTCOMES AND CRISIS MAGNITUDE

The new minister of defense, Moshe Arens, who replaced Rabin, did not make any drastic changes in Israeli policy toward the Intifada. In fact, the Intifada was overshadowed by the outbreak of a new international crisis—the conquest of Kuwait by Saddam Hussein. For the next nine months, from August 1990 through March 1991, the Intifada fell dormant. The Intifada came to a further halt in the interval between the end of Desert Storm in March 1991 and the Madrid conference of October 1991.[35] Arafat and the PLO officially backed Saddam Hussein during the Gulf crisis, thus linking the Gulf crisis and the interethnic Intifada. However, between the dancing of Palestinians on the rooftops in the territories while Scuds fell in Tel-Aviv and the desperate situation of 400,000 Palestinians from Kuwait and Saudi Arabia, the Intifada took a time out. Very soon after the end of the Gulf war, diplomatic activity in the Arab-Israeli arena resumed, as did a low scale version of the Intifada. This time, however, along with demonstrations and stone throwing, Palestinians took to shooting at passing Israeli cars and against Israeli soldiers and civilians alike.

The Intifada faded away with the opening of the Madrid conference on 30 October 1991. However, we can see in the diplomatic process that emerged in the wake of Madrid only a partial outcome, to use ICB language, of the interethnic crisis. The Oslo agreement, stipulated the withdrawal of the IDF from Gaza and the major cities of the West Bank. Our final evaluation of crisis termination must await analysis of the Gulf crisis and the second Intifada of October 2000.

THE GULF CRISIS: APRIL 1990–MARCH 1991

Brecher considered the Gulf crisis of 1990–1991 a "bilateral international crisis" between Iraq and Kuwait at its outset, and a "global crisis" by the time it ended. From our perspective, the threats uttered by both Israel and Iraq, the involvement of at least one superpower, the application of violence by one regional party, the escalation and de-escalation of threats, and the violent management technique exhibited by the U.S.-led alliance all qualify the confrontation as a major event in Arab-Israeli relations. At the same time, its theoretical relevance lies in the tension it embodies between power politics and international institutionalism. Though the Gulf crisis was defined by the ICB project as a confrontation outside the Arab-Israeli conflict, we analyze it here in terms of its core CMI attributes and assess its implications for conflict transformation.

CONTEXT AND CRISIS MAGNITUDE

On 2 April 1990, the Iraqi president Saddam Hussein announced that he would light a fire to eat up half of Israel with his binary chemical weapons. He repeated the threat on May 30 during the Arab summit in Baghdad. The Iraqi army, at the time the fourth largest in the world, reinforced Iraq's chemical capability. Israeli intelligence warned that Iraq was on the verge of being able to produce nuclear weapons without external assistance. In July 1990, one month prior to the Iraqi conquest of Kuwait, Israeli minister of defense Moshe Arens flew to the United States to alert the U.S. defense establishment regarding the Iraqi conventional and nuclear threat.[36]

The Iraqi invasion of Kuwait on 2 August 1990 triggered an international crisis on a global scale. Throughout the crisis there existed the potential of an Israeli preemptive and then retaliatory attack on Iraq.[37] Other states directly menaced were the Gulf oil states, particularly Saudi Arabia. Indirectly threatened were the Western industrial states, vulnerable to potential Iraqi control of Middle Eastern oil. As the leader of the Western world, the United States was also sensitive to the Iraqi blow to the international order and U.S. leadership. The Arab states, which had competed for power since the emergence of the modern state system, worried about the specter of Iraqi regional supremacy. In addition, the invasion of Kuwait opened the whole question of the integrity of borders arbitrarily delineated by the colonial powers; the de-legitimization of the Iraq-Kuwait border potentially de-legitimized most of the state borders in the region.[38]

Iraq's threats against and then attacks on Israel were aimed at restoring the traditional pan-Arab coalition by dragging Israel into the war. Saddam expected that an Iraq-Israel war would disrupt the U.S. effort to build an anti-Iraq coalition that included the Arab states. Iraq possessed missiles that could reach Israeli urban centers, and also had chemical weapons with which to threaten Israel's civilian population. But Israel's nonconventional capacity meant that an existential threat was also in the making against Iraq.

On the whole, the mutual implied threats to use nonconventional weapons in the confrontation between Iraq and Israel were new in the range of weapons they involved, but the high gravity threats they entailed accord well with the profile of interstate-type crises.

Analysis is more complex when we turn to the number of crisis actors involved, since Iraq was interacting with many actors but on different levels of intensity. The Gulf confrontation clearly fits the interstate profile with its many actors, marking its overall high magnitude. The U.S.-led coalition included twenty-eight states, but only six were actively involved in the hostilities. The brunt of warfare, however, was borne by two states—the United States and Iraq.[39] Iraq hurled missiles as well as threats at Israel, despite the fact that the latter adopted a "low profile" policy. In terms of the Arab–Israeli conflict, there were but two actors: Iraq and Israel. The occurrence of the crisis during the period of Soviet decline and disintegration allowed for U.S. predominance to an unprecedented degree. The ultimate direct military involvement of the United States in heading a grand coalition against Iraq constituted a major new precedent in the Middle East, as well as for the Arab–Israeli conflict.

During the Cold War, Soviet behavior constrained American involvement in the Middle East. The Soviet factor in this crisis was marginal, making American behavior as a sole superpower quite novel.[40] This was the first crisis where the United States could almost ignore a Soviet response. In terms of the distribution of power, U.S. superiority was clear. Nevertheless, Washington was careful to concoct a coalition that would provide the United States with legitimacy to intervene against Iraq under a collective security formula.[41] The intense U.S. role in this confrontation follows our expectation regarding large scale superpower participation in interstate crises. In accordance with its war strategy, the United States sought to avert Israeli military activity so as to keep the coalition intact. The prevention of Israeli involvement required, at a minimum, the removal of the Scud batteries firing on Israel. Incredibly, Israel did not respond, despite the U.S. failure to remove the Scud threat against Israel.

PROCESS AND CRISIS MAGNITUDE

Ten days after the conquest of Kuwait, Saddam Hussain attempted to make a clear linkage between the Gulf crisis and the Palestine question. In light of the outrage that greeted the invasion of Kuwait, internationally and in the Arab world, he sought to revive the anti-Israeli coalition.[42] At a meeting on 9 January 1991 between U.S. secretary of state James Baker and Iraqi foreign minister Tariq Aziz, Aziz demanded an "Arab Solution," which would constitute a comprehensive settlement of all the Middle Eastern disputes, particularly the liberation of Kuwait, in return for the liberation of Palestine. The inability of the Iraqi dictator to mobilize the Arab states behind his linkage strategy reflected both the severe response to his Kuwait operation, even in the Middle East, and the new emerging realities of moderation, identified earlier.

In both the Desert Shield and Desert Storm periods of the crisis, linkage did not succeed in dragging Israel into the confrontation. This failure prevented the transformation of the crisis from an inter-Arab to an Arab–Israeli confrontation. On 18 January 1991 Iraq struck Israel with eight separate missiles, and Iraqi crisis management escalated from nonviolent military to violent. The Shamir government's restrained crisis management in the subsequent weeks, and the controlled Arab response in the face of counterthreats by the Israeli air force provided additional support for the emergence of moderation in the area and the transformed nature of the Arab-Israeli conflict.

Many Arab states, including Egypt and Syria, the two states that had participated in every Arab-Israeli war, joined the American-led coalition. The Egyptians assured President Bush and Secretary of State Baker that they would not leave the coalition if Iraq attacked Israel and Israel retaliated.[43] The two states even joined, to a very limited extent, in the fighting against Iraq alongside Saudi Arabia, the United States, the UK, and France.[44] The escalation of the Gulf crisis thus differed from the regular pattern of Arab-Israeli crises in that Israel and the Arab states did not find themselves automatically at war with each other. Nor were they pitted against each other in rigid camps or competing alliance configurations.

Israel's behavior deviated from its traditional national security doctrine in two respects. First, despite the open threats coming from Iraq and Israeli intelligence confirming the existence of a huge Iraqi army with a nonconventional capability, Israel abstained from a preemptive attack, such as it had launched in the past. Second, despite Israeli warnings that it would retaliate if attacked, the Jewish state abstained from responding to the multiple Iraqi Scud missile hits, which caused grave damage to civilian property. Both policies contradicted the traditional Israeli deterrence strategy.[45]

Israeli inactivity from outbreak of the crisis on 2 August 1990 until the end of the war in February was novel.[46] From 18 January through 25 February 1991 Israel absorbed thirty-nine ground to ground missile strikes, launched on seventeen separate occasions. In the past, Israel had suffered attacks on its frontier-civilian centers, but since the 1948 war, the Israeli heartland had never been threatened. Besides the material losses, the Scud attacks caused the disturbance of daily life for a long period of time, and induced psychological distress in Israeli society. The flight of civilians from major cities, especially Tel-Aviv and Ramat-Gan, was unprecedented and reached 40 percent in some areas of these cities.[47]

Israeli leaders had warned Iraq since the inception of the crisis that Israel would retaliate for any attack. Many argued that the surprising lack of an Israeli military response harmed Israel's deterrence credibility. Keeping a reputation for carrying out threats is an important element in maintaining deterrence.[48] Nonresponse was especially significant as far as Israel's deterrence posture was concerned, in light of an accumulation of failures by the IDF to inflict decisive victories in response to Arab violence.[49] Even those who argued that Israeli deterrence had successfully prevented a chemical or a biological attack admitted that in this regard Israel's credibility had been impaired.[50] We relate Israeli inactivity, inter alia, to the transformation of the strategic environment of the Arab-Israeli conflict that had started to evolve after 1973.

OUTCOMES AND CRISIS MAGNITUDE

The end of the Gulf crisis came on 28 February 1991, when a ceasefire went into effect between the U.S.-led coalition and Iraq. The formal ceasefire occurred on 12 April 1991. In the interim period the international community hashed out its demands for an end to hostilities, imposed on Iraq by Security Council Resolution 687. The conditions embodied in the resolution were severe and included the elimination of Iraq's nonconventional weapons and its payment of reparations to states damaged in the war, Iraq's acceptance of the 1963 border with Kuwait, and a pledge that Iraq would deny bases for terrorist organizations and accept demilitarized zones.[51]

The "imposed agreement" that ended the crisis on the global level did not carry over to the Iraq-Israel axis. Since Israel was not formally a belligerent in the war and never had a formal interstate relationship with Iraq, the war ended as it had started, by way of a unilateral act. Unilateral conclusions of wars are not extraordinary in the Israel-Iraq milieu. The crisis followed a pattern similar to the one between the two countries during the 1947–1949 war. Resolution 687 did include Israel as one of the states to be compensated by Iraq, even though it was clear that the probability of Iraq paying compensation to Israel was remote. This formal decision to compensate Israel was also new for UN resolutions on the Middle East.

Saddam's replacement might have legitimized the return of Iraq to the fold of the Arab world. Saddam survived because the coalition stopped the war once Iraq had been evicted from Kuwait, but before Iraq itself had been defeated. At the close of this crisis, Saddam used brutal means to suppress two internal upheavals, one in the north by the Kurds, and one in the south by the Shi'ite minority. Despite these domestic events and Saddam's persistence in power, his falling out with much of the Arab world meant that Iraq was effectively marginalized for the immediate future. With time, it became clear that Iraq's army had not been destroyed and that elite units of the Republican Guard had survived. In terms of the Arab-Israeli conflict this meant that Iraq could not be counted out completely for the long run.[52] Indeed, Iraq was partially rehabilitated during Intifada 2000 when it participated in the October Arab summit.

Iraq's defeat implied the temporary disruption of Israel's eastern front, thus transforming the conventional balance of power. The inspection regime established by the UN and its partial destruction of Iraq's nonconventional weapons further strengthened the strategic status quo. The minimal Russian role throughout the crisis confirmed that the Middle East had fallen under the influence of one superpower—the United States. Washington's paramount role in the crisis and in the region bore implications for both the distribution of power as well as for institutionalism.

A unilateral termination of a crisis is not conducive to a stable post-crisis system. However, American preeminence in the Middle East did not allow the unilateral termination of the Israel-Iraq encounter to suspend the Middle East peace process. Officially, the U.S. administration rejected Saddam's linkage strategy, but in fact, the United States had accepted a Gulf war nexus with the Arab-Israeli conflict.[53] Hence, in March 1991 while the details of the formal cease-fire with Iraq were being worked out, the secretary of state headed for the Middle East in hopes of reviving the Middle East peace process, which had been interrupted by the Gulf crisis.

The Bush-Baker administration decided to try to advance the peace process via a "two track concept," which in itself insinuated both the linkage principle and the compound conflict structure. The two track negotiations that followed the war envisioned a Palestinian-Israeli dialogue coupled with a regional conference among Israel and the Arab states. By separating the two strands, Baker highlighted the difference between the two conflicts: one interethnic and the other interstate. Yet by organizing them simultaneously, he also reassured the Arab states that the United States was aware of the overlap between them. The timing of Baker's Middle East trip, while the terms of the ceasefire were being worked out, indicated that the advancement of the Arab-Israeli peace process was an integral part of the termination of the Gulf crisis, a quid pro quo for the role the Arab states had played in it and a basic condition for a stable Middle East.

Realizing that a window of opportunity for movement on the Arab-Israeli peace process had opened up in the wake of Gulf crisis, Secretary Baker recommended to President Bush that he undertake personal diplomacy. In the spring and summer of 1991, Baker opened a round of shuttle diplomacy that ultimately generated two major events: the Madrid conference and the Oslo process. The fact that two separate administrations in Israel and the United States advanced each event indicated the strength of the process at the system level.[54]

FROM MADRID TO OSLO: CHANGE AT THE
ETHNIC-STATE LEVEL

The 30 October 1991 Madrid conference and the various diplomatic encounters between Arabs and Israelis that evolved in the early 1990s emanated partly from the Intifada and more immediately from the Gulf crisis. The robustness of the negotiations, however, stemmed from the broader process that had started in the mid-1970s.[55]

Several characteristics of the Madrid conference reflected the major obstacles that both sides had to overcome. First, Madrid was dubbed a "peace" conference due to Shamir's objection to an "international" conference, a term that could allow the Arabs to claim that they had participated in indirect negotiations. The attendance of the United States and the Soviet Union, as well as the participation of the UN and European delegations, would have provided such a cover. Technically co-sponsored by the two superpowers, in essence the United States exercised preeminent control at the conference. Second, Israel insisted that only state delegates participate in the conference, effectively block-ing the PLO and limiting the Palestinians to participating as part of the Jordanian delegation. Third, no negotiations would be conducted nor decisions made at the plenary. The negotiations were to continue via two formats: (1) three sets of direct, bilateral negotiations between Israel and a Jordanian-Palestinian delegation, Israel and Syria, and Israel and Lebanon, and (2) multi-lateral negotiations about arms control, water, economic development, refugees, and the environment in which many countries would participate.

The basis of Madrid was the distinction between bilateral and multilateral issues. The bilateral negotiations aimed at resolving purely political areas of dis-agreement and were devised to be direct face to face negotiations. The multi-lateral format dealt with regional concerns that can be classified as cross-state or transnational issues, some of which the literature considers "functional," and we can dub it as institution building.[56] International institutionalism appeared also in the form of a Middle East Development Bank. Baker envisioned a bank in which the more prosperous regional states would invest so that the bank could finance regional development.[57]

Although Baker had stated before the House Foreign Operations Subcommittee that the peace process would "proceed simultaneously along two tracks involving direct negotiations between Israel and the Arab states and between Israel and the Palestinians,"[58] the ethnonational Palestinian issue formally was embedded in the bilateral negotiations between Israel and the joint Jordanian-Palestinian delegation. When the Madrid bilateral talks moved to Washington, the Palestinians insisted on separate negotiations, which the Israeli delegation rejected. Unable to reach a compromise on this procedural matter, unofficial negotiations took place in the corridor pending an official resolution. In January 1992 the mul-tilateral conference on arms control opened in Moscow, including Israel, Egypt, Jordan, and also Saudi Arabia, Oman, Morocco, and Tunis. The Palestinians showed up but left when they were refused independent representation. Syria and Lebanon refused from the outset to participate in the multilateral negotiations, preferring to focus the bargaining on the bilateral issues. From behind the scenes, the PLO directed the Palestinian delegation at the talks in Washington to block progress pending recognition of the PLO itself. Even after the change of government in Israel from a Likud to a Labor-led coalition, in June 1992, Elayakim Rubinstein remained as the head of the Israeli delegation in Washington and the PLO kept as its delegate Haider Abdul- Shafi. But in early March 1993, Rabin agreed to allow Faisal Husseini, who had been rejected by Shamir because of his Jerusalem resi-dence, to join the Palestinian delegation.[59] Despite this gesture, the Palestinian del-egation pressed its demands: the PLO wanted recognition from Israel. A Palestinian delegate to the Washington talks, Saeb Erakat, stated openly at a conference at Bir Zeit University that the PLO strategy was to block progress in Washington in order to prompt Rabin to deal directly with Arafat.[60]

The PLO plan succeeded. On 20–22 January 1993, Foreign Minister Peres authorized Israeli academicians to meet PLO officials in Sarpsborg, near Oslo.

Prime Minister Yitzhak Rabin was informed of the opening of the Oslo talks in early February.[61] Ongoing Israeli negotiations with top Arafat deputies and PLO leaders Ahmed Qurai (Abu Alaa) and Mahmoud Abbas (Abu Mazen) ultimately provided the PLO with a path to recognition by Israel. The PLO was adamant that any progress in the negotiations would come in Oslo, where Israel was dealing with the PLO, and not in Washington, where Israel was talking to Palestinians from the territories. With time, the center of gravity moved from the formal avenue in Washington to the informal one in Norway. The product of the Oslo talks was the 13 September 1993 agreement between the PLO and the state of Israel and a formal cessation of the Intifada by the PLO.[62]

The Rabin government's goal in the emerging agreement was to accomplish partition, a traditional Labor approach to resolving the Palestinian-Jewish interethnic protracted conflict. The importation of terror to Israeli cities convinced Israelis that they must separate from the Palestinians. It was this notion of "separation," a code word for partition, that Prime Minister Rabin used in the wake of the wave of indiscriminate anti-Israeli terrorism that followed the signing of Oslo.[63] While ready to terminate all acts of PLO terrorism and accept responsibility for PLO actions, Arafat either could not or would not rein in Hamas terror.[64]

Iraq's repeated missile attacks on Israeli cities reinforced the positions of those asserting that the territories did not provide Israel with absolute security. The Gulf crisis was also responsible for the international low status of Arafat, who had supported Saddam Hussein. The discovery of an advanced Iraqi nuclear program convinced Rabin and other Israeli security-oriented policy makers that Israel must make peace with its immediate Arab neighbors before the more distant hostile Arab and Moslem states acquired mass destruction capability[65]. Moreover, the Scuds demonstrated to the Israeli public how radical regimes could abuse the Palestinian problem to advancing their own goals.[66]

The Israeli-Palestinian mutual recognition and negotiations allowed King Hussein to work out a peace agreement with Israel, signed on 26 October 1994. The treaty between Hussein and Rabin ensured the Hashemites a special role in managing the holy places in Jerusalem especially the Dome of the Rock and Al Aqsa Mosques, a fact not appreciated by the Palestinians. The issue of the holy places was to re-emerge in the July 200 Camp David summit leading to the breakdown of the talks between Prime Minister Ehud Barak and Chairman Ararfat. It was clear from any perspective that the peace with Jordan was much warmer than the one signed with the PLO and even with Egypt.[67]

The Israeli-Jordanian treaty reflected both the linkage between the interstate and interethnic dimensions and the differences between the two domains. Jordan could formalize its peace with Israel only following Oslo, but once transformation in the ethnic-state domain took place the institutional arrangements set up proved more solid than those between Israel and the Palestinians. The major issues comprising the Israeli-Jordanian peace treaty were classically interstate: borders, water, and security. On both border and water issues Israel accepted Jordan's claims and agreed to compensate its eastern neighbor. On the security issue, Jordan rewarded Israel with what had always concerned its national security makers—a Jordanian commitment not to allow a third country (i.e., Iraq) to deploy forces in that country. Other important areas included a Jordanian role in Moslem shrines in Jerusalem, economic cooperation, interconnection of the two nations' electricity grids, and other issues of interdependence.[68] With the United States as a guarantor, the peace treaty constituted a package of security elements and components of promoting interdependence, both reinforced by international institutions.

The Israeli–Palestinian track proved more bumpy. The difficulties of resolving the ethnic-state dimension of the conflict were demonstrated in the two years that followed the Declaration of Principles (DOP). Arafat arrived in Gaza on 1 July 1994 and installed a new Palestinian Authority (PA) in Gaza and Jericho. Negotiations between Israel and the PA produced another agreement, known as Oslo II, in September 1995.

Extremist forces opposed to the peace process from both camps tried to derail the agreement with violence. The Hebron massacre of Palestinians at prayer by Dr. Baruch Goldstein on 25 February 1994 and Hamas suicide bombings in the heart of major Israeli cities epitomized the determination of hardline Jews and Arabs to halt the peace process. Despite the outbreak of indiscriminate violence, Israel and the PA tried to overcome their domestic opposition; with Oslo II Israel agreed to transfer all eight Arab cities (area A) in the West Bank (with the exception of the Jewish part of Hebron) to the PA, thus alleviating Israel from contact with a major share of the Palestinian populace. Area B, which included the Arab villages, was under Arab civilian control and an "overriding" Israeli security authority. Area C encompassed the rest of the West Bank (approximately 70 percent) and fell under total Israeli jurisdiction.[69] In short, Oslo reflected the quest for a termination of the ethnic dimension of the Arab–Israeli conflict.

The Syrian–Israeli negotiations were the third track that opened in Madrid. But this path was much harder than the Jordanian one. The Golan Heights was primarily a security issue and a factor in the balance of power, but an Israeli–Syrian peace would also denote the formal conclusion of the Arab–Israeli interstate conflict. As such it carried also some institutional bearings. The formula proposed by Prime Minister Rabin in May 1993, that the depth of withdrawal would be equivalent to the depth of peace, reflected a combination of security and institutional arrangements. Controversy persisted over the strength and breadth of institutions erected to support an Israeli–Syrian peace. Negotiations concentrated on territorial withdrawal and the depth of peace, as well as Confidence and Security Building Measures (CSBMs). But negotiations were hampered by symbols and gestures loaded with mistrust. While Israel expected a gesture along the lines of Sadat's Jerusalem visit in 1977, President Hafez Assad saw in allowing his chief of staff or, later on, his foreign minister to negotiate with Israel a major motion. During intensive negotiations between Syria and the Rabin-Peres government the distance between the positions of the two sides narrowed, but three major issues resisted resolution:(1) The depth of withdrawal: while Syria demanded a return to the 4 June 1967 border, the Rabin-Peres government proposed a return to the international border, already a deviation from the traditional position that Israel must stay at least on the ridges of the Golan. The 4 June 1967 line meant Syrian control of the slopes of the Banias River, Hamat Gader, and the eastern bank of the Sea of Galilee; (2) The extent of peace: while Israel demanded a comprehensive peace supported by full economic, political, and cultural relations and open borders, Damascus perceived a full peace in more narrow terms of a termination of the state of war. The difference between the positions meant conflicting opinions as to the breadth of institutions supporting the peace, with Damascus interested in a narrow scope and Israel in the broadest range possible; (3) Security arrangements and CSBMs: two issue-areas remained problematic. First, Israel demanded a ratio of 9:1 demilitarization between the two countries, while Syria finally dropped its insistence on symmetrical demilitarization and limited-force zones and suggested a 10:6 ratio . Second, Israel wanted early warning stations on the Golan and Mount Hermon while Syria opposed the establishment of any surveillance and verification systems on its territory, even if manned by Americans, not Israelis. Another issue of contention concerned the establishment of a regional arms control regime, with Syria demanding an Israeli signature on the Non-Proliferation Treaty (NPT).[70]

After Prime Minister Rabin's assassination in November 1995, Syrian-Israeli talks resumed in 1996 at the Wye plantation in Virginia. When Prime Minister Shimon Peres called for early national elections, the Syrian-Israeli track was suspended for the campaign period. The election of Binyamin Netanyahu of the right-wing Likud party seemed to close the Syrian peace track. Nevertheless, indirect talks continued between Jerusalem and Damascus via the services of American Jewish leader Ron Lauder and later president of Major Jewish Organizations. The details of proposals that Netanyahu forwarded to Assad were the subject of debate between Labor and Likud following the May 1999 Barak victory. In the ensuing period the new Labor government tried to resume the Israeli-Syrian negotiations, with direct talks between Barak and the Syrian foreign minister taking place in Wye. An Assad-Clinton Geneva meeting in March 2000 failed to accomplish any breakthrough. Assad insisted on full Israeli withdrawal to the pre–June 1967 borders. Assad's death in June 2000 brought the peace process to a halt.

OPERATION GRAPES OF WRATH, 1996

It was during the April 1996 pre-election period in Israel that Prime Minister Peres launched Operation Grapes of Wrath in Lebanon. This crisis was not included in the ICB since it occurred after completion of the project but its attributes accord with the ICB definition of an international crisis. According the typology presented in chapter 1, the crisis belongs to the ethnic-state category, the most prevalent one during the post-1973 years. In many ways, the crisis is a twin to the 1993 Operation Accountability. The persistence of near-identical low level magnitude crisis attributes three years after Operation Accountability ended demonstrates that the transformation of the conflict in the 1990s into low intensity and ethnic was in effect.

The context of the crisis was essentially the Peres government's fear of seeming "soft" in the low intensity war it was fighting with the Moslem-fundamentalist Hizbullah in Lebanon. Syria, frustrated with the lack of Israeli concessions on the Golan Heights, supported the Shia Hizbullah extremists who were conducting a prolonged guerilla campaign to expel the IDF from Lebanon. Israel aspired to reach some security regime arrangements on its northern border, probably also entailing the maintenance of its South Lebanon "Security Zone." By contrast, Hizbullah rejected the status quo and pursued a more daring policy toward Israel. Syria, Lebanon, and Iran were also involved in this conflict, as was the United States.

The crisis started on 9 April 1996 when Hizbullah fired thirty Katusha rockets into Kiryat-Shmona in northern Israel and the next day four Israeli soldiers were killed in Lebanon. Israel responded on 11 April with a strike against Hizbullah bases and targets as far north as Beirut. Lebanon followed its routine procedure in crises and called for a UN Security Council meeting. Lebanese Prime Minister Rafik El-Hariri traveled to Damascus to consult with Assad and then went on to Cairo and Paris to achieve support against Israel. The Israeli attacks on Lebanon were primarily by air, artillery, and Precise Guided Munitions (PGM), imitating the Gulf war. The operation ended badly when an Israeli missile missed its target and hit a UN post in Qana, killing more than 100 refugees. Worldwide condemnation forced Israel to lower its terms for a full ceasefire agreement.

The manner in which the crisis was handled puts it in the CMT category of multiple techniques including violence. Throughout the crisis, Israeli-Hizbullah low level violence was simultaneously accompanied by negotiations involving several Arab states, Israel, Hizbullah, the United States, and France.[71]

The official ceasefire settlement was a semiformal agreement drafted by the United States between Israel and Hizbullah, with Lebanon, Syria, and France behind. Lebanon also gave the United States a non-written pledge to restrain Hizbullah and agreed to the establishment of a followup committee. The United States, Israel, Lebanon, Syria, and France comprised the committee established to monitor alleged ceasefire violations. The commitment to halt the firing, however, was limited to civilian targets on both sides, implicitly condoning continued conflict in the security zone between Hizbullah and the Southern Lebanese Army supported by the IDF.

Operation Grapes of Wrath is a typical crisis of the 1990s; it contains many of the attributes of the transformed Arab-Israeli conflict. It was an ethnic-state confrontation in which rival state actors, including the U.S. superpower, played major roles. During the crisis the violence included three levels of weapons and warfare: sub-conventional, conventional, and PGM weapons that had proven themselves in the Gulf war. Negotiations accompanied the violence throughout the crisis. Finally, the outcome was not unilateral, as had been customary in previous ethnic-state crises, but rather a combination of semiformal and formal agreements. Despite the agreements, however, the confrontation continued in the post-crisis period, at a low intensity warfare level. In May 2000, Israel's new prime minister Ehud Barak made good on an election campaign promise and ordered a unilateral withdrawal from Lebanon. Four and one-half months later, at the outset of a new Palestinian Intifada, the Hizbullah kidnaped three Israeli soldiers as bargaining chips for the release of Lebanese and Palestinian prisoners in Israel. This act, in addition to the Hizbullah demand for the return of the Shebaa farm, put an end to Israeli hopes that its implementation of UN Resolution 425 and the announcement by the UN secretary general Kofi Annan that Israel had fulfilled all the requirements in terms of the border between the two states would end the conflict. This continuation of the conflict and inconclusive denouement resembled that of other compound conflicts elsewhere around the globe and especially the Israeli-Palestinian one.

INTIFADA 2000

Indeed, the Israeli-Palestinian relationship continued to be conflict ridden despite the series of accommodations brought about by the first and second Oslo agreements in 1993 and 1995 respectively. A major wave of violence erupted in the spring of 1996 when Hamas executed a series of terror acts by blowing up buses inside Israel, causing dozens of Israeli deaths. Hamas terrorism soured Labor voters on the peace process and led to the election in 1996 of Likud leader Binyamin Netanyahu. A second outbreak of major violence occurred in September 1996 after the Netanyahu government authorized the opening of a tunnel in Jerusalem that led to the Temple Mount, although the tunnel did not structurally impinge upon the Muslim holy sites.

The Netanyahu government, which openly objected to the Oslo accords, nonetheless continued negotiating with Arafat's Palestinian Authority and reached the Hebron agreement of January 1997, which included almost a full Israeli pullback from the last Palestinian city. In October 1998 Netanyahu signed the Washington (Wye) agreement, where he promised to transfer another 13 percent of the West Bank to the PA. However, in March 1999, unable to implement the Wye agreements, the Netanyahu government fell. Netanyahu's years in power were characterized overall by a mixture of halfhearted negotiations, perceived provocations by the Arabs, and low intensity sporadic violence in both Lebanon and the territories.

Prime Minister Ehud Barak, having run on a platform promising a final peace agreement, turned immediately to fulfilling his promise. Recruiting

President Mubarak, he convened the Sharm conference and signed an agreement with Chairman Arafat to implement the withdrawal promised by Netanyahu. In addition, they agreed to reach a final framework peace accord within fifteen months. The two leaders failed to agree on the framework a year later, in July 2000, at Camp David under the auspices of President Clinton. Chairman Arafat walked away from an unprecedented Israeli offer, which reportedly included around 95 percent of the West Bank, all of the Gaza Strip, and even parts of Jerusalem in exchange for a full peace. Despite its early threat to declare a state on 13 September, leaders in the United States, Europe, and some Arab states persuaded the PA to postpone that highly charged decision.

But hopes for the further winding down of the Jewish-Palestinian conflict came to a halt two weeks later with the outbreak of a second Intifada, dubbed the Al Aqsa Intifada, by the Palestinians. The trigger to the outbreak of violence was officially the September 28 visit to the Temple Mount by opposition leader Ariel Sharon. In the ensuing violent demonstrations twenty Israeli policemen and ten Palestinians were wounded. The next day, following the Friday sermons at the Haram al-Sharif, as the Temple Mount is called by Moslems, in violent clashes seven Palestinians were killed. The widening of the demonstrations brought more casualties. A significant expansion of the conflict occurred on 1 October when Israeli Arabs joined the demonstrations and blocked strategic passes between the coast and the Galilee such as the Vadi Ara. In skirmishes with the Israeli police over the course of several days, thirteen Israeli Arabs were killed. The linkage between the two groups reinforced the interethnic character of the Israeli-Palestinian conflict. Most threatening to Israel was the linkage between the self-identification of Israeli Arabs nationally as Palestinians and the riots in the West Bank and Gaza. To the Israeli Arabs, most intimidating was the fact that the Israeli police used live bullets against Israeli citizens.

While the Palestinian Intifada seemed detached from the Lebanese withdrawal, the Palestinians saw Hizbullah success in getting Israel out of Lebanon as a model they could use to get the IDF out of the West Bank and Gaza and maybe beyond. On the Israeli side, the initial threat of the Arab violence was the Lebanonization of the Israeli-Palestinian conflict. A series of side road explosions in the Gaza Strip in September preceded the Sharon visit, emulating the warfare in Lebanon that ultimately resulted in an Israeli unilateral withdrawal. Following the Israeli pullback Arafat repeatedly proclaimed that he also demanded a total Israeli withdrawal in the West Bank and Gaza similar to that in Lebanon. The linkage with Lebanon was further strengthened on 7 October when Hizbullah penetrated the international border between Israel and Lebanon and captured three Israeli soldiers. In late October, UN secretary general Kofi Annan came to the Middle East to negotiate both the Palestinian and Hizbullah confrontations with Israel, without much success.

Another concern of Israel was the renewed threat by Arafat to declare independence unilaterally, an act several times pledged and then postponed.

Presumably, the borders set forth by the PA would be at least the pre-1967 lines and Eastern Jerusalem, thus including more than a hundred Israeli settlements with a combined population of 200,000 Jews. For Israel the threat was a territorial one. The Palestinians also faced at most a territorial threat. Given the close watch by the international media and the potential of Arab states' intervention on their behalf, an existential threat or even one of grave damage did not seem impending. Israel has threatened that should the PA unilaterally declare a state Israel would retaliate with a unilateral annexation of territories in the West Bank and the Gaza Strip. The territories to be annexed by Barak were not specified. However, the fall of the Labor government brought in its wake a Likud government, which threatened to annex a large share of West Bank territories, but not conquer the Palestinian cities.

Despite Arafat's attempt to pull in other Arab states, the main crisis actors remained the Israelis and the Palestinians. The encounter, to be sure, evoked popular support in many Arab countries, with strong religious expressions in Moslem countries. Egyptian President Mubarak convened an Arab summit for 21 October.[72] In the ensuing weeks and despite ongoing violence moderate states such as Egypt and Jordan warned against the use of violence. At the Arab summit all the Arab states supported the Palestinian Intifada, putting full blame on Israel. The call to break relations was limited to the Arab states that did not sign an official peace treaty, thus excluding Jordan and Egypt which ultimately did call back their ambassadors for consultations. The more extreme bloc led by Syria, Yemen, and Iraq demanded more radical resolutions.[73] Saddam Hussein moved some of Iraq's military divisions to western Iraq, closer to Jordan's borders. Israel's concern was that this was more an attempt by Saddam to assault the nuclear reactor in Dimona, as retaliation for the IDF's 1981 strike, than a military intervention.[74]

The great powers carried on primarily as actors in crisis. President Clinton's characterization of Arafat as intransigent at Camp David was one of the prods to the PA chairman's decision to order the Tanzim (Arafat's militia) to escalate the crisis.[75] With Clinton hoping that the Middle East peace process would be the crown jewel in his legacy, the United States tried to end the crisis from its inception by forcing the sides to stop the violence. But Washington was not alone. The Europeans, especially France and Russia, had long aspired to reduce the overwhelming U.S. role in the peace process. Thus, less than a week into the crisis Barak and Arafat were summoned to Paris on 4 October, where Secretary of State Albright was visiting, so that she could try to impose a cease-fire agreement. Ironically, French president Jacques Chirac's wanting to jump in spoiled the agreement, by strengthening Arafat's demand for an international inquiry. Barak, insulted by the French approach, abstained from participating the next day in another conference in Sharm-el-Sheikh with President Mubarak.[76]

U.S. entanglement derived not only from the personal aspirations of its president. On 9 October a terrorist bombing of the U.S.S. *Cole* while refueling in the port of Yemen killed seventeen U.S. sailors. While the attack was linked to international terrorist groups such as the Aden-Abyen Islamic Army or followers of Osama Bin Laden, the act further induced the United States to intervene in the crisis in order to stabilize the situation. An eruption of the Arab-Israeli conflict did not serve American interests in the region. With ongoing violence between Israelis and Palestinians reaching new heights with the lynching of two Israeli soldiers by a mob in Ramallah, the American president arranged for a another round of personal diplomacy in Sharm el-Sheikh on 16 October. At this conference, President Clinton engineered a ceasefire plan between Arafat and Barak, but violent events on the ground overtook almost immediately. President Clinton did not give up and appointed the Mitchell Committee on 8 November. The mandate of this committee was to inquire who brought about the outbreak of violence and to suggest remedies.

Intensive diplomatic involvement by the United States in the crisis throughout the fighting determined the process of crisis management as one encompassing both negotiations and coercion, or to use ICB language, multiple including violence. From the outset, the Israeli government did not abandon the peace process even while expressing doubts as to whether it had a partner to peace.[77] Israel and the PA maintained their ties both at the military level, where officers continued meeting, and at the political level, where envoys were passing messages between Barak and Arafat. Kofi Annan, UN Secretary General, and U.S. officials including CIA Director George Tenet also served as diplomats in this crisis. Tenet, despite some criticism from within his organization, served as a personal presidential envoy between Arafat and Barak while reporting to his boss on the status of the crisis[78]. While violence claimed casualties on both sides on a daily basis, Clinton carried on with personal telephone calls to both leaders.

In terms of levels of violence, from an interethnic perspective, we define the process of interaction as serious clashes. According to the B'tselem, the Israel Information Center for Human Rights, and the Palestinian Red Crescent, at the end of December 2000 the Palestinian toll reached 278 dead and over 10,000 wounded.[79] The Israeli casualty toll was 42 dead and almost 500 wounded.[80] Undoubtedly, Intifada 2000 was higher in violence than the 1987 Intifada since, from its inception, the Palestinians in the more recent crisis were using firearms and even antitank rockets, while Israel struck with tanks and Cobra helicopters. In these incidents the PA police joined the Tanzim militia, turning demonstrations and other confrontations into battles between opposing military forces. The imbalance between the two militaries resulted in an imbalance in casualties in Israel's favor.

During the last decade of the twentieth century Arab-Israeli crises thus continued to reflect the main themes of this book: the winding down of the conflict that had started in the mid-1970s and the reality of ongoing ethnonational instability and crises. Along with the decline in interstate confrontations, an Israeli-Jordanian peace treaty, and an emergent Israeli-Palestinian peace process, the ethnonational dimension and the threat from weapons of mass destruction moved to center stage. The two Intifadas, the Gulf war, and the two military encounters in Lebanon with Hizbullah illustrate these points. The first Intifada was a limited form of ethnonational rebellion ultimately followed by Israeli-Palestinian direct negotiations. The Gulf war, despite the Iraqi Scud attacks, did not turn into a full-fledged Arab-Israeli confrontation; Israel refrained from implementing its right to retaliate and the peace process accelerated after the war. Operation Accountability and the Grapes of Wrath campaign did not go beyond the ethnic-state level and ended with tacit/semiformal agreements, and ultimately led to a unilateral Israeli withdrawal according to UN Resolution 425. In their eventual arrival at negotiated settlements, the crises of the 1990s differed greatly from those of the pre-1973 period. The primacy of ethnic-state crises indicated the new features of the ongoing Arab-Israeli conflict. Their linkage with the interstate level is something yet to be determined, an issue we leave for the concluding chapter.

CHAPTER 7

UNDERSTANDING
TRANSFORMATION IN THE
ARAB-ISRAELI CONFLICT

The main purpose of this book was to measure and explain change in the Arab-Israeli conflict. In its examination of conflict, crisis and war, this study posed three core questions: 1. Was there change in the attributes of international crises over time? 2. If yes, in which dimensions and directions did change take place? 3. Why did changes in conflict occur? In addressing these queries we purposely drew on multiple scholarly approaches thereby making three theoretical contributions to the international relations field. First, in explaining change we articulated our theory in a terminology taken from both major contending schools in contemporary international relations theory: realism and institutionalism. Second, our empirical research combined quantitative and qualitative methods of analysis. Third, we integrated the ethnonational dimension into our analysis.

This book, as noted at the onset, is divided thematically into seven chapters. Chapter 1 presented the theoretical framework for all further analysis. Chapters 2, 3 and 4 analyzed the interstate dimension, while chapters 5 and 6 focussed primarily on the ethnic dimension of the conflict. Chapter 7 now integrates the interstate and ethnic aspects and suggests directions for new research.

The findings from Chapters 2, 3 and 4 point to a clear conclusion regarding all three core questions guiding this research: change occurred, but not in the same degree or with identical timing in all crisis attributes, and the theoretical conditions for change provide a viable basis for the explanation of change in conflict dynamics. In the ethnonational dimension of the conflict, analyzed in chapters 5 and 6, the trends and explanations are less pronounced but still affirmative. Our conclusions below will unfold according the structure of the book and its research questions. At the end of the chapter we shall add some policy comments regarding our ability to analyze the direction of the conflict.

We conducted our research of this book in the midst of a post-Oslo trend suggesting the winding down of the Arab-Israeli conflict. We tried to test this apparently positive inclination with empirical evidence. Indeed, despite the outbreak of strife and violence in the Israeli-Palestinian arena in September 2000, our theoretical framework and empirical evidence supported the perhaps surprising argument that at the close of the twentieth century, the fierceness of the Arab-Israeli conflict has been subsiding. Taking a broad and comprehensive view of almost a hundred years of conflict and over fifty years of international crises, we discovered that for the last two decades and a half a gradual decline has occurred in the frequency and magnitude of international crises in the Arab-Israeli arena. Against this trend, we also noticed the vigorousness of ethnic-state and interethnic types of crises. While we observed some modification in the Jewish-Palestinian sphere of the conflict, it was less pronounced than in the interstate domain. The evaluation of these changes gains significance given the enduring condition of the conflict. The question we leave open is whether the ethnic elements will pull the entire conflict back to its former rigid and hostile nature.

DETECTING CHANGE

In order to respond to our core questions, we devised an index for measuring magnitude and explaining change in crises. An international crisis among states was designated in this study as a critical stage in the transition from stability to the use of force in world politics. We assumed that the reduction of such occurrences, or modifications in the mode of behavior within them, would reflect both change in the pattern of relations among the involved actors as well as the introduction of rules and regulations. An international crisis can deteriorate into war but it can also shift toward stability. Hence, we chose state behavior in international crises as an indicator of a potential transition from an anarchical order to one that is more stable. The duration of a crisis was regarded as a period characterized by the dynamics of transition from normal relations range to violent interactions and back. On the basis of the above, we assumed that an international crisis—a microcosm of international politics and condensed change—would be an effective vehicle through which to evaluate the potential transformation from total conflict to a more regulated rivalry and perhaps even further, to some level of cooperation in a protracted conflict.

To capture the dual nature of conflict, with its static and dynamic components, we chose to focus on the core attributes of international crises as operational indicators of conflict trends. Thus, the role played by crisis, an event that can be observed, is to represent the unobserved variable of international conflict.

Cumulative evaluations of the "state of the art" of international relations theory and its contribution to our understanding of past and present world politics specify several criteria that should be applied: description, causal explanations, and prediction.[1] To meet the criterion of description—that is, to analyze the course of change and to detect nuances that characterize the dynamics of conflict over time—we adopted international crisis and its associated empirical evidence; specifically, data from the Middle East section of Michael Brecher and Jonathan Wilkenfeld's International Crisis Behavior (ICB) project.

Our own index of crisis magnitude (CMI) enabled measurement of the extent of change in crisis attributes, which is critical in the accomplishment of all other goals in this study. As developed in chapter 1, the CMI consists of three realms: context, process, and outcome. Within each domain, specific crisis attributes have been designated as core indicators of magnitude, designed to capture the extent of distortion that occurs during an international crisis and reflect nuances of change when such take place. By methodically analyzing our three context indicators (threat escalation reduction, the number of actors, and the level of superpower involvement), assessing the two process variables (types of crisis management and the scope of violence) and taking into account the extent of accommodation marking crisis termination, our research identified key dimensions of change. We turn now to the findings related to each of the CMI indicators.

TRENDS AND AREAS OF CHANGE

Our second task was to identify the main trends and areas of change in crisis and link these changes in crises with trends in the conflict; to evaluate whether change in crises dynamics reflects upon trends in conflict. We began our analysis with an exploration of the Arab-Israeli protracted conflict in search for nuances of change and transformation. Using our CMI, the first general conclusion we reached was that change did take place. All of the magnitude indicators measured in this study suggested that in the years 1974–2000 the Arab-Israeli conflict has been winding down. Over time, the gravity of crises has diminished, the number of crisis actors has shrunk, and the level of both military and political involvement by superpowers has decreased. This trend was matched, to a more limited extent, by a decline in the severity of crisis violence and a move to more peaceful modes of crisis management. Further evidence of the winding down of the Arab-Israeli conflict emerged from analysis of the accommodative/nonaccommodative types of crisis outcomes.

Our CMI findings are outlined in the first part of chapter 4. At this stage we underline two insights. First, within the context indicators that point to reduced magnitude marked *inter alia* by more limited scope of superpower participation, the relationship between superpower role in crisis and high magnitude is the smallest of all CMI components. Furthermore, the role of the USSR was more central, with five cases where the primary role was not only diplomatic: 1955 Gaza raid; 1956 Suez war; 1969 War of Attrition; 1973 war; and 1982 Lebanon war, while the United States played such a role only in the 1973 war. All but one of these crises occurred in the first period. Thus, while the superpowers' activity in the Arab-Israeli conflict has exacerbated hostilities through arms shipments and ideological rivalry, during crisis periods they often also played the role of moderating agents. We can explain this difference between the escalating impact of the superpowers in the conflict as a whole, and their moderating role during crises by their fear of confrontation spillover from the regional to a global arena. The balance of power between the superpowers hence, led to both arms races and restraints during international crises.

Second, change in the process realm was relatively smaller than that identified in context, thereby marking a more limited decline in overall crisis magnitude. More specifically, the reduction in scope of violence is somewhat smaller than that of other CMI elements, revealing the strength of modes of operation. Once the Normal Relations Range in this conflict subsumed a certain threshold of violence, it was difficult to change this hostile mode of behavior. The violence-accommodation rationale links adaptation to high levels of violence. It explains why, despite the relatively high levels of violence that characterized most crises, they ended in relative accommodation.

On the whole, the indicators representing context proved to be the most salient in terms of change, followed by those in the realm of outcomes. Indicators of process were the last ones to reveal change. This pattern accorded well with the expectations of the different theories of international politics referenced throughout this book. Indeed, the indicators of context—threat, number of actors, and superpower involvement—concur with power realities, while process indicators and type of outcomes correspond more with the tenets of institutionalism, reflecting insights from the constructivist school.

EXPLAINING CHANGE

Four schools of thought contend to explain conflict and international order: neorealism, which regards order as directly linked to structure; neoliberalism and realism which, while differing on the degree, perceive a role for institutions in promoting order; and constructivism, which totally rejects structure and views cooperation as a result of changing the practice of thought and behavior. Our study sought to bridge the gaps among differing elements from within these various approaches. We acknowledged a prior inclination toward realism as the perspective most appropriate to the study of conflict, crisis, and war in the Middle East. While the institutional approach focused primarily on a specific geographic area or on functional areas, by applying it to a case study of intense conflict where violence is still a viable option, we articulated a more rigorous test for the relevance of institutions in contributing to international order.

Our task was therefore to detect whether the Middle East exhibits the genesis of cooperation coupled with international institution building and regime formulation that might promote regional international order.

On the basis of the four approaches we identify a set of conditions that can be conducive to the transition from an anarchic international system to order or to moderation in a protracted interstate conflict: balance of power, legitimacy, unbearable cost of war, and institutional arrangements. In explaining the transformation of the conflict, we examined, in chapter 4, critical turning points in the evolution of the Arab-Israeli conflict. Only one of the five turning points, in 1973, embraced all four conditions according to our theoretical stipulations. Significantly, the winding down did not begin until all four of the key conditions for conflict transformation simultaneously coexisted. Institutional arrangements in the form of Arab-Israeli armistice agreements had been present since the termination of the first 1947–1949 Palestine partition crisis. A balance of power between Israel and its core Arab adversaries emerged from the Suez war of 1956–1957. Following the 1967 war, the balance of power tilted toward the status quo power—Israel. It was then that the conflict started moving out of its zero-sum determinant, since Israel possessed assets that could be exchanged for legitimacy. But two wars, the 1969 War of Attrition and the 1973 war, broke out before genuine interstate accommodation could be established. During those years, institutional arrangements such as those in UN Resolution 242 and the Rogers A & B plans were suggested and some aspects fully or partially agreed upon. But genuine transformation came only following 1973, when the staggering cost of war became apparent to all the combatants. The lesson to draw from this comparative analysis is that, at least in the Middle East, neither a balance of power structure nor the conclusion of agreements and the establishment of institutions, in themselves, can promote stability.

Institutional elements involving legitimacy, norms, and regime formulation supplement structural realities. The gradual emergence of norms, involving mutual acceptance and the awareness of overwhelming costs of war by all parties, complemented the balance of power and made the initiation of crisis, violence, and war seem increasingly unreasonable. In addition, over time increased legitimacy surfaced from the diverse institutional arrangements that were reached between the parties, such as the 1949 ceasefire boundaries, the coupling of peace and security for all the Middle East countries introduced in UN Resolution 242, and the Camp David accords, which all contributed to an incremental buildup of mutual recognition and the joint use of regulative measures to prevent escalation. As Intifada 2000 has indicated, the Arab-Israeli conflict is far from being resolved and the gap in core interests between rivals still remains a barrier to long-term peace and stability in the region. But even during periods of crisis and swelling popular anti-Israel sentiment in the Arab world, the maintenance of the peace treaties between Israel and states such as Egypt and Jordan has led to compromise, accommodation, and conflict regulation, often without crossing the threshold of either crisis or violence and sometimes through a combined use of controlled violence and negotiations. At different points in the first months of Intifada 2000, both Egypt and Jordan registered displeasure with Israel, but significantly, via diplomatically appropriate means such as delaying the arrival of the new Jordanian ambassador to Israel and the recalling of the Egyptian ambassador.

Our book embraces both a rigorous quantitative approach that advocates the use of comparative analysis as the only appropriate form of research to validate theory, and the qualitative approach, which supports individualized case-study research as the core tool that enables scholars to understand the nuances of regional attributes and the fine details reflecting change over a prolonged time. Rather than taking a stand on the merits of each approach, we used both so as to gain from the advantages each offers. In chapters 2, 3, and the first half of 4 we used ICB derived data, variables, and quantitative modes of data analysis to establish trends in crisis magnitude and to identify the dynamics of change in conflict. In the second part of chapter 4, we complemented our quantitative approach with a qualitative comparison of major potential and real turning points in the conflict that embodied part or all of the conditions we had outlined earlier as the sources of change. Parts of chapter 5 and all of 6 continued the traditional case-study approach.

This convergence between quantitative-oriented analysis of trends and attributes based on ICB data and explanations derived from traditional-qualitative comparative analysis strengthened the validity of our conclusions regarding the effects of structure, legitimacy, costs of war, and institutionalism—our four explanatory conditions. We therefore expect that these conditions will apply to other conflicts as well and can add to a better understanding of conflict transformation and stability in world politics.

THE ETHNIC DIMENSION

From a theoretical standpoint, another major novelty in our study of the Arab-Israeli conflict is the inclusion of the ethnic dimension, together with the traditional-realist study of international conflict, crisis, and war. Recognizing that one of the special features of the Arab-Israeli conflict was the role of ethnic actors in triggering and escalating crises and their intense involvement in defining the issues on the interstate conflict agenda, we complemented our realist-institutional framework for explaining conflict transformation with an ethnic perspective.

The transformation that came about in the mid-1970s denoted dual change in magnitude and in domain. This was true for the respective types of crises identified in this study: interstate crises—namely, events involving at least two states in which the ethnic factor does not play any role; ethnic-state crises —that is, incidents in which a Non-State ethnic Actor (NSA) is preeminent in triggering a crisis between or among states, defining the issues at stake, and/or participating in hostilities; and interethnic crises—consisting of hostile encounters between two or more ethnic groups within one polity that do not involve an interstate confrontation.

From 1947 to 1973 crisis magnitude was high, the number of interstate cases was not significantly higher than that of the ethnic-state type crisis, but the main contribution to high magnitude came from the interstate domain. By contrast, in the post-1973 period, overall magnitude declined and it is clear that the ethnic-state domain became the major source of regional instability. Significantly, changes in the interstate domain preceded those in the ethnic-state one. At the same time ethnicity seems to be the primary source for the enduring nature of the conflict. This conclusion accords with Edward Azar's notion that ethnic elements cultivate the endurance of protracted conflicts.

The importance of the ethnonational factor in the Arab-Israeli conflict is evident from the chronological history of the dispute. The Palestinian-Jewish ethnonational rivalry preceded (1917–1948), coexisted with (1948–1973), and will probably outlast the interstate Arab-Israeli conflict. In the 1917–1948 period, the interethnic conflict played a central role. In the 1948–1973 period, the high magnitude wars between contiguous states drew attention away from the ethnonational dimension of the conflict. And yet, our analysis of crisis attributes revealed that even during the interstate period, almost half of the crises contained an ethnic element. Throughout this period ethnic NSAs were able to draw states into actions of severe violence. At the same time these actors were much less successful in initiating war or in concluding crisis by compromise embodied in formal agreements. But interstate power relations did make a difference; the Palestinians could drag the weaker Jordanians into war, but not the stronger Egyptians. Similarly, they could turn weak Lebanon into a battlefield, but not strong Syria. In the post-1973 period, the emergence of the PLO as the recognized representative of the Palestinians allowed Egypt, who was faced with the set of conditions mentioned above, to extricate itself from the confrontation. In turn, the withdrawal of Egypt ultimately forced the PLO to compromise its positions and to reduce its destabilizing impact on the conflict. We ascertained thus the centrality of interstate power relations even in ethnonational conflicts. Similarly, during the Intifada 2000, the Palestinian Authority, recognizing the centrality of the interstate power relations, was trying to introduce more involvement of the Arab states and/or an international observer force into the conflict.

The beginning of stabilization in the Arab-Israeli conflict coincided with the ascendancy of the Palestinian- Jewish ethnonational rivalry. The 1974 Rabat conference, a byproduct of the 1973 war, constituted a major victory for the PLO. This resolution implied that the Arab world considered the West Bank and the Gaza Strip to constitute a separate entity and the PLO its rightful masters. The PLO victories in the 1976 municipal elections, followed by the victory of the Likud in Israel's national 1977 elections and then an Israeli settlement drive in the West Bank and the Gaza Strip, reflected the ascendance of ethno-nationalism, both Palestinian and Israeli. However, these occurrences did not impede the peace process between Israel and Egypt and the corollary winding down of the Arab-Israeli conflict.

Strategic realities, as well as institutional developments at the interstate level, influenced the ethnonational level. The slow and painful acceptance of Israel's presence in the Middle East by pivotal Arab states such as Egypt, Jordan, and Morocco also penetrated the Jewish-Palestinian ethnonational struggle over the Land of Israel/Palestine. The two national movements had to learn to bear with each other. The process that started at Camp David in 1978, despite some ethnic detours in Lebanon and the Intifada, led to Oslo in 1993. But this trend is not a linear one and setbacks, even very violent ones, such as the Intifada 2000, are to be expected.

Our study compared ethnic-state crises in two periods: one when the interstate conflict was very intense, and one when it had started to wane. As we discovered even during the first period, ethnic-state crises in general were more limited in magnitude in comparison to interstate ones. Most significant was the fact that in the second period, while ethnic-state crises constituted an absolute majority, they also scored lower in terms of threat, violence, and outcome than the same kind of crises in the previous period. Similarly, even the 1982 Lebanon crisis, which deteriorated to war, was limited to the destruction of the PLO (goals), to Lebanon (space), and neither Syria nor Israel used the whole arsenal at its disposition (means). The 1987 Intifada was distinguished by ordinary weapons such as stones, knives, bombs, and explosives, means of violence distinct from the advanced conventional weapons that had appeared in the six previous wars between Arabs and Israelis.

At the same time, on the ethnonational level the conflict was widening. In the 1987 Intifada the Palestinians residing in the West Bank and Gaza engaged in collective and territory-wide action and a prolonged use of violence, all new patterns in the Palestinian-Israeli conflict. With time, targets were expanded from Israeli soldiers to civilians, a process that contradicted the moderation trend detected in the conflict. In Intifada 2000 the level of violence has grown further in comparison to 1987. Hence, we must conclude that while the conflict was declining in overall crisis magnitude and reflecting increased stabilization in the interstate domain, it was also expanding in some interethnic confrontations.

In sum, to meet the criteria of description, we defined our "research puzzle" as encompassing the nature and scope of change from intense conflict to some form of regulation and the gradual emergence of institutionalism in a conflict-ridden regional system. We detected trends of change in conflict dynamics over time and emphasized that the two variants of international crises, interstate and ethnic-state, manifest different profiles of crisis attributes.

When taken at face value, our findings about the magnitude of ethnic crises seem to contradict, at least in part, others in the literature. Brecher and Wilkenfeld discovered that ethnicity-driven crises, especially within protracted conflicts, were more susceptible to violence, were characterized by a higher level of threat, offered the great powers little moderating influence, but did present lasting agreements as outcomes.[2] In our study we found that in terms of distinct magnitude components, interstate crises revealed more extreme values than ethnic-state ones, in all CMI indicators and especially in the scope of violence attribute, that is, these crises fell into two broad categories of either very high magnitude—war— or very low magnitude—no use of violence. By contrast, ethnic-state crises in the 1947–1973 era tended to be midsize events characterized by a gravity of threat that did not reach peak levels, involving only two or three actors, limited superpower involvement, violent crisis management techniques with minor or serious clashes but rarely crossing the threshold of war. Their outcomes were generally unilateral in type.

We reconcile our findings with those mentioned above by situating the Arab-Israeli protracted conflict within the category of compound conflicts, which in our definition involve spillover effects between their interstate and the ethnic-state type attributes. From the outset we turned down the Brecher-Wilkenfeld "ethnic-driven" category in our framework but rather distinguished between interstate and ethnic-state crises within the ethnic-related conflict. This study goes beyond the Brecher and Wilkenfeld findings by offering a potentially more nuanced analysis that highlights the midsize flavor of ethnic-state crises, reflecting the fact that both diplomacy and war were more pertinent in interstate crises, where sovereign governments manage the confrontation, than in ethnic-state interactions, where NSAs play by different rules. While ethnic-related crises in protracted conflicts might be harsh, they are not likely to spawn war. In a nutshell, states make wars, not ethnic groups. Similarly, states make peace, not ethnic groups.

Because of the different profiles characteristic of the interstate and the ethnic domains, we discovered that the set of conditions that influenced the interstate setting spilled over to the ethnonational domain, but with a time lag. Accordingly, only after the stabilization of a balance of power on the interstate level (our first condition for change) did the PLO start to look for a political solution. Since PLO threats against Israel posed no danger to Israel's existence, as opposed to threats from the Arab states, the PLO generally evoked a more moderate Israeli response. At the same time, we must take into account that a balance of power between ethnic actors is less efficient in stabilizing the system.

Acceptance of the legitimacy of a system, our second condition for conflict transformation, depends predominantly on the major actors, a fact that an ethnic actor must nevertheless take into account. Egypt's turn into a status quo actor ultimately influenced the PLO to modify its positions and to join the camp of willing-to-compromise moderates who gradually accepted Israel's existence. The Israeli recognition of Palestinian rights made its debut in the Camp David accords, but gained momentum only after a decade and one-half in the Oslo agreements. The high costs of interstate war in an age of nuclear weapons, our third condition for conflict moderation, induced the Palestinians to adopt a that best fit an epoch of nonconventional weapons on the ‚main—the Intifada. Prolonged low level confrontation had its toll ‚ Israel and the Palestinians, leading to a political solution for the upris‚ over a military one.

Adding its input to the moderating trends mentioned above, the 1990–1991 Gulf crisis and the Iraqi threat to attack Israel with mass destruction weapons proved that regional instability was extremely dangerous for all participants. Despite the early phase of zero-sum goals between Israel and the PLO, some institutionalism took root. Starting with the initial 1976 tacit agreement in Lebanon regarding the Litani River, which included the PLO, via the U.S.-mediated 1982 agreement, the PLO's November 1988 renunciation of terror, and its acceptance of UN Resolution 242, led to Oslo and the ensuing Oslo II and Wye agreements. In sum, the four conditions that prevailed on the interstate level also contributed to the evolution, albeit a delayed one, of the ethnic conflict. The failure in July 2000 of the Camp David summit and the outbreak of Intifada 2000, however, indicated the limits of these conditions in the ethnic sphere.

This occurrence touches upon a most pertinent question, raised in chapter 1, regarding the durability of agreements in ethnic conflicts. According to Licklider's studies, negotiated settlements that "end" ethnic wars do not last. The experience of Rwanda and the Balkans, for instance, confirms the precariousness of institutionalism in ethnic conflicts. The formal termination of interethnic conflicts in the above cases did not decimate ethnonational sentiments but only postponed them for a while. Another reason for instability and unsteadiness of agreements is the precariousness of the balance of threats in ethnic conflicts.

This observation leads us to the third and hardest task of theory building after description and explanation—the premise of reliable prediction. Our main puzzle is whether the magnitude of interstate crises would continue to decline and resist the pressures from the interethnic axis, even if the distribution of power in the Arab-Israeli interstate system stays constant. The chances of further winding down at the Israeli-Palestinian ethnonational level is even less certain. In more general terms, this question focuses on the effects of a compound conflict involving both interstate and ethnic-state elements. Can solid interstate agreements lead to ethnic-based negotiated compromises? Or would the opposite be the case, namely, that the ethnic elements would diminish the stability of interstate accords?

And does this imply that Israeli-Palestinian agreements, even if achieved, will not hold? This question is related to another evaluation: whether the internationalization of an ethnic-type conflict, namely, the establishment of a Palestinian state, would end the ethnic conflict. Would the enhancement of such an agreement with international institutions provide sufficient stamina for the perseverance of these actors? Or would the creation of a Palestinian state with strong irredentist aspirations destabilize the region? Related questions touch upon the relevance of the periphery—the Gulf area—to the future dynamics at the core Arab-Israeli conflict zone. So far, stability between Israel and its Arab neighbors has not promoted less hostility between Israel and its distant opponents, Iraq and Iran.

At this point a special note about ICB's classification of crises into protracted conflict clusters is in order. We discovered that despite its global reach, ICB clusters of crises are insufficient in certain ways as far as the Arab-Israeli conflict is concerned. Due to the ICB's working definition of crises and protracted conflicts, it omitted both the Intifada and the Gulf war from the Arab-Israeli cluster. This absence results from its theoretical definition of core actors and issues in interstate crises. However, these two kinds of crises may constitute the most expected form of contention in the Arab-Israeli conflict, representing the thesis developed in this book regarding the most likely trends in future crises attributes being primarily ethnic-state, interethnic, or interstate at the periphery of the conflict, namely in the Gulf region and focusing on nonconventional weapons. This application of the ICB variables and data for measuring change from conflict to order allows the ICB to function in a way perhaps unintended by its creators, namely, to focus on conflict transformation, rather than applying ICB concepts and data to measure change in crisis attributes alone.

Where do we go from here? Our research has identified four conditions that explain conflict transformation. Although this cluster of mutually supporting elements may not be exhaustive, we believe it enhances our understanding of the dynamics of conflict and accomodation in the Arab-Israeli conflict. Additional research should be devoted to the task of identifying other supporting conditions for conflict transformation and applying them to the study of the Arab-Israeli conflict. The nonintegration of the realist and institutionalist paradigms required us to look farther afield in our search for explanations of systemic fluctuations from anarchy to order. Our contribution has been to incorporate ethno-nationalism with the realist and institutional approaches. A genuine synthesis would be useful not only in questions of war and peace but also for international relations at large.

Another direction to be pursued is a closer examination of the superpower role, and more specifically that of the United States as the only superpower in the post–Cold War years. With time, our conclusions regarding the distinctive nature of this new era will benefit from more academic research, and it will be possible to address the links between changes in the global structure and emergence of regional stability. More specifically, will the fact of a unipolar system change the role of the United States from a structural component to that of an institutional agent? In the ICB project, the U.S. role was one of a dominant power affecting the structural elements of the international/regional system(s). With our attempt to integrate the contending paradigms and especially following the new role of the United States, students of international politics must look at its role as an institution-promoting actor.

To advance the goal of a generalized explanation of anarchy and order in world politics, we encourage our colleagues to apply and test our framework for understanding the dynamics of conflict transformation on other protracted conflicts, using ICB data as well as other data-sets or based upon the incorporation of qualitative case-study analysis. The emergence of such comparable findings will enable us to reach more general conclusions and to decide whether the attributes identified herein for the Arab-Israeli conflict are unique or if they generically characterize other compound protracted conflicts in world politics.

Besides inspiring new directions for future research, this study has utility not only for IR and area specialists but for policy makers as well. The overview and exploration of continuity and change in a conflict that has persisted for more than a half-century contain some perhaps uncommon policy implications for decision makers who are used to operating in conflict emergencies, but are perhaps less attuned to transformations in the conflict's core attributes over time. From a long-term analysis of crisis outcomes, we conclude that temporary arrangements often last longer than originally planned, and create a setting for long lasting and legitimate accords. This is especially true in the interstate domain but sometimes also in the ethnic-state one. Hence, short-term compromises that may seem insignificant at the time could and should be regarded as contributions to the gradual process of change in the conflict.

Moreover, in a compound protracted conflict such as the Arab-Israeli case, with all its complexity and multiple interstate and ethnic-state crises, a step-by-step process of accommodation is inherently created via the links among the different outcomes of crisis. The two domains of interstate and ethnic-state conflict affect one another. Hence, even without investing in the intensive negotiation efforts needed for formally demarcating linkages between the interstate and ethnic topics in official documents, over time the coupling of issues frequently exists de facto and the transfer of behavioral regularities, as well as the establishment of new norms of behavior, occurs.

Finally, we must recall that our evaluation—that the Arab-Israeli conflict has been winding down since the mid-1970s—is counterbalanced by the spillover effects that are at work between the interstate and the ethnic-state domains. While perhaps moderating the Israeli-Palestinian conflict, the interstate conflict will remain sensitive to the ethnonational one. Progress and enhanced stability should not be automatically regarded as an irreversible process. Turmoil may emulate from the interethnic or ethnic-state domain back to the relatively calm interstate zone. The endurance of unresolved matters of short- or long-term importance between Israel and the Palestinians might impinge upon the interstate peace process. Lack of agreement and the outbreak of violence at the sub-state level is more likely than not to strain the relatively new practice of nonviolent conflict management that currently characterizes the interstate domain. A similar linkage exists in the Israel/Lebanon /Syria triangle, which is itself linked to the Israeli-Palestinian one.

With these dangers in mind, policy makers in the region should be aware that interethnic violence might escalate rapidly and transcend the initial level of low strife. It may trigger an escalation cycle that would upset the delicate interstate equilibrium of vaguely defined regulations, norms, and slowly emerging regimes. Our study highlighted the fact that regional stability is thus far supported via diverse factors, all indicating transformation in the nature of the Arab-Israeli conflict. To strengthen the advent of long-range stability, future moderation must be achieved in both interstate and ethnic confrontations.

GLOSSARY OF CRISES IN THE
ARAB-ISRAELI CONFLICT

1. PALESTINE PARTITION-FIRST ARAB-ISRAEL WAR

The first of twenty-six crises in the Arab-Israeli conflict is classified as an *ethnic-state* case that consisted of two main phases: interethnic and interstate. The Jewish-Arab intercommunal strife that had characterized the period of the British Mandate in Palestine intensified with the UN General Assembly resolution of 29 November 1947, which called for the partition of Palestine into two independent states—Arab and Jewish. The end of the Mandate, the proclamation of the State of Israel on 14–15 May 1948, and the invasion of Israel by the armies of Egypt, Iraq, Jordan, Lebanon, and Syria marked the transition of the crisis into the interstate domain. The existence of Israel was the core issue of contention among adversaries who used both violence and diplomacy to advance their goals. The UN and major/super powers from outside the region were intensely involved, arranging four truce agreements and leading Israel and four of the five Arab protagonists to negotiate armistice agreements through the mediation of Count Folke Bernadotte and, after his assassination, UN Under Secretary General Ralph Bunche. Acting indirectly through Czechoslovakia, the USSR served as the major supplier of weapons for the State of Israel, while the United States and the UK were involved diplomatically within and alongside the UN. The crisis de-escalated gradually: Egypt and Israel signed an armistice agreement on 24 February 1949, followed by Lebanon and Israel (29 March 1949), Jordan and Israel (3

---

*The purpose of this glossary is to provide the reader with a historical narrative of each crisis analyzed in the book. These summaries take the ICB data as their point of departure. In addition we highlighted the ethnic dimension and updated the sources for each case summary. All the sources, including those used by the ICB project, are listed in the bibliography.

April 1949), and Syria and Israel (20 July 1949). Iraq withdrew from the battlefield in July 1948, but negotiated no formal agreement with Israel.[1]

2. SINAI INCURSION

This *interstate* crisis of 28 December 1948–10 January 1949 was, in effect, a violent escalation within the context of the Palestine partition crisis and involved
Egypt, the UK, and Israel. Egypt's initial refusal to negotiate an armistice
agreement led Israel to increase its military pressure by launching Operation
Horev, an attack into Egypt's Sinai Peninsula. Intense diplomatic activity
accompanied the violence. Cairo attempted to rally the Arab League states to
its aid while also requesting the UK to press for a Security Council resolution
demanding an Israeli withdrawal. Britain then issued an ultimatum to Israel on
31 December, demanding that Israel evacuate Egyptian territory within one
week. Israeli compliance with major power pressure was gradual, at first simply
changing the direction of its military forces while keeping them in Sinai. Peak
escalation occurred when Israel shot down five British planes sent to observe
the withdrawal process, to which Britain responded by reinforcing its military
presence in Aqaba, Jordan. Only then did Israel order its troops out of the Sinai;
full compliance was achieved on 10 January 1949 when Israel completed its
withdrawal.[2]

3. HULA DRAINAGE

The second *interstate* crisis in the Arab-Israeli conflict occurred between Syria
and Israel over water resources and activity in the Demilitarized Zone (DMZ)
along the border and lasted from 12 February to 15 May 1951. The crisis began
in February when Israel commenced work on a national drainage project
designed to drain Lake Hula, reclaim the land for agriculture, and use the accu-
mulated water to irrigate other parts of Israel. Syria perceived this project as a
violation of the 1949 armistice agreement, which designated the DMZ a "no
man's land," and worried about an adverse change in the balance of power as a
consequence of Israel's territorial gain in the contested area. Syria's initial use of
diplomacy via an appeal to the UN Security Council failed to halt the Israeli
operation. Further escalation occurred in March and April with several instances
in which the two sides exchanged fire in the DMZ. On 8 May the UN Security
Council issued a resolution calling for a ceasefire and the withdrawal of all military forces from the DMZ. The UN Mixed Armistice Commission (MAC)
negotiated an agreement by which Israel agreed to halt its works, except on
Jewish-owned land, but Syria rejected the proposed settlement. The issue
remained unresolved and the crisis resurfaced during the 1963–1964 Jordan
waters confrontation. [3]

4. QIBYA

During this second *ethnic-state* crisis, Jordan and the Palestinian Fedayeen (guerillas) confronted Israel over the issues of Palestinian cross-border infiltrations and harsh Israeli reprisals. Palestinian Arab refugees from the first Arab-Israeli war, living in Jordanian camps, rapidly translated their personal frustrations into political and military activity against Israel. Infiltrations from Jordan into Israel began in 1951 but on 12 October 1953 the situation escalated with the murder of an Israeli woman and her two children at Yahud, a settlement east of Tel-Aviv. In a severe Israeli retaliatory attack two days later, against the Jordanian village of Qibya, sixty-nine civilians were killed and forty-five houses were destroyed. Jordan appealed through diplomatic channels to the United States, Britain, the Arab League, and the UN Security Council. Each of the latter forums condemned Israel. Israeli public opinion questioned the effectiveness of the severe military retaliation policy, after which infiltrations stopped for only a few months. The basic ethnic-state source of turbulence went without resolution. 4

5. GAZA RAID / CZECH ARMS

A third *ethnic-state* crisis involving Egypt, the Palestinians, and Israel lasted from 28 February 1955 to 23 June 1956. In addition to the tension on its eastern border with Jordan, Israel also suffered repeated terrorist attacks from Egyptian-controlled Gaza on its southwestern border. Between 1950 and 1955 Israel launched five reprisal operations, but only the raid into Gaza on 28 February 1955, which killed thirty-nine Arabs and injured thirty-two, was considered severe enough by the ICB to cross the normal relations range threshold and constitute a crisis. The crisis escalated when Israel responded to continued terrorist attacks with four more raids, culminating on 5 April 1956 with a massive sweep into Gaza, which resulted in significant Arab casualties. Both Egypt and Israel used diplomacy (though not direct bilateral contact) to manage the crisis and stabilize the situation. On 20 March Egypt appealed to the UN Security Council and the Arab League and also used the Chinese channel to secure Russian arms supplies. The Security Council passed a resolution condemning Israel for the Gaza raid and the Secretary General tried unsuccessfully to mediate between the two parties. On 28 September 1955 the Soviets approved an arms deal between Egypt and Czechoslovakia, tilting the regional balance of power in favor of Cairo and exacerbating Israeli insecurity. With the goal of countering the Egyptian effort to gain regional supremacy, Israel negotiated several massive arms purchases from France. The crisis ended on 23 June 1956 when a third Franco-Israeli arms deal clearly reasserted Israeli military superiority in the region. What had begun as ethnic-triggered turmoil led to an inter-state flexing of military preparedness and an escalated arms race.5

6. SUEZ NATIONALIZATION—SINAI CAMPAIGN

A third *interstate* crisis involved six states: Egypt, France, Israel, the Soviet Union, the United Kingdom, and the United States. The crisis lasted from 26 July 1956 until 13 March 1957 and focused on two major issues—regional decolonization and balance of power/security among newly established states. In July 1952 the Free Officers overthrew the Egyptian monarchy and Colonel Abdel Nasser emerged as the dominant Egyptian decision maker, with aspirations to act as leader of the Third World and nonaligned countries. As such he supported the Algerian nationalists in their struggle against France and opposed the continued presence of 70,000 British troops in the canal zone. On 26 July 1956, Nasser proclaimed the nationalization of the Suez Canal. France, Israel, and Britain secretly joined forces against their common enemy. On 29 October 1956 Israel invaded the Sinai; two days later British and French forces landed in the canal zone. Egypt reacted with a mix of military and diplomatic measures. The former effort saw limited resistence to the invasion, a call for general mobilization, and an appeal to the Soviet Union for military and diplomatic assistance. The Soviet response marked the peak of the crisis: on 5 November Moscow dispatched a harsh note to the three invading powers and the United States, referring to the "dangerous consequences" of the aggression against Egypt and warning that London, Paris, and Tel Aviv lay under the threat of Soviet missiles. Bowing to superpower pressure, Britain and France agreed to a ceasefire and the withdrawal of their troops. The United States declared a semi-alert and indicated that it would not stand idly by if Russian bombs began to fall. On 8 November Israel agreed to evacuate as soon as the United Nations Emergency Force (UNEF) arrived to act as a buffer in Sinai and Gaza. On 12 March 1957 Israel completed its withdrawal, ending the crisis. 6

7. QALQILYA

A fourth *ethnic-state* crisis involving Jordan and the Palestinians versus. Israel followed a pattern similar to the Qibya case and lasted from 13 September until mid-October 1956. As in the early 1950s, so too during July and August 1956 Palestinian infiltrators escalated tensions along the Israel-Jordan border, severely testing Israel's post-Qibya restraint. Israel finally responded with three raids. On 13 September 1956 the IDF blew up a police station in the Jordanian village of Garandal, followed by a second strike, this time against the Jordanian village of Husan, and a third attack on 10 October against Qalqilya, this in response to the Jordanian ambush of an Israeli bus. The deteriorating situation prompted Jordan to request the dispatch of Iraqi forces to Jordan. Iraq's positive response threatened to disrupt the local equation of forces. For Israel, the presence of Iraqi troops in Jordan constituted a long standing *casus belli*; what had begun as ethnically derived strife rapidly brought the three states to the brink of war. But confrontation was avoided when Jordan clarified that Iraqi forces would enter Jordan only if Israel attacked. The crisis faded toward the end of October and the regional balance remained unchanged. The problem of the Palestinians, and of the Fedayeen, however, remained similarly unresolved. 7

8. OPERATION "ROTTEM"

This fourth *interstate* crisis involved Egypt and Israel and lasted for three weeks in February and March 1960. Egypt and Syria had decided to form a single political entity, the United Arab Republic, and tensions between it and Israel ran high due to Palestinian cross-border attacks from Syria and severe Israeli retaliation. On 15 February 1960 President Nasser received Soviet information claiming that Israel was massing troops on its northern border with the intention of attacking Syria. To counter this challenge Egypt began secretly sending troops across the Suez Canal and into Sinai toward the Israeli border. Four days into these maneuvers, Israel learned that a major portion of the Egyptian army had crossed the Suez Canal and was situated near Israel's southern border. Israel promptly responded with "Operation Rottem," a series of IDF countermaneuvers. Despite the receipt and processing of the misinformation and the resulting escalation, violence did not occur and de-escalation began on 1 March when Egyptian forces began to return to their bases west of the canal and Israel similarly terminated its war preparation. On 8 March Israel's prime minister departed for an official visit to the United States, indicating that the situation had returned to normal. 8

9. JORDAN WATERS

Five state actors, Egypt, Israel, Jordan, Lebanon, and Syria, participated in this fifth *interstate* crisis between 11 December 1963 and 5 May 1964. To a great extent it resulted from the unresolved water problem that had led earlier to the Hula drainage crisis in 1953 (see above Case 3). Throughout the prolonged dispute between Israel and the neighboring Arab states concerning the utilization of the Jordan waters, only the Johnston Plan of 1955 earned both Arab and Israeli approval, at the technical level. The Arab League Political Committee rejected the plan in principle, however, because of a perceived bias toward Israel. In the absence of an agreement, both Jordan and Israel proceeded to develop their own unilateral water projects. Jordan initiated a water plan in 1958; in 1959 Israel began its program for carrying water from the Sea of Galilee to the Negev, Israel's arid southern region. Once again, as in the early fifties, the Arab states interpreted the prospect of a water-rich Israel in territorial and power terms, leading to an increased sense of insecurity in the Arab world. The Arab chiefs of staff met in Cairo in December 1963 to devise a common Arab strategy against the Israeli diversion plan. Confrontation seemed inevitable once Israel declared its intention to complete the National Water Carrier project despite external opposition. Both superpowers, as well as the United Nations, called for restraint and warned Israel and the Arabs against using force. At an Arab League summit conference in Cairo in January 1964, all thirteen members of the League agreed upon a plan to divert the three tributaries of the Jordan River and to set up a unified military command. Before the Arab states took any further action, Israel announced the completion of its water project, scheduled to become operational in the summer of 1964. This confrontation over water ended without aggression from either side. [9]

10. EL SAMU

The fifth *ethnic-state* crisis in the Arab-Israeli conflict involved Israel, Jordan, and the Palestinians from 12 to 15 November 1966, and can be considered a prelude to the 1967 June war. It followed a period of several months of escalating tension along Israel's eastern border due to a series of border infiltrations. Events crossed the threshold of a full-fledged crisis on 12 November when an Israeli army command car hit a mine near the border with Jordan. The next day Israel launched a reprisal raid against the village of El Samu in Jordan, a Palestinian stronghold. Jordan mobilized its army and heavy fighting commenced before Israel withdrew its forces. In addition to its military response, Jordan also declared an internal state of alert and resorted to diplomacy by appealing to the Security Council, which sent the secretary general to confer with the Israeli and Jordanian ambassadors. Jordan canceled the state of alert on 15 November, indicating the termination of this ethnic-state case. [10]

11. JUNE—SIX DAY WAR

The sixth *interstate* crisis in the Arab-Israeli conflict also constituted the third war involving Israel, Egypt, Jordan, Syria, the Soviet Union, and the United States. On 14 May, Syria and Egypt announced a state of emergency, based upon Soviet reports that Israel was concentrating troops on its northern border. But the situation crossed the threshold of crisis on 17 May, when Egyptian planes flew over Israel's nuclear research center at Dimona, and additional Egyptian troops moved into Sinai. The next day UN Secretary General U Thant acceded to President Nasser's demand that he withdraw the United Nations Emergency Force (UNEF) from Sinai, removing the buffer between Israel and Egypt, both of whom mobilized their army reserves.

On 23 May Egypt closed the Straits of Tiran, blockading the Israeli port of Eilat. On 30 May Jordan and Egypt signed a defense pact, enhancing Arab cohesion and increasing Israeli insecurity. On 5 June, Israel launched a preemptive air attack on Egypt's air force bases, totally destroying Egyptian air power. Jordan escalated the crisis by shelling Jerusalem; Egypt and Syria also joined the military counterattack. In the ensuing war, Israel destroyed the Jordanian air force and captured the Jordanian-controlled Old City of Jerusalem; by 9 June its advances on the Golan Heights threatened Damascus. These rapid changes in the regional balance of power drew both superpowers into the crisis. On 6 June the USSR used the "hot line" telephone to warn the United States of imminent Soviet action. The United States countered by ordering the Sixth Fleet to sail within fifty miles of the Syrian coast, indicating a willingness to use force if the Soviets joined the war. The dangerous prospect of a superpower clash marked the peak of this crisis and led to a de-escalation process. On 11 June a UN Security Council ceasefire resolution came into effect for all the adversaries, thus ending this interstate war. [11]

12. KARAMEH

This sixth *ethnic-state* crisis in the Arab-Israeli conflict between Israel and Jordan and the Palestinians lasted from 18 to 22 March 1968. It followed several months of increased tension along the Israel-Jordan border, with multiple cross-border infiltrations resulting in significant casualties among Israeli soldiers and civilians alike. On 18 March an Israeli school bus hit a mine in the Arava valley near Be'er Ora, close to the Jordanian border, killing two adults and wounding more than twenty children. As a warning to Jordan that it must terminate Fedayeen activity, Israel attacked the village of Karameh in Jordan, a Fedayeen base. Jordan dispatched its armed forces to the site, where armed members of the Palestine Liberation Organization (PLO) joined in the heavy fighting. The IDF finally withdrew, with severe losses on both sides. Jordan used a mix of military and diplomatic measures to manage the crisis, including an appeal to the United Nations. This case is remarkable, however, for the particularly strong Palestinian resistence to the Israeli attack, which introduced a step-level increase in ethnic involvement in international crises. On 22 March Jordan reopened the Allenby bridge, linking it with the Israel-occupied West Bank and Jordan, thus signaling a return to the pre-crisis situation. The Palestinian problem, and the turmoil caused by Fedayeen activities, however, remained unresolved. [12]

13. BEIRUT AIRPORT

The seventh *ethnic-state* crisis in the Arab-Israeli conflict signaled the opening of a new zone of confrontation: Lebanon. Although in ICB terms Lebanon was the only "crisis actor" in the 1968 airport incident, the fight was actually between Israel and the Palestinians over the issue of Palestinian activity along the Israel-Lebanon border and, indeed, within Lebanon. The catalyst for this airport episode was a 26 December attack by the Lebanon-based Popular Front for the Liberation of Palestine (PFLP) on an Israeli passenger plane in Athens. A passenger was killed and one air crew member was injured. The crisis began two days later when Israel undertook a retaliatory raid on Beirut International Airport, designed to deter Arab states from facilitating the Palestinians in their assaults against Israel or Israeli targets abroad. The Israeli attackers destroyed thirteen jetliners belonging to Middle East Airlines and some privately owned Lebanese planes and then departed as quickly as they had come. The crisis did not escalate to further violence, however. Lebanon's response was to lodge a complaint against Israel with the Security Council, declare a state of alert, and mobilize reserve forces. The international community roundly condemned Israel for the operation. Both superpowers supported Lebanon's position and on 7 January 1969 France reiterated its embargo of all military supplies destined for Israel. The crisis faded in January 1969 as tensions related to the ethnic-state domain temporarily subsided. [13]

14. WAR OF ATTRITION

The seventh *interstate* crisis witnessed a prolonged confrontation that escalated into an all-out war between Israel and Egypt and even included some direct military participation by the USSR. Unlike the 1956 war, which was followed by a decade of relative calm, the 1967 war led to only a temporary lull in the violence. In the fall of 1968 tension along the Israeli-Egyptian border rose when Egyptian artillery bombarded Israeli positions on the east bank of Suez Canal and Israel destroyed Egypt's power station at Naj Hamadi. On 8 March 1969 Egypt launched the War of Attrition, shelling positions along Israel's Bar Lev Line and generally seeking to extract a steady toll in Israeli casualties without provoking a full-scale war. Israeli air raids against SAM-2 batteries and Egyptian anti-aircraft systems indicated that Israel was not willing to shoulder the heavy cost of low level warfare alone. The crisis reached its most acute phase after Israel initiated intensified deep-penetration bombing raids into Egypt in January 1970. The USSR came to Egypt's aid by installing Soviet missile batteries near the canal in March, but Israel promptly attacked them; the stakes rose farther in April with a direct Soviet - Israeli aircraft encounter. Intense U.S. diplomatic efforts to halt the increasing instability in the area finally produced a ceasefire on 7 August based upon Secretary of State Rogers's Plan B, thus ending the War of Attrition. [14]

15. LIBYAN PLANE

The eighth *ethnic-state* crisis resulted from rumors and the unexpected appearance of a Libyan plane over Israeli territory on 21 February 1973. Israel had learned of a possible terrorist plan to hijack a civilian plane and explode it over an Israeli city, an unfortunately plausible scenario within the context of the ethnic Israeli-Palestinian confrontation. Thus, the lone Libyan Boeing-727 with 113 passengers on board and headed in the direction of Israel's nuclear plant in Dimona rang particularly loud alarm bells. Israeli fighter planes intercepted the plane, which refused to respond to Israeli warnings and signals. The air-force finally received orders to shoot down the plane, and only after it crashed did Israel determine that it had indeed been only a stray passenger plane with no hostile intent. This short crisis ended with Israel paying compensation to the families of the dead. [15]

16. ISRAEL MOBILIZATION

The eighth *interstate* crisis and a prelude to the 1973 war involved Israel and Egypt and lasted from 10 April to late June 1973. Seeking to eradicate the results of their 1967 defeat, Egypt and Syria coordinated their activities and planned for a joint attack against Israel in May 1973. In April, Israel received intelligence reports detailing an imminent Egyptian attack and reporting the arrival of thirty-two fighter planes from Iraq and Libya in Egypt. To deter Egypt from opening hostilities, Israel placed its army on alert, called reserve units into active service, and began war preparations. In the context of both Israel's military preparedness and the superpower talks between Nixon and Brezhnev in June 1973, Israel became convinced that Egypt did not intend to go to war at that time; Israel relaxed its state of alert and the crisis ended. But the high economic cost of the April mobilization would constitute a crucial factor in Israel's reluctance to order a general mobilization four months later during the warning phase of the 1973 war. [16]

17. OCTOBER—YOM KIPPUR WAR

The ninth *interstate* crisis lasted from 5 October 1973 until 31 May 1974 and involved Egypt, Israel, the Soviet Union, Syria, and the United States. Despite a September 1973 buildup of Syrian forces along the Israeli-Syrian border and a high state of alert for the IDF, the crisis did not begin until 5 October 1973, when Egyptian forces advanced toward the Suez Canal. Although Israel put its army on high alert, it was still unprepared for the simultaneous attack by Egyptian and Syrian forces on 6 October. Egypt's successful crossing of the Suez Canal on the 7 October and Syria's advance on the Golan Heights indicated a change in the regional balance of power, leading Israel to begin implementing its nuclear "Samson Option." Between 10–14 October, however, Israel's forces regained control over developments in the north, allowing it to return its nuclear weapons to storage, thus ending one of the most acute phases of this confrontation.

Egypt and Syria's rejection of Israel's offer of a ceasefire one week into the war led to intense superpower involvement and brinkmanship. The Soviets placed seven airborne divisions on an increased state of readiness and began a huge resupply of arms to the Arab states; the United States responded with its own massive resupply of Israel. Egyptian-Israeli fighting intensified in the south over the fate of the Egyptian Third Army, trapped by Israel when the IDF crossed the canal. As in 1956 and 1967, Moscow warned that it might intervene unilaterally unless Israel halted at once. While pressuring Israel to release the encircled Egyptian troops, the United States also placed most of its armed forces, including the Strategic Air Command with its nuclear capability, on a high state of alert. The arrival of a Soviet vessal in Alexandria reportedly carrying nuclear weapons further escalated the crisis. On 26 October 1973 all of the parties accepted a Security Council ceasefire resolution co-sponsored by the United States and USSR. Three months of mediation by U.S. secretary of state Kissinger produced the Egyptian-Israeli disengagement agreement of 18 January 1974. Four more months of intense shuttle diplomacy by Kissinger between Damascus and Jerusalem were required before Israel and Syria signed a disengagement agreement on 31 May 1974, allowing for a UN buffer force along their border and ending this prolonged war. [17]

18. ENTEBBE

The ninth *ethnic-state* crisis focused on a spectacular Palestinian hijacking operation and the fate of Israeli and other hostages held in Uganda from 27 June to 4 July 1976. The crisis began on 27 June when the Popular Front for the Liberation of Palestine (PFLP), accompanied by members of Germany's Bader-Meinhof gang, hijacked an Air France plane en route from Tel Aviv to Paris. The terrorists forced the plane to fly to Libya and then on to Entebbe, Uganda, where they released all of their hostages except for the Israeli and Jewish passengers and the French crew. The hijackers demanded that Israel release hundreds of Palestinian prisoners in Israeli jails in exchange for the remaining captives in Uganda. Instead, Israel chose to attempt a clandestine rescue operation. On 3 July three Hercules transport planes carrying Israeli commando troops surprised the Ugandan soldiers guarding the Entebbe airport. After a brief firefight with the Ugandans and the hijackers, the Israelis successfully liberated all of the hostages. The crisis ended on 4 July when the rescue team, together with the former hostages, landed in Israel. [18]

19. SYRIA MOBILIZATION

The origins of the tenth *ethnic-state* crisis, in the winter of 1976, lay in the dispatch of some 30,000 Syrian troops into Lebanon, at the request of the

Lebanese government which was faring poorly in the civil war that had erupted in April 1975, in which the Palestinians played a crucial role. In the middle of October 1976, the Arab Heads of State convened a summit in Riyadh, Saudi Arabia, to establish a program for halting the violence between the Palestinian and Lebanese factions in Lebanon. Their plan was to send an Arab Deterrent Force (ADF), consisting almost entirely of Syrian troops, to pacify Lebanon. Syrian troops moved into Lebanon en masse; of particular concern to Israel was Syrian control of all the key points in Lebanon along the Litani River which marked, by tacit agreement, a "red line" between Syrian and Israeli zones of influence in their weaker neighbor. On 21 November, Syrian troop movements suggested a move south, across the river and toward the border with Israel, thus jeopardizing the status quo, which was re-established only after Israel and the United States reacted with a mix of military and diplomatic means. Katusha rockets fired from Lebanon landed in the northern Israeli city of Naharia and Israel requested the United States. to warn Syria that such Ethnic-NSA activity will lead to undesirable escalation. Israel also requested the Christian forces in southern Lebanon to refrain from reacting to provocations in order to stabalize the situation and concentrated forces along its northern border with Lebanon. United States political pressure persuaded the Syrians to halt at the Litani River. By 13 December the situation stabilized. Syrian forces reconcentrated their attention and efforts on the complex Lebanese battleground into which they had waded, and left standing the red line between it and Israel along the Litani. [19]

20. OPERATION "LITANI"

This eleventh *ethnic-state* crisis, characteristic of the post-1973 crises, involved a severe Israeli retaliatory raid against PLO bases in southern Lebanon in the spring of 1978. The catalyst was a fatal attack by PLO terrorists against civilian vehicles on the coastal highway between Tel-Aviv and Haifa on 11 March 1978. On 14 March Israel invaded Lebanon in force and pushed the guerillas across Lebanon's Litani River, which became a "red line" whose violation would provoke further Israeli action. Militarily helpless, Lebanon managed the crisis through diplomatic channels, primarily in the UN Security Council, which quickly passed Resolution 425, which called for Israel's immediate withdrawal and the establishment of a UN buffer force in south Lebanon. Israel withdrew on 13 June 1978 and the United Nations Interim Force in Lebanon (UNIFIL) took up their positions. UNIFIL soon proved unable to prevent violence across the Israeli-Lebanese border, but remained in place during subsequent ethnic-state crises in the country. [20]

21. IRAQI NUCLEAR REACTOR

Iraq and Israel created the tenth *interstate* crisis in the Arab-Israeli conflict and the only one to break out in the post-1973 period. This episode signaled a shift in primary Arab actors from the Arab states bordering Israel to Iraq, once removed. This also constituted a shift in the in foci of conflict, from local territorial disputes among adversaries to the strategic-nuclear balance of power among them. Iraq had declared the goal of achieving nuclear parity with Israel, and in 1975 secured a French commitment to construct in Osirak a nuclear reactor. Israeli efforts to persuade France to abandon the project failed, and the French announcement in January of 1981 that the reactor would be fully operational by mid-July, prompted the Israeli cabinet to approve a plan to obstruct the completion of the reactor. On 7 June 1981, Israeli jets destroyed the reactor, dashing Iraq's attempt to challenge Israel's regional nuclear supremacy. Widespread world condemnation of Israel followed the attack, but after the 1990–1991 Gulf War, Israel offered the 1981 operation as an important element in Saddam's defeat and in favor of regional stability. [21]

22. AL-BIQA MISSILES I

Lebanon was also the venue for the twelfth *ethnic-state* crisis, a confrontation between Syria and Israel over influence in Lebanon. Thirty thousand Syrian troops, under the nominal aegis of the Arab Deterrent Force (ADF) had occupied Lebanon's Biqa Valley by invitation of the Lebanese government during the Lebanese civil war, which began in 1975. In the spring of 1981 the Lebanese Forces, the largest independent Lebanese Christian militia, came into conflict with Syrian forces in the vicinity of the Zahle, astride the Beirut-Damascus highway. Responding to calls for assistance from the Lebanese Forces, Israeli warplanes shot down two Syrian helicopters on 28 April 1981.

The Syrian response was to deploy SAM-3 ground-to-air missiles in the Biqa and press its attack on the Christian militia in Zahle. Israel destroyed the Syrian missile bases on 28 May, and the cycle of violence threatened to spiral into a Syrian-Israeli war. The United States sent special envoy Philip Habib to mediate an end to the crisis, which he successfully did.

The PLO also increased its prominence in Lebanon at this time, threatening to eject itself into the crisis. Habib was also able to separately negotiate an Israeli-PLO ceasefire (in the guise of an Israeli-Lebanese agreement). Its implementation on 24 July terminated this crisis, but with the growing Palestinian military presence in Lebanon and Israel's determination to paralyze the PLO, additional escalation was only a matter of time. This crisis also hinted at the Israeli-Christian cooperation that would later lead to further conflict. [22]

23. WAR IN LEBANON

The thirteenth *ethnic-state* crisis in the Arab-Israeli system evolved out of the unstable circumstances prevailing in Lebanon. Observing heightened PLO activity in Lebanon under cover of the 1981 ceasefire, the government of Menachem Begin adopted on 21 April 1982 a decision in principle to uproot PLO bases there. An assassination attempt against Israel's ambassador to the United Kingdom on 3 June provided the trigger point for a full-scale Israeli invasion of Lebanon, code-named "Peace for Galilee." Israel's primary purpose was to destroy the PLO, but subsidiary goals were to diminish Syrian influence in Lebanon, facilitate the consolidation of a pro-Israel Lebanese government, and win Israel its second peace treaty with an Arab state. In the first days of the war Israeli and Syrian forces clashed on the ground and in the skies over the Biqa Valley, with severe Syrian losses. United States envoy Philip Habib returned to the region and mediated an 11 June ceasefire between Syria and Israel, but the Israeli campaign in Lebanon continued. The IDF cornered the PLO in Beirut, but its siege of the city brought worldwide condemnation. Satisfaction at Habib's successful negotiation of the PLO's evacuation from Lebanon in September 1981 was cut short by the assassination of Israel's Lebanese ally, Bashir Gemayel, and the subsequent massacre of Palestinian civilians by Christian militiamen in an area under ostensible Israeli control. The latter provoked further international fury at Israel and revolted Israelis, who demanded an end to their country's involvement in Lebanon.

U.S. secretary of state George Shultz mediated the agreement of 17 May 1983 between the Lebanese and Israeli governments, which looked like the peace accord Israel had wanted and called for an IDF withdrawal, but Syrian pressure and challenges from rival Lebanese groups led to the quick abrogation of the accord by Beirut. Unable to wrest political or military victory from the Begin government's invasion of Lebanon, Prime Minister Shimon Peres ordered a unilateral withdrawal in 1985, leaving behind a small number of Israeli troops to reinforce a "security zone" in southern Lebanon. There the IDF hoped that an indigenous South Lebanese Army (SLA) militia, trained and armed by Israel, would serve as a buffer between Israel and hostile forces in Lebanon. [23]

24. AL-BIQA MISSILES II

The fourteenth *ethnic-state* crisis found Syria and Israel wrangling again in Lebanon's Biqa Valley in the winter of 1985–1986. In a skirmish on 19 November 1985, Israeli planes shot down two Syrian MIG aircraft over

Lebanon; Syria responded on 24 November by deploying SAM-6 missiles in the Biqa Valley and along the Beirut-Damascus highway. American pressure made Syria withdraw those missiles, but the crisis resumed in mid-December when Syria redeployed SAM-6 and SAM-8 missiles close to the Lebanon border. Israel also accused Syria of deploying long-range SAM-2 missiles in southwestern Syria, posing a threat to mutually agreed-upon Israeli reconnaissance missions over Lebanon. The Syrian government claimed the redeployment was defensive only; Israel warned that if the Syrian missiles would not be removed and the shelling of Katusha rockets by the Palestinians to the northern region of Israel would not come to a halt, it would unilaterally remove the missiles. De-escalation occurred in early January 1986 as a result of United States mediation. Syria agreed not to interfere with Israeli air reconnaissance missions, Israel promised not to attack Syrian missile sites in return, and both sides considered the crisis ended. [24]

25. OPERATION "ACCOUNTABILITY"

The fifteenth *ethnic-state* crisis occurred in Lebanon between Israel and Lebanon's Shia Muslim fundamentalist guerilla group, Hizbullah (Party of God), in July 1993. Formed in the years following Israel's 1982 invasion, Hizbullah sought a total Israeli withdrawal from Lebanon and the liquidation of the security zone. Funded by Iran and encouraged by Syria, Hizbullah squads mobilized to drive Israel out of Lebanon and succeeded in inflicting high casualties on both the SLA and the IDF.

After a spate of cross-border Katyusha attacks into northern Israel, three lethal Hizbullah attacks in July 1993 against IDF patrols in the security zone within a two week span triggered a full-blown crisis for Israel. Israel launched Operation "Accountability," characterized by heavy air raids and intense artillery attacks on Hizbullah bases all over Lebanon. Also targeted were South Lebanese villages, which forced large numbers of civilians to flee northward, where Israel hoped they would pressure Beirut to pressure Damascus to pressure Hizbullah to stop its activities. Instead, Israel faced global condemnation and Hizbullah emerged from the battles bloodied but unbowed.

On 31 July United States mediators facilitated a ceasefire between the IDF and Hizbullah, by which the IDF agreed to desist from military operations against villages north of the security zone, and Hizbullah pledged to stop firing missiles into northern Israel. This ended the immediate crisis and removed civilians on both sides from the line of fire, but the respite could be only temporarysince the Hizbullah-Israeli conflict within the security zone remained unresolved. [25]

26. OPERATION "GRAPES OF WRATH"

The failure of Operation Accountability (Case 25, above) to resolve the conflict along the Israeli-Lebanese border was manifest by the outbreak of a sixteenth *ethnic-state* crisis in the same region. The deaths of several South Lebanese civilians by alleged SLA fire infuriated Hizbullah on 9 April 1996, which responded by launching thirty Katyusha rockets against the northern Israeli town of Kiryat Shmona. The next day, four Israeli soldiers died in a security zone gunfight with Hizbullah. Together, the two events triggered a crisis for Israel, which unleashed Operation "Grapes of Wrath," a full frontal assault into Lebanon aimed to break Hizbullah's ability to undertake military attacks within southern Lebanon and into northern Israel by destroying Hizbullah camps, supply lines, arms depots, and fighters. A flood of refugees north toward the capital and Israeli attacks against targets in Beirut triggered a crisis for Lebanon.

As in 1993, Israel hoped that suffering civilians in the south would blame the Hizbullah elements in their midst for provoking Israel's wrath. Both hopes failed. Lebanese across the sectarian spectrum, even those with little sympathy for Hizbullah's wider aspirations (such as creating an Islamic state), rallied behind the refugees and against Israel.

Israel vowed not to cease its campaign until it had won better terms than Operation "Accountability" had produced in 1993. But it inadvertently undercut its own position when an IDF missile struck a UN compound in Qana, killing more than a hundred civilians who had sought shelter there. Worldwide condemnation pushed Israel to the negotiating table, where Israel and Hizbullah ended up reconfirming the 1993 ceasefire terms designed to limit Israeli and Lebanese civilian injuries, thereby ending the crisis on 27 April 1996. This agreement also established a followup committee composed of the United States, Israel, Lebanon, Syria, and France, which would hear complaints from any party about alleged ceasefire violations by another. The proposition that neither side would target the other's civilians, however, implicitly validated continued warfare in the security zone, where Hizbullah hit-and-run strikes promptly resumed. Maintenance of the security zone entailed increasingly costly Israeli sacrifices in blood, money, and international opinion, and set off a vigorous debate within Israel over the pros and cons of a unilateral withdrawal. [26]

NOTES

CHAPTER 1. THEORETICAL APPROACHES TO CONFLICT AND ORDER IN INTERNATIONAL POLITICS

1. One of the first major books that put the debate in this light was Robert O. Keohane, ed., *Neorealism and Its Critics* (New York: Columbia University Press, 1986); See also Joseph S. Nye, "Neorealism and Neoliberalism," *World Politics* 40, No.2 (1988): 235–251.

2. The debate on institutions versus realism and especially the mechanism of balance of power goes back to the idealist-realist dichotomy during the late 1930s and may be traced to ancient times as K. J. Holsti does in *The Dividing Discipline* (Boston: Allen and Unwin, 1985). See also John Herz, "Idealist Internationalism and the Security Dilemma," *World Politics* 2, No. 2 (January 1950): 157–180; Herbert Butterfield, *History and Human Relations* (London: Collins, 1950), 19–20; Robert Jervis, "Cooperation under the Security Dilemma", *World Politics* 30 (January 1978): 167–214; and George Liska, *International Equilibrium* (Cambridge: Harvard University Press, 1957). For a comprehensive book presenting the debate see David A. Baldwin, ed., *Neorealism and Neoliberalism* (New York: Columbia University Press, 1993). For a recent debate on neorealism see articles by John Vasquez, Kenneth Waltz, and others in *American Political Science Review* 91, No. 4 (December 1997): 899–935.

3. For arguments recommending the inclusion of ethnic nationalism in international politics see Anthony D. Smith, *The Ethnic Revival* (Cambridge: Cambridge University Press, 1981), xii–xiii and Anthony D. Smith, "Ethnic Identity and World Order," *Millennium* 12, No.2 (June 1982): 307–327. See also special issues on the ethnic problem in international politics in *Millennium* 20, No. 3 (Winter 1991), and *Survival* 36, No. 1 (1993).

4. On the need for modifying realism with ethno-nationalism see Shmuel Sandler, "Ethno nationalism and the Foreign Policy of Nation States," *Nationalism and Ethnic Politics* 1, No. 2 (Summer 1995): 250–269.

5. For an early account of this dilemma see Thucydides, *The Peloponnesian War*, translated by Rex Warner (Baltimore: Penguin Books, 1972). See also George Liska, *War and Order*, (Baltimore: The Johns Hopkins University Press, 1970); and George Liska, *States in Evolution: Changing Societies and Traditional Systems in World Politics* (Baltimore: Johns Hopkins University Press, 1973).

198   THE ARAB-ISRAELI CONFLICT TRANSFORMED

6. John Herz, *The Nation State and the Crisis of World Politics* (New York: David McKay, 1976), Introduction and chapter 1.

7. Kenneth N. Waltz, "Evaluating Theories," *American Political Science Review* 91, No. 4 (December 1997): 913.

8. Baldwin, *Neorealism and Neoliberalism,* 147–148.

9. Many chapters in Morgenthau's book on international politics deal with international institutions; see for instance *Politics Among Nations* (New York: Knopf, 1956), chapters 23–30. See also Inis Claude, *Power and International Relations* (New York: Random House, 1962), especially chapters 2–8.

10. John Grieco, in Baldwin, *Neorealism and Neoliberlism,* 335.

11. John Mearsheimer, "The False Promise of International Institutions," *International Security* 19, No. 3 (1995):13. For neorealists institutions are a dependent variable, for neoliberals regimes may have an independent impact on international politics.

12. Baldwin, *Neorealism and Neoliberalism,* 14.

13. Mearsheimer, "The False Promise of International Institutions": 8. It is significant that Mearsheimer refrained from adding norms and principles to his definition of international order.

14. Stephen Krasner, *International Regimes* (Ithaca: Cornell University Press, 1983), 2.

15. Robert Jervis, "Security Regimes," *International Organizations* 38, No.2 (1982): 357.

16. See the Forum section in *American Political Science Review,* quoted in EN 2.

17. For the role of institutions in classical realists see Morgenthau, *Politics among Nations,* 365–465. George Liska's emphasis on international equilibrium and the organization of security could be seen as an early version of intstitutionalism. See Liska, *International Equilibrium.* In E. H. Carr's *The Twenty Years Crisis, 1919-1939* (New York: Harper, 1964, originally published in 1939 by Macmillan), see especially part four. See also Patricia Stein Wrightson, "Morality, Realism, and Foreign Affairs," in Benjamin Frankel, ed., *Roots of Realism* (London: Frank Cass, 1996), 354–386.

18. Krasner, *International Regimes,* 3.

19. Ibid,. p. 8.

20. Ibid.

21. Baldwin, *Neorealism and Neoliberalism,* 329.

22. John Mearsheimer, "Back to the Future: Instability in Europe after the Cold War," *International Security* 15, No. 1 (Summer 1990): 5–56. See also some remarks made by Waltz on the future of NATO in Robert O. Keohane, "Institutional Theory and the Realist Challenge after the Cold War," in Baldwin, *Neorealism and Neoliberalism,* 286–287.

23. Alexander Wendt, "Anarchy Is What States Make Out of It," *International Organization* 46, No.2 (Spring 1992): 417.

24. Ibid. 394–395, On this approach, which highlights the role of process, see also: Emanuel Adler, "Seizing the Middle Ground: Constructivism in World Politics," *European Journal of International Relations* 3, No. 3 (September 1997):319–363; Ted Hopf, "The Promise of Constructivism in International Relations Theory," *International Security* 23 No. 1 (Summer 1998): 171–200; Peter J. Katzenstein, ed., *The Culture of National Security: Norms and Identity in World Politics* (New York: Columbia University Press, 1996); Yosef

Lapid and Friedrich V. Kratochwil, eds. *The Return of Culture and Identity in International Relations Theory* (Boulder: Lynne Rienner, 1996).

25. Mearsheimer, too, in the "The False Promise of International Institutions,": 42–44, pointed out that clearly realism was the hegemonic discourse or theory in world politics at least since the emergence of the Westphalian interstate system.

26. Krasner, "Regimes and the Limits of Realism: Regimes as Autonomous Variables," in Stephen Krasner, ed. *International Regimes,* 357.

27. Arthur Stein, "Coordination and Collaboration: Regimes in an Anarchic World," in Baldwin, *Neorealism and Neoliberalism,* 50–51.

28. Krasner, *International Regimes,* 3–4.

29. Hans Morgenthau's *Politics Among Nations* (1956 edition), pages 205–535 are dedicated to the limitations of power, international organization, and accommodation.

30. Henry Kissinger, *A World Restored* (Boston: Houghton Mifflin, 1957), 145.

31. Ibid., 2.

32. Ibid., 6.

33. Ibid., 1.

34. Michael Mandelbaum, *The Nuclear Revolution* (Cambridge: Cambridge University Press, 1981), 51–86.

35. Jervis, "Security Regimes": 187; Charles Lipson, "Are Security Regimes Possible? Historical Cases and Modern Issues," in Efraim Inbar, ed., *Regional Security Regimes* (Albany: State University of New York Press, 1995), 12–17.

36. Jervis "Security Regimes": 179. See also Lipson, 12–17.

37. Jervis, "Security Regimes": 185. For further analysis of the balance of power systems, see Stanley Hoffman, "International Systems and International Law," in Klaus Knor and Sidney Verba, eds., *The International System* (Princeton: Princeton University Press, 1961), 205–237.

38. See for instance Waltz, "Evaluating Theories," 915. See also Stephen Walt, "The Progressive Power of Realism," *American Political Science Review* 91, No. 4 (December 1997): 932. See in the same issue, Thomas J. Christensen and Jack Snyder, "Progressive Research on Degenerate Alliances,": 920.

39. Randall Schweller, "Bandwagoning for Profit: Bringing the Revisionist State Back In," *International Security* 19, No. 1 (Summer 1994): 72–107. See also by the same author, *Deadly Imbalances: Tripolarity and Hitler's Strategy of World Conquest* (New York: Columbia University Press, 1998).

40. Morgenthau, *Politics Among Nations,* 179–184. The significance of a balance of power that is reinforced by an external power is related to reassurances that a sudden transition of power is not a realistic option. For the threat of a transition of power see A. F. K. Organski, *World Politics* (New York: Alfred A. Knopf, 1968); For a whole volume dedicated to this question see Jack Kugler and Douglas Lemke, eds., *Parity and War* (Ann Arbor: University of Michigan Press, 1996).

41. For two articles summarizing the debate between neoliberals and neorealists on absolute and relative gains see Duncan Snidal, "Relative Gains and Patterns of International Cooperation," and Robert Powell, "Absolute and Relative Gains in International Relations," in Baldwin, *Neorealism and Neoliberalism,* 170–249.

42. Herz, "Idealist Internationalism and the Security Dilemma" : 157–180; See also

Butterfield, *History and Human Relations,* 19–20; Jervis, "Cooperation under the Security Dilemma" 167–214.

43. Kissinger, *A World Restored,* 145.

44. Ibid. See also Helen Milner, "The Assumption of Anarchy in International Relations," in Baldwin, *Neorealism and Neoliberalism,* 163–164.

45. Stein, "Coordination and Collaboration: Regimes in an Anarchic World," 38–45.

46. Ibid., 53.

47. Jervis, "Security Regimes" :178; Mearsheimer, "Back to the Future": 14–15.

48. On preventive war see Jack Levy, "Declining Power and the Preventive Motivation for War," *World Politics* 40, No. 1 (1987): 82–107. On the contribution of arms races see Randolph M. Siverson and Paul F. Diehl, "Arms Races, the Conflict Spiral, and the Onset of War," in Manus Mildarsky, ed. *Handbook of War Studies* (Boston: Unwin Hyman, 1989), 195–218 and in the same book Michael D. Intriligator and Dagobert L. Brito, "Richardsonian Arms Race Models," 219–236.

49. For a more comprehensive definition and its application to the Middle East see Yair Evron, "Confidence and Security-Building Measures in the Arab-Israeli Context," in Efraim Inbar and Shmuel Sandler, eds., *Middle Eastern Security, Prospects for an Arms Control Regime* (London: Frank Cross, 1995) 152–153.

50. Indeed, the first condition that Jervis posits for the establishment of a security regime is the support of the great powers. See Jervis, "Security Regimes": 176.

51. Jervis, "Security Regimes": 189.

52. Efraim Inbar and Shmuel Sandler, "The Changing Israeli Strategic Equation: Toward a Security Regime," *Review of International Studies* 21, No. 1 (1995): 41–59.

53. For an overview of crisis literature see: Michael Brecher, *Crises in World Politics: Theory and Reality* (Oxford: Pergamon, 1993), 8–25; Michael Haas, "Research on International Crisis: Obsolescence of an Approach?" *International Interactions* 13, No. 1: (1986): 23–57; and Raymond Tanter, "International Crisis Behavior: An Appraisal of the Literature," *The Jerusalem Journal of International Relations* 3, Nos. 2–3, (1978): 340–374.

54. To update the analysis of crises in the Arab-Israeli conflict for the fifty year time span analyzed in this book, an additional case that accords with the ICB definitions was added—the 1996 Operation Grapes of Wrath.

55. Michael Brecher and Hemda Ben-Yehuda, "System and Crisis in International Politics," *Review of International Studies* 11, No. 1 (1985) :23.

56. On the integration of the different phase models to a unified model of international crisis see Brecher, *Crises in World Politics,* 351–403.

57. On crossing the threshold between conflict and crisis, see John Vasquez, *The War Puzzle* (Cambridge: Cambridge University Press, 1993), 83. The Vasquez analysis is especially relevant for the Middle East since it deals with wars of rivalry, namely, wars between adversaries with small power gaps between them.

58. The usage of crisis as both agent of change and indicator appears in Michael Brecher and Patrick James, *Crisis and Change in World Politics* (Boulder: Westview Press, 1986).

59. For a more detailed exposition of the linkages between and among conflict, crisis, and war, see Patrick James, *Crisis and War* (Montreal and Kingston: McGill-Queen's

University Press, 1988). The concept formation in the present study also is distinguished from the traditions of events data and psychological modeling. Conflict is not understood to be measured in terms of something like the normal relations range on the one hand or presumed manifestations of hostility at the psychological level on the other. Instead, it is recognized that, to date, no compelling operational definition of conflict has been derived from a conceptual framework. Thus, the use of international crises to assess the level of conflict within a dyad (or, for that matter, a larger grouping) is a product of concerns about the need for face validity and the less appealing nature of the other salient options within the literature. As will become apparent, the key variable in the remainder of this study, magnitude, represents (a) something more than behavior alone (i.e., normal relations range); and (b) a deductively derived construct that is capable of providing the foundation for empirical measurement that is placed within the theoretical frame of reference traced to the conceptual definition of an international crisis.

60. For a similar approach to core issues and stakes in interstate rivalry see Vasquez, John *The War Puzzle,* and John Vasquez, "Why Global Conflict Resolution Is Possible," in John Vasquez et al., eds., *Beyond Confrontation: Learning Conflict Resolution in the Post–Cold War Era* (Ann Arbor: University of Michigan Press, 1995), 131–153.

61. The categories for this variable, as well as their application in chapters 2 and 3, follow the values of the ICB variables.

62. An international crisis consists of two adversaries or more, with at least one of them experiencing a foreign policy crisis, which is defined by ICB as a situation derived from three interrelated perceptions of: 1) threat to one or more basic values; 2) finite time for response; and 3) heightened probability of involvement in military hostilities before the challenge is overcome (for both definitions see Brecher, *Crises in World Politics: Theory and Reality,* 3.

63. In process we include only interactions which take place between the adversarial states located in the region. To illustrate, during the October-Yom Kippur War, superpower military moves, as well as the diplomatic mediation efforts carried out by the U.S. Secretary of State Henry Kissinger, are analyzed as a contextual element while the military and diplomatic moves of Israel-Egypt-Syria are described as part of the process realm.

64. See fn. 61 above.

65. On this issue of the linkage between diplomacy and force, see the classic work of Thomas Schelling, *Arms and Influence* (New Haven: Yale University Press, 1966), especially ch. 1.

66. These crises and others will be analyzed in chapters 2–5. A summary of all the crises in the Arab-Israeli conflict is found in the Glossary of the book.

67. Brecher and James, Crisis and Change in World Politics, 31–54.

68. These indicators will be added in the future when a cross regional analysis of crisis magnitude will be carried out. However, it should be noted that if strategic salience, heterogeneity, and number of issues add to magnitude, and receive high values when characterizing the Middle East, then findings on change in magnitude over time in the Middle East would be even more significant.

69. Michael Brecher "International Crises and Protracted Conflicts," *International Interactions* 11, No. 3 (1984): 237–297; Brecher and Wilkenfeld, *A Study of Crisis* (Ann Arbor: University of Michigan Press, 1997), 820–834.

70. Edward Azar, Paul Jureidini, and Ronald McLaurin, "Protracted Social Conflict,"*Journal of Palestine Studies* 8, No. 1 (Autumn 1978): 51–52. See also Brecher, *Crisis in World Politics: Theory and Reality,* 4–7 and Brecher and Wilkenfeld, *A Study of Crisis,* 5–7.

71. Brecher and Ben-Yehuda differentiate between equilibrium and stability, See Brecher and Ben Yehuda, "System and Crisis in International Politics": 21–23. On protracted conflicts see also Brecher, "International Crises and Protracted Conflicts": 237–297; and Zeev Maoz and Ben D. Mor, "Enduring Rivalries: The Early Years," *International Political Science Review* 17, No. 2 (1996): 141–160.

72. Azar, et al., "Protracted Social Conflict" 41–60.

73. Shmuel Sandler, "The Protracted Arab Israeli Conflict: A Temporal-Spatial Analysis," *The Jerusalem Journal of International Relations* 10, No. 4 (1988): 55.

74. Other conflicts that fall in this category are those in: Cyprus, India-Pakistan, Lebanon, Northen Ireland, some of the former republics of the Soviet Union, and the former Yugoslavia.

75. To illustrate the lack of literature at the time, in a comprehensive collection, entitled *Handbook of Political Conflict,* the two major articles surveying the literature on international conflict failed to look at ethnic conflicts; See Ted Robert Gurr, *Handbook of Political Conflict: Theory and Research* (New York: Free Press, 1980), chs. 8–9. Change could be detected if we examine another major work: David Singer and Melvin Small's *Resort to Arms.* Although their earlier reports to the Correlates of War project were limited to interstate wars, they dedicated an entire section of their 1982 edition to modern civil wars from 1816 to 1980. Nevertheless, the book lacks any reference to ethnic violence or conflict and is primarily concerned with internationalized civil wars; see David J. Singer and Melvin Small, *Resort to Arms* (Beverly Hills: Sage, 1982). Gurr himself turned to ethno-national conflict; see Ted Robert Gurr, *Minorities at Risk: A Global View of Ethnopolitical Conflicts* (Washington, DC: United States Institute of Peace, 1993). For more of Gurr's work see below.

76. Ted Robert Gurr and Barbara Harf, *Ethnic Conflict in World Politics* (Boulder: Westview Press, 1994), 15.

77. Ted Robert Gurr, "Why Minorities Rebel: A Global Analysis of Communal Mobilization and Conflict since 1945," *International Political Science Review* 14, No. 2 (1993): 165.

78. Ted Robert Gurr, "Peoples Against States: Ethnopolitical Conflict and the Changing World System," *International Studies Quarterly* 38, No. 3 (September 1994): 355–358.

79. A. D. Smith, *The Ethnic Revival,* ch. 1; Walker Connor, "Nation Building or Nation Destroying?" *World Politics* 24, No. 3 (April 1972): 332; See also Smith, "Ethnic Identity and World Order" : 158–159.

80. David Carment provided a three-way typology: irredenta, secession, and decolonization; see "The International Dimensions of Ethnic Conflict: Concept, Indicators, and Theory," *Journal of Peace Research* 30, No. 2 (April 1993): 139–140.

81. Efraim Inbar and Shmuel Sandler, "The Risks of Palestinian Statehood," *Survival* 39, No. 2 (Summer 1997): 32–33

82. Roy Licklider, "The Consequences of Negotiated Settlements in Civil Wars, 1945–1993," *American Political Science Review* 89, No. 3 (September 1995): 685. See also

Robert Harrison Wagner, " The Causes of Peace," in Roy Licklider, ed., *Stopping the Killing* (New York: New York University Press, 1993), 257–263.

83. For an insightful discussion of this relationship see R. Harrison Wagner, "Peace, War, and the Balance of Power," *American Political Science Review* 88, No. 3 (September, 1994): 593–607.

84. Licklider, "The Consequences of Negotiated Settlements": 683. See also William I Zartman, "The Unfinished Agenda: Negotiating Internal Conflicts," in Licklider, ed., *Stopping the Killing,* 32–34.

85. For a good recent summary of the argument see Chaim Kaufman, "Possible and Impossible Solutions to Ethnic Civil Wars," *International Security* 20, No. 4 (Spring 1996): 138–161.

86. Separation, to a lesser degree, can be materialized by partition but also via power-sharing arrangements, which include territorial autonomy or cultural autonomy. See for instance, Kamal S. Shehadi, "Ethnic Self-Determination and the Break-up of States," *Adelphi Paper* No. 283 (December 1993). See also articles by Ivo D. Duchacek, John Kincaid, Marcel Korn, and Shmuel Sandler in Daniel J. Elazar, ed., *Constitutional Design and Power Sharing in the Postmodern Epoch* (Lanham, MD: University Press of America, 1991), and Daniel J. Elazar, ed., *Federalism and Political Integration* (Lanham, MD: University Press of America, 1979).

87. See p.23 for the definitions of these distinct types of crisis.

88. We do not accept the notion that the Middle East, like any other region is *sui generis.* Stephen Walt, *The Origins of Alliances,* (Ithica: Cornell University Press, 1987) 14.

89. Brecher and Wilkenfeld, *A Study of Crisis,* 780.

90. Ibid., part 4, 779–802. Similarly, but with emphasis on different types of ethnic crises Carment, and Carment and James, elaborated on the unique attributes of ethnic cases. See for example: Carment, "The International Dimensions of Ethnic Conflict : Concepts, Indicators, and Theory": 137–150; David Carment, and Patrick James. "The United Nations at 50: Managing Ethnic Crises—Past and Present," *Journal of Peace Research* 35, No. 1 (1998): 61–82; David Carment, and Patrick James, "Ethnic Conflict at the International Level: An Appraisal of Theories and Evidence," in David Carment and Patrick James, eds., *Wars in the Midst of Peace* (Pittsburgh: University of Pittsburgh Press, 1997), 252–264; and David Carment, and Patrick James, "Internal Constraints and Interstate Ethnic Conflict: Towards a Crisis-Based Assessment of Irredentism," *Journal of Conflict Resolution* 39, No. 1 (1995): 82–109.

91. Brecher and Wilkenfeld, *A Study of Crisis,* 787–788.

92. Carment, "The International Dimensions of Ethnic Conflict, Concepts, Indicators, and Theory": 137–150.

93. For a summary of findings on "ethnic related" and "ethnic driven" variables, see Brecher and Wilkenfeld, *A Study of Crisis,* 801–802.

94. Ethnic conflicts, they argued in accordance with the traditional typology, derive from two main sources: secessionist and irredentist, Brecher and Wilkenfeld, *A Study of Crises,* 780–802. A secessionist conflict involves one or more ethnic groups, who demand a reduction of control or autonomy from a central authority through political means. These groups refuse to recognize the political state authorities and induce internal challenge to existing regimes, thereby creating an international crisis. In addition, secessionist-oriented ethnic groups may trigger a crisis for the state's allies, or seek external sup-

port from other groups/states. Secessionism recognizes the central role ethnic elements play in provoking interstate struggles. By contrast, in an irredentist case, core attention is given to state actors, since an irredentist conflict is defined as a state's claim to territory of an entity, usually of a state adversary, in which an ethnic group is in a numerical minority. In these situations, state adversaries use ethnic minorities to promote their national interests. See Carment and James, "The United Nations at 50: Managing Ethnic Crises—Past and Present": 69.

95. See Carment, "The International Dimensions of Ethnic Conflict, Concepts, Indicators, and Theory" :140.

96. This notion of irredentism was advanced by Carment, "The International Dimension of Ethnic Conflicts" :139.

CHAPTER 2. CONTEXT, CRISIS MAGNITUDE, AND CHANGE

1. The description of CMI attributes in this chapter as well as in chapters 3 and 4 is based on the ICB data-set. Accordingly, we focus on the twenty-five crises in the Arab-Israeli conflict identified by the ICB project and on an additional case in 1996 that is compatible with ICB definitions of crisis but was not coded by ICB coders because the project is only updated until 1994.

2. This chapter and the one that follows are organized around analytical concepts rather than historical narrative. This approach accords with the theoretical framework presented in chapter 1 and makes the testing of the winding down thesis, presented in the book, possible. A summary of each crisis is presented in the Glossary (the last section of the book), making it easy to pick up the sequence of events. For each crisis a detailed list of references is provided, replacing the need to repeat sources in this chapter on multiple occasions as they continue to be used in the analysis.

3. See chapters 5 and 6 for an analysis of ethnicity in the Arab-Israeli conflict.

4. We start with 1948 since the last months of 1947 only included minimal reactions to UN Resolution 181 and the core of the crisis began after the declaration of Israel's independence in May 1948.

5. As noted in Table 2, the years free of crisis were: 1950, 1952, 1954, 1957–1959, 1961–1962, 1964–1965, and 1971–1972. One or more midrange cases occurred in 1951, 1953, 1963, 1966, and 1968.

6. One or more major crisis erupted or continued in 1948–1949, 1955–1956, 1967, 1969–1970 and 1973–1974.

7. These include: 1975, 1977, 1979, 1984, 1986–1992, and 1994.

8. The former included 1976, 1978, 1985, and 1993, while the latter involved the 1980–1983 period.

9. Operation Accountability in 1993, coded by ICB, and Operation Grapes of Wrath in 1996, which accords with ICB crisis definitions.

10. The findings on changes in the frequency of crisis over time are also supported by findings on crisis magnitude, to be discussed in chapter 4.

11. These gravity of threat categories follow the values of the GRAVITY variable in the ICB project.

12. This crisis is also known as the first Arab-Israeli war. We follow ICB titles in the crises we analyze for the sake of clarity and consistency.

13. See Brecher and Wilkenfeld, *A Study of Crisis,* 281 and Nadav Safran, *From War to War: The Arab-Israeli Confrontation, 1948–1967* (New York: Pegasus, 1969), 268, who mentions also an earlier escalation, on the fourteenth when the Egyptian Army was put into a state of alert.

14. On the nuclear elements in the conflict see chapter 3 fn. 7.

15. For details on the Israeli threat perception see Moshe Dayan, *Diary of the Sinai Campaign* (New York: Harper and Row, 1966), 1-19.

16. On the cycle of terror and counterterror see: Ian Black, and Benny Morris, *Israel's Secret Wars: A History of Israel's Intelligence Services* (New York: Grove Weidenfeld, 1991); David Maimon (Heb.), *The Terrorism that was Beaten: the Suppression of the Terrorism in the Gaza Strip, 1971–1972* (Jerusalem: Steimatzky, 1993); Ariel Merari and Shlomi Elad (Heb.), *Sabotage Abroad: Palestinian Terrorism Abroad, 1968–1986* (Tel-Aviv: Kibbutz Hameuchad, 1986).

17. See, Brecher and Wilkfield, *A Study of Crisis*, 277.

18. See Case no. 6 in the Glossary.

19. On the domestic threat in international crises and internal regime changes see also: Andrew J. Enterline, "Regime Changes, Neighborhoods, and Interstate Conflict, 1816–1992," *Journal of Conflict Resolution* 42, No. 6 (December 1998): 804–829.

20. Given the indirect nature of these threats they are designated as low level threats, different from direct threats that for authoritarian regimes are regarded as high level threats.

21. See Shmuel Sandler, *The State of Israel, the Land of Israel* (Westport: Greenwood Press,1993), 121–129.

22. On the long spiral of cross-border penetrations and reprisals see also: Hanan Alon, *Countering Palestinian Terrorism in Israel: Toward a Policy Analysis of Countermeasures.* Rand Report No. 1567 (Santa Monica: Rand, 1980); Shlomo Ahronson and Dan Horowitz, "The Strategy of Controlled Retaliation—The Israeli Example," *Medina u'Mimshal* 1, No.1 (1971): 77–99; Barry M. Blechman, "The Impact of Israel's Reprisals on Behavior of the Bordering Arab Nations Directed at Israel," *Journal of Conflict Resolution* 16, No. 2 (June 1972): 155–81; Benny Morris, *Righteous Victims: A History of the Zionist-Arab Conflict 1881–1999* (New York: Alfred A.Knopf, 1999), 269–284; Benny Morris, *Israel's Border Wars, 1949–1956* (Oxford: Clarendon Press, 1993); Ehud Ya'ari (Heb.), *Egypt and the Fedayeen 1953–1956* (Givat Haviva: Center for Arab and Afro-Asian Studies, 1975).

23. On the dangers of arms races and the need for arms control in the conflict see: Shai Feldman, "The Middle East Arms Control Agenda: 1994–95," *The International Spectator* 29, No. 3 (July-Sept. 1994): 67–82; Peter Jones, "Arms Control in the Middle East: Some Reflections on ACRS," *Security Dialogue* 28, No.1 (1997): 57–70; Aaron Karp, "Ballistic Missile Proliferation," *SIPRI Yearbook* 1991: 317–343; Dinsha Mistry, "Ballistic Missile Proliferation and the MTCR, a Ten Year Review," *Contemporary Security Policy 18,* No. 3 (1997): 59–82; Gerald Steinberg, "Israeli Security and the Peace Process," *Security Dialogue* 25, No. 1 (March 1994): 51–62; Gerald Steinberg, "Israeli Arms Control Policy: Cautious Realism," *Journal of Strategic Studies* 17, No. 2 (June 1994): 1–16.

24. In 1957 there were 125 incidents between Israel and Syria, in 1958: 100, 1959: 50, 1960: 67. David Ben-Gurion, *The Restored State of Israel* (Tel Aviv: Am Oved, 1969), 688.

25. By contrast, six years later during the Six Day War crisis, a similar movement of forces escalated into an existential threat and involved full-scale war between Israel and its Arab adversaries; see Case no. 11 in the Glossary.

26. The identification of influence as the most salient threat in the crisis is true when international rather than foreign policy crises are analyzed, as indeed ICB approached this case on the system level. When we shift to the ethnic realm for the PLO and Israel, Palestinian presence in Lebanon, intercommunal order, and grave war related damage were all at stake. These aspects will be further elaborated in chapter 6.

27. On the broader issue of economics and armaments and their impact on conflict dynamics see David Kinsella, "Conflict in Context: Arms Transfers and Third World Rivalries during the Cold War," *American Journal of Political Science* 38, No. 3 (1994): 557–581; David Kinsella and Herbert K. Tillema,"Arms and Aggression in the Middle East: Overt Military Interventions, 1948–1991," *Journal of Conflict Resolution* 39, No. 2 (1995): 306–329; Jim Lederman, "Economics of the Arab-Israeli Peace Process," *Orbis* 39, No. 4 (Fall 1995): 549–566; Robert E. Looney,"The Economics of Middle East Military Expenditures: Implications for Arms Reduction in the Region," *Bulletin of Peace Proposals* 22, No. 4 (December 1991): 407–417; Jochen Mayer and Ralph Rotte, "Arms and Aggression in the Middle East, 1948–1991—a Reappraisal," *Journal of Conflict Resolution* 43, No. 1 (Feb. 1999): 45–57.

28. On the rivalry over water resources in the conflict see also: Natasha Beschorner, *Water and Instability in the Middle East* Adelphi Papers No. 273. (London: Brassey's, 1992); Mostafa Dolatyar, "Water Diplomacy in the Middle East,"*Iranian Journal of International Affairs* 7, No. 3 (1995): 599–615; Marcia Drezon-Tepler, "Contested Waters and the Prospects for Arab-Israeli Peace," *Middle Eastern Studies* 30, No. 2 (April 1994): 281–303; Godfrey H. Jansen, "The Problem of the Jordan Waters," *World Today* 20, No. 2 (Feb. 1964): 60–68; Fred Khouri, "The Policy of Retaliation in Arab-Israeli Relations," *The Middle East Journal* 20, No. 4 (Autumn 1966): 435–455; Miriam R. Lowi, "Bridging the Divide:Transboundary Resource Disputes and the Case of West Bank Water," *International Security* 18, No. 1 (Summer 1993): 113–138; Donald Neff,"Israel-Syria: conflict at the Jordan River, 1949–1967," *Journal of Palestine Studies* 23, No. 4 (Summer 1994): 26–40; Donald Neff, "The U.S. , Iraq, Israel, and Iran: Backdrop to War," *Journal of Palestine Studies* 20, No. 4 (Summer 1991): 23–41; Yoram Nimrod, "Conflict Over the Jordan—Last Stage," *New Outlook* 8, No. 6 (September 1965): 5–18; Yoram Nimrod,"The Jordan's Angry Waters," *New Outlook* 8, No. 5 (July-August 1965): 19–33; Sara Reguer, "Controversial Waters: Exploitation of the Jordan River, 1950–1980," *Middle Eastern Studies* 29, No. 1 (January 1993): 53–90; Samir N. Saliba, *The Jordan River Dispute* (The Hague: Nijhoff, 1968); Hillel Shuval, "Towards Resolving Conflicts over Water between Israel and Its Neighbours:The Israeli-Palestinian Shared Use of the Mountain Aquifer as a Case Study," *Israel Affairs* 2, No.1 (Autumn 1995): 215–238.

29. See chapter 1 pp. 11.

30. In this case, as well as in all the following crises, the participating states are listed in the sequence that they join the international crisis: Egypt was the first crisis actor in the 1947–1948 case and Israel was the last to encounter the three necessary and sufficient conditions of an ICB crisis. The Palestinians were not considered by the ICB

data-set as a crisis actor, due to the realist orientation of the project. As noted earlier in this chapter as well as in chapters 3 and 4, we follow the ICB definitions strictly. However, we are aware that Palestinian participation played an important role in this crisis as well as in other cases defined in this book as ethnic crises. To supplement this lacuna the ethnic dimensions in crises are described in depth and analyzed in chapters 5 and 6.

31. For an in-depth analysis on the role of superpowers in the conflict see also the sections on process and outcomes in chapter 3 as well as the individual case descriptions in the Glossary, found at the end of the book.

32. The limited resort to violence by a nonregional power was illustrated by the British involvement in 1948 and in the1969 case in which the USSR alone employed a strategy of direct military involvement, but its activity was considerably confined and manifested itself in a single air battle with the Israeli air force. See Case no. 14 in the Glossary.

33. On the policy, role and impact of the major powers and other European states in the conflict see also: David Allen and Alfred Pijpers eds., *European Foreign Making and the Arab-Israeli Conflict* (The Hague: Nijhoff, 1984); Alan L. G. Bullock, *Ernest Bevin: Foreign Secretary, 1945–1951* (London: Heinemann, 1983); Michael Cohen, *Palestine and the Great Powers, 1945–48* (Princeton: Princeton University Press, 1982) Michael Cohen, *Palestine: Retreat from the Mandate, the Making of British policy, 1936–45* (London: Paul Elek, 1978); Paul Marie De La Gorce, "Europe and the Arab-Israel Conflict: a Survey," *Journal of Palestine Studies* 26, No. 3 (Spring 1997): 5–16; Halford L. Hoskins, "The Guardianship of the Suez Canal: A View of Anglo-Egyptian Relations," *Middle East Journal* 4, No. 2 (April 1950): 143–154; Ilan Pappe, *The Making of the Arab-Israeli Conflict, 1947-51.* London: I.B.Tauris, 1992; I. Pappe, *Britain and the Arab-Israeli Conflict, 1948–51* (New York: St. Martin's, 1988); Mohamed Rabie, "The U.S.-PLO Dialogue: The Swedish Connection," *Journal of Palestine Studies* 21, No. 4 (Summer 1992): 54–66; James L. Richardson, *Crisis Diplomacy: The Great Powers since the Mid-Nineteenth Century* (Cambridge: Cambridge University Press, 1994). On major power intervention over the 1918–1988 period see Paul K. Huth, "Major Power Intervention in International Crises, 1918–1988," *Journal of Conflict Resolution* 42 No. 6 (Dec. 1998): 744–770.

34. On the specifics and effects of UN involvement in crises see also: Carment and James, "The United Nations at 50: Managing Ethnic Crises—Past and Present," : 61–82; On the UN in the Arab-Israeli conflict see: Phyllis Bennis, "The United Nations and Palestine: Partition and Its Aftermath," *Arab Studies Quarterly* 19, No. 3 (Summer 1997): 47–75; General Odd Bull, *War and Peace in the Middle East* (London: Leo Cooper, 1976); Michael Comay, *U.N. Peacekeeping in the Israel-Arab Conflict, 1948–1975: An Israel Critique.* Jerusalem Papers on Peace Problems No. 17–18. (Jerusalem: Leonard Davis Institute for International Relations, Hebrew University of Jerusalem, 1976); Gerald L. Curtis, "The United Nations Observation Group in Lebanon," *International Organization* 18 (Autumn 1964): 738–765; F. S. Hamezeh, *U.N. Conciliation for Palestine, 1949–67* (Beirut: Institute for Palestine Studies, 1968); James O. C. Jonah, "The Military Talks at Kilometer 101: The U.N's Effectiveness as a Third Party," *Negotiation Journal* 6, No.1 (January 1990): 53–70; Arthur Lall, *The United Nations and the Middle East Crisis, 1967,* 2nd ed. (New York: Columbia University Press, 1970); Istvan S. Pogany, *The Security Council and the Arab-Israeli Conflict* (London: Gower Publishing Company, 1984); Gideon Rafael, *Destination Peace: Three Decades of Israeli Foreign Policy* (New York: Stein and Day, 1981).

208 THE ARAB-ISRAELI CONFLICT TRANSFORMED

35. The ethnic dimension in the Arab-Israeli conflict will be elaborated in chapters 5 and 6.

36. See chapter 5.

37. Nasser testified that it was the Gaza raid that made him negotiate for Soviet arms. See Ewrnest Stock, *Israel on the Road to Sinai 1949-1956* (Ithaca: Cornell University Press, 1967), 115, based on an interview in the *New York Times*, 6 Oct 1955 p. 1.

38. For an analysis of the Gulf war and its implications on the Arab-Israeli conflict see chapter 6.

39. The ICB project does not regard the Palestinian elements as independent crisis actors, and Israel, in these instances, was not a crisis actor because its level of stress did not cross the threshold of crisis, that is, it did not perceive high threat, limited time, or high probability of violence.

40. On the concept of an opportunity crisis and it application see Hemda Ben-Yehuda, "Opportunity Crisis: Framework and Findings, 1918–1994," *Conflict Management and Peace Science* 17, No. 1: 69–102.

41. These superpower-involvement categories follow the values of the USINV and USSRINV variables in the ICB project.

42. On the superpower role in crises see also: Yaacov Bar-Siman-Tov, *Israel, the Superpowers, and the War in the Middle East* (New York: Praeger, 1987); Abraham Ben-Zvi, "The Superpower Option for Resolving the Arab-Israeli Conflict: Precedents, Preconditions, and Prospects," *Conflict* 10, No. 1 (1990): 63–81; Bruce Bueno de-Mesquita, "Multilateral Negotiations: A Spatial Analysis of the Arab-Israeli Dispute," *International Organization* 44, No. 3 (Summer 1990): 317–340; Helena Cobban, *The Superpowers and the Syrian-Israeli Conflict* (New York: Praeger, 1991); Fred Halliday, "The Great Powers and the Middle East," *Middle East Report* 151 (March–April 1988): 3–6; David Korn, *Stalemate: The War of Attrition and Great Power Diplomacy in the Middle East, 1967–70* (Boulder: Westview Press, 1992); Louis Kriesberg, *International Conflict Resolution: The US-USSR and Middle East Cases* (New Haven: Yale University Press, 1992); Peter Margold, *Superpower Intervention in the Middle East* (New York: St. Martin's, 1978); Jeffrey Milstein, "American and Soviet Influence, Balance of Power and Arab-Israeli Violence" in *Peace, War, Numbers, and International Relations*, ed. Bruce Russett (Beverly Hills: Sage Publications, 1972), 139–166; Barry Rubin, "Reshaping the Middle East," *Foreign Affairs* 69, No. 3 (Summer 1990): 131–146; Gerald L. Sorokin, "Patrons, Clients and Allies in the Arab-Israeli Conflict," *Journal of Strategic Studies* 20, No. 1 (March 1997): 46–71; Alan R. Taylor, *The Superpowers and the Middle East* (New York: Syracuse University Press, 1991); Saadia Touval, *The Peace-Brokers: Mediators in the Arab-Israeli Conflict, 1948–79* (Princeton: Princeton University Press, 1982); Gregory F. Treverton, *Crisis Management and the Superpowers in the Middle East* (Farnborough: Gower, 1981); Panayiotis Jerasimof Vatikiotis, *Arab and Regional Politics in the Middle East* (London: Croom Helm, 1984).

43. There might be an overlap in cases where the superpowers are crisis actors and high role involvement is observed, such as during the 1956 Suez war or 1973 October War cases, but the two attributes differ conceptually, enabling us to view the unique aspects of superpower involvement in crises.

44. For details on the U.S. policy and its role in the conflict see: Nabeel Abraham, "The Conversion of Chairman Arafat," *American-Arab Affairs* 31 (Winter 1989): 53–69; Dean Acheson, *Present at the Creation: My Years in the State Department* (New York: New

American Library, 1969); Stephen E. Ambrose, *Eisenhower: The President 1952–1969, Vol. 2* (London: George Allen and Unwin, 1984); Moshe Arens, *Broken Covenant: American Foreign Policy and the Crisis Between the US and Israel* (New York: Simon and Schuster, 1995); Robert J. Art, "A Defensible Defense: America's Grand Strategy after the Cold War," *International Security* 15, No. 4 (Spring 1991): 5–53; Naseer H. Aruri, "The U.S. and the Arabs: A Woeful History," *Arab Studies Quarterly* 19, No. 3 (Summer 1997): 29–45; Nasser H. Aruri, "The United States and Palestine: Reagan's Legacy to Bush," *Journal of Palestine Studies* 18, No. 3 (Spring 1989): 3–21; James A. Baker, III., *The Politics of Diplomacy* (New York: G.P. Putnam, 1995); George Ball, "The Unbalanced Triangle: The United States, Israel and Palestine," *Arab Studies Quarterly* 10, No. 4 (Fall 1988): 375–383; Zbigniew Brzezinski, *Power and Principle: Memoirs of the National Security Adviser 1977–1981* (New York: Farrar, Straus, Giroux, 1983); Jimmy Carter, "The Middle East Consultation: A Look to the Future," *Middle East Journal* 41, No. 1 (Winter 1987): 187–191; Jimmy Carter, *Keeping Faith: Memoirs of a President* (New York: Bantam Books, 1982); Kathleen Christison, "Bound by a Frame of Reference, Part 2: U.S. Policy and the Palestinians, 1948–88," *Journal of Palestine Studies* 27, No. 3 (Spring 1988): 20–34; Duncan L. Clarke, "U.S. Security Assistance to Egypt and Israel: Politically Untouchable?" *Middle East Journal* 51, No. 2 (Spring 1997): 200–214; Steven R. David, "The Continuing Importance of American Interests in the Middle East after the Cold War," *Israel Affairs* 2 Nos. 3–4 (Spring-Summer 1996): 94–106; Robert J. Donovan, *Conflict and Crisis: The Presidency of Harry S. Truman, 1945–1948* (New York: Norton, 1977); Robert J. Donovan, *Tumultuous Years: The Presidency of Harry S. Truman 1949–1953* (New York: Norton, 1977); Alan Dowty, *Middle East Crisis: U.S. Decision-Making in 1958, 1970, and 1973* (Berkeley: University of California Press, 1984); Herbert Druks, *From Truman Through Johnson: A Documentary History* (New York: Robert Speller, 1971); Dwight D. Eisenhower, *The White House Years Vol. 2: Waging Peace, 1956–1961* (Garden City: Doubleday, 1965); Dwight D. Eisenhower, *The White House Years Vol. 1: Mandate for Change 1953–1956* (Garden City: Doubleday, 1963); Rowland Evans, and Robert Novak, *Nixon in the White House: The Frustration of Power* (New York: Random House, 1971); Rowland Evans and Robert Novak, *Lyndon B. Johnson: The Exercise of Power* (London: Allen and Unwin, 1967); Mahmud A. Faksh, "U.S. Policy in the Middle East: Incongruity in Political Strategy and Action," *American-Arab Affairs* 23 (Winter 1987–88): 38–46; Herman Finer, *Dulles Over Suez: The Theory and Practice of His Diplomacy* (Chicago: Quadrangle, 1964); Steven Z. Freiberger, *Dawn over Suez: The Rise of American Power in the Middle East, 1953–1957* (Chicago: I.R. Dee, 1992); Adam M. Garfinkle, "U.S. Decision-Making in the Jordan Crisis: Correcting the Record," *Political Science Quarterly* 100, No. 1 (1985): 117–138; Alexander M. Haig, Jr., *Caveat: Realism, Reagan, and Foreign Policy* (New York: Macmillan, 1984); Martin Indyk, "Beyond the Balance of Power: America's Choice in the Middle East," *National Interest* 26 (Winter 1991–92): 33–43; Martin Indyk, "Peace without the PLO," *Foreign Policy* 83, (Summer 1991): 30–38; Lyndon B. Johnson, *The Vantage Point: Perspectives of the Presidency 1963–1969* (New York: Holt, Rinehart and Winston, 1971); Marvin and Bernard Kalb *Kissinger* (Boston: Little, Brown, 1974); Henry Kissinger, *Diplomacy* (New York: Simon and Schuster, 1994); Henry Kissinger, *Years of Upheaval* (London: Weidenfeld and Nicolson, 1982); Henry Kissinger, *The White House Years* (London: Weidenfeld and Nicolson, 1979); Bruce Kuniholm, "Retrospect and Prospects: Forty Years of US Middle East Policy," *The Middle East Journal* 41, No. 1 (Winter 1987): 7–25; Fred H. Lawson, "Can U.S. Economic Assistance Alter Syria's Posture toward Israel?" *Middle East Policy* 4, No. 4 (October

1996): 102–109; George Lenczowski, *American Presidents and the Middle East* (Durham: Duke University Press, 1990); Charles Lipson, "American Support for Israel: History, Sources, Limits," *Israel Affairs* 2, Nos. 3–4 (Spring-Summer 1996): 128–146; W. Roger Louis, *The British Empire in the Middle East 1945–51: Arab Nationalism, the United States, and Postwar Imperialism* (Oxford, England: Clarendon Press, 1984); Edward N. Luttwak, "Strategic Aspects of U.S-Israeli Relations," *Israel Affairs* 2, Nos. 3–4 (Spring-Summer 1996)· 198–211· Madiha Rashid Al Madfai, *Jordan, the United States, and the Middle East Peace Process, 1974-1991* (Cambridge: Cambridge University Press, 1993); Thomas R. Mattair, "The Bush Administration and the Arab-Israeli Conflict," *American-Arab Affairs* 36, (Spring 1991): 52–72; Richard M. Nixon, *The Memoirs of Richard Nixon* (New York: Grosset and Dunlop, 1978); William B. Quandt, *Peace Process: American Diplomacy and the Arab-Israeli Conflict since 1967* (Washington, DC: Brookings Institution; and Berkeley: University of California Press, 1993); William B. Quandt, *The Middle East: Ten Years after Camp David* (Washington DC: Brookings Institution, 1988); William B. Quandt, *Camp David: Peacemaking and Politics* (Washington DC: Brookings Institution, 1986); William B. Quandt, "Reagan's Lebanon Policy: Trial and Error," *Middle East Journal* 38, No. 2 (Spring 1984): 237–254; William B. Quandt, "Lebanon, 1958, and Jordan, 1970," in Barry Blechman and Stephen S. Kaplan, eds. *Force Without War: U.S. Armed Forces as a Political Instrument* (Washington, DC: Brookings Institution, 1978); William B. Quandt, *Decade of Decisions: American Policy Toward the Arab-Israeli Conflict, 1967–1976* (Berkeley: University of California Press, 1977); Rabie, "The U.S.-PLO Dialogue: The Swedish Connection": 54–66; Edward R. R. Sheehan, *The Arabs, Israelis, and Kissinger—A Secret History of American Diplomacy in the Middle East* (New York: Reader's Digest Press, 1976); Arthur M. Schlesinger Jr., *Robert Kennedy and His Times* (Boston: Houghton Mifflin, 1978); David Schoenbaum, *The United States and the State of Israel* (New York: Oxford University Press, 1993); Haim Shaked and Itamar Rabinovitch, eds., *The Middle East and the United States* (New Brunswick: Transaction Books, 1980); Steven L. Spiegel, *The Other Arab-Israeli Conflict: Making America's Middle East Policy from Truman to Reagan* (Chicago: University of Chicago Press, 1985); Shibley Telhami, "The United States and the Middle East Peace: The Case for Arbitrating Israeli-Palestinian Disputes," *Brookings Review* 13, No. 44 (Fall 1995): 32–35; Harry S. Truman, *Years of Trial and Hope. The Memoirs of Harry Truman, Vol. 2* (New York: Doubleday, 1956); Harry S. Truman, *Year of Decisions: 1945. The Memoirs of Harry Truman, Vol. 1* (New York: Doubleday, 1955); Cyrus Vance, *Hard Choices: Critical Years in America's Foreign Policy* (New York: Simon and Schuster, 1983); Stephen Zunes, "The Israeli-Jordanian Agreement: Peace or Pax Americana?" *Middle East Policy* 3, No. 4 (April 1995): 57–68.

45. For further information on the distinct modes of USSR involvement during the Cold War as well as the policies of the USSR successor republics see: Shlomo Avineri, "The Impact of Changes in the Soviet Union and Eastern Europe on the Arab-Israeli Conflict," *Mediterranean Quarterly* 2, No. 1 (Winter 1991): 45–57; Uri Hannah, and John P. Bar-Joseph, "Intervention Threats in Short Arab-Israeli Wars: an Analysis of Soviet Crisis Behavior," *The Journal of Strategic Studies* 2, No. 4 (Dec 1988):436–467; Michael Confino and Shimon Shamir *The USSR and the Middle East* (Jerusalem: Israel University Press, 1973); Edward Crankshaw, *Khrushchev: A Biography* (London: Collins, 1966); Karen Dawisha, "The USSR in the Middle East: Superpower in Eclipse," *Foreign Affairs* 6, No. 2 (Winter 1982/83): 438–451; Robert, O Freedman." Israeli-Russian Relations since the Collapse of the Soviet Union," *Middle East Journal* 49, No. 2 (1995): 233–247; Robert Freedman, "Israel and the Successor States of the Soviet Union: a Preliminary Analysis,"

Mediterranean Quarterly 4, No. 2 (Spring 1993): 64–89; Robert O. Freedman, *Soviet Policy Toward the Middle East since 1970* third ed. (New York: Praeger, 1982); Jon D. Glassman, *Arms for the Arabs: The Soviet Union and War in the Middle East* (Baltimore: Johns Hopkins University Press, 1975); Galia Golan, *Moscow and the Middle East: New Thinking on Regional Conflict* (London: Pinter, 1992); Galia Golan, "The Soviet Union and the War in Lebanon," *The Middle East Journal* 40, No. 2 (Spring 1986): 285–305; Galia Golan, "Soviet Decisionmaking in the Yom Kippur War," in Jiri Valenta and William Potter, eds., *Soviet Decision-making for National Security* (London: George Allen and Unwin, 1984): 185–217; Galia Golan, *Yom Kippur and After: The Soviet Union and the Middle East Crisis* (Cambridge: Cambridge University Press, 1977); Melvin A. Goodman and Carolyn McGiffert Ekedahl, "Trends in Soviet Policy in the Middle East and the Gulf," *International Journal* 45, No. 3 (1990): 603–630; Melvin A. Goodman and Carolyn McGiffert Ekedahl, "Gorbachev's 'New Directions' in the Middle East," *Middle East Journal* 41, No. 1 (Winter 1987): 571–586; Baruch Hazan, *Soviet Propaganda: A Case Study of the Middle East Conflict* (New York: Wiley, 1976); Mohamed Heikal, *The Sphinx and the Commissar: The Rise and Fall of Soviet Influence in the Middle East* (New York: Harper and Row, 1978); Ilana Kass, *Soviet Involvement in the Middle East* (Boulder: Westview, 1978); Walter Z. Laqueur, *The Soviet Union and the Middle East* (New York: Fredrick A. Preager Publishers, 1959); Alvin Z. Rubinstein, *Red Star on the Nile* (Princeton: Princeton University Press, 1977); Marshall Shulman, *Stalin's Foreign Policy Reappraised* (Cambridge: Belknap Press, 1963); Oles M. Smolanski, *The Soviet Union and the Arab East Under Khrushchev* (Lewisburg: Bucknell University. Press, 1974); Jan F. Triska and David D. Finley, *Soviet Foreign Policy* (New York: Macmillan, 1968); Adam B. Ulam, *Expansion and Coexistence: A History of Soviet Foreign Policy, 1917–73* (New York: Praeger, 1973).

46. *Middle Eastern Affairs* (Dec. 1953): 384.

47. Michael Brecher with Benjamin Geist, *Decisions in Crisis: Israel 1967 and 1973* (Berkeley: University of California Press, 1980), 282–285.

48. In the analysis of process only states acting under crisis-generated stress are considered.

49. For a full discussion on the conditions of conflict regulation and crisis moderation see chapter 4. Another explanation, which we will develop in chapters 5 and 6, concerns the element of ethnicity. Contextual attributes indicate that lower gravity, dyadic or single actor cases, and minimal superpower involvement, usually marked the intertwining of the interstate and ethnic-state dimensions. These cases escalate from the sub-state domain to the interstate arena, as did crises between Israel and Jordan or Israel and Egypt in the 1950s and 1960s, and those related to the Lebanese civil war in the 1970s and 1980s. Clearly then, our picture of change in conflict will not be complete until we enhance it with an analysis of the relationship between the interstate and ethnic domains of crises in the Arab–Israeli conflict.

CHAPTER 3. PROCESS, OUTCOMES, OVERALL CRISIS MAGNITUDE, AND CHANGE

1. The Description of CMI attributes in this chapter is organized around analytical concepts rather than historical narrative. This approach accords with the theoretical framework presented in chapter 1 and makes the testing of the winding-down thesis,

presented in the book, possible. A summary of each crisis is presented in the Glossary (the last section of the book), making it easy to pick up the sequence of events. For each crisis a detailed list of references is provided, replacing the need to repeat sources in this chapter on multiple occasions as they continue to be used in the analysis.

2. Even in these three crises that were managed via negotiations, hostile acts did take place, though not by the threatened state, i.e., the one targeted by Israeli reprisal activity. In all these cases Israel was not recorded by ICB data-set as a crisis actor since the three conditions of high threat, finite time, and perceived high probability of violence were absent. On the whole, ICB did not find that sub-state hostility in these cases was severe enough to induce Israeli decision makers into a crisis-generated stress situation. On the distinction between crisis actors and actors in crisis see chapter 1 pp. 14–16 and chapter 2 p. 42. An ICB international crisis begins only when at least two states confront one another. Hence, the role of the Palestinians is minimized in the present analysis. In chapters 5 and 6 our perspective changes and we adopt an ethnic orientation in order to fill the gap missing here.

3. On the Israel-Syria relationship in the protracted conflict see: Alon Ben-Meir, "Israel and Syria: The Search for a 'Risk-Free' Peace," *Middle East Policy* 4, No.1–2 (Sept. 1995): 140–155; Shebonti Ray Dadwal, "Syria Continues to Hold the Key to Peace in West Asia," *Strategic Analysis* 18, No. 1 (1995): 127–140; Zhair M. Diab, "Syrian Security Requirements in a Peace Settlement with Israel," *Israel Affairs* 1, No. 4 (Summer, 1996): 71–88; Zhair M. Diab, "Have Syria and Israel Opted for Peace?" *Middle East Policy* 3, (1994): 77–90; Y. Evron, *War and Intervention in Lebanon: The Israeli-Syrian Deterrence Dialogue* (Baltimore: Johns Hopkins University Press, 1987); Joel M. Guttman, "The Explanatory Power of Game Theory in International Politics: Syrian-Israeli Crisis Interactions, 1951–87," *Economics and Politics* 9, No. 1 (March 1997): 71–85; Raymond A. Hinnebusch, "Does Syria Want Peace? Syrian Policy in the Syrian-Israeli Peace Negotiations," *Journal of Palestine Studies* 26, No. 1 (Fall 1996): 42–57; Raymond A. Hinnebusch, "Syria: The Politics of Peace and Regime Survival," *Middle East Policy* 3, No. 4 (April 1995): 74–87; Brian S. Mandell, "Getting to Peacemaking in Principal Rivalries—Anticipating an Israel-Syria Peace Treaty," *Journal of Conflict Resolution* 40 No. 2 (June 1996): 238–271; Moshe Ma'oz, "Syrian-Israeli Relations and the Middle East Peace Process," *Jerusalem Journal of International Relations* 14, No. 3 (1992): 1–21; Muhammad Muslih, "The Golan, Israel, Syria, and Strategic Calculations," *Middle East Journal* 47, No. 4 (Autumn 1993): 611–632; Itamar Rabinovich (Heb.), *The Brink of Peace: Israel and Syria, 1992–96.* (Tel Aviv: Yediot Ahronot Books, 1998); Itamar Rabinovich, "Israel, Syria, and Lebanon," *International Journal* 45, No. 3 (Summer 1990): 529–552; Talcott Seelye, "Syria and the Peace Process," *Middle East Policy* 2, No. 2 (1993): 104–109; Eyal Zisser, "Syria and Israel: From War to Peace," *Orient* 36, No. 3 (Sept. 1995): 487–498; Eyal Zisser, "Assad of Syria—the Leader and the Image," *Orient* 35, No. 2 (June 1994): 247–260.

4. We use the term *coercive diplomacy* following Thomas Schelling, *Arms and Influence* to describe the use of diplomacy and violence—one alongside the other in order to increase credulity and maximize foreign policy gains.

5. Though violence was extensive and magnitude high, this crisis led to the establishment of some regulative mechanisms, in the form of the UN emergency force, which provided several years of stability along the Egypt-Israel border. Janice Gross Stein defined the relationship between Israel and Egypt in the ensuing years as a "security regime," in a study on "Deterrence and Learning in an Enduring Rivalry: Egypt and

Israel, 1948–1973," *Security Studies* 6, No. 1 (Autumn 1996): 104–152. The fact that the regulative mechanism between Egypt and Israel did not lead to peace points to the limits of process inputs alone in the establishment of international institution building.

6. On the Israel-Egypt axis in the conflict and the transformation in its characteristics see: William Ayres, "Mediating International Conflicts: Is Image Change Necessary?" *Journal of Peace Research* 34, No. 3 (Nov. 1997): 431–447; Mitchell G. Bard, "How Fares the Camp David Trio?" *Orbis* 34, No. 2 (Spring 1990): 227–240; Ismail Fahmy, *Negotiation for Peace in the Middle East* (London: Croom Helm, 1983); Mazen Gharaibeh, "Sadat's Decision to Visit Jerusalem: A Decision-Making Approach," *Administrative Change* 19, No.1–2 (July 1991-June 1992): 38–58; Ibrahim A. Karawan, "Sadat and the Egyptian-Israeli Peace Revisited," *International Journal of Middle East Studies* 26, No. 2 (May 1994): 249–266; Zeev Maoz and Allison Astorino, "The Cognitive Structure of Peace-Making: Egypt and Israel, 1970–1978," *Political Psychology* 13, No.4 (1992): 647–662; Mordechai Nisan, "The Camp David Legacy," *Global Affairs* 5, No. 1 (Winter 1990): 96–115; Michael B. Oren, "Secret Egypt-Israel Peace Initiatives Prior to the Suez Campaign," *Middle Eastern Studies* 26, No. 3 (July 1990): 351–370; Kenneth W. Stein, "Continuity and Change in Egyptian-Israeli Relations, 1973-97," *Israel Affairs* 3, Nos. 3–4 (Spring-Summer 1997): 296–320.

7. On the nuclear issue in the Arab-Israeli conflict see: Shlomo Ahronson with Oded Brosh, *The Politics and Strategy of Nuclear Weapons in the Middle East: Opacity, Theory, and Reality, 1966–1991, An Israeli Perspective* (Albany: State University of New York Press, 1992); Louis Beres, "The Growing Threat of Nuclear War in the Middle East," *Jerusalem Journal of International Relations* 12, No. 1 (Jan. 1990): 1–27; Shyam Bhatia, *Nuclear Rivals in the Middle East* (New York: Routledge, 1988); Barry M. Blechman and Douglas M. Hart, "The Political Utility of Nuclear Weapons: The 1973 Middle East Crisis," *International Security* 7, (Summer 1982): 132–156; Avner Cohen, "The Nuclear Issue in the Middle East in a New World Order," in Efraim Inbar and Shmuel Sandler, eds., *Middle Eastern Security Prospects for an Arms Control Regime* (London: Frank Cass, 1995), 49–70; Avner Cohen and Marvin Miller, "How to Think About—and Implement—Nuclear Arms Control in the Middle East," *Washington Quarterly* 16, No. 2 (Spring 1993): 101–113; Yair Evron, *Israel's Nuclear Dilemma* (London: Routledge, 1994); Yair Evron, "Gulf Crisis and War: Regional Rules of the Game and Policy and Theoretical Implications," *Security Studies* 4, No. 1 (Autumn 1994): 115–154; Shai Feldman, Israeli *Nuclear Deterrence: A Strategy for the 1990s* (New York: Columbia University Press, 1982); Robert E. Harkavy, "Triangular or Indirect Deterrence/Compellence: Something New in Deterrence Theory?" *Comparative Strategy* 17, No. 1 (1998): 63–81; Avigdor Haselkorn, "Arab-Israeli Conflict: Implications of Mass Destruction Weapons," *Global Affairs* 3, No.1 (Winter 1988): 120–137; Efraim Inbar, "Israel and Nuclear Weapons since October 1973," in Louis Irene Beres, ed., *Security or Armageddon, Israel's Nuclear Strategy* (Lexington, MA: Lexington Books, 1986); Emily B. Landau, *Israel's Nuclear Image: Arab Perceptions of Israel's Nuclear Posture* (Tel-Aviv: Jaffe Center for Strategic Studies, 1994); Ariel Levitte and Emily Landau, *Israel's Nuclear Image: Arab Perceptions of Israel's Nuclear Posture* (Tel Aviv: Jaffe Center for Strategic Studies, 1994; Mandelbaum, *The Nuclear Revolution;* Paul F. Power, "Middle East Nuclear Issues in Global Perspective," *Middle East Policy* 1–2, (1995): 188–209, Peter Pry, *Israel's Nuclear Arsenal* (Boulder: Westview, 1984); Yohanan Ramati, "Israel and Nuclear Deterrence," *Global Affairs* 3, No. 2 (Spring 1988): 175–185; Scott D. Sagan, "Nuclear Alerts and Crisis Management," *International Security* 9, No. 4 (1985): 99–139; Scott D. Sagan, "Lessons of

the Yom Kippur Alert," *Foreign Policy* 36 (Fall 1979): 160–177; Haim Shaked "The Nuclearization of the Middle East: The Israeli Raid of Osirak," *The Middle East Contemporary Survey* 5(1980–1981): 182–213; Leonard S. Specter, *The Undeclared Bomb* (Cambridge: Ballinger,1988); Steve Weissman and Herbert Krosney, *The Islamic Bomb:The Nuclear Threat to Israel and the Middle East* (New York:Times Books, 1981); Avner Yaniv, "Non-Conventional Weapons and the Future of Arab-Israeli Deterrence," *Israel Affairs* 2, No.1 (Autumn 1995): 135–149.

8. The ethnic aspects of the crisis will be dealt with in chapters 5 and 6. Here we focus primarily on the interstate dimensions of these cases.

9. For a full analysis of overall magnitude see chapter 4.

10. On the local level, war implied an IDF advantage over the Egyptian army. But the fact that Israel needed the help of external powers suggested a different distribution of power. On the global level, the crisis revealed the depths of Cold War penetration into the Middle East, a factor that promised future instability.

11. For an overview of this transformation and the conditions that led to it see chapter 4.

12. Yaacov Bar-Siman-Tov, *The Israeli-Egyptian War of Attrition, 1969-1970: A case Study of Limited Local War* (New York: Columbia University Press, 1980), 187–208.

13. On the Israel-Jordan relationship in the conflict see also: Arun Kumar Banerji, "The Israeli-Jordanian Peace Treaty, Jordan's Long Quest for Security and Identity," *Strategic Analysis* 17, No. 11 (Feb. 1995): 1419–1430; Robert J. Bookmiller, "Approaching the Rubicon: Jordan and the Peace Process," *SAIS Review* 14, No. 2 (Summer-Fall 1994): 109–123; Bob Boker, "Jordan and Israel: The Problems of Bringing Peace to Fruition," *Pacific Research* 8, No. 1 (February 1995): 9–11; Ali Jarbawi, "The Triangle of Conflict," *Foreign Policy* 100, (Fall 1995): 92–108; Ramati "Israel and Nuclear Deterrence,"; Moshe Zak, "Israel and Jordan: Strategically Bound," *Israel Affairs* 3, No.1 (Autumn 1996): 39–60.

14. On the Islamic elements in the conflict see also: Richard W. Bulliet, "The Future of the Islamic Movement," *Foreign Affairs* 72, No. 5 (Nov.-Dec. 1993): 38–44; Nizar A. Hamzeh, "Clan Conflicts, Hizballah, and the Lebanese State," *Journal of Social, Political and Economic Studies* 19, No. 4 (Winter 1994): 433–446; Nizar A. Hamzeh, and Hrair R. Dekmejian, "The Islamic Spectrum of Lebanese Politics," *Journal of South Asian and Middle Eastern Studies* 16, No. 3 (Spring 1993): 25–42; Meir Hatina, "Iran and the Palestinian Islamic Movement," *Orient* 38, No. 1 (1997): 107–120; Mahmood Monshipouri, "The PLO Rivalry with Hamas: The Challenge of Peace, Democratization, and Islamic Radicalism," *Middle East Policy* 4 No. 3 (March 96): 84–105; Mark Tessler and Jodi Nachtwey, "Islam and Attitudes toward International Conflict," *Journal of Conflict Resolution* 42, No. 5 (Oct. 1998): 619–636; Eyal Zisser, "Hizballah in Lebanon: At the Crossroads," *Terrorism and Political Violence* 8, No. 2 (1996): 90–110.

15. A full elaboration of these crises and their special attributes is found in chapters 5 and 6.

16. Five cases that involved a tacit understanding were also grouped into the accommodative-type terminations. See p. 82 on cases designated "other" by ICB data-set, and assigned herein as a nonaccommodative type crisis termination. So too were the 1967 war crisis, identified by the ICB data-set as an imposed agreement.

17. Two additional nonaccommodative cases of different termination type will be discussed on p. 82.

18. Notable were the 1985 Al Biqa II, 1993 Operation Accountability, and 1996 Operation Grapes of Wrath, in which full-scale war was avoided.

19. Moshe Dayan, who served both as Israeli defense and foreign minister, articulated the notion that because of the special circumstances in the Arab world, Israel had no choice but to accede to tacit agreements, because the alternative was no agreement at all. The best example of this kind of agreement were the "open bridges" between the territories and Jordan, which Dayan initiated without any formal agreement. It was this logic that also guided Dayan to support a "unilateral autonomy" by Israel to the Palestinians, following the Camp David accords.

20. See Fn. 17 for two additional crises with non-accommodative outcomes

21. For an elaborate analysis of the background to the decision of Israel based on indepth interviews with the decision-making elite at the time see Michael Brecher, *Decisions in Israel's Foreign Policy* (London: Oxford University Press, 1974), 282–291. See also Dayan, *Diary of the Sinai Campaign,* 185–186.

22. As such these cases deviate from the violence-accommodation pattern mentioned in our book.

23. See chapter 4 for an analysis of the conditions for change primarily in the interstate realm.

CHAPTER 4. CRISIS MAGNITUDE AND CONFLICT TRANSFORMATION

1. We added the 1996 Operation Grapes of Wrath, the only additional ICB-compatible case throughout the 1995–2000 years, to the twenty-five ICB crises (the project is updated to 1994). This case enables us to assess trends throughout the 1947–2000 period. It is also included in the Glossary of cases.

2. Due to the centrality of the Palestinian factor in the Arab–Israeli conflict, we added the Non State Actor category. Palestinian involvement ranges from triggering an interstate crisis (six out of twenty-six cases throughout the period); involvement in crisis (eleven out of twenty-six crises); and participation in crisis resolution. The first participation of the PLO in resolution of violence between itself and Israel was during the July 1981 artillery exchanges in Lebanon. It is further indicated in the prolonged negotiations that led to the 1993 Oslo accords and mutual Israel-PLO recognition as well as PLO participation in resolving the Intifada. These developments are not recorded by the ICB, which focuses on interstate crisis only. It is however most significant that the PLO's moderation was associated with a decline in crisis initiation by Israel and/or Arab states.

3. See chapter 6.

4. All the crises that were termed by the ICB project as undefined endings or dubbed as faded were reevaluated by us as belonging to the nonaccommodative type.

5. Karl Deutsch et al., *Political Community in the North Atlantic Area* (Princeton: Princeton University Press,1957).

6. For a detailed analysis of crisis frequency see the first section of chapter 2.

7. Aware of the multifaceted interpretations given to this basic theory and concept, in this study we presume it to mean a rough distribution of force. For a thoughtful study see Claude, *Power and International Relations,* chapters 2–3; See also Steven R. David, "Explaining Third World Alignment," *World Politics* 43, No. 2 (Jan.1991): esp. 234–235.

8. Brecher and Ben Yehuda, "System and crisis in International Politics,": 21–22.

9. Avi Kober, *Military Decision in the Arab-Israeli War* (Tel-Aviv: Maarchot/Israeli Defense Ministry Press, 1995), 198–199.

10. Ibid., 198–204.

11. See for instance, Malcolm Kerr, "Regional Arab Politics and the Conflict with Israel," in Paul Y. Hammond and S. Alexander, eds., *Political Dynamics in the Middle East* (New York: 1972). See also Michael C. Hudson, *Arab Politics: The Search for Legitimacy* (New Haven: Yale University Press, 1977) and James A. Bill and Carl Leiden, *Politics in the Middle East* (Boston: Little, Brown, 1983), chapters 5–7.

12. Fred J. Khouri, *The Arab-Israeli Dilemma* (Syracuse: Syracuse University Press, 1985), 73–101.

13. Ariyeh Shalev, *Co-operation under the Shadow of Conflict, The Israeli-Syrian Armistice Regime 1949–1955* (Boulder: Westview, 1994). See also Khouri, *The Arab-Israeli Dilemma,* 185–191.

14. Dan Schueftan, *A Jordanian Option* (Tel-Aviv: Yad-Tabenkin, 1986), 187–224; Itamar Rabinovich, *The Road not Taken: Early Arab-Israeli Negotiations* (Jerusalem: Keter, 1991), chapter 4; Mohamed Heikal, *Secret Channels The Inside Story of Arab-Israeli Negotiations* (London: Harper Collins, 1996), 75–86.

15. For studies on the linkage between retaliation and war see: Milstein, "American and Soviet Influence"; Ahronson and Horowitz, "The Strategy of Controlled Retaliation"; and Blechman, "The Impact of Israel's Reprisals"; Khouri, "The Policy of Retaliation in Arab-Israeli Relations."

16. Rabinovich, *The Road not Taken,* chapter 5; Safran, *From War to War,* 42–46.

17. For other elements in the Arab-Israeli balance of power see Yigal Allon, *The Making of the Israeli Army* (London: Sphere Books, 1970), 66, and Dayan, *Diary of the Sinai Campaign,* 58–60.

18. For an analysis of the distribution of forces during that war see Kober, *Military Decision in the Arab-Israeli War 1984–1982,* 241–248. See also Col. Trevor N. Dupuy, *Elusive Victory: The Arab-Israeli Wars 1947–1974* (New York: Harper and Row, 1978), 212–215; Haddad, "Arab Peace Efforts," 196–200.

19. Walt, *The Origins of Alliances,* chapter 8.

20. In Israel's perceptions, Nasser's Egypt represented a threat to its existence. The largest and strongest Arab state, led by a charismatic pan-Arab leader, was being armed with the most advanced weapons. The combination of several trends—(1) modernization, which the new regime in Egypt was committed to accomplishing; (2) the potential of the new leader to mobilize Arab masses in other Arab societies through pan-Arab slogans; and (3) the backing of a superpower, whom Ben-Gurion and many of the ruling elite never trusted—constituted an acute strategic threat. The extreme anti-Israel oratory emanating from Cairo, Egypt's rejection of the Eisenhower-sponsored Anderson peace initiative, and the continuous Fedayeen incursions from Gaza indicated to many of the Israeli leadership that Egypt was acquiring both the will and the capability to destroy Israel. Dayan, *Diary of the Sinai Campaign,* 3–19. See also Stock, *Israel on the Road*

to Sinai, 1949–1956, 79–95 and 147–153.

21. Levy, "Declining Power and the Preventive Motivation for War": 102.

22. Brecher, *Decisions in Israel's Foreign Policy,* chapter 6; Finer, *Dulles over Suez.*

23. Janice Gross Stein, "Detection and Defection: Security 'Regimes' and the Management of International Conflict,"*International Journal* 40, No. 4 (1985): 616–618.

24. Safran, *From War to War,* 267.

25. Kober, *Military Decision,* 287; Dupuy, *Elusive Victory,* 337; and Safran *From War to War,* Appendix B.

26. This evaluation is based on Safran, *From War to War to War,* 317–320; Brecher, *Decisions in Israel's Foreign Policy,* 324–325; and Avner Yaniv, *Deterrence without the Bomb* (Lexington: Lexington Books, 1987), 75–81.

27. See for instance, Safran, *From War to War,* chapter 6, and Brecher, *Decisions in Israel's Foreign Policy,* chapter 7; and Walter Laqueur, *The Road to Jerusalem,* (New York: Macmillan, 1968).The panic that the Israeli leadership portrayed following Nasser's military moves also disqualifies any collusion theory. On the Arab side see Samir A. Mutawi, *Jordan in the 1967 War,* (Cambridge: Cambridge University Press, 1987), 108–11.

28. On Israel's geostrategic doctrine see Sandler, *The State of Israel,The Land of Israel,* 118–120 and Michael Brecher, *The Foreign Policy System of Israel* (London: Oxford University Press, 1972), 67. Complementing Israel's deterrence doctrine was the preemptive war strategy; Israel must preempt when war becomes inevitable. On the relationship between balance of power considerations and preemptive war, see Organski, *World Politics,* chapter 12; and A. F. K. Organski and Jacek Kugler, *The War Ledger* (Chicago: University of Chicago Press, 1980), chapters 1 and 3; and Levy, "Declining Power and the Preventive Motivation for War": 90. On Israel's application of deterrence see Yaniv, *Deterrence without the Bomb,* 20 and chapters 2–3; and Dan Horowitz, "Israel's National Security Conception (1948–1978)," in Benyamin Neuberger, ed., *Diplomacy and Confrontation, Selected Issues in Israel's Foreign Policy 1948–1978* (Tel-Aviv: Everyman's University, 1984), 124–134.

29. Nasser understood that Israel had little choice but open war. He miscalculated the exact time and the strength of the IDF, but he and his close adviser Muhamad Hassanain Haykal anticipated that Israel had no other alternative. For Haykal's analysis of why Israel must attack see his column in Al Ahram 26 May 1967, in Walter Laqueur and Barry Rubin, eds., *The Israel-Arab Reader* (New York Penguin Books, 1991), 179–185. See also Safran, *From War to War,* 299–302; and Brecher, *Decisions in Israel's Foreign Policy,* 393; Mutawi, *Jordan in the 1967 War,* 111–112.

30. Ben-Gurion's principle that Israel needs the support of at least one major power constrained the IDF's demand for a first strike. Ultimately, the Eshkol government succeeded in ensuring the United States' tacit support and initiated war without impairing Israel's national security doctrine as it evolved over the years. On Ben-Gurion's attitude toward the great powers see Shabtai Teveth, *Moshe Dayan: A Biography* (Tel-Aviv: Shocken, 1972), 561–562 (in Hebrew).

31. Khouri, *The Arab-Israeli Dilemma,* 285–287; A. El-Gamasy, *The October War* (Cairo: The American University in Cairo Press, 1993), 78–79.

32. For the full text of the Resolution see Laqueur and Rubin, *The Israel-Arab Reader,* 365–366.The value of territories according to the Israeli ruling elite at the time

was double: enhancing deterrence and a bargaining chip to be exchanged for peace. For Labor, excluding certain strategic spots, the territories did not constitute a pivotal element in the balance of power. This conception changed after the Likud's victory in May 1977. See Sandler, *The State of Israel, The Land of Israel*, 188–196.

33. Malcolm H. Kerr, *The Arab Cold War* (Oxford: Oxford University Press, 1971), 131–132; El-Gamasy, *The October War*, 78–79 and 103–105; Khouri, *The Arab-Israeli Dilemma*, 318–319.

34. On the strategy of pain and compellence see Schelling, *Arms and Influence*, chapter 1; On the Arab view of the War of Attrition see El-Gamasy, *The October War*, 108–126.

35. See Walt, *The Origins*, 109. According to Walt, by the end of 1970 between fifteen and twenty thousand Soviet troops were stationed in Egypt. See also El-Gamasy, *The October War*, 117–118.

36. Yaniv, *Deterrence without the Bomb*, 176; El-Gamasy, *The October War*, 123–125.

37. Kalb and Kalb, *Kissinger*, 215–241. Brecher, *Decisions in Israel's Foreign Policy*, 454–457.

38. Dayan as minister of defense had doubts regarding the military wisdom of the post-1967 lines. See Yaniv, *Deterrence without the Bomb*, 136–137 and 181–182.

39. Brecher, *Decisions in Israel's Foreign Policy*, 455 and 504; Khouri, *The Arab-Israeli Dilemma*, 319.

40. Kober, *Military Decision*, chapter 10, and especially 317. See also Bar-Siman Tov, *The Israeli-Egyptian War of Attrition*, 189; El-Gamasy, *The October War*, 123–126.

41. For the role of the 1967 war in promoting peace see Yoram Meital, *Egypt's Struggle for Peace, Continuity and Change 1967–1977* (Gainsville: University Press of Florida, 1998). For the relationship between balance of power and game theory see Bruce Bueno de Mesquita, "Theories of International Conflict: An Analysis and an Appraisal," in Ted Robert Gurr, ed., *Handbook of Political Conflict* (New York: The Free Press, 1980), 368–374.

42. Stein, "Detection and Defection": 599. For a study of a legitimation process see Yehudit Auerbach, "Legitimation for Turning-Point Decisions in Foreign Policy: Israel vis-à-vis Germany 1952 and Egypt 1957," *Review of International Studies* 15, No. 2 (Oct. 1989): 329–340.

43. El-Gamasy, *The October War*, 78. The Syrian goals were more extreme than the Egyptian ones but since the latter were the decisive factor it is possibe to define the goals of war accordingly. Patrick Seale, *Assad: The Struggle for the Middle East* (London: Taurus, 1988), chapter 13; Kober, *Military Decision*, 327–331; Nadav Safran, *Israel: The Embattled Ally* (Cambridge: The Belknap Press of Harvard University Press, 1978), chapter 24.

44. Hassan El Badri, Taha El Magdoub, Mohammed Dia El Din Zohdy, *The Ramadan War, 1973* (Dunn Loring: T.N. Dupuy Associates, 1978), 15–19; Heikal, *Secret Channels*, 181–184: Anwar el-Sadat, *In Search of Identity: An Autobiography* (New York: Harper and Row, 1977), 242. See also John Mearsheimer, *Conventional Deterrence* (Ithaca: Cornell University Press, 1982), 53–56 and 155–162.

45. See Morton H. Halpern, *Limited War in the Nuclear Age* (New York: John Wiley, 1963) and *Contemporary Military Strategy* (Boston: Little, Brown, 1967), 95.

46. Kalb and Kalb, *Kissinger*, 223–224 and chapter 19. Heikal, *Secret Channels*, 165–179.

47. Walt, *The Origins of Alliances*, 125–128; Khouri, *The Arab-Israeli Dilemma*, 373–374.

48. Kissinger comprehended the significance of Sadat's international orientation shift; see Stephen R. Graubard, *Kissinger, Portrait of a Mind* (New York: Norton, 1974), especially the last chapter, entitled "Epilogue, The Testing of Theory," 171–191. See also Khouri, *The Arab-Israeli Dilemma*, 367–371; Jonah, "The Military Talks at Kilometer 101": 53–70.

49. Efraim Inbar, *Outcast Countries in the World Community,* Monograph Series in World Affairs (Denver: University of Denver Press, 1985). See also Adel Safty, "Egyptian Negotiations and Decision Making from Sinai to Camp David: The Preponderance of the Psychological Perceptions of the Leader as Decision-Maker," *International Studies* 28, No. 4 (Oct.-Dec. 1991): 409–442.

50. Efraim Inbar, "Israeli Strategic Thinking after 1973," *Journal of Strategic Studies* 6 (March 1983):41–45. See also Ariel Levitte, *Offense and Defense in Israeli Military Doctrine* (Boulder: Westview, 1989).

51. For the two main views in this regard see Yigal Allon, "Israel: The Case for Defensible Borders," *Foreign Affairs* 55, No. 1 (Oct. 1976):38–53 and Dayan in *The Jerusalem Post,* 15 May 1973. For an analysis of the role of the territories as inviting or deterring war see Shmuel Sandler, "Partition versus Sharing in the Arab-Israeli Conflict," in Daniel J. Elazar, ed., *Governing Peoples and Territories* (Philadelphia: ISHI, 1982), 234–245. See also Brecher, *Decisions in Israel's Foreign Policy,* 460–-462.

52. For a detailed analysis of Israeli attitudes see Asher Arian, *Security Threatened, Surveying Israeli Opinion on Peace and War* (Cambridge: Cambridge University Press,1995), 94–104.

53. See for instance, General Avraham Tamir, "The Use of Military Force: An Israeli Analysis," in Judith Kipper and Harold H. Saunders, eds., *The Middle East in Global Perspective* (Boulder: Westview, 1991), 219–230. See also Ahmed Khalidi and Hussein Agha, "The Syrian Doctrine of Strategic Parity," ibid., 186–187; Muhamad Feisal Abd al Manam, "The Arab Deterrence and the Shattering of Israeli Strategy," in Emmanuel Sivan, ed., *The Arab Lessons from the October War* (Tel-Aviv: Am Oved, 1974), 25–27 (Heb.).

54. Kober, *Military Decision,* 360. For a view that dowgrades the rate of attrition see Dupuy, *Elusive Victory,* 593.

55. See Shlomo Ahronson with Oded Brosh, *The Politics and Strategy of Nuclear Weapons in the Middle East* (Albany: State University of New York Press, 1992), chapter 5; For a more cautious approach see Avner Cohen, "Cairo, Dimona, and the June 1967 War," *Middle East Journal* 50, No. 2 (Spring 1996): 190–210. For an opposing view see Evron, *Israel's Nuclear Dilemma,* 45–50.

56. Prior to the war Sadat stated that he was ready to sacrifice "a million casualties," a fact that was interpreted as a reference to Israel's nuclear capability. See Levitte and Landau, *Israel's Nuclear Image,* 41–43.

57. For details on this incident see: *Time Magazine,* 12 April 1976; Aronson, *Nuclear Weapons in the Middle East,* chapter 7; Amir Oren, in *Haaretz,* 23 May 1997.

58. *Maariv,* 2 December 1974.

59. Levitte and Landau, *Israel's Nuclear Image,* 179. In this debate the main figure was Moshe Dayan who published a series of articles between March and November 1976 on the rationale of an Israeli nuclear deterrence. Fostering the nuclear debate that erupted in the wake of the Yom Kippur War was also the new Arab economic strength brought

about by petrodollars. This enhanced economic power assured them of the upper hand in any arms race, thus threatening the future balance of power. In light of these trends, the argument was advanced that the only solution to Israel's defense problems was to introduce the ultimate deterrence—nuclear weapons. The reduced role of the territories in deterrence even led some analysts to suggest an Israeli-declared nuclear option in exchange for territorial withdrawal.

60. On the nuclear debate following the Yom Kippur War, see Inbar, "Israel and Nuclear Weapons since October 1973," 61–78. See also Dan Horowitz, *Continuity and Change in Israel's Security Doctrine* (Jerusalem: Leonard Davis Institute, 1982), 48–54 and Avner Cohen, *Israel and the Bomb* (New York: Columbia University Press, 1998).

61. Ibid., 77–78.

62. On the nuclear threat passed on to Egypt and the subsequent debate in the Israeli national security establishment see: Etel Solingen, "Domestic Aspects of Strategic Postures: The Past and Future in a Middle East Nuclear Regime," in Inbar and Sandler, eds., *Middle Eastern Security,* 130–151.

63. Sandler, *The State of Israel, The Land of Israel,* 203–210.

64. This step-by-step policy was designed to promote security arrangements between Israel and both Egypt and Syria, the construction of devices against cheating, and the establishment of confidence-building measures (CBMs).

65. See "The Egyptian-Israeli Accord on Sinai (September 1, 1975)," in Laqueur and Rubin, eds., *The Arab-Israel Reader,* 572–582.

66. Stein, "Detection and Defection": 601–627. See also Art, "A Defensible Defense."

67. Yair Evron, *Conflict and Security Building Measures in the Arab-Israeli Context* (Tel-Aviv: Tel-Aviv University, 1995), 45–53; Itamar Rabinovich, "Controlled Conflicct in the Middle East: The Syrian-Israeli Rivalry in Lebanon," in *Conflict Management in the Middle East* ed. Gabriel Ben-Dor and David De-Witt. (Lexington: Lexington Books 1987); Stein, "Detection and Defection."

68. Auerbach and Ben-Yehuda, "Attitudes toward an Existence Conflict: Begin and Dayan on the Palestinian Issue," *International Interactions 13* (1987), 323–351. See also Ayres, "Mediating International Conflicts"; Joseph Alpher, "Israel's Security Concerns in the Peace Process," *International Affairs* 70, No. 2 (April 1994): 229–241 and Ben Yehuda, Hemda. "Attitude Change and Policy Transformation: Yitzhak Rabin and the Palestinian Question, 1967–1995," *Israel Affairs* 3, Nos. 3–4 (1997): 201–224.

CHAPTER 5. ETHNIC CRISES IN A
COMPOUND CONFLICT

1. From the Israeli viewpoint the outset of the Arab-Israeli ethno-national conflict was in the early 1880s, at the era of the First Aliyah (migration) and the first Moshavot (settlements). Some historians and also Israel's first prime minister David Ben-Gurion argued to this effect. See Yosef Gorny, *The Arab Question and the Jewish Problem* (Tel-Aviv: Am Oved, 1985), part I; Neville J. Mandel, *The Arabs and Zionism before World War I* (Berkeley: University of California Press, 1976); Ben-Gurion, *The Restored State of Israel,* 18–51. For the Arab view on the origis of the conflict, see George Antonius, *The Arab*

Awakening (New York: Capricorn Books, 1946). See also Baruch Kimmerling and Joel S. Migdal, *The Palestinians: The Making of a People* (New York: The Free Press, 1993).

2. The book most identified with the correlation between the onset of the conflict and the Mandate is Christopher Sykes, *Cross roads to Palestine: Palestine from Balfour to Bevin* (London: first published by Collins, 1965, Mentor, 1967).

3. For an analysis of the Yishuv along these lines see Dan Horowitz and Moshe Lissak, *The Origins of the Israeli Polity* (Tel-Aviv: Am Oved, 1977). The concept "Dual Authority Polities" is taken from Dan Horowitz, "Dual Authority Polities," *Comparative Politics* 14, No. 3 (April 1982): 329–349.

4. The analysis of the Palestinian community is based on Yehoshua Porat, *The Emergence of the Palestinian Arab National Movement* (Tel-Aviv: Am-Oved, 1976), chapters 4 and 6. See also Joel Migdal, "State and Society in a Society Without a State," in Gabriel Ben-Dor, ed., *The Palestinians and the Middle East Conflict* (Princeton: Princeton University Press, 1979), 381–391, and Joel Migdal et al., *Palestinian Politics and Society* (Princeton: Princeton University Press, 1979). Ann Lesch, *Arab Politics in Palestine, 1917–1939* (Ithaca: Cornell University Press, 1979); Ibrahim Abu-Lughod, ed., *The Transformation of Palestine* (Evanston: Northwestern University Press, 1971).

5. On the Jewish community see Elyakim Rubinstein, "From the Yishuv to the State: Institutions and Parties," in Benyamin Eliav, *The Jewish National Home: From the Balfour Declaration to Independence* (Jerusalem: Keter, 1976), 135–195.

6. Porat, *The Emergence*, 75–81, and 103–104; Sykes, *Cross Roads to Israel*, chapters 2–3.

7. From a foreign policy perspective it also qualified as a crisis as the Zionist leadership perceived the outbreak of riots as a severe threat to the Zionist enterprise, fearing an abolition of the Balfour Declaration. See Shaul Avigur, Yehuda Slutzky, and Gershon Rivlin, *The Short Version of the History of the Haganah*. (Tel-Aviv: Ma'arachot/Ministry of Defense, 1978), chapters 5 and 7. The Palestinians also perceived the international declarations that indeed triggered the violence as threatening their existence in the long run and steps with grave damage or at least a threat to their influence in the short run. Porat, *The Emergence*, chapter 2.

8. On the neotiations to terminate the crisis see Porat, *The Emergence*, 108–128.

9. On the relationship of the Palestine ethno-national conflict, Arab nationalism, and state building see Bill and Leiden, *Politics in the Middle East*, 329–330.

10. Yehoshua Porat, *From Riots to Rebellion, The Palestinian Arab National Movement, 1929–1939* (Tel-Aviv: Am Oved, 1978), 25–28. (Hebrew). See also Philip Mattar, *The Mufti of Jerusalem—Al-Hajj Amin Husseini and the Palestine National Movement* (New York: Columbia University Press, 1988).

11. The two documents can be found in Laqueur and Rubin, eds., *The Israel-Arab Reader*, 45–56.

12. See Porat, *From Riots to Rebellion*, 15–57.

13. Ibid., 58.

14. The issue of collective action is very comprehensive in the rebellion literature. For the main themes see Ted Robert Gurr, *Why Men Rebel* (Princeton: Princeton University Press, 1970) and Charles Tilly, *From Mobilization to Revolution* (Reading: Addison-Wesley, 1978). See also Harry Eckstein, "Theoretical Approaches to Explaining Collective Political Violence," in Ted Robert Gurr, ed., *Handbook of Political Conflict:*

Theories and Research (New York: The Free Press, 1980), 135–136.

15. On summary of the debate on this issue see Yaacov Shavit, *"Self-Restraint"* or *"Reaction"* (Ramat-Gan: Bar-Ilan University Press, 1983). On the debate in the Arab side see, Porat, *From Riots to Rebellion,* chapter 9.

16. Sykes, *Crossroads to Israel,* 161.

17. On the reactions to the Peel Commission see C. Merchavia, ed., *Zionism, A Collection of Political Documents* (Jerusalem: Ahiassaf, 1943), 471–480; Lois A. Aroian and Richard P. Mitchell, *The Modern Middle East and North Africa* (New York: Macmillan, 1984), 236–237; Porat, *From Riots to Rebellion,* 271–276, Shmuel Dothan, *Partition of Eretz-Israel in the Mandatory Period, the Jewish Controversy* (Jerusalem: Yad Yitzhak Ben-Zvi, 1979); Yitzhak Galnoor, "The Territorial Partition of Palestine: The Decision of 1937," in *Studies in Israel's Independence* (Sde Boker: Ben-Gurion University, 1991), 211–239.

18. Aroian, and Mitchell, *The Modern Middle East and North Africa,* 237.

19. Yossi Katz, "The Formation of the Jewish Agency's Partition Proposal of Borders, 1937–1938," *Zion* 56, No. 4 (1992): 401–439.

20. See Document 17 in Laqueur and Rubin, eds., *The Israel-Arab Reader,* 64–75.

21. On the Jewish reaction see Ibid., 76. On the Arab reaction see Porat, *From Riots to Rebellion,* chapter 10.

22. Heikal, *Secret Channels,* 74–86. For the Biltmore Program declarations see Document 19 in Laqueur and Rubin, eds., *The Israel-Arab Reader,* 77–78.

23. On the Israeli perceptions of threat see for instance David Ben-Gurion, *In Battle* (Tel-Aviv: Am-Oved, 1957), Vol. 5, p. 225, and *The War of Independence: Ben-Gurion's War Diary* (Tel-Aviv: Misrad Habitachon, 1982), Vol. 1, 3–11, and throughout the diary, see for instance 155, 342, and 416. See also Moshe Sharett, *At the Threshold of Statehood* (Tel-Aviv: Am-Oved, 1966), 155–172.

24. Avigur et al., *The Short Version of the Story of the Hahaganah,* chapters 32–33. Khouri, *The Arab-Israeli Dilemma,* 73–81.

25. Based on Benny Morris, *The Birth of the Palestinian Refugee Problem, 1947–1949* (Cambridge: Cambridge University Press, 1987), see especially the conclusions of Morris in 57–60 and 128–131. See also Roberto Bachi, *The Population of Israel* (Jerusalem: The Hebrew University of Jerusalem and Prime Minister's Office, 1974), 53–54.

26. Kerr, *The Arab Cold War;* Alan Taylor, *The Arab Balance of Power* (Syracuse: Syracuse University Press, 1982). See also Khouri, *The Arab-Israeli Dilemma.*

27. See Yezid Sayigh, *Armed Struggle and the Search for a State: The Palestine National Movement 1949–1993* (Oxford: Clarendon Press, 1997). On the place and orientation of the Palestinians between Jordan and Egypt see Eli'ezer Be'eri, *The Palestinians under Jordanian Rule—Three Issues* (Jerusalem: The Magness Press, 1978).

28. Schueftan, *A Jordanian Option,* 269–270. Haddad, "Arab Peace Efforts and the Solution of the Arab-Israeli Problem," 196.

29. Kalb and Kalb, *Kissinger,* 226–240. See also Kerr, *The Arab Cold War,* 145–149.

30. Sandler, *The State of Israel, the Land of Israel,* chapter 4; Michael C. Hudson, *Arab Politics*; John Waterbury, *The Egypt of Nasser and Sadat: The Political Economy of Two Regimes* (Princeton: Princeton University Press, 1983); Bruce Maddy-Weitzman, *The*

Crystallization of the Arab State System (Syracuse: Syracuse University Press, 1993).

31. Leonard Binder, "The Middle East as a Subordinate International System," *World Politics* 10. No. 3 (April 1958):408–29; See also Brecher, *The Foreign Policy System of Israel,* chapter 3.

32. See chapter 6.

33. See for instance Yehoshafat Harkabi, *The Palestinian Covenant and Its Meaning* (London:Valentine, Mitchell, 1979); Avner Yaniv, *PLO—A Profile* (Haifa: Israel Universities Study Group for Middle Eastern Affairs, 1974); Rashid Hamid, "What Is the PLO?", *Journal of Palestine Studies* 4 No. 4 (Summer 1975): 90–109.

34. On the evolution of the PLO see Helena Cobban, *The Palestine Liberation Organization: People, Power, and Politics* (Cambridge: Cambridge University Press, 1984). On the relationship between the PLO and the territories see Emile Sahliyeh, *In Search of Leadership:West Bank Politics since 1967* (Washington, DC: Brookings Institution, 1968).

35. It was this reality that influenced Brecher's worldwide study to count the 1970 September tension as a Jordanian-Syrian international crisis instead of an Arab-Israeli one. For a somewhat different approach see Dowty, *Middle East Crisis.*

36. Rashid Khalidi, "Policymaking within the Palestinian Polity," in Judit Kipper and Harold H. Saunders, eds., *The Middle East in Global Perspective* (Boulder, Westview, 1991), 63–80.

37. For further analysis of the ascendancy of ethnonationalism among both communities see Sandler, *The State of Israel, The Land of Israel,* 142–179.

38. Hamzeh and Dekmejian, "The Islamic Spectrum of Lebanese Politics": 25–42; Nizar A. Hamzeh, "Lebanon's Hizbullah: From Islamic Revolution to Parliamentary Accomodation," *Third World Quarterly* 14, No. 2: 321–337; Judith Palmer Harik, " Between Islam and the System, Sources and Implications of Popular Support for Lebanon's Hizballah," *Journal of Conflict Resolution* 40, No. 1 (March 1996): 41–67.

39. Zisser, "Hizballah in Lebanon."

40. Halliday, "The Great Powers and the Middle East"; Goodman and Ekedahl, "Trends in Soviet Policy."

41. Philip Habib, *Diplomacy and the Search for Peace in the Middle East* (Georgetown: Institute for the Study of Diplomacy, 1985); Rashid Khalidi, *Under Siege: PLO Decision Making during the 1982 War* (New York: Columbia University Press, 1986). See also Quandt, "Reagan's Lebanon Policy."

42. Laura Zittrain Eisenberg, "Israel's South Lebanon Imbroglio," *Middle East Quarterly* 4, No. 2 (June 1997): 60–69.

43. See "Arab League Summit Communique," in Laqueur and Rubin, eds., *The Israel-Arab Reader,* 616–617.

44. Ibid., 611–613.

45. Shmuel Sandler and Hillel Frisch, *Israel, the Palestinians and the West Bank* (Lexington, MA:Lexington, 1984), chapters 6–7.

.46 See also Herbert C. Kelman, "The Palestinization of the Arab-Israeli Conflict," *Jerusalem Quarterly* 46 (Spring 1988): 3–15.

47. Brecher and Ben Yehuda, "System and Crisis in International Politics": 21–22.

CHAPTER 6. NEW DIMENSIONS IN THE ARAB-ISRAELI
CONFLICT: FROM THE INTIFADA 1987 TO INTIFADA 2000

1. Zeev Schiff and Ehud Ya'ari, *Intifada* (Jerusalem: Schocken, 1990) 9–11.

2. Arie Shalev, *The Intifada, Causes and Effects* (Tel-Aviv: The Jaffe Center for Strategic Studies, 1990), 45; see especially fn. 28 for the other occurrences and Appendix A, 209. See also Schiff and Yaari, *Intifada, 26.*

3. For Rabin's view on the Intifada see Ben-Yehuda, Hemda "Attitude Change and Policy Transformation: Yitzhak Rabin and the Palestinian Question, 1967–95," *Israel Affairs* 3, Nos. 3–4 (1997): 201–224; Efraim Inbar, "Israel's Small War: The Military Response to the Intifada," *Armed Forces and Society* 18, No. 1 (Fall, 1991): 33.

4. To be sure, to a certain segment of the Jewish population, the settlers and members of the believers in the "integrity of the land of Israel," such an outcome might have been perceived as an existential threat. See Schiff and Yaari, *Intifada,* 161–65. The publication expressing most accurately the views of the settlers is *Nekuda*, and the right wing, *Nativ*. See these two journals during the months of the Intifada.

5. On the Intifada and its impact on national unity government see ""Who Is the Boss Today? Coalition Government in Israel," in Daniel J. Elazar and Shmuel Sandler, *Who is the Boss in Israel? Israel at the Polls, 1988–1989* (Detroit: Wayne State University Press, 1992), 277–302.

6. Sandler and Frisch, *Israel, the Palestinians, and the West Bank,* chapter 5.

7. For a summary of the Arab states' involvement in the Intifada see Laurie A. Brand, "The Intifada and the Arab World: Old Players, New Roles," *International Journal* XLV, No. 3 (Summer 1990): 501–527. On the London agreement and Hussein's withdrawal see Gerald Steinberg, "Israel among the Nations: Foreign Policy and the Peace Process," in Daniel J. Elaazar and Shmuel Sandler, *Who Is the Boss in Israel?* 176–183.

8. Muhammad Muslih, "Towards Coexistence: An Analysis of the Resolutions of the Palestine National Council," *Journal of Palestine Studies* 19, No. 4 (Summer 1990): 3–29. See also Brand, "The Intifada and the Arab World": 509.

9. This analysis is based on Schiff and Yaari, *Intifada,* chs. 6–8. See also Hillel Frisch, "If Things Are So Much Better, How Come They Are Worse: The Political Fragmentation of the Arab Community and the Marginalization of Arab National Politics," in Daniel J. Elazar and Shmuel Sandler, eds., *Who Is the Boss in Israel?* 130–150.

10. In accordance with the Algerian and Vietnamese models, Palestinian civilians were to serve as a "human forest" in which the guerillas could hide, and hold general strikes and demonstrations, while the role of the fighters was to wear out the enemy. Yehoshafat Harkabi, *On the Guerrilla* (Tel Aviv: Ma'archot/Israeli Defense Ministry 1971), 303–352. See also Abraham Sela, "The PLO, the West Bank, and Gaza Strip," *The Jerusalem Quarterly* 8 (Summer, 1978): 66–67.

11. Sandler and Frisch, *Israel, The Palestinians, and the West Bank,* chapter 5.

12. Schiff and Yaari, *Intifada,* 61–63.

13. In fact, one can argue that the Intifada gradually faded out and never reached a formal conclusion, which is in itself a common feature of interethnic struggles. Unlike interstate wars, interethnic crises are characterized by nonformal or unilateral endings, which may explain why they tend to linger on at different levels of violence.

14. Shalev, *The Intifada,* 82

15. For the major works in this field see Eckstein, "Theoretical Approaches to Explaining Collective Political Violence"; Tilly, *From Mobilization to Revolution;* Gurr, *Why Men Rebel;* Jack Goldstone, ed., *Revolutions. Theoretical, Comparative and Historical Studies* (San Diego: Harcourt Brace Jovanovich, 1986).

16. Aryeh Shalev estimated that at least 10 percent of the Palestinian population in Gaza and the West Bank participated in violent activities. The uprising enjoyed virtually unanimous Palestinian support, Shalev, *The Intifada,* 86; Yezid Sayigh, "The Intifada Continues: Legacy, Dynamics, and Challenges," *Third World Quarterly* 11, No. 3 (July 1989): 20–49. See also William B. Vogele, "Learning and Nonviolent Struggles in the Intifada," *Peace and Change* 17, No. 3 (July 1992): 312–340. See also a special issue on "Israel and the Arabs since the Intifada," in *International Journal* 45, No. 3 (Summer 1990).

17. Shalev, *The Intifada,* 84–86. See also *B'tselem, 1992/1993*(Jerusalem: The Israeli Information Center for Human Rights, n.d.), Table A p.20 and 27–28.

18. On the process of change in the PLO positions see Sandler and Frisch, *Israel, the Palestinians, and the West Bank,* 58–70. See also documents supporting this trend in *Journal of Palestine Studies* 8, No. 2 (Winter 1979): 166; and Appendix 1, in Cobban, *The Palestinian Liberation Organization, People Power and Politics,* 265.

19. Appendix 18, Shalev, *The Intifada,* 245–246.

20. Ibid., 247. See Yezid Sayigh, "Struggle Within, Struggle Without: The Transformation of PLO Politics since 1982," *International Affairs* 65, No. 2 (Spring 1989): 247–271.

21. In March 1988 Rabin stated that "just by using force within the framework of what is allowed, through detentions as permitted by law, we will be unable to stop the violence . . . the only solution to the underlying causes of the violence is a political one," On the views of the IDF generals see Schiff and Yaari, *Intifada,* 128–134. See also interviews with Shomron, in *Haaretz,* 17 March 1989, B-2,and *Maariv,* 17 May 1988, A-3.

22. Gad Barzilai and Efarim Inbar, "The Use of Force: Israeli Public Opinion on Military Options," *Armed Forces and Society* 23, No. 1 (Fall 1996): 54–56. See also Don Peretz, "The Intifada and the Middle East Peace," *Survival* 32, No. 5 (Sept.-Oct. 1990): 387–401.

23. Arian, *Security Threatened,* 80-81. For an opposing view see Azmy Bashara, "Israel Faces the Uprising, A Preliminary Assessment," *Middle East Report* 157 (March-April 1989): 6–14. For the impact of the Intifada on American Public Opinion see Fouad M. Moughrabi, "Public Opinion, Public Policy, and the Israeli-Palestinian Conflict," *American-Arab Affairs* 30 (Fall 89): 40–51.

24. Ian Lustick in a review article on the Intifada summarized the strategic rationale for the Intifada as a "calibrated mobilization designed to effect profound changes in Israeli public opinion and Israeli government policies," Ian Lustick, "Writing the Intifada," *World Politics* 45, No. 4 (1993): 579. This is also the sense one gets from the nine books under review by Lustick, all researching the Palestinian side of the Intifada.

25. See the incident of Ezer Weizmann, in Steinberg, "Israel among the Nations," Foreign Policy and the Peace Process," 183.

26. On changes in PLO positions see Khalidi, "Policymaking within the Palestinian Polity," 69–79. See also Heikal, *Secret Channels,* 343–344 and Sayigh, "Struggle Within, Struggle Without,": 247–271.

27. This was done in defiance of Prime Minister Yitzhak Shamir's policy.

28. Shalev, *The Intifada,* appendix 20, 258–259. For the deceleration of independ-ence and the PNC resolutions see appendixes: 17, 18, 21. See also Telhami, "The United States and the Middle East Peace."

29. Moshe Arens, *Peace and War in the Middle East 1988–1992* (Tel-Aviv: Yehiot Ahronot, 1995), 21–22.

30. For the full text of Rabin's address, Shamir's plan, and the government peace plan, See Shalev, *The Intifada,* Appendices 22–24, 266–279.

31. President Husni Mubarak: Ten-Point Plan (September 1989), in Laqueur and Rubin, eds., *The Israel-Arab Reader,* 551

32. Robert O. Keohane and Joseph S. Nye Jr., eds., *Transnational Relations and World Politics* (Cambridge: Harvard University Press, 1970), 381–382.

33. Secretary of State James Baker: Five Points Plan (October 1989), in Laqueur and Rubin, eds., *The Arab-Israel Reader,* 556

34. Arens, *War and Peace in the Middle East,* 116.

35. Salah Khalaf (Abu-Iyad), "Lowering the Sword," *Foreign Policy* 78 (Spring 1990): 92–112. For the triggers of Madrid and Oslo see Laura Zittrain Eisenberg and Caplan, *Negotiating Arab-Israeli Peace* 75–81.

36. Arens, *War and Peace in the Middle East,* 157.

37. Laura Zittrain Eisenberg, "Passive Belligerency: Israel and the 1991 Gulf War," *Journal of Strategic Studies* 15, No. 3 (September 1992): 304–29.

38. Michael Barnett, "Identity and Alliances in the Middle East," in Peter Katzenstein, ed., *The Culture of National Security* (New York: Columbia University Press, 1996), 400–421–432. See also Kerr, *The Arab Cold War,* Taylor, *The Arab Balance of Power,* and Walt, *The Origins of Alliances.*

39. Brecher, *Crises in World Politics,* 410. According to Gazit, thirty-three states par-ticipated in the coalition. See Shlomo Gazit, "The Gulf War, The Political and Military Process," in *War in the Gulf; Report of a JCSS Study Group* (Tel-Aviv: Papyrus, 1991), 40.

40. On the novelty of the U.S. role see for instance Robert W. Tucker, "Origins of the New World Order," in G. Barzilai, A. Klieman, and G. Shidlo, eds., *The Gulf Crisis and Its Global Aftermath* (London: Routledge, 1993).

41. The problematics of this concept when used against a rival state can found in Arnold Wolfers, *Discord and Collaboration* (Baltimore: Johns Hopkins University Press, 1962), chs. 11–12.

42. On August 10, a majority of twelve Arab states at the Arab League summit in Cairo voted in favor of a resolution condemning Iraq's invasion, calling for Iraqi with-drawal, and even supporting UN economic sanctions and the dispatch of Arab troops to the region. Only the PLO and Libya rejected the resolution, while the other delegates either abstained or approved with reservation. See Brecher, *Crises in World Politics,* 431–432.

43. Brecher, *Crises in World Politics,* 445. On the negotiations see Baker, III, *The Politics of Diplomacy,* 308 and 375–376.

44. Russia, which had always sided with Iraq and was its main arms supplier, also participated in the American-led coalition. On the negotiations with the Soviet foreign minister on the linkage between the two crises, see Baker, *The Politics of Diplomacy,* 15.

45. For a broad analysis of Israel's deterrence doctrine and its modifications in the wake of the Gulf crisis see Efraim Inbar and Shmuel Sandler, "Israel's Deterrence Strategy Revisited," *Security Studies* 3, No. 2 (Winter 1993/94): 330–358. For a first hand analysis of the changes in Israeli thinking see Yitzhak Rabin, "Israeli Strategic Thinking After Desert Storm," in *Thoughts on the Concept of National Security* (Ramat-Gan: Bar-Ilan Center for Strategic Studies, August 1991) (Heb.). See also Yaniv, *Deterrence without the Bomb*.

46. Israel's preventive and preemptive approaches were an integral part of its national security strategy. That doctrine assumed a worst-case scenario, in which the Arab goal remained the destruction of the Jewish state and therefore required that, when threatened, Israel must take the initiative and attack the enemy, first. On Israel's preemptive and/or preventive doctrine see Dan Horowitz, "The Constant and the Changing in Israeli Strategic Thinking," in Joseph Alpher, ed., *War by Choice* (Tel-Aviv: Hakibbutz Hameuchad, 1985), 58–77. See also Levitte, *Offense and Defense in Israeli Military Doctrine*, 25–62. For a general review of the problem see Levy, "Declining Power and the Preventive Motivation for War."

47. Yehuda Ben-Meir, "The Internal Israeli Scene during the Gulf War," in *War in the Gulf* (Boulder: Westview, 1992) 292–300. During this war, thirteen Israeli civilian deaths were caused directly and indirectly by the scuds, hundreds of private homes and thousands of apartments and businesses were damaged.

48. Schelling, *Arms and Influence*, 55–59.

49. For an evaluation of the effects on Israel's deterrence posture see Inbar and Sandler, "Israel's Deterrence Strategy Revisited," and Aharon Levran, *The Storm's Interpretation*, 81–96. See also Amatzia Baram, "Israeli Deterrence, Iraqi Responses," *Orbis* 36, No. 3 (Summer 1992): 397–409.

50. Shai Feldman, "The Israeli Deterrence in the Test of the Gulf War," in *War in the Gulf,* 183. Saddam refrained from using his nonconventional weapons, although there is every evidence that he possessed chemical capabilities, which he had previously used against Iran and Kurdish opposition at home. In this light, Israel's deterrence against nonconventional attack was effective. An Israeli nonconventional response was so grave that he chose to abstain from crossing the threshold, demonstrating rationality on Saddam's part. Efraim Karsh, "Survival at All Costs: Saddam Hussien as Crisis Manager," in Barzilai, Klieman, and Shidlo, eds., *The Gulf Crisis and the Global Aftermath,* 477–482.

51. Brecher, *Crises in World Politics,* 477–482.

52. *New York Times,* 24 April 1992, A6.

53. Secretary Baker admitted this much in his memoirs. "In putting together the diplomatic and military coalition against Iraq, I had repeatedly pledged that the United States would address the larger issues of the Middle East after the crisis had been resolved. In large measure, this promise had enabled me to repel efforts to link the invasion of Kuwait with the Arab-Israeli dispute. Having given my word in this regard, I felt a moral obligation to follow through," Baker, *The Politics of Diplomacy,* 414.

54. Eisenberg and Capaln, *Negotiating Arab-Israeli Peace,* chapters 4 and 6. For a different view see Indyk, "Peace without the PLO."

55. Eisenberg and Caplan, *Negotiating Arab-Israeli Peace,* 103–104. See also the sources cited in this book, especially the books by Neil Caplan, *Futile Diplomacy* 1–2 (London: Frank Cass, 1983 and 1986).

THE ARAB-ISRAELI CONFLICT TRANSFORMED

228   THE ARAB-ISRAELI CONFLICT TRANSFORMED

56. The literature here is very broad. Enclosed is the most general and basic book: Keohane and Nye, eds., *Transnational Relations and World Politics*; Charles Pentland, *International Theory and European Integration* (New York: The Free Press, 1973), especially chs. 1 and 4.

57. Baker, *The Politics of Diplomacy*, 413.

58. *Guide to the Mideast Peace Conference* (Washington: AIPAC, 1991), 10. See also "The Israel PLO Peace Process," Israel Law Review 28 Nos. 2–3 (Summer 1994): 207–434.

59. David Makovsky, *Making Peace with the PLO* (Boulder: Westview, 1996), 26.

60. Ibid., 39. For the Palestinian approach toward the forthcoming negotiations see Jamil Hilal, "PLO Institutions: The Challenge Ahead," *Journal of Palestine Studies* 23, No. 1 (Autumn, 1993): 46–60. For a theoretical interpretation see Jacob Bercovitch, "Conflict Management and the Oslo Experiences: Assessing the Success of Israeli-Palestinian Peacemaking," *International Negotiation* 2 No. 2 (1997): 217–235.

61. Makovsky, *Making Peace with the PLO* (Boulder: Westview, 1996), 25.

62. Burhan Dajani, "The September 1993 Israeli-PLO Documents: A Textual Analysis," *Journal of Palestine Studies* 23 No. 3 (Spring 1994): 5–23; Kumaraswamy, "The Gaza-Jericho Agreement: An Asymmetrical Accord," *Strategic Analysis* 17 No. 4 (May 1994): 219–232; Yossi Beilin, *Touching Peace* (Tel-Aviv: Yedioth Ahronoth Books, 1997), 107. See also Herbert C. Kelman, "Some Determinants of the Oslo Breakthrough," *International Negotiation* 2, No. 2 (1997): 183–194 and William I. Zartman, "Explaining Oslo," *International Negotiation* 2, No. 2 (1997): 195–215.

63. Makovsky, *Making Peace with the PLO*, 89–90.

64. Monshipouri, "The PLO Rivalry with Hamas"; Makovsky, *Making Peace with the PLO*, 79–80. See also Bulliet, "The Future of the Islamic Movement."

65. Makovsky, *Making Peace with the PLO*, 107–114. See also Shimon Peres, *The New Middle East* (Tel-Aviv: Steimatsky, 1993), 41–45.

66. Makovsky advances this assumption based on an interview with pollster Kalamn Geyer. Makovsky, *Making Peace with the PLO*, 132.

67. Jarbawi, "The Triangle of Conflict"; Banerji, "The Israeli-Jordanian Peace Treaty"; Bookmiller, "Approaching the Rubicon."

68. For the peace treaty see Laqueur and Rubin, eds., *The Israel-Arab Reader*, 665–674. See also Boker, "Jordan and Israel"; Makovsky, *Making Peace with the PLO*, 157–160. For a theoretical analysis of the negotiations see Bueno De Mesquita, "Multilateral Negotiations: A Spatial Analysis of the Arab-Israeli Dispute."

69. David Makovsky, *The Jerusalem Post*, 8 October 1995, 3, and *Making Peace with the PLO*, 151. For a Palestinian view see Naseer H. Aruri, "Early Empowerment for the Palestinians: The Burden, not the Responsibility," *Journal of Palestine Studies* 24, No. 2 (Winter 1995): 33–39.

70. This analysis is based on Moshe Ma'oz, *Syria and Israel: From War to Peace Making* (Tel-Aviv: Maariv Books, 1996), chapter 11; Diab, " Syrian Security Requirements in a Peace Settlement with Israel"; and Efraim Inbar, "Israeli Negotiations with Syria," *Israel Affairs* 1, No.4: 89–100; Laurie A. Brand, "Asad's Syria and the PLO: Coincidence or Conflict of Interests?" *Journal of South Asian and Middle Eastern Studies* 14, No. 2 (1990): 22–43. On the issue of an Arms control regime see Inbar and Sandler, eds., *Middle Eastern Security*: 152–194.

71. Despite the Qana village tragedy, the general level of violence was that of minor clashes.

72. *Ha'aretz,* 8 October 2000, A8.

73. *Yediot Ahronot,* 22 October 2000, 2–3; 23 October, 11.

74. *Ha'aretz,* 1 Nov. 2000, A1.

75. See Johanna Mc Geary, "The Many Minds of Arafat," *Time* (23 October 2000): 48–54.

76. *Time* (16 October 2000): 48.

77. See interview with Barak, in *Time* (23 October 2000): 41.

78. Ibid.: 39.

79. www.btselem.org.il

80. *Ha'aretz,* 1 November 2000, A2.

CHAPTER 7. UNDERSTANDING TRANSFORMATION IN
THE ARAB-ISRAELI CONFLICT

1. Highlighting the need to improve our scientific achievements, Michael Brecher, in his presidential address to the annual convention of the International Studies Association in 1999, stressed the need to improve description, explanation, and prediction in IR research. Toward that end he called for efforts toward a synthesis between contending schools of thought in international relations and warned against continuing fixation on flawed dichotomies that obsess the discipline. Michael Brecher, "International Studies in the Twentieth Century and Beyond: Flawed Dichotomies, Synthesis, Cumulation," *International Studies Quarterly* 43, No. 2 (June 1999): 213–264.

2. Brecher and Wilkenfeld, *A Study of Crisis,* 802.

GLOSSARY

1. See also Jacob Bercovitch and Richard Jackson, *International Conflict: A Chronological Encyclopedia of Conflicts and Their Management 1945–1995* (New York: Congressional Quarterly Inc., 1997), 57–58; Brecher and Wilkenfeld, *A Study of Crisis* 269–271, and sources listed therein; Robert Lyle Butterworth with Margaret. E. Scranton, *Managing Interstate Conflict, 1945–74: Data with Synopses* (Pittsburgh: University of Pittsburgh, 1976), 66; Caplan, *Futile Diplomacy*; Ruth E. Lapidoth and Moshe Hirsch, *The Arab-Israel Conflict and its Resolution: Selected Documents* (Boston: M. Nijhoff, 1992), 33–102; Netanel Lorch, *History of the War of Independence* (Tel Aviv: Massada, 1966); Benny Morris, "Refabricating 1948," *Journal of Palestine Studies* 27, No. 2 (Winter 1998): 81–95; Pappe, *Britain and the Arab-Israeli Conflict, 1948–51.* For the pre-state era see Yosef Gorny, (Heb.) *Zionism and the Arabs, 1881–1948: A Study of Ideology* (Tel-Aviv: Am Oved, 1985).

2. See also Brecher and Wilkenfeld, *A Study of Crisis,* 271 and sources listed therein; Morris, *Righteous Victims*; 245–249.

3. See also Bercovitch and Jackson, *International Conflict,* 69; Brecher and Wilkenfeld, *A Study of Crisis,* 272–273 and sources listed therein.

230   THE ARAB-ISRAELI CONFLICT TRANSFORMED

4. See also Bercovitch and Jackson, *International Conflict*, 76; Brecher and Wilkenfeld, *A Study of Crisis*, 273 and sources listed therein; Butterworth with Scranton *Managing Interstate Conflict*, 124; Morris, *Righteous Victims*, 278–279.

5. See also Mordechai Bar-On, *The Gates of Gaza: Israel's Road to Suez and Back, 1955–1957* (New York: St. Martin's Press, 1994); Brecher and Wilkenfeld, *A Study of Crisis*, 274 and sources listed therein; Motti Golani, ed., (Heb.) *Black Arrow: Gaza Raid and the Israeli Policy of Retaliation during the Fifties* (Holon: Ma'arachot/Israeli Defense Ministry Press, 1994); Morris, *Righteous Victims*, 282–288; Michael B. Oren, "Escalation to Suez: The Egyptian-Israeli Border War, 1949–56," *Journal of Contemporary History* (April 1989): 347–374.

6. See also Bercovitch and Jackson, 71–72, 84–85; Brecher and Wilkenfeld, *A Study of Crisis*, 275–276 and sources listed therein; Harry Browne, *Suez and Sinai* (London: Longman, 1971); Butterworth with Scranton, *Managing Interstate Conflict*, 156–158, 219–221; Matthew A. Fitzsimons, *The Suez Crisis and the Containment Policy* (Indianapolis: Bobbs-Merrill, 1957); Motti Golani, (Heb.) *There Will Be War Next Summer . . . The Road to the Sinai War, 1955–56* (Tel Aviv: Ma'arachot/Israeli Defense Ministry Press, 1997); Anthony Gorst and W. Scott-Lucas, "Suez 1956: Strategy and the Diplomatic Process," *Journal of Strategic Studies* 11, No. 4 (1988): 391–436; Lapidoth and Hirsch, *The Arab-Israel Conflict and its Resolution*, 117–119; Scott W. Lucas, *Divided We Stand: Britain, The United States, and the Suez Crisis* (London: Hodder and Stoughton, 1991); John Marlowe, *Anglo-Egyptian Relations, 1800–1953* (London: Cresset, 1954); Morris, *Righteous Victims*, 288–300; Edgar O'Ballance, *The Sinai Campaign, 1956* (New York: Praeger, 1959); Avi Shlaim, "The Protocol of Sevres, 1956: Anatomy of a War Plot," *International Affairs* 73, No. 3 (July 1997): 509–530; Donald C. Watt, *Britain and the Suez Canal* (London: Oxford University Press, 1957).

7. See also Brecher and Wilkenfeld, *A Study of Crisis*, 277–278 and sources listed therein.

8. See also Brecher and Wilkenfeld, *A Study of Crisis*, 278–279 and sources listed therein.

9. See also Brecher and Wilkenfeld, *A Study of Crisis*, 279–280 and sources listed therein; Cohen, "Cairo, Dimona, and the June 1967 War"; Reguer, "Controversial Waters."

10. See also Brecher and Wilkenfeld, *A Study of Crisis*, 280–281 and sources listed therein; Morris, *Righteous Victims*, 302–303.

11. See also Bercovitch and Jackson, *International Conflict*, 134–135; Brecher and Wilkenfeld, *A Study of Crisis*, 281–282 and sources listed therein; Butterworth with Scranton, *Managing Interstate Conflict*, 226–227, 417–419; Lapidoth and Hirsch, *The Arab-Israel Conflict and its Resolution*, 120–135; Morris, *Righteous Victims*, 305–329, Richard Parker, "The June 1967 War: Some Mysteries Explored," *Middle East Journal* 46. No. 2 (1992); William B. Quandt, "Lyndon Johnson and the June 1967 War: What Color Was the Light?" *Middle East Journal* 46, No. 2 (1992): 177–198; Robert A. Wagner, *Crisis-Decision Making: Israel's Experience in 1967 and 1973* (New York: Praeger, 1974).

12. See also Brecher and Wilkenfeld, *A Study of Crisis*, 282–283 and sources listed therein; Dupuy, *Elusive Victory*, 350–356; Morris, *Righteous Victims*, 368–370.

13. See also Bercovitch and Jackson, *International Conflict*, 128–129 for background information; Brecher and Wilkenfeld, *A Study of Crisis*, 283–284 and sources listed therein; Morris, *Righteous Victims*, 376–379 and 380–383, on the continuation of PLO terror after the crisis ended.

14. See also Brecher and Wilkenfeld, *A Study of Crisis,* 284–285 and sources listed therein; Butterworth with Scranton, *Managing Interstate Conflict,* 422–424; Dupuy, *Elusive Victory,* 361–369; Korn, *Stalemate*; Lapidoth, and Hirsch, *The Arab-Israel Conflict and its Resolution,* 361–369; Morris, *Righteous Victims,* 347–363; Dan Schueftan, (Heb.) *Attrition: Egypt's Postwar Political Strategy, 1967–70* (Tel-Aviv: Ma'arachot/Israeli Defense Ministry Press 1989).

15. See also Brecher and Wilkenfeld, *A Study of Crisis,* 285–286 and sources listed therein; Eli Ze'ira, (Heb.) *The Yom Kippur War* (Tel-Aviv: Idanim, 1993).

16. See also Brecher and Wilkenfeld, *A Study of Crisis,* 286–287 and sources listed therein; Morris, *Righteous Victims,* 398–400.

17. See also Bercovitch and Jackson, *International Conflict,* 147, 150; Brecher and Wilkenfeld, *A Study of Crisis,* 287–290 and sources listed therein; Butterworth with Scranton, *Managing Interstate Conflict,* 468–470; Michael I. Handel, *Perception, Deception, and Surprise: The Case of the Yom Kippur War. Jerusalem Papers on Peace Problems # 19* (Jerusalem: Leonard Davis Institute for International Relations, Hebrew University of Jerusalem, 1976); Victor Israelyan, "The October War: Kissinger in Moscow," *Middle East Journal* 49 No. 2 (1995): 248–267; Lapidoth and Hirsch, *The Arab-Israel Conflict and its Resolution,*145–155; Morris, *Righteous Victims,* 398–441; Ze'ira, *The Yom Kippur War.*

18. See also Brecher and Wilkenfeld, *A Study of Crisis,* 290–291 and sources listed therein; Morris, *Righteous Victims,* 383–385; Shimon Peres, (Heb.) *Entebbe Diary* (Tel-Aviv: Idanim, 1991).

19. See also Reuven Avi-Ran, "The Syrian Military-Strategic Interest in Lebanon," *Jerusalem Quarterly* 46, (Spring 1988):131–144; Brecher and Wilkenfeld, *A Study of Crisis,* 291 and sources listed therein; Raymond A. Hinnebusch, "Syrian Policy in Lebanon and the Palestinians," *Arab Studies Quarterly* 8, No. 1 (1986): 1–20; and Morris, *Righteous Victims,* 497–505, for background and consequences of this case.

20. See also Bercovitch and Jackson, *International Conflict,* 177, 182–183; Brecher and Wilkenfeld, *A Study of Crisis,* 292 and sources listed therein; Hinnebusch, "Syrian Policy in Lebanon and the Palestinians"; Lapidoth, and Hirsch, *The Arab-Israel Conflict and its Resolution,*193–194; Morris, *Righteous Victims,* 591.

21. See also Brecher and Wilkenfeld, *A Study of Crisis,* 292–294 and sources listed therein; Lapidoth, and Hirsch, *The Arab-Israel Conflict and its Resolution,* 258–259; Shlomo Nakdimon, *First Strike: The Exclusive Story of how Israel Foiled Iraq's Attempt to Get the Bomb* (New York: Summit Books, 1987).

22. See also Bercovitch and Jackson, *International Conflict,* 191; Brecher smd Wilkenfeld, *A Study of Crisis,* 294–295 and sources listed therein; Hinnebusch, "Syrian Policy in Lebanon and the Palestinians"; Patrick Seale, "A Game of Masters and Proxies (in Lebanon)," *European Journal of International Affairs* 5 (Summer 1989): 108–120.

23. See also Bercovitch and Jackson, *International Conflict,* 201; Brecher and Wilkenfeld, *A Study of Crisis,* 295–297 and sources listed therein; Trevor Dupuy, and Paul Martell, *Flawed Victory: The Arab-Israeli Conflict and the 1982 War in Lebanon* (Fairfax, VA: Hero Books, 1986); Hinnebusch, "Syrian Policy in Lebanon and the Palestinians"; Lapidoth and Hirsch, *The Arab-Israel Conflict and its Resolution,* 285–286; Morris, *Righteous Victims,* 510–551; Arye Naor, (Heb.) *Cabinet at War, The Functioning of the Israeli Cabinet During the Lebanon War (1982)* (Israel: Lahav, 1986); Zeev Schiff and Ehud Ya'ari, *Israel's Lebanon War* (London: Unwin, 1986).

24. See also Bercovitch and Jackson, *International Conflict,* 213–214; Brecher and Wilkenfeld, *A Study of Crisis,* 298 and sources listed therein. On Israel-Syria struggle in Lebanon see: Raymond Cohen, "Threat Assessment in Military Intelligence: The Case of Israel and Syria, 1985–86," *Intelligence and National Security* 4 (October 1989):735–786; Adam M. Garfinkle, "Israel's Abiding Troubles in Lebanon," *Orbis* 41, No. 4 (Fall 1997): 603–612; Hudson, *Arab Politics.*

25. See also Bercovitch and Jackson, *International Conflict,* 213–214; Brecher and Wilkenfeld, *A Study of Crisis,* 299–300 and sources listed therein; Morris, *Righteous Victims,* 551–560, 618–619.

26. See also Bercovitch and Jackson, *International Conflict,* 213–214; Peter A. Lupsha, and John Fullilove, "Beyond State Terror: The 'Grapes of Wrath'," *Low Intensity Conflict and Law Enforcement* 5, No.3 (Winter 1996): 301–333, for background data; and Morris, *Righteous Victims,* 639.

BIBLIOGRAPHY

Abdullah King of Jordan. *My Memoirs Completed: Al-Takmilah.* New York: Longman, 1978.

Abidi, Aqil H. *Jordan: A Political Study, 1948–1957.* London: Asia Publishing House, 1965.

Abir, Mordechai. *Oil, Power, and Politics.* London: Frank Cass, 1974.

Abraham, Nabeel. "The Conversion of Chairman Arafat," *American-Arab Affairs* 31 (Winter 1989): 53–69.

AbuKhalil, Asad. "Ideology and Practice of Hizbullah in Lebanon: Islamization of Leninist Organizational Principles," *Middle Eastern Studies* 27, No. 3 (July 1991): 390–403.

AbuKhalil, Asad. "Internal Contradictions in the PFLP: Decision-Making and Policy Orientation," *Middle East Journal* 41, No. 3 (Summer 1987): 361–378.

Abu-Lughod, Ibrahim. (ed.) *The Transformation of Palestine.* Evanston: Northwestern University Press, 1971.

Acheson, Dean. *Present at the Creation: My Years in the State Department.* New York: New American Library, 1969.

Adams, Michael. *Suez and After—Year of Crisis.* Boston: Beacon, 1958.

Adler, Emanuel. "Seizing the Middle Ground: Constructivism in World Politics," *European Journal of International Relations* 3, No. 3 (September 1997): 319–363.

Adan, Avraham. *On the Banks of the Suez.* San Francisco: Presidio, 1980.

Adomeit, Hannes. *Soviet Risk-Taking and Crisis Behavior.* London: Allen and Unwin, 1982.

Agwani, Mohammed S. *The Lebanese Crisis, 1958: A Documentary Study.* London: Asia Publishing House, 1965.

Ahronson, Shlomo. *Conflict and Bargaining in the Middle East: An Israeli Perspective.* Baltimore: Johns Hopkins University Press, 1978.

Ahronson, Shlomo, with Oded Brosh. *The Politics and Strategy of Nuclear Weapons in the Middle East: Opacity, Theory, and Reality, 1966–1991, An Israeli Perspective.* Albany: State University of New York Press, 1992.

Ahronson, Shlomo, and Dan Horowitz. "The Strategy of Controlled Retaliation—The Israeli Example," *Medina u'Mimshal* 1, No. 1 (1971). 77–99.

Ajomo, M. Ayo. "The Entebbe Affair: Intervention in International Law." Lagos: Nigerian Institute of International Affairs, *Lecture Series*, No. 13, 1977.

Alamuddin, Najib. *Turmoil: The Druzes, Lebanon, and the Arab-Israeli Conflict*. London: Quartet, 1993.

Albin, Cecilia. "Negotiating Intractable Conflicts: On the Future of Jerusalem," *Cooperation and Conflict* 32, No. 1 (March 1997): 29–77.

Alexander, Yonah, and Nicholas N. Kittrie. (eds.) *Crescent and Star: Arab and Israeli Perspectives on the Middle East Conflict*. New York: AMS Press, 1973.

Allen, David, and Alfred Pijpers. (eds.) *European Foreign Policy Making and the Arab-Israeli Conflict*. The Hague: M. Nijhoff, 1984.

Allon, Yigal. "Israel: The Case for Defensible Borders," *Foreign Affairs* 55, No. 1 (October 1976): 38–53.

Allon, Yigal. *The Making of the Israeli Army*. London: Sphere Books, 1970.

Al Madfai, Madiha Rashid. *Jordan, the United States, and the Middle East Peace Process, 1974–1991*. Cambridge: Cambridge University Press, 1993.

Alon, Hanan. *Countering Palestinian Terrorism in Israel: Toward a Policy Analysis of Countermeasures*. Rand Report No. 1567. Santa Monica: Rand, 1980.

Alpher, Joseph. "Israel's Security Concerns in the Peace Process," *International Affairs* 70, No. 2 (April 1994): 229–241.

Alpher, Joseph. "Security Arrangements for a Palestinian Settlement," *Survival* 34, No. 4 (Winter 1992–3): 49–67.

Ambrose, Stephen E. *Eisenhower: The President 1952–1969*. Vol. 2. London: Allen and Unwin, 1984.

Amirahmadi, Hooshang, and Nader Entessar. *Iran and the Arab World*. New York: St. Martin's, 1993.

Amos, John W. *Arab-Israeli Military-Political Relations: Arab Perceptions and the Politics of Escalation*. New York: Pergamon, 1979.

Anderson, Ewan W. "The Vulnerability of Arab Water Resources," *Arab Affairs* (Summer/Fall 1988): 73–81.

Anderson, Ray, Robert F. Seibert, and Jan G. Wagner. *Politics and Change in the Middle East: Sources of Conflict and Accommodation*. Englewood Cliffs: Prentice-Hall, 1990.

Andoni, Lamis. "Redefining Oslo: Negotiating the Hebron Protocol," *Journal of Palestine Studies* 26, No. 3 (Spring 1997): 17–30.

Andriole, Stephen J. "The Levels of Analysis Problems and the Study of Foreign, International, and Global Affairs: A Review Critique and Another Final Solution," *International Interactions* 5, No. 2–3 (1978): 113–133.

Andriole, Stephen J., Jonathan Wilkenfeld, and Gerald W. Hopple. "A Framework for the Comparative Analysis of Foreign Policy Behavior," *International Studies Quarterly* 19, No. 2 (June 1975): 160–198.

Antonius, George. *The Arab Awakening*. New York: Capricorn Books, 1946.

Arens, Moshe. *Peace and War in the Middle East 1988–1992*. Tel-Aviv: Yediot Ahronot, 1995.

Arens, Moshe. *Broken Covenant: American Foreign Policy and the Crisis Between the US and Israel*. New York: Simon and Schuster, 1995.

Arian, Asher. *Security Threatened, Surveying Israeli Opinion on Peace and War.* Cambridge: Cambridge University Press. Tel-Aviv: Tel-Aviv University, 1995.

Aroian, Lois A., and Richard P. Mitchell. *The Modern Middle East and North Africa.* New York: Macmillan, 1984.

Art, Robert J. "A Defensible Defense: America's Grand Strategy After the Cold War," *International Security* 15, No. 4 (Spring 1991): 5–53.

Aruri, Nasseer H. "The Wye Memorandum: Netanyahu's Oslo and Unreciprocal Reciprocity," *Journal of Palestine Studies* 28, No. 2 (Summer 1999): 17–28.

Aruri, Naseer H. "The U.S. and the Arabs: A Woeful History," *Arab Studies Quarterly* 19, No. 3 (Summer 1997): 29–45.

Aruri, Naseer H. "Early Empowerment for Palestinians: The Burden, Not the Responsibility," *Journal of Palestine Studies* 24, No. 2 (Winter 1995): 33–40.

Aruri, Naseer H. "The United States and Palestine: Reagan's Legacy to Bush," *Journal of Palestine Studies* 18, No. 3 (Spring 1989): 3–21.

Aruri, Naseer H. (ed.) *Middle East Crucible: Studies on the Arab-Israeli War of October 1973.* Wilmette, IL: The Medina University Press International, 1975.

Atherton, Alfred Leroy Jr. "The Shifting Sands of Middle East Peace," *Foreign Policy* 86 (Spring 1992): 114–133.

Atran, Scott. "Stones against the Iron Fist, Terror within the Nation: Alternating Structures of Violence and Cultural Identity in the Israeli-Palestinian Conflict," *Politics and Society* 18, No. 4 (December 1990): 481–526.

Auerbach, Yehudit. "Legitimation for Turning-Point Decisions in Foreign Policy: Israel vis-à-vis Germany 1952 and Egypt 1977," *Review of International Studies* 15, No. 4 (Oct. 1989): 329–340.

Auerbach, Yehudit, and Hemda Ben-Yehuda. "Attitudes towards an Existence Conflict: Rabin and Sharon on the Palestinian Issue," In *Conflict and Social Psychology,* ed. Knud S. Larsen. International Peace Research Institute, Oslo (PRIO), London: Sage, 1993.

Auerbach, Yehudit, and Hemda Ben-Yehuda. "Attitudes towards an Existence Conflict: Begin and Dayan on the Palestinian Issue," *International Interactions* 13, No. 4 (1987): 323–351.

Avigur, Shaul, Yehuda Slutzky, and Gershon Rivlin. *The Short Version of the History of the Haganah.* Tel-Aviv: Ma'archot/Israeli Defense Ministry, 1978.

Avineri, Shlomo. "Israel and the End of the Cold War: The Shadow has Faded," *The Brookings Review* 11, No. 2 (Spring 1993): 26–31.

Avineri, Shlomo. "The Impact of Changes in the Soviet Union and Eastern Europe on the Arab-Israeli Conflict," *Mediterranean Quarterly* 2, No. 1 (Winter 1991): 45–57.

Avi-Ran, Reuven. (Heb.) *The Lebanon War: Documents and Arab Sources, 2, The War.* Tel-Aviv: Ma'archot/Israeli Defense Ministry, 1997.

Avi-Ran, Reuven. "The Syrian Military-Strategic Interest in Lebanon," *Jerusalem Quarterly* 46 (Spring 1988): 131–144.

Avi-Ran, Reuven. (Heb.) *Syrian Involvement in Lebanon, 1975–1985.* Tel-Aviv: Ma'archot/Israeli Defense Ministry, 1986.

Awartani, H., Klieman E. "Economic Interactions among Participants in the Middle East Peace Process," *Middle East Journal* 51 (Spring 1997): 215–229.

Ayoob, Mohammed. *Defusing the Middle East Time Bomb: A State for the Palestinians.*

Working Paper No. 35. Canberra: Strategic and Defence Studies Center, Australian National University, 1981.

Ayres, William. "Mediating International Conflicts: Is Image Change Necessary?" *Journal of Peace Research* 34, No. 3 (November 1997): 431–447.

Azar, Edward E. "Protracted International Conflicts: Ten Propositions," *International Interactions* 12, No. 1 (1985): 59–70.

Azar, Edward E. "Peace Amidst Development: A Conceptual Agenda for Conflict and Peace Research," *International Interactions* 6, No. 2 (1979): 123–143.

Azar, Edward E. "Conflict Escalation and Conflict Reduction in an International Crisis: Suez, 1956," *Journal of Conflict Resolution* 16, No. 2 (1972): 183–201.

Azar, Edward E., Paul Jureidini, and Ronald McLaurin. "Protracted Social Conflict: Theory and Practice in the Middle East," *Journal of Palestine Studies* 8, No. 1 (1978): 41–60.

Baaklini, Abdo I. *Legislative and Political Development, Lebanon, 1842–1972.* Durham: Duke University Press, 1976.

Bachi, Roberto. *The Population of Israel.* Jerusalem: Hebrew University; Institute of Contemporary Jewry, 1976.

El Badri, Hassan, Taha El Magdoub, and Mohammed Dia El Din Zohdy. *The Ramadan War 1973.* Dunn Loring, Virginia: T. N. Dupuy Associates, 1978.

Bailey, Clinton. *Jordan's Palestinian Challenge, 1948–1983: A Political History.* Boulder: Westview, 1984.

Bailey, Sydney D. *Four Arab-Israeli Wars and the Peace Process.* New York: St. Martin's, 1990.

Baker, James A. III. *The Politics of Diplomacy.* New York: G. P. Putnam, 1995.

Baldwin, David A. (ed.) *Neorealism and Neoliberalism.* New York: Columbia University Press, 1993.

Ball, George. "The Unbalanced Triangle: The United States, Israel, and Palestine," *Arab Studies Quarterly* 10, No. 4 (Fall 1988): 375–383.

Bandmann, Yona, and Yishai Cordova. "The Soviet Nuclear Threat Towards the Close of the Yom Kippur War," *Jerusalem Journal of International Relations* 5, No. 1 (1980): 94–110.

Banerji, Arun Kumar. "The Israeli-Jordanian Peace Treaty, Jordan's Long Quest for Security and Identity," *Strategic Analysis* 17, No. 11 (February 1995): 1419–1430.

Baram, Amatzia. "Israeli Deterrence, Iraqi Responses," *Orbis* 36, No. 3 (Summer 1992): 397–409.

Baram, Amatzia. "After the Iran-Iraq War—What?" *Jerusalem Quarterly* 49 (Winter 1989): 85–96.

Bard, Mitchell G. "How Fares the Camp David Trio?" *Orbis* 34, No. 2 (Spring 1990): 227–240.

Barker, Arthur J. *Suez: The Seven Day War.* London: Faber and Faber, 1964.

Barnett, Michael. "Identity and Alliances in the Middle East." In *The Culture of National Security,* ed. Peter Katzenstein. New York, Columbia University Press, 1996.

Barnett, Michael. "Sovereignty, Nationalism, and Regional Order in the Arab States System," *International Organization* 49, No. 3 (Summer 1995): 479–510.

Barnett, Michael. "Institutions, Roles, and Disorder: The Case of the Arab States

System," *International Studies Quarterly* 37, No. 3 (1993): 271–296.

Barnett, Michael. *Confronting the Costs of War: Military Power, State and Society in Egypt and Israel*. Princeton: Princeton University Press, 1992.

Bartov, Hanoch. *Dado: Forty Eight Years and Another Twenty Days*, 2 Vols. Tel-Aviv: Ma'ariv Library, 1981.

Barzilai, Gad, and Efraim Inbar. "The Use of Force: Israeli Public Opinion on Military Options," *Armed Forces and Society* 23, No. 1 (Fall 1996): 54–56.

Barzilai, Gad, Aharon Klieman, and Gil Shidlo. (eds.) *The Gulf Crisis and the Global Aftermath*. London: Routledge, 1993.

Barzilai, Gad, and Yossi Shain. "Israeli Democracy at the Crossroads: a Crisis of Non-Governability," *Government and Opposition* 26, No. 3 (Summer 1991): 345–367.

Bar-Ilan, David. "Palestinian Nationalism—Unguided Missile," *Global Affairs* 3, No. 4 (Fall 1988): 87–98.

Bar-Joseph, Uri, and John P. Hannah. "Intervention Threats in Short Arab-Israeli Wars: An Analysis of Soviet Crisis Behavior," *The Journal of Strategic Studies* 2, No. 4 (Dec. 1988): 436–467.

Bar-On, Mordechai. *The Gates of Gaza: Israel's Road to Suez and Back, 1955–1957*. New York: St. Martin's Press, 1994.

Bar-On, Mordechai. "Israeli Reactions to the Uprising," *Journal of Palestine Studies* 17, No. 4 (Summer 1988): 46–65.

Bar-Siman-Tov, Yaacov. "The Arab-Israeli Conflict: Learning Conflict Resolution," *Journal of Peace Research* 31, No. 1 (1994): 75–92.

Bar-Siman-Tov, Yaacov. *Israel, the Superpowers and the War in the Middle East*. New York: Praeger, 1987.

Bar-Siman-Tov, Yaacov. *Linkage Politics in the Middle East: Syria between Domestic and External Conflict, 1961–1970*. Boulder: Westview, 1983.

Bar-Siman-Tov, Yaacov. *The Israeli-Egyptian War of Attrition, 1969–1970: A Case-Study of Limited Local War*. New York: Columbia University Press, 1980.

Bar-Yaacov, Nissim. *The Israel-Syrian Armistice: Problems of Implementation, 1949–66*. Jerusalem: Magnes, 1967.

Bar-Zohar, Michael. (Heb.) *Ben-Gurion: A Political Biography*. Vols 1, 2, and 3. Tel-Aviv: Am Oved, 1978.

Bar-Zohar, Michael. *Embassies in Crisis: Diplomats and Demagogues Behind the Six Day War*. Englewood Cliffs: Prentice-Hall, 1970.

Bar-Zohar, Michael. *Ben-Gurion: The Armed Prophet*. Englewood Cliffs: Prentice-Hall, 1967.

Bar-Zohar, Michael. *Suez: Ultra Secret*. Paris: Librairie Fayard, 1964.

Bassiouni, M. Chelif. "An Analysis of Egyptian Peace Policy Toward Israel: From Resolution 242 (1967) to the 1979 Peace Treaty," *New Outlook* (January 1981): 27–33.

Beaufre, Andre. *The Suez Expedition 1956*. London: Faber and Faber, 1969.

Bechor, Guy. (Heb.) *Lexicon of the PLO*. Tel-Aviv: Ma'archot/Israeli Defense Ministry, 1991.

Becker, Jillian. *The PLO: The Rise and Fall of the Palestine Liberation Organization*. New

York: St. Martin's, 1984.

Be'eri, Eliezer. *The Palestinians under Jordanian Rule—Three Issues.* Jerusalem: Magness 1978.

Beilin, Yossi. *Touching Peace.* Tel-Aviv: Yedioth Ahronot, 1997.

Bennis, Phyllis. "The United Nations and Palestine: Partition and its Aftermath," *Arab Studies Quarterly* 19, No. 3 (Summer 1997): 47–75.

Ben-Dor, Gabriel, and David Brian Dewitt. *Conflict Management in the Middle East.* Lexington, MA: Lexington Books, 1987.

Ben-Gurion, David. *The War of Independence: Ben-Gurion's War Diary.* Tel-Aviv: Ma'archot/Israeli Defense Ministry, 1982.

Ben-Gurion, David. *Israel: A Personal History.* Tel-Aviv: Sabra, 1972.

Ben-Gurion, David. *Recollections.* Tel-Aviv: Am Oved, 1971.

Ben-Gurion, David. *The Restored State of Israel.* Tel-Aviv: Am Oved, 1969.

Ben-Gurion, David. *The Sinai Campaign.* Tel-Aviv: Am Oved, 1964.

Ben-Gurion, David. *Israel: Years of Challenge.* New York: Holt, Rinehart and Winston, 1963.

Ben-Gurion, David. *In Battle.* Vol. 5 Tel-Aviv: Am Oved, 1957.

Ben-Meir, Alon. "Why Syria Must Regain the Golan to Make Peace," *Middle East Policy* 5, No. 3 (1997): 104–112.

Ben-Meir, Alon. "Israel and Syria: The Search for a "Risk-Free" Peace," *Middle East Policy* 4, No.1–2 (Sept. 1995): 140–155.

Ben-Meir, Alon. "The Israeli-Syrian Battle for Equitable Peace," *Middle East Policy* 3, No. 1 (1994): 70–83.

Ben-Meir, Alon. "Israelis and Palestinians: Harsh Demographic Reality and Peace," *Middle East Policy* 2, No. 2 (1993): 74–86.

Ben-Meir, Alon. "The Palestinian-Israeli Conflict. Five Principles on Which Peace Must Be Constructed," *Society and Politics* 32, No. 3–4 (1993): 5–28.

Ben-Porat, Yeshayahu, and Ze'ev Schiff. *Entebbe Rescue.* London: Delacorte Press, 1977.

Ben-Rafael, Eliezer. *Israel-Palestine: a Guerrilla Conflict in International Politics.* New York: Greenwood, 1987.

Ben-Yehuda, Hemda. "Territoriality Crisis and War in the Arab-Israel Conflict," *Journal of Conflict Studies* 21, No.2 (January 2002):78–108.

Ben-Yehuda, Hemda. "Opportunity Crisis: Framework and Findings, 1918–1994," *Conflict Management and Peace Science* 17, No. 1 (1999): 69–102.

Ben-Yehuda, Hemda. "Attitude Change and Policy Transformation: Yitzhak Rabin and the Palestinian Question, 1967–1995," *Israel Affairs* 3, Nos. 3–4 (1997): 201–224.

Ben-Yehuda, Hemda. "The ICB Project: Evolution, Evaluation, and Impact." Paper presented at the *International Studies Association Annual Convention,* San Diego, 1996.

Ben-Yehuda, Hemda, and Meirav Mishali. "Ethnicity, Crisis, and Conflict: Applied to the Arab-Israeli Domain 1947–1997." Paper presented at the *International Studies Association Annual Convention,* March 1998.

Ben-Yehuda, Hemda, and Shmuel Sandler. "Crisis Magnitude and Interstate Conflict: Changes in the Arab-Israel Dispute," *Journal of Peace Research* 35, No. 1 (1998): 83–109.

Ben-Yehuda, Hemda, and Yehudit Auerbach. "Attitudes to an Existence Conflict: Allon and Peres on the Palestinian Issue, 1967–1987," *Journal of Conflict Resolution* 35, No. 3 (1991): 519–546.

Ben-Zvi, Abraham. "The Superpower Option for Resolving the Arab-Israeli Conflict: Precedents, Preconditions, and Prospects," *Conflict* 10, No. 1 (1990): 63–81.

Bercovitch, Jacob. "Conflict Management and the Oslo Experiences: Assessing the Success of Israeli-Palestinian Peacemaking," *International Negotiation* 2, No. 2 (1997): 217–235.

Bercovitch, Jacob, and Richard Jackson. *International Conflict: A Chronological Encyclopedia of Conflicts and Their Management 1945–1995.* New York: Congressional Quarterly Inc., 1997.

Bercovitch, Jacob, and Brian Mandell. "Conflict Management and Peace-Making in the Middle East in the Wake of the Gulf War: Objectives, Achievement, and Prospects," *Society and Politics* 32, No. 1–2 (1993): 55–70.

Beres, Louis Rene. "The Growing Threat of Nuclear War in the Middle East," *Jerusalem Journal of International Relations* 12, No. 1 (January 1990): 1–27.

Beres, Louis Rene. (ed.) *Security or Armageddon, Israel's Nuclear Strategy.* Lexington, MA: Lexington Books, 1986.

Bergus, Donald C. "'Forty Years on'—Israel's Quest for Security," *Middle East Journal* 42, No. 2 (1988): 202–208.

Bernstein, Marver H. "Israel: Turbulent Democracy at Forty," *Middle East Journal* 42, No. 2 (1988): 193–201.

Beschorner, Natasha. *Water and Instability in the Middle East.* Adelphi Papers No. 273. London: Brassey's, 1992.

Bethell, Nicholas. *The Palestine Triangle.* London: Andre Deutsch, 1979.

Bhatia, Shyam. *Nuclear Rivals in the Middle East.* New York: Routledge, 1988.

Bill, James A., and Carl Leiden. *Politics in the Middle East.* Boston: Little, Brown, 1983.

Binder, Leonard. "The Middle East as a Subordinate International System," *World Politics* 10, No. 3 (April 1958): 408–429.

Bishara, Azmy. "Israel Faces the Uprising: a Preliminary Assessment," *Middle East Report* 157 (March-April 1989): 6–14.

Bishara, Ghassan. "The Political Repercussions of the Israeli Raid on the Iraqi Nuclear Reactor," *Journal of Palestine Studies* 11, No. 3 (Spring 1982): 58–76.

Bishop, Donald H. "The Israeli-Palestinian Conflict, Past, Present, and Future," *Scandinavian Journal of Development Alternatives* 9, No.1 (March 1990): 5–38.

Black, Ian, and Benny Morris. *Israel's Secret Wars: A History of Israel's Intelligence Services.* New York: Grove Weidenfeld, 1991.

Blechman, Barry M. "The Impact of Israel's Reprisals on Behavior of the Bordering Arab Nations Directed at Israel," *Journal of Conflict Resolution* 16, No. 2 (June 1972): 155–181.

Blechman, Barry M., and Douglas M. Hart. "The Political Utility of Nuclear Weapons: The 1973 Middle East Crisis," *International Security* 7 (Summer 1982): 132–156.

Boker, Bob. "Jordan and Israel: The Problems of Bringing Peace to Fruition," *Pacific Research* 8, No. 1 (February 1995): 9–11.

Bookmiller, Robert J. "Likud's Jordan Policy," *Middle East Policy* 5, No. 3 (1997): 90–103.

Bookmiller, Robert J. "Approaching the Rubicon: Jordan and the Peace Process," *SAIS Review* 14, No. 2 (Summer-Fall 1994): 109–123.

Bowie, Robert R. *Suez 1956: International Crises and the Role of Law.* New York: Oxford University Press, 1974.

Bowyer Bell, John. *The Long War: Israel and the Arabs Since 1946.* Englewood Cliffs, NJ: Prentice-Hall, 1969.

Boyer, Mark A., and Jonathan Wilkenfeld. "Third Party Intervention II: The Superpowers as Crisis Managers." Ch. 6 in Michael Brecher and Jonathan Wilkenfeld, *Crisis, Conflict and Instability.* Oxford: Pergamon, 1996.

Boyle, Francis A. "Create the State of Palestine," *Scandinavian Journal of Development Alternatives* 7, No. 2–3 (June-Sept. 1988): 25–58.

Brand, Laurie A. "Asad's Syria and the PLO: Coincidence or Conflict of Interests?" *Journal of South Asian and Middle Eastern Studies* 14, No. 2 (1990): 22–43.

Brand, Laurie A. "The Intifada and the Arab World: Old Players, New Roles," *International Journal* 45, No. 3 (Summer 1990): 501–527.

Brawer, Moshe. "The Boundaries of Peace," *Israel Affairs* 1, No. 1 (Autumn 1994): 41–63.

Brecher, Michael. "International Studies in the Twentieth Century and Beyond: Flawed Dichotomies, Synthesis, Cumulation," *International Studies Quarterly* 43, No. 2 (June 1999): 213–264.

Brecher, Michael. "International Crises: Reflections on the Future," *Security Studies* 3, No. 4 (1994): 650–677.

Brecher, Michael. *Crises in World Politics. Theory and Reality.* Oxford: Pergamon, 1993.

Brecher, Michael. "International Crises and Protracted Conflicts," *International Interactions* 11, No. 3 (1984): 237–297.

Brecher, Michael. *Decisions in Israel's Foreign Policy.* London: Oxford University Press, 1974.

Brecher, Michael. "Israel and the Rogers Peace Initiatives: Decisions and Consequences," *Orbis* 18, No. 2 (Summer 1974): 402–426.

Brecher, Michael. *The Foreign Policy System of Israel.* London: Oxford University Press, 1972.

Brecher, Michael, and Hemda Ben-Yehuda. "System and Crisis in International Politics," *Review of International Studies* 11, No. 1 (1985): 17–36.

Brecher, Michael, with Benjamin Geist. *Decisions in Crisis: Israel 1967 and 1973.* Berkeley: University of California Press, 1980.

Brecher, Michael, and Patrick James. "Crisis Management in the Arab-Israeli Conflict." In *Conflict Management in the Middle East,* ed. Gabriel Ben-Dor and David B. Dewitt. Lexington, MA: Lexington Books, 1987.

Brecher, Michael, and Patrick James. *Crisis and Change in World Politics.* Boulder: Westview Press, 1986.

Brecher, Michael, Blema Steinberg, and Janice Stein Gross. "A Framework for Research on Foreign Policy Behavior," *Journal of Conflict Resolution* 13, No. 1 (1969): 75–101.

Brecher, Michael, and Jonathan Wilkenfeld. *A Study of Crisis.* Ann Arbor: University of Michigan Press, 1997.

Brecher, Michael, and Jonathan Wilkenfeld. *International Crisis Behavior Project,*

1918–1988. ICPSR 9286, Inter-University Consortium for Political and Social Research, Ann Arbor, MI, 1992.

Brecher, Michael, and Jonathan Wilkenfeld. *Crisis, Conflict and Instability.* Oxford: Pergamon, 1989.

Brecher, Michael, and Jonathan Wilkenfeld. "International Crisis Behavior Datasets." *DDIR* (Data Development for International Research) 4, No.1 (1989): 1–12.

Brecher, Michael, and Jonathan Wilkenfeld. *Crises in the Twentieth Century: Vol. 1. Handbook of International Crises.* Oxford: Pergamon, 1988.

Bremer, Stuart A. "Advancing the Scientific Study of War," *International Interaction* 19, Nos. 1–2 (1993): 1–26.

Bromberger, Merry and Serge. *Secrets of Suez.* London: Pan Books, 1957.

Brown, Leon Carl. *International Politics and the Middle East: Old Rules, Dangerous Game.* London: I.B. Tauris, 1984.

Browne, Harry. *Suez and Sinai.* London: Longman, 1971.

Brynen, Rex. *Sanctuary and Survival: The PLO in Lebanon.* Boulder: Westview, 1976.

Brzezinski, Zbigniew. *Power and Principle: Memoirs of the National Security Adviser 1977–1981.* New York: Farrar, Straus, Giroux, 1983.

B'tselem. Jerusalem: The Israeli Information Center for Human Rights and www.b`tselem.org.il.

Bueno de Mesquita, Bruce. "Multilateral Negotiations: A Spatial Analysis of the Arab-Israeli Dispute," *International Organizations* 44, No. 3 (Summer 1990): 317–340.

Bueno de Mesquita, Bruce. "Theories of International Conflict: An Analysis and an Appraisal." In *Handbook of Political Conflict: Theory and Research,* ed. Ted Robert Gurr. New York: The Free Press, 1980.

Bull, General Odd. *War and Peace in the Middle East.* London: Leo Cooper, 1976.

Bulliet, Richard W. "The Future of the Islamic Movement," *Foreign Affairs* 72, No. 5 (Nov.-Dec. 1993): 38–44.

Bullock, Alan L. G. *Ernest Bevin: Foreign Secretary, 1945–1951.* London: Heinemann, 1983.

Burdett, Winston. *Encounter with the Middle East: An Intimate Report of What Lies Behind the Arab-Israeli Conflict.* London: Andre Deutsch, 1970.

Butterfield, Herbert. *History and Human Relations.* London: Collins, 1950.

Butterworth, Charles E., and Ira William Zartman. (eds.) *Political Islam.* Newbury Park, CA: Sage, 1992.

Butterworth, Robert Lyle, with Margaret E. Scranton. *Managing Interstate Conflict, 1945–74: Data with Synopses.* Pittsburgh: University of Pittsburgh, 1976.

Caplan, Neil. *Futile Diplomacy,* Vols. 1–2. London: Frank Cass, 1983 and 1986.

Capitanchik, David B., and Wyllie James. *The Middle East: Conflict and Stability.* Oxford: Blackwell, 1989.

Carlton, David. *Britain and the Suez Crisis.* Oxford: Blackwell, 1989.

Carment, David. "The International Dimensions of Ethnic Conflict: Concepts, Indicators, and Theory," *Journal of Peace Research* 30, No. 2 (1993): 137–150.

Carment, David, and Patrick James. "The United Nations at 50: Managing Ethnic Crises—Past and Present," *Journal of Peace Research* 35, No. 1 (1998): 61–82.

Carment, David, and Patrick James. "Ethnic Conflict at the International Level: An Appraisal of Theories and Evidence." In *Wars in the Midst of Peace*, ed. David Carment and Patrick James. Pittsburgh: University of Pittsburgh Press, 1997.

Carment, David, and Patrick James. "Internal Constraints and Interstate Ethnic Conflict: Towards a Crisis-Based Assessment of Irridentism," *Journal of Conflict Resolution* 39, No. 1 (March 1995): 82–109.

Carment, David, and Dane Rowlands. "Evaluating Third-Party Intervention in Intrastate Conflict," *Journal of Conflict Resolution* 42, No. 5 (October 1998): 572–599.

Carr, Edward. *The Twenty Years Crisis, 1919–1939*. New York: Harper, 1964.

Carter, Jimmy. "The Middle East Consultation: A Look to the Future," *Middle East Journal* 41, No. 1 (Winter 1987): 187–191.

Carter, Jimmy. *The Blood of Abraham: Insights into the Middle East*. Boston: Houghton Mifflin, 1985.

Carter, Jimmy. *Keeping Faith: Memoirs of a President*. New York: Bantam Books, 1982.

Cattan, Henry. *Palestine and International Law: The Legal Aspects of the Arab-Israeli Conflict*. 2nd Ed. London: Longman, 1976.

Cattan, Henry. *Palestine, the Arabs and Israel: The Search for Justice*. London: Longman, 1969.

Chang, Gordon H. *Friends and Enemies: The United States, China, and the Soviet Union, 1948–1972*. Stanford: Stanford University Press, 1990.

Childers, Erskine B. *The Road to Suez: A Study of Western-Arab Relations*. London: Macgibbon and Kee, 1962.

Chomsky, Noam. "The United States and the Middle East," *Journal of Palestine Studies* 16, No. 3 (Spring 1987): 25–42.

Chomsky, Noam. *Peace in the Middle East? Reflections on Justice and Nationhood*. London: Fontana/Collins, 1975.

Christensen, Thomas J., and Jack Snyder. "Progressive Research on Degenerate Alliances," *American Political Science Review* 91, No. 4 (1997): 919–922.

Christison, Kathleen. "Bound by a Frame of Reference, Part 2: U.S. Policy and the Palestinians, 1948–88," *Journal of Palestine Studies* 27, No. 3 (Spring 1988): 20–34.

Churchill, Randolph S., and Winston S. Churchill. *The Six Day War*. London: Heinemann, 1967.

Clarke, Duncan L. "U.S. Security Assistance to Egypt and Israel: Politically Untouchable?" *Middle East Journal* 51, No. 2 (Spring 1997): 200–214.

Claude, Inis L. Jr. *Power and International Relations*. New York: Random House, 1962.

Clausewitz, Karl. *On War*. Trans. and ed. Michael Howard and Peter Paret. Princeton: Princeton University Press, 1976. (First published in German, 1832).

Cobban, Helena. *The Superpowers and the Syrian-Israeli Conflict*. New York: Praeger, 1991.

Cobban, Helena. *The Making of Modern Lebanon*. Boulder: Westview, 1985.

Cobban, Helena. *The Palestinian Liberation Organization, People, Power and Politics*. Cambridge: Cambridge University Press, 1984.

Cohen, Avner. *Israel and the Bomb*. New York: Columbia University Press, 1998.

Cohen, Avner. "Cairo, Dimona, and the June 1967 War," *Middle East Journal* 50, No. 2 (Spring 1996): 190–210.

Cohen, Avner. "The Nuclear Issue in the Middle East in a New World Order." In *Middle*

Eastern Security. ed. Efraim Inbar and Shmuel Sandler. London: Frank Cass, 1995.

Cohen, Avner, and Marvin Miller. "How to Think About—and Implement—Nuclear Arms Control in the Middle East," *Washington Quarterly* 16, No. 2 (Spring 1993): 101–113.

Cohen, Michael. *Palestine and the Great Powers, 1945–48.* Princeton: Princeton University Press, 1982.

Cohen, Michael. *Palestine: Retreat from the Mandate, the Making of British Policy, 1936–45.* London: Paul Elek, 1978.

Cohen, Raymond. "Culture Gets in the Way (of Syria and Israel)," *Middle East Quarterly* 1, No. 3 (September 1994): 45–53.

Cohen, Raymond. *Culture and Conflict in Egyptian-Israeli Relations: A Dialogue of the Deaf.* Bloomington: Indiana University Press, 1990.

Cohen, Raymond. "Threat Assessment in Military Intelligence: The Case of Israel and Syria, 1985–86," *Intelligence and National Security* 4 (October 1989): 735–786.

Cohen, Raymond. *Vision and Conflict in the Holy Land.* New York: St. Martin's, 1985.

Comay, Michael. *U.N. Peacekeeping in the Israel-Arab Conflict, 1948–1975: An Israel Critique.* Jerusalem Papers on Peace Problems No. 17–18. Jerusalem: Leonard Davis Institute for International Relations, Hebrew University of Jerusalem, 1976.

Confino, Michael, and Shimon Shamir. *The USSR and the Middle East.* Jerusalem: Israel University Press, 1973.

Connor, Walker. "Nation Building or Nation Destroying?" *World Politics* 24, No.3 (April 1972): 319–355.

Cooley, John K. *Green March, Black September: The Story of the Palestinian Arabs.* London: Frank Cass, 1973.

Cordesman, Anthony H. *After the Storm: The Changing Military Balance in the Middle East.* Boulder: Westview, 1988.

Cordesman, Anthony H. "The Middle East and the Cost of the Politics of Force," *Middle East Journal* 40, No. 1 (Winter 1986): 5–15.

Crankshaw, Edward. *Khrushchev: A Biography.* London: Collins, 1966.

Crawford, Beverly. "The New Security Dilemma under International Economic Interdependence," *Millenium* 23 (1994): 25–55.

Cremeans, Charles D. *The Arabs and the World: Nasser's Arab Nationalist Policy.* New York: Praeger, 1963.

Curtis, Gerald L. "The United Nations Observation Group in Lebanon," *International Organization* 18 (Autumn 1964): 738–765.

Curtis, Michael, Joseph Nyer, Chaim Waxman, Allen Pollack. (eds.) *The Palestinians: People, History, Politics.* New Brunswick, New Jersey: Transaction Books, 1975.

Dadwal, Shebonti Ray. "Syria Continues to Hold the Key to Peace in West Asia," *Strategic Analysis* 18, No. 1 (1995): 127–140.

Dajani, Burhan. "The September 1993 Israeli-PLO Documents: A Textual Analysis," *Journal of Palestine Studies* 23, No. 3 (Spring 1994): 5–23.

Dan, Uri. *Operation Uganda.* Jerusalem: Keter, 1976.

Dann, Uriel. *Iraq under Qassem, a Political History 1958–1963.* New York: Praeger, 1969.

David, Peter. "Israel and the Palestinians; the Price of Immobility," *The World Today* 44

(November 1988): 184–186.

David, Steven R. "Explaining Third World Alignment," *World Politics* 43, No. 2 (Jan. 1991): 233–257.

David, Steven R. "The Continuing Importance of American Interests in the Middle East after the Cold War," *Israel Affairs* 2, Nos. 3–4 (Spring-Summer 1996): 94–106.

Davis, L., E. Roseman, and J. Z. Rubin. (eds.) *Myths and Facts 1989: A Concise Record of the Arab-Israeli Conflict.* Washington, DC: Near East Report, 1988.

Davis, David R., and Will H. Moore. "Ethnicity Matters: Transnational Ethnic Alliances and Foreign Policy Behavior," *International Studies Quarterly* 41, No. 1 (1997): 171–184.

Dawisha, Adeed I. *Syria and the Lebanese Crisis.* London: Macmillan, 1980.

Dawisha, Karen. "The USSR in the Middle East: Superpower in Eclipse," *Foreign Affairs* 6, No. 2 (Winter 1982–1983): 438–451.

Dawisha, Karen. "Soviet Decision-Making in the Middle East: The 1973 October War and the 1980 Gulf War," *International Affairs* 57, No. 1 (Winter 1980–81): 43–59.

Dayan, Moshe. *Breakthrough: A Personal Account of the Egypt-Israel Peace Negotiations.* New York: Knopf, 1981.

Dayan, Moshe. *Story of My Life.* New York: Morrow, 1976.

Dayan, Moshe. *Diary of the Sinai Campaign.* New York: Harper and Row, 1966.

Deeb, Marius. *The Lebanese Civil War.* New York: Praeger, 1980.

Deitchman, Seymour J. *Limited War and American Defense Policy.* Washington, DC: Institute of Defense Analysis, 1964.

De La Gorce, Paul Marie. "Europe and the Arab-Israel Conflict: a Survey," *Journal of Palestine Studies* 26, No. 3 (Spring 1997): 5–16.

Delvoie, Louis. "Canada and Egypt: From Antagonism to Partnership," *International Journal* 52, No.4 (1997):657–676.

Deutsch, Karl. *Politics and Government,* 2nd ed. Boston: Houghton Mifflin, 1974.

Deutsch, Karl, and J. David Singer. "Multipolar Power Systems and International Stability." *World Politics* 16, No.3 (1964): 390–406.

Deutsch, Karl, et al. *Political Community in the North Atlantic Area.* Princeton: Princeton University Press, 1957.

Diab, M. Zhair. "Syrian Security Requirements in a Peace Settlement with Israel," *Israel Affairs* 1, No. 4 (Summer 1996): 71–88.

Diab, M. Zhair. "Have Syria and Israel Opted for Peace?" *Middle East Policy* 3 (1994): 77–90.

Dion, Douglas. "Competition and Ethnic Conflict: Artifactual?" *Journal of Conflict Resolution*, 41, No. 5 (Oct. 1997): 638–648.

Dishon, Daniel. (ed.) *Middle East Record* 3. Shiloah Center for Middle Eastern and African Studies, Tel-Aviv University: Israel Universities Press, 1971.

Dolatyar, Mostafa. "Water Diplomacy in the Middle East," *Iranian Journal of International Affairs* 7, No. 3 (1995): 599–615.

Donovan, Robert J. *Conflict and Crisis: The Presidency of Harry S. Truman, 1945–1948.* New York: Norton, 1977.

Donovan, Robert J. *Tumultuous Years: The Presidency of Harry S. Truman 1949–1953.* New

York: Norton, 1977.

Dothan, Shmuel. *Partition of Eretz-Israel in the Mandatory Period, the Jewish Controversy.* Jerusalem:Yad Yitzhak Ben-Zvi, 1979.

Dowty, Alan. *Middle East Crisis: U.S. Decision-Making in 1958, 1970, and 1973.* Berkeley: University of California Press, 1984.

Dowty, Alan. "The U.S. and the Syria–Jordan Confrontation, 1970," in "Studies in Crisis Behavior," *The Jerusalem Journal of International Relations* (Special Issue) 3, Nos. 2–3 (1978): 172–196.

Draper, Theodore. *Israel and World Politics: Roots of the Third Arab-Israeli War.* New York: Viking Press, 1968.

Drezon-Tepler, Marcia. "Contested Waters and the Prospects for Arab-Israeli Peace," *Middle Eastern Studies* 30, No. 2 (April 1994): 281–303.

Druks, Herbert. *From Truman Through Johnson: A Documentary History.* New York: Robert Speller, 1971.

Drysdale, Alaisdair, and Raymond A. Hinnebusch. *Syria and the Middle East Peace Process.* New York: Council on Foreign Relations Press, 1991.

Duff, Reginald Eustance Bluett. *100 Years of the Suez Canal.* Brighton: Clifton, 1969.

Duncan, Andrew. "Land for Peace: Israel's Choice," *Israel Affairs* 2, No. 1 (Autumn 1995): 59–72.

Dupuy, Trevor. *Elusive Victory: The Arab-Israeli Wars 1947–1974.* New York: Harper and Row, 1978.

Dupuy, Trevor, and Paul Martell. *Flawed Victory: The Arab-Israeli Conflict and the 1982 War in Lebanon.* Fairfax, VA: Hero Books, 1986.

East, Maurice A. "Size and Foreign Policy Behavior: A Test of Two Models," *World Politics* 25 (July 1973): 556–576.

East, Maurice A., and Charles F. Hermann. "Do Nation-Types Account for Foreign Policy Behavior." In *Comparing Foreign Policies: Theories, Findings, and Methods,* ed. James N. Rosenau. New York: John Wiley, 1974.

Eban, Abba. *Personal Witness: Israel Through My Eyes.* New York: G.P. Putnam's Sons, 1992.

Eban, Abba. "Camp David: The Unfinished Business," *Foreign Affairs* 57, No. 2 (Winter 1978–1979): 343–354.

Eban, Abba. *An Autobiography.* Tel-Aviv: Steimatzky, 1977.

Eban, Abba. *My Country: The Story of Modern Israel.* London: Weidenfeld and Nicolson, 1972.

Ebert, Barbara Gregory. "The Gulf War and Its Aftermath: An Assessment of Evolving Arab Responses," *Middle East Policy* 1, No. 4 (1992): 77–95.

Eckstein, Harry. "Theoretical Approaches to Explaining Collective Political Violence." In *Handbook of Political Conflict: Theories and Research,* ed. Ted Robert Gurr. New York: The Free Press, 1980.

Eden, Anthony Earl of Avon. *The Suez Crisis of 1956.* Boston: Beacon Press, 1968.

Eilts, Herman. *A Conversation with Ambassador Herman Eilts: The Dilemma in the Persian Gulf.* Washington, DC: American Enterprise Institute for Public Policy Research, 1980.

Eisenberg, Laura Zittrain. "Israel's South Lebanon Imbroglio," *Middle East Quarterly* 4,

No. 2 (June 1997): 60–69.

Eisenberg, Laura Zittrain. *My Enemy's Enemy*. Detroit: Wayne State University Press, 1994.

Eisenberg, Laura Zittrain. "Passive Belligerency: Israel and the 1991 Gulf War," *Journal of Strategic Studies* 15, No. 3 (September 1992): 304–329.

Eisenberg, Laura Zittrain, and Neil Caplan. *Negotiating Arab-Israeli Peace*. Bloomington: Indiana University Press, 1998.

Eisendorf, Richard. "The Middle East: The Peace and Security Building Process," *SIPRI Yearbook* 1994: 97–124.

Eisenhower, Dwight D. *The White House Years Vol. 2: Waging Peace, 1956–1961*. Garden City: Doubleday, 1965.

Eisenhower, Dwight D. *The White House Years Vol. 1: Mandate for Change 1953–1956*. Garden City: Doubleday, 1963.

Elazar, Daniel J. (ed.) *Constitutional Design and Power Sharing in the Postmodern Epoch*. Lanham, MD: University Press of America, 1991.

Elazar, Daniel J. (ed.) *Governing Peoples and Territories*. Philadelphia: ISHI, 1982.

Elazar, Daniel J. (ed.) *Federalism and Political Integration*. Lanham, MD: University Press of America, 1979.

Elazar, Daniel J. *The Camp David Framework for Peace: A Shift Toward Shared Rule*. Washington, DC: American Enterprise Institute for Public Policy Research, 1979.

Elazar, Daniel J., and Shmuel Sandler. "The 1992 Knesset Elections Revisited: Implications for the Future," *Israel Affairs* 1, No. 2 (Winter 1994): 209–226.

Elazar, Daniel J., and Shmuel Sandler. *Who is the Boss in Israel? Israel at the Polls, 1988–1989*. Detroit: Wayne State University Press, 1992.

Elazar, Daniel J., and Shmuel Sandler. "Governing under Peres and Shamir." In *Israel's Odd Couple, The 1984 Knesset Election and the National Unity Government*, ed. Daniel J. Elazar and Shmuel Sandler. Detroit: Wayne State University Press, 1990.

Elias, Robert, and Jennifer Turpin. *Rethinking Peace*. Boulder: Lynne Rienner, 1994.

Ellis, Marc H. "The Future of Israel/Palestine: Embracing the Broken Middle," *Journal of Palestine Studies* 26, No. 3 (Spring 1997): 56–66.

Elman, Colin, and Miriam Fendius Elman. "Lakatos and Neorealism: A Reply to Vasquez," *American Political Science Review* 91, No. 4 (1997): 923–926.

Elmusa, Sharif S. "The Jordan-Israel Water Agreement: A Model or an Exception?" *Journal of Palestine Studies* 24, No. 3 (Spring 1995): 63–73.

Enterline, Andrew J. "Regime Changes, Neighborhoods, and Interstate Conflict, 1816–1992," *Journal of Conflict Resolution* 42, No. 6 (December 1998): 804–829.

Epstein, Leon D. *British Politics in the Suez Crisis*. London: Pall Mall, 1964.

Esman, Milton J. *Ethnic Politics*. New York: Cornell University Press, 1994.

Esposito, John L. *The Islamic Threat: Myth or Reality*. New York: Oxford University Press, 1992.

Evans, Rowland, and Robert Novak. *Nixon in the White House: The Frustration of Power*. New York: Random House, 1971.

Evans, Rowland, and Robert Novak. *Lyndon B. Johnson: The Exercise of Power*. London: Allen and Unwin, 1967.

Evron, Yair. "Confidence and Security-Building Measures in the Arab-Israeli Context." In *Middle East Security*, ed. Efraim Inbar and Shmuel Sandler. London: Frank Cass, 1995.

Evron, Yair. *Conflict and Security Building Measures in the Arab-Israeli Context*. Tel-Aviv: Tel-Aviv University, 1995.

Evron, Yair. *Israel's Nuclear Dilemma*. London: Routledge, 1994.

Evron, Yair. "Gulf Crisis and War: Regional Rules of the Game and Policy and Theoretical Implications," *Security Studies* 4, No. 1 (Autumn 1994): 115–154.

Evron, Yair. *War and Intervention in Lebanon: The Israeli-Syrian Deterrence Dialogue*. Baltimore: Johns Hopkins University Press, 1987.

Fahmy, Ismail. *Negotiation for Peace in the Middle East*. London: Croom Helm, 1983.

Faksh, Mahmud A. "Assad's Westward Turn: Implications for Syria," *Middle East Policy* 2, No. 3 (1993): 49–61.

Faksh, Mahmud A. "U.S. Policy in the Middle East: Incongruity in Political Strategy and Action," *American-Arab Affairs* 23 (Winter 1987–88): 38–46.

Farnie, Douglas A. *East and West of Suez: The Suez Canal in History, 1854–1956*. Oxford: Clarendon Press, 1969.

Feith, Douglas J. "The Inner Logic of Israel's Negotiations: Withdrawal Process, not Peace Process," *Middle East Quarterly* 3, No.1 (March 1996): 12–20.

Feldman, Shai. "The Middle East Arms Control Agenda: 1994–95," *The International Spectator* 29, No. 3 (July–Sept. 1994): 67–82.

Feldman, Shai. "The Israeli Deterrence in the Test of the Gulf War." In *War in the Gulf*. Boulder: Westview, 1992.

Feldman, Shai. *Israeli Nuclear Deterrence: A Strategy for the 1990s*. New York: Columbia University Press, 1982.

Feldman, Shai, and Heda Rechnitz-Kijner. *Deception, Consensus, and War: Israel in Lebanon*. Tel-Aviv: Tel-Aviv University, Jaffee Center for Strategic Studies, Paper No. 27, 1984.

Fervann, Gunnar. "Peace in the Middle East: A Window of Opportunity?" *International Challenges* 14, No. 2 (1994): 32–40.

Finer, Herman. *Dulles Over Suez: The Theory and Practice of His Diplomacy*. Chicago: Quadrangle, 1964.

Fischer, Stanley. *Securing Peace in the Middle East*. Cambridge: MIT Press, 1994.

Fitzsimons, Matthew A. *The Suez Crisis and the Containment Policy*. Indianapolis: Bobbs-Merrill, 1957.

Flapan, Simha. *The Birth of Israel: Myths and Realities*. New York: Pantheon Books, 1987.

Ford, Gerald. *A Time to Heal*. New York: Harper and Row, 1979.

Freedman, Robert O. "Israeli-Russian Relations since the Collapse of the Soviet Union," *Middle East Journal* 49, No. 2 (1995): 233–247.

Freedman, Robert O. "Israel and the Successor States of the Soviet Union: a Preliminary Analysis," *Mediterranean Quarterly* 4, No. 2 (Spring 1993): 64–89.

Freedman, Robert O. *Soviet Policy Toward the Middle East Since 1970*. 3rd ed. New York: Praeger, 1982.

Freedman, Lawrence, and Efraim Karsh. *The Gulf Conflict, 1990–91: Diplomacy and War in the New World Order*. Princeton: Princeton University Press, 1993.

Frei, Daniel. (ed.) *Managing International Crises.* Beverly Hills: Sage, 1982.

Freiberger, Steven Z. *Dawn over Suez: The Rise of American Power in the Middle East, 1953–1957.* Chicago: I.R. Dee, 1992.

Friedlander, M.A. *Sadat and Begin:The Domestic Policies of Peacemaking.* Boulder:Westview, 1983.

Friedman,Thomas L. *From Beirut to Jerusalem.* NewYork: Farrar, Strauss, Giroux, 1989.

Frisch, Hillel. "Ethnicity,Territorial Integrity, and Regional Order: Palestinian Identity in Jordan and Israel," *Journal of Peace Research* 34, No. 3 (August 1997): 257–269.

Frisch, Hillel. "From Repression to Facilitation: The Effects of Israeli Policies on Palestinian Mobilization in the West Bank, 1967–87," *Terrorism and Political Violence* 8, No. 1 (Spring 1996): 1–21.

Frisch, Hillel. "The PLO and the Arabs in Israel 1967–93: Politicization or Radicalization?" *Nationalism and Ethnic Politics* 2, No. 3 (Autumn 1996): 446–464.

Frisch, Hillel. "IfThings Are So Much Better, How Come They Are Worse:The Political Fragmentation of the Arab Community and the Marginalization of Arab National Politics." In *Who is the Boss in Israel? Israel at the Polls 1988–1989,* ed. Daniel J. Elazar and Shmuel Sandler. Detroit:Wayne State University Press (1992): 130–150.

Fullick, Roy, and G. Powell. *Suez:The Double War.* London: Hamish Hamilton, 1979.

Gabriel, Richard A. *Operation Peace for Galilee:The Israeli-PLO War in Lebanon.* NewYork: Hill and Wang, 1984.

Gainsborough,J. Russell. *The Arab-Israeli Conflict:A Politico-Legal Analysis.* Aldershot, UK: Gower, 1986.

Galnoor, Yitzhak. "The Territorial Partition of Palestine: The Decision of 1937." In *Studies in Israel's Independence.* Sde Boker: Ben-Gurion University, 1991.

El-Gamasy, Mohamed Abdel Ghani. *The October War.* Cairo: American University of Cairo Press, 1993.

Garnham, David. "The Causes of War: Systemic Findings." In *Polarity and War,* ed. Alan Ned Sabrosky. Boulder:Westview, 1985.

Garfinkle, Adam M. "Israel's Abiding Troubles in Lebanon," *Orbis* 41, No. 4 (Fall 1997): 603–612.

Garfinkle,Adam M. "Israel and Palestine: a Precarious Partnership," *Washington Quarterly* 20, No. 3 (Summer 1997): 3–22.

Garfinkle, Adam M. "U.S. Decision-Making in the Jordan Crisis: Correcting the Record," *Political Science Quarterly* 100, No. 1 (1985): 117–138.

Gazit, Shlomo. "Israel and the Palestinians: FiftyYears ofWars andTurning Points," *Annals of the American Academy of Political and Social Science* 555 (1998): 82–96.

Gazit, Shlomo. "The Gulf War, The Political and Military Process." In *War in the Gulf; Report of a JCSS Study Group.* Tel-Aviv: Papyrus, 1991.

Gazit, Shlomo. (Heb.) *The Stick and the Carrot.* Tel-Aviv: Zmora Bitan, 1985.

George, Alexander L. *Bridging the Gap:Theory and Practice in Foreign Policy.* Washington, DC: U.S. Institute for Peace Press, 1993.

George, Alexander L. (ed.) *Avoiding War: Problems of Crisis Management.* Boulder: Westview, 1991.

George,Alexander L. *Managing U.S.-Soviet Rivalry.* Boulder:Westview, 1983.

George, Alexander L. *Presidential Decisionmaking in Foreign Policy: The Effective Use of Information and Advice.* Boulder: Westview, 1980.

George, Alexander L., and Richard Smoke. *Deterrence in American Foreign Policy: Theory and Practice.* New York: Columbia University Press, 1974.

Gerner, Deborah J. *One Land, Two Peoples: The Conflict over Palestine.* Boulder: Westview, 1991.

Gerson, Joseph. "Legacies of the Storm: Desert Shield, Desert Storm, and the Diplomacy of the Israeli-Palestinian-Arab Conflict," *Scandinavian Journal of Development Alternatives* 12, No. 2–3 (June-Sept. 1993): 63–77.

Ghadban, Najib. "Arms Control in the Middle East: a Synthesis of Major Issues," *Middle East Affairs Journal* 2, No. 1 (1994): 49–62.

Gharaibeh, Mazen. "Sadat's Decision to Visit Jerusalem: A Decision-Making Approach," *Administrative Change* 19, No.1–2 (July 1991–June 1992): 38–58.

Gilbar, Gad, and Asher Susser. (eds.) (Heb.) *In the Eye of the Conflict: The Intifada.* Tel-Aviv: Kibbutz Hameuchad, 1992.

Gilboa, Eitan. "The Palestinian Uprising: Has It Turned American Public Opinion?" *Orbis* 33, No. 1 (Winter 1989): 21–37.

Gilboa, Eitan, and Mordechai Naor. (Heb.) *The Arab-Israeli Conflict.* Tel-Aviv: Ma'archot/Ministry of Defense, 1981.

Gilbert, Martin. *Atlas of the Arab-Israeli Conflict.* New York: Macmillan, 1974.

Gilmour, David Robert. *Lebanon: The Fractured Country.* New York: St. Martin's, 1984.

Gilmour, David Robert. *Dispossessed: The Ordeal of the Palestinians.* London: Shere, 1980.

Glassman, Jon D. *Arms for the Arabs: The Soviet Union and War in the Middle East.* Baltimore: Johns Hopkins University Press, 1975.

Gochman, Charles S., and Zeev Maoz. "Militarized Interstate Disputes, 1816–1976: Procedures, Patterns, and Insights," *Journal of Conflict Resolution* 28, No. 4 (1984): 585–616.

Golan, Aviezer. *Sinai Campaign 29/10/56–5/11/56.* Tel-Aviv: Ma'archot/Ministry of Defense, Israel Defense Forces, Department of Instruction and Information, 1958.

Golan, Galia. "A Palestinian State from an Israeli Point of View," *Middle East Policy* 3, No. 1 (1994): 56–69.

Golan, Galia. *Moscow and the Middle East: New Thinking on Regional Conflict.* London: Pinter, 1992.

Golan, Galia. "The Soviet Union and the War in Lebanon," *The Middle East Journal* 40, No. 2 (Spring 1986): 285–305.

Golan, Galia. "Soviet Decision-making in the Yom Kippur War." In *Soviet Decision-making for National Security,* ed. Jiri Valenta and William Potter. London: George Allen and Unwin, 1984.

Golan, Galia. *Yom Kippur and After: The Soviet Union and the Middle East Crisis.* Cambridge: Cambridge University Press, 1977.

Golan, Matti. *The Secret Conversations of Henry Kissinger: Step-by-Step Diplomacy in the Middle East.* New York: Bantam Books, 1976.

Golani, Motti. (Heb.) *There Will Be War Next Summer... The Road to the Sinai War, 1955–56.* Tel-Aviv: Ma'arachot/Ministry of Defense, 1997.

Golani, Motti. (ed.) (Heb.) *Black Arrow: Gaza Raid and the Israeli Policy of Retaliation during the Fifties.* Tel-Aviv: Ma'arachot/Israel Defense Ministry, 1994.

Gold, Dore. "Where is the Peace Process Going," *Commentary* 100, No. 2 (Aug. 1995): 38–42.

Gold, Dore. *America, the Gulf and Israel: Centcom and Emerging U.S. Regional Security Policies in the Middle East.* Boulder: Westview, 1989.

Goldberg, Giora. "Ben-Gurion and Jewish Foreign Policy," *Jewish Political Studies Review* 3, No. 1–2 (Spring 1991): 91–102.

Goldmann, Kjell. "Detente and Crisis," *Cooperation and Conflict* 18 (1983): 215–232.

Goldstone, Jack. (ed.) *Revolutions. Theoretical, Comparative, and Historical Studies.* San Diego: Harcourt Brace Jovanovich, 1986.

Goodman, Melvin A., and Carolyn McGiffert Ekedahl. "Trends in Soviet Policy in the Middle East and the Gulf," *International Journal* 45, No. 3 (1990): 603–630.

Goodman, Melvin A., and Carolyn McGiffert Ekedahl. "Gorbachev's 'New Directions' in the Middle East," *Middle East Journal* 41, No. 1 (Winter 1987): 571–586.

Gorny, Yosef. (Heb.) *The Arab Question and the Jewish Problem.* Tel-Aviv: Am Oved, 1985.

Gorny, Yosef. (Heb.) *Zionism and the Arabs, 1881–1948: A Study of Ideology.* Tel-Aviv: Am Oved, 1985.

Gorst, Anthony, and W. Scott-Lucas. "Suez 1956: Strategy and the Diplomatic Process," *Journal of Strategic Studies* 11, No. 4 (1988): 391–436.

Graubard, Stephen Richards. *Kissinger, Portrait of a Mind.* New York: Norton, 1974.

Green, Leslie C. "Rescue at Entebbe—Legal Aspects," *Israel Yearbook on Human Rights* 6 (1976): 312–329.

Greaves, Col. Fielding V. "Peace in Our Time—Fact or Fable?" *Military Review* (Dec. 1962): 55–58.

Grieco, Joseph. *Cooperation among Nations: Europe, America, and the Non-tariff Barriers to Trade.* Ithaca: Cornell University Press, 1990.

Grieco, Joseph. "Realist Theory and the Problem of Cooperation," *Journal of Politics* 50, No. 3 (1988): 600–624.

Grossier, Philip. L. *The United States and the Middle East: New Thinking on Regional Conflict.* London: Pinter, 1992.

Gurr, Ted Robert. "Peoples Against States: Ethnopolitical Conflict and the Changing World System," *International Studies Quarterly* 38, No. 3 (1994): 347–377.

Gurr, Ted Robert. "Why Minorities Rebel: A Global Analysis of Communal Mobilization and Conflict Since 1945," *International Political Science Review* 14, No. 2 (1993): 161–201.

Gurr, Ted Robert. *Minorities At Risk: A Global View of Ethnopolitical Conflicts.* Washington, DC: Institution of Peace Press, 1993.

Gurr, Ted Robert. *Handbook of Political Conflict.* New York: Free Press, 1980.

Gurr, Ted Robert. *Why Men Rebel.* Princeton: Princeton University Press, 1970.

Gurr, Ted Robert, and Barbara Harff. *Ethnic Conflict in World Politics.* Boulder: Westview, 1994.

Guttman, Joel M. "The Explanatory Power of Game Theory in International Politics:

Syrian-Israeli Crisis Interactions, 1951–87," *Economics and Politics* 9, No. 1 (March 1997): 71–85.

Haas, Ernst B. *Nationalism, Liberalism and Progress.* New York: Cornell University Press, 1997.

Haas, Ernst B. "Regime Decay: Conflict Management and International Organizations, 1945–1981," *International Organization* 37, No. 2 (1983): 189–256.

Haas, Ernst B., Joseph S. Nye, and Robert L. Butterworth. *Conflict Management by International Organizations.* Morristown, NJ: General Learning Press, 1972.

Haas, Michael. "Research on International Crisis: Obsolescence of an Approach?" *International Interactions* 13, No.1 (1986): 23–58.

Haas, Michael. "International Subsystems: Stability and Polarity," *American Political Science Review* 64, No. 2 (1970): 98–123.

Haass, Richard N. "The Middle East: No More Treaties," *Foreign Affairs* 75, No. 5 (Sept.-Oct. 1996): 53–63.

Haber, Eitan, Ehud Ya'ari, and Ze'ev Schiff. (Heb.) *The Year of the Dove.* Tel-Aviv: Zmora, Bitan, Modan, 1980.

Habib, Philip. *Diplomacy and the Search for Peace in the Middle East.* Georgetown: Institute for the Study of Diplomacy, 1985.

Hadar, Leon T. "The 1992 Electoral Earthquake and the Fall of the Second Israeli Republic," *Middle East Journal* 46, No. 4 (Autumn 1992): 594–616.

Hagopian, Elaine G. "Is the Peace Process a Process for Peace? A Retrospective Analysis of Oslo," *Arab Studies Quarterly* 19, No. 3 (Summer 1997): 1–27.

Hagopian, Elaine G. "Maronite Hegemony to Maronite Militancy: The Creation and Disintegration of Lebanon," *Third World Quarterly* 11, No. 4 (1989): 101–117.

Haig, Alexander M. Jr. *Caveat: Realism, Reagan, and Foreign Policy.* New York: Macmillan, 1984.

Hajjar, Sami G. "The Israel-Syria Track," *Middle East Policy* 6, No. 3 (Feb. 1999): 112–130.

Halliday, Fred. "The Great Powers and the Middle East," *Middle East Report* 151 (March-April, 1988): 3–6.

Halpern, Morton H. *Contemporary Military Strategy.* Boston: Little, Brown, 1967.

Halpern, Morton H. *Limited War in the Nuclear Age.* New York: John Wiley, 1963.

Hamezeh, F. S. *U.N. Conciliation for Palestine, 1949–67.* Beirut: Institute for Palestine Studies, 1968.

Hamid, Rashid. "What Is the PLO?" *Journal of Palestine Studies* 4, No. 4 (Summer 1975): 90–109.

Hamizrachi, Beate. *The Emergence of the South Lebanon Security Belt: Major Saad Haddad and the Ties with Israel, 1975–78.* New York: Praeger, 1988.

Hammarsttrom, Mats. "Theory-Building and the Study of Crisis," *Journal of Peace Research* 32, No. 2 (1995): 233–238.

Hamzeh, Nizar A. "Lebanon's Hizbullah: From Islamic Revolution to Parliamentary Accomodation," *Third World Quarterly* 14, No. 2 (1993): 321–337.

Hamzeh, Nizar A. "Clan Conflicts, Hizballah, and the Lebanese State," *Journal of Social, Political and Economic Studies* 19, No. 4 (Winter 1994): 433–446.

Hamzeh, Nizar A., and Hrair R. Dekmejian. "The Islamic Spectrum of Lebanese

Politics," *Journal of South Asian and Middle Eastern Studies* 16, No 3 (Spring 1993): 25–42.

Handel, Michael I. "Perception, Deception, and Surprise: The Case of the Yom Kippur War," *Jerusalem Papers on Peace Problems No. 19*. Jerusalem: Leonard Davis Institute for International Relations, Hebrew University of Jerusalem, 1976.

Hareven, Alouf. "Is Another Arab War Coalition Possible?" *Jerusalem Quarterly* 49 (Winter 1989): 97–120.

Harik, Judith Palmer. "Between Islam and the System, Sources and Implications of Popular Support for Lebanon's Hizbullah," *Journal of Conflict Resolution* 40, No.1 (March 1996): 41–67.

Harkabi, Yehoshafat. *The Palestinian Covenant and its Meaning*. London: Vallentine, Mitchell, 1979.

Harkabi, Yehoshafat. *On the Guerrilla*. Tel-Aviv: Ma'archot/Israeli Defense Ministry, 1971.

Harkavy, Robert E. "Triangular or Indirect Deterrence/Compellence: Something New in Deterrence Theory?" *Comparative Strategy* 17, No. 1 (1998): 63–81.

Harris, William W. *Taking Root: Israeli Settlement in the West Bank, the Golan, and Gaza-Sinai, 1967–80*. New York: John Wiley and Sons, 1980.

Hart, Alan. *Arafat: A Political Biography*. Bloomington: Indiana University Press, 1989.

Hart, Jeffrey A. "Power and Polarity in the International System." In *Polarity and War*, ed. Alan Ned Sabrosky. Boulder: Westview, 1984.

Haselkorn, Avigdor. "Arab-Israeli Conflict: Implications of Mass Destruction Weapons," *Global Affairs* 3, No.1 (Winter 1988): 120–137.

Hassouna, Hussein A. *The League of Arab States and Regional Disputes*. Dobbs Ferry, NY: Oceana Publications, 1975.

Hatina, Meir. "Iran and the Palestinian Islamic Movement," *Orient* 38, No. 1 (1997): 107–120.

Hazan, Baruch A. *Soviet Propaganda: A Case Study of the Middle East Conflict*. New York: Wiley, 1976.

Heikal, Mohamed. *Secret Channels: The Inside Story of Arab-Israeli Negotiations*. London: Harper Collins, 1996.

Heikal, Mohamed. *Cutting the Lion's Tail: Suez through Egyptian Eyes*. London: Deutsch, 1986.

Heikal, Mohamed. *Autumn of Fury: The Assassination of Sadat*. New York: Random House, 1983.

Heikal, Mohamed. *The Sphinx and the Commissar: The Rise and Fall of Soviet Influence in the Middle East*. New York: Harper and Row, 1978.

Heikal, Mohamed. *The Road to Ramadan*. London: Collins, 1975.

Heikal, Mohamed. *The Cairo Documents*. New York: Doubleday, 1973.

Heller, Mark A. "Towards a Palestinian State," *Survival* 39, No. 2 (Summer 1997): 5–22.

Heller, Mark A. "The Middle East: Out of Step with History," *Foreign Affairs* 69, No. 1 (1990): 152–171.

Heller, Mark, and Sari Nusseibeh. *No Trumpets, No Drums: A Two-State Settlement of the Israeli-Palestinian Conflict*. New York: Hill and Wang, 1991.

Heller, Mark, Dov Tamari, and Zeev Eytan. *The Middle East Military Balance 1984*. Tel-

Aviv: Jaffee Center for Strategic Studies, and Boulder: Westview, 1985.

Heller, Peter B. "The Syrian Factor in the Lebanese Civil War," *Journal of South Asian and Middle Eastern Studies* 4, No. 1 (Fall 1980): 56–76.

Heraclides, Alexis. "Conflict Resolution, Ethnonationalism, and the Middle East," *Journal of Peace Research* 26, No. 2 (May 1989): 197–212.

Hermann, Charles F. (ed.) *International Crises: Insights from Behavioral Research*. New York: Free Press, 1972.

Hermann, Charles F. *Crisis in Foreign Policy: A Simulation Analysis.* Indianapolis: Bobbs-Merrill, 1969.

Hermann, Charles F. "International Crisis as a Situational Variable." In *International Politics and Foreign Policy: A Reader,* ed. James N. Rosenau. New York: Free Press, rev. ed., 1969.

Hermann, Charles F. "Some Consequences of Crisis which Limit the Viability of Organizations," *Administrative Science Quarterly* 8 (June 1963): 61–82.

Hermann, Margaret G., and Charles W. Kegley. "The U.S. Use of Military Intervention to Promote Democracy: Evaluating the Record," *International Interactions* 24, No. 2 (1998): 91–114.

Hersh, Seymour M. *The Price of Power: Kissinger in the Nixon White House.* New York: Simon and Schuster, 1983.

Hertzberg, Arthur. "The End of the Dream of the Undivided Land of Israel," *Journal of Palestine Studies* 25, No. 2 (1996): 35–46.

Herz, John H. *The Nation State and the Crisis of World Politics.* New York: David McKay, 1976.

Herz, John H. "Rise and Demise of the Territorial State," *World Politics.* 9, No. 4 (1957): 473–493.

Herz, John H. "Idealist Internationalism and the Security Dilemma," *World Politics* 2, No. 2 (January 1950): 157–80.

Herzog, Chaim. *The Arab-Israeli Wars.* New York: Random House, 1982.

Herzog, Chaim. *The War of Atonement.* London: Weidenfeld and Nicolson, 1975.

Hilal, Jamil. "PLO Institutions: The Challenge Ahead," *Journal of Palestine Studies* 23, No. 1 (Autumn, 1993): 46–60.

Hiltermann, Joost. *Behind the Intifada.* Princeton: Princeton University Press, 1991.

Hinnebusch, Raymond A. "Does Syria Want Peace? Syrian Policy in the Syrian-Israeli Peace Negotiations," *Journal of Palestine Studies* 26, No. 1 (Fall 1996): 42–57.

Hinnebusch, Raymond A. "Syria: The Politics of Peace and Regime Survival," *Middle East Policy* 3, No. 4 (April 1995): 74–87.

Hinnebusch, Raymond A. "Syrian Policy in Lebanon and the Palestinians," *Arab Studies Quarterly* 8, No. 1 (1986): 1–20.

Hiro, Dilip. *Desert Shield to Desert Storm: The Second Gulf War.* New York: Routledge, 1992.

Hoffman, Stanley. "International Systems and International Law." In *The International System,* ed. Klaus Knorr and Sidney Verba. Princeton: Princeton University Press, 1961.

Hofstadter, Dan. (ed.) *Egypt and Nasser.* New York: Facts on File, 1973.

Holsti, Kalevi J. *The State, War, and the State of War.* Cambridge: Cambridge University Press, 1996.

Holsti, Kalevi J. *The Dividing Discipline.* Boston: Allen and Unwin,1985.

Holsti, Kalevi J. *International Politics,* 4th ed. Englewood Cliffs, NJ: Prentice-Hall, 1983.

Holsti, Kalevi J. "Resolving International Conflicts: A Taxonomy of Behavior and Some Figures on Procedures," *Journal of Conflict Resolution* 10, No. 3 (1966): 272–296.

Holsti, Ole R. "Theories of Crisis Decision-Making." In *Diplomacy: New Approaches in History, Theory, and Policy,* ed. Paul G. Lauren. New York: Free Press, 1979.

Holsti, Ole R. *Crisis, Escalation, War.* Montreal: McGill-Queens University Press, 1972.

Hopf, Ted. "The Promise of Constructivism in International Relations Theory," *International Security* 23, No.1 (Summer 1998): 171–200.

Hopple, Gerald W., and Paul J. Rossa. "International Crisis Analysis: Recent Developments and Future Directions." In *Cumulation in International Relations Research,* ed. P. Terrence Hopmann, Dina A. Zinnes, and J. David Singer. Denver: Monograph Series in World Affairs, Vol. 18, Book 3, 1981.

Horowitz, Dan. "The Constant and the Changing in Israeli Strategic Thinking." In *War by Choice,* ed. Joseph Alpher. Tel-Aviv, Hakibbutz Hameuchad, 1985.

Horowitz, Dan. "Israel's National Security Conception, 1948-1978." In *Diplomacy and Confrontation, Selected Issues in Israel's Foreign Relations, 1948-1978,* ed. Benyamin Neuberger. Tel-Aviv: Everyman's University, 1984.

Horowitz, Dan. "Dual Authority Polities," *Comparative Politics* 14, No. 3 (April, 1982): 329–349.

Horowitz, Dan and Moshe Lissak. *The Origins of the Israeli Polity.* Tel-Aviv: Am Oved, 1977.

Hoskins, Halford L. "The Guardianship of the Suez Canal: A View of Anglo-Egyptian Relations," *Middle East Journal* 4, No. 2 (April 1950): 143–154.

Hourani, Albert H. *A History of the Arab Peoples.* Cambridge: Belknap Press, 1991.

Hourani, Albert H. *Syria and Lebanon: A Political Essay.* London: Oxford University Press, 1946.

Howard, Michael, and Robert E. Hunter. *Israel and the Arab World: The Crisis of 1967.* Adelphi Papers No. 41. London: IISS 1967.

Hudson, Michael C. *Arab Politics: The Search for Legitimacy.* New Haven: Yale University Press, 1977.

Hurewitz, Jacob. *The Struggle for Palestine.* New York: Greenwood Press, 1968.

Huth, Paul K. "Major Power Intervention in International Crises, 1918–1988," *Journal of Conflict Resolution* 42, No. 6 (Dec. 1998): 744–770.

Inbar, Efraim. "Israeli Negotiations with Syria," *Israel Affairs* 1, No. 4 (Summer 1996): 89–100.

Inbar, Efraim. "Israel's Small War: The Military Response to the Intifada," *Armed Forces and Society.* 18, No.1 (Fall 1991): 29–51.

Inbar, Efraim. "Israel and Nuclear Weapons Since October 1973." In *Security or Armageddon, Israel's Nuclear Strategy,* ed. Louis Irene Beres. Lexington, MA: Lexington Books, 1986.

Inbar, Efraim. *Outcast Countries in the World Community.* Denver: University of Denver

Press, 1985.

Inbar, Efraim. "Israeli Strategic Thinking after 1973," *Journal of Strategic Studies* 6, No. (March 1983): 41–45.

Inbar, Efraim, and Shmuel Sandler. "The Risks of Palestinian Statehood," *Survival* 39, No.2 (Summer 1997): 23–42.

Inbar, Efraim, and Shmuel Sandler. (eds.) *Middle Eastern Security: Prospects for an Arms Control Regime.* London: Frank Cass, 1995.

Inbar, Efraim, and Shmuel Sandler. "The Changing Israeli Strategic Equation," *Review of International Studies* 21, No. 1 (1995): 41–59.

Inbar, Efraim, and Shmuel Sandler. "Israel's Deterrence Strategy Revisited," BESA *Policy Studies* No. 17, 1994.

Indyk, Martin. "Watershed in the Middle East," *Foreign Affairs* 71, No. 1 (Winter 1992): 70–93.

Indyk, Martin. "Beyond the Balance of Power: America's Choice in the Middle East," *National Interest* 26 (Winter 1991–92): 33–43.

Indyk, Martin. "Peace without the PLO," *Foreign Policy* 83 (Summer 1991): 30–38.

Insight Team of the London Sunday Times. *The Yom Kippur War.* New York: Doubleday, 1974.

Intriligator, Michael D. "Research of Conflict Theory," *Journal of Conflict Resolution* 26, No. 2 (June 1982): 307–329.

Intriligator, Michael D., and Dagobert Brito. "Richardsonian Arms Race Models." In *Handbook of War Studies,* ed. Manus Mildarsky. Boston: Unwin Hyman, 1989.

Isaacson, Walter. *Kissinger: A Biography.* New York: Simon and Schuster, 1992.

"The Israel-PLO Peace Process," *Israel Law Review* 28, Nos. 2–3 (Summer 1994): 207–434.

Israelyan, Victor. "The October War: Kissinger in Moscow," *Middle East Journal* 49, No. 2 (1995): 248–267.

James, Patrick. "Structural Realism and the Causes of War," *Mershon International Studies Review* 39, No. 2 (1995): 181–208.

James, Patrick. "The Great Powers and Crisis-Generated Instability: Some Preliminary Findings," *The Journal of International Studies* 30 (1993): 1–25.

James, Patrick. *Crisis and War.* Montreal and Kingston: McGill-Queen's University Press, 1988.

Jansen, Godfrey H. "The Problem of the Jordan Waters," *World Today* 20, No. 2 (Feb. 1964): 60–68.

Jarbawi, Ali. "The Triangle of Conflict," *Foreign Policy* 100 (Fall 1995): 92–108.

Jervis, Robert. "Security Regimes," *International Organization* 36, No. 2 (1982): 357–378.

Jervis, Robert. "Cooperation under the Security Dilemma," *World Politics* 30, No. 2 (1978): 167–214.

Joffe, E. George H. "Relations Between the Middle East and the West," *Middle East Journal* 48, No. 2 (Spring 1994): 250–267.

Johnson, Lyndon B. *The Vantage Point: Perspectives of the Presidency 1963–1969.* New York: Holt, Rinehart and Winston, 1971.

Johnson, Paul. *The Suez War.* London: Macgibbon and Kee, 1957.

Jonah, James O. C. "The Military Talks at Kilometer 101: The U.N's Effectiveness as a Third Party," *Negotiation Journal* 6, No. 1 (January 1990): 53–70.

Jones, Peter. "Arms Control in the Middle East: Some Reflections on ACRS," *Security Dialogue* 28, No. 1 (1997): 57–70.

Jones, Peter. *The Middle East Peace Process (in 1996)*. SIPRI Yearbook (1997): 83–101.

Jones, Peter. *The Middle East Peace Process*. SIPRI Yearbook (1996): 161–189.

Jukes, Geoffrey. *Hitler's Stalingrad Decisions*. Berkeley: University of California Press, 1985.

Kacowicz, Arie M. "The Process of Reaching Peaceful Territorial Change: The Arab-Israeli Conflict in Comparative Perspective," *Journal of Interdisciplinary History* 27, No. 2 (Autumn 1996): 215–245.

Kadi, Laila Salim. *The Arab-Israeli Conflict: The Peaceful Proposals, 1948–1972*. Beirut: Palestine Research Center, 1973.

Kahan Commission of Enquiry. *The Beirut Massacre: The Complete Kahan Commission Report*. Princeton: Kars-Cohl, 1983.

Kalb, Marvin and Bernard. *Kissinger*. Boston: Little, Brown, 1974.

Kamil, Muhammad Ibrahim. *The Camp David Accords: A Testimony*. Boston: Routledge and Kegan Paul, 1986.

Kaplan, Morton A. *System and Process in International Politics*. New York: John Wiley, 1957.

Kaplan, Stephen S. *Diplomacy of Power: Soviet Armed Forces as a Political Instrument*. Washington, DC: Brookings Institution, 1981.

Karam, Simon. "Lebanon, Collapse and Revival: Society and the Nation-State in the Arab World," *Middle East Policy* 2, No. 1 (1993): 15–24.

Karawan, Ibrahim A. "Sadat and the Egyptian-Israeli Peace Revisited," *International Journal of Middle East Studies* 26, No. 2 (May 1994): 249–266.

Karp, Aaron. "Ballistic Missile Proliferation," *SIPRI Yearbook* 1991: 317–343.

Karsh, Efraim. "Survival at all Costs: Saddam Hussein as Crisis Manager." In *The Gulf Crisis and the Global Aftermath,* eds. Gad Barzilai, Aharon Klieman, and Gil Shidlo. London: Routledge, 1993.

Karsh, Efraim. "Neutralization: The Key to an Arab-Israeli Peace," *Bulletin of Peace Proposals* 22, No. 1 (March 1991): 11–23.

Kass, Ilana. *Soviet Involvement in the Middle East*. Boulder: Westview, 1978.

Katz, Yossi. "The Formation of the Jewish Agency's Partition Proposal of Borders, 1937–1938," *Zion* 56, No. 4 (1992): 401–439.

Katzenstein, Peter. (ed.) *The Culture of National Security: Norms and Identity in World Politics*. New York: Columbia University Press, 1996.

Kaufmann, Chaim. "Possible and Impossible Solutions to Ethnic Civil Wars," *International Security* 20, No. 4 (1996): 136–175.

Kaufman, Stuart J. "An 'International' Theory of Inter-Ethnic War," *Review of International Studies* 22, No. 2 (1996): 149–171.

Kauppi, Mark V., and R. Craig Nation. *The Soviet Union and the Middle East in the 1980s: Opportunities, Constraints, and Dilemmas*. Lexington, MA: Lexington Books, 1983.

Kearns, Doris. *Lyndon Johnson and the American Dream*. New York: Harper and Row, 1976.

Keller, Adam. "Israel and the Palestinians," *New Politics* 2, No. 1 (Summer 1988): 41–54.

Kelman, Herbert C. "Some Determinants of the Oslo Breakthrough," *International Negotiation* 2, No. 2 (1997): 183–194.

Kelman, Herbert C. "The Palestinization of the Arab-Israeli Conflict," *Jerusalem Quarterly* 46 (Spring 1988): 3–15.

Kemp, Geoffrey, and Jeremy Pressman. "The Middle East in 1994: Continuation of the Peace Process," *SIPRI Yearbook* (1995): 171–196.

Kende, Istvan. "Wars of Ten Years (1967–1976)," *Journal of Peace Research* 15, No. 3 (1978): 227–241.

Kende, Istvan. "Twenty-five Years of Local Wars," *Journal of Peace Research* 1 (1971): 5–22.

Keohane, Robert O. "Institutional Theory and the Realist Challenge after the Cold War." In *Neorealism and Neoliberalism,* ed. David A. Baldwin. New York: Columbia University Press, 1993.

Keohane, Robert O. (ed.) *Neorealism and Its Critics.* New York: Columbia University Press, 1986.

Keohane, Robert O., and Joseph S. Nye. *Transnational Relations and World Politics.* Cambridge: Harvard University Press, 1970.

Kerr, Malcolm H. "The Lebanese Civil War." In *The International Regulation of Civil Wars,* ed. Evan Luard. London: Thames and Hudson, 1972.

Kerr, Malcolm H. "Regional Arab Politics and the Conflict with Israel." In *Political Dynamics in the Middle East,* ed. Paul Y. Hammond and S. Alexander. New York: 1972.

Kerr, Malcolm H. *The Arab Cold War.* London: Oxford University Press, 1971.

Khalaf Salah (Abu-Iyad). "Lowering the Sword," *Foreign Policy* 78 (Spring 1990): 92–112.

Khalidi, Ahmed, and Hussein Agha. "The Syrian Doctrine of Strategic Parity." In *The Middle East in Global Perspective,* ed. Judith Kipper and Harold H. Saunders. Boulder: Westview, 1991.

Khalidi, Rashid. "Policymaking within the Palestinian Polity." In *The Middle East in Global Perspective,* ed. Judith Kipper and Harold H. Saunders. Boulder: Westview, 1991.

Khalidi, Rashid. "The Uprising and the Palestinian Question," *World Policy Journal* 5, No. 3 (Summer 1988): 497–517.

Khalidi, Rashid. *Under Siege: PLO Decision-Making During the 1982 War.* New York: Columbia University Press, 1986.

Khalidi, Walid. "Selected Documents of the 1948 Palestine War," *Journal of Palestine Studies* 27, No. 3 (Spring 1998): 60–105.

Khalidi, Walid. "The Half-Empty Glass of Middle East Peace," *Journal of Palestine Studies* 19, No. 3, Issue 75 (1990): 14–38.

Khalidi, Walid. *Conflict and Violence in Lebanon.* Cambridge: Harvard University Press, 1979.

Khouri, Fred J. *The Arab-Israeli Dilemma,* 3rd ed. Syracuse: Syracuse University Press, 1985.

Khouri, Fred. "The Policy of Retaliation in Arab-Israeli Relations," *The Middle East Journal* 20, No. 4 (Autumn 1966). 435–455.

Khouri, Fred J. "The U.S., the U.N., and the Jordan River Issue," *Middle East Forum* 40, No. 4 (May 1964): 20–24.

Kimche, David. "The Arab-Israeli Peace Process," *Security Dialogue* 27, No. 2 (June 1996): 135–148.

Kimche, David, and Dan Bawly. *The Sandstorm: The Arab-Israeli War of 1967.* London: Secker and Warburg, 1968.

Kimmerling, Baruch, and Joel S. Migdal. *The Palestinians: The Making of a People.* New York: The Free Press, 1993.

Kinsella, David. "Conflict in Context: Arms Transfers and Third World Rivalries During the Cold War," *American Journal of Political Science* 38, No. 3 (1994): 557–581.

Kinsella, David, and Herbert K. Tillema. "Arms and Aggression in the Middle East: Overt Military Interventions, 1948–1991," *Journal of Conflict Resolution* 39, No. 2 (1995): 306–329.

Kipper, Judith, and Harold Saunders. *The Middle East in Global Perspective.* Boulder: Westview, 1991.

Kissinger, Henry. *Years of Renewal.* New York: Simon and Schuster, 1999.

Kissinger, Henry. *Diplomacy.* New York: Simon and Schuster, 1994.

Kissinger, Henry. *Years of Upheaval.* London: Weidenfeld and Nicolson, 1982.

Kissinger, Henry. *The White House Years.* London: Weidenfeld and Nicolson, 1979.

Kissinger, Henry. *A World Restored.* Boston: Houghton Mifflin, 1957.

Klein, Menachem. "Between Right and Realization: the PLO Dialectics of the 'Right of Return,'" *Journal of Refugee Studies* 11, No. 1 (March 1998): 1–19.

Kober, Avi. *Military Decision in the Arab-Israeli War.* Tel-Aviv: Ma'arachot/Israeli Defense Ministry, 1995.

Korn, David. *Stalemate: The War of Attrition and Great Power Diplomacy in the Middle East, 1967–70.* Boulder: Westview, 1992.

Kosut, Hal. *Israel and the Arabs: The June 1967 War.* New York: Facts on File, 1968.

Krasner, Stephen. *International Regimes.* Ithaca: Cornell University Press, 1983.

Kriesberg, Louis. *International Conflict Resolution: The US-USSR and Middle East Cases.* New Haven: Yale University Press, 1992.

Krosnick, Jon, and Shibley Telhami. "Public Attitudes Toward Israel: A Study of the Attentive and Issue (U.S.) Publics," *International Studies Quarterly* 39, No. 4 (December 1995): 535–554.

Kugler, Jack, and Douglas Lemke. (eds.) *Parity and War.* Ann Arbor: The University of Michigan Press, 1996.

Kumaraswamy, P. R. "The Gaza-Jericho Agreement: An Asymmetrical Accord," *Strategic Analysis* 17, No. 4 (May 1994): 219–232.

Kuniholm, Bruce R. "Retrospect and Prospects: Forty Years of U.S. Middle East Policy," *Middle East Journal* 41, No. 1 (Winter 1987): 7–25.

Kunz, Diane B. *The Economic Diplomacy of the Suez Crisis.* Chapel Hill: University of North Carolina Press, 1991.

Kurzman, Dan. *Genesis 1948: The First Arab-Israeli War.* New York: World Publishing Co., 1970.

Krasner, Stephen D. (ed.) *International Regimes.* Ithaca: Cornell University Press, 1983.

Kyle, Keith. *Suez.* New York: St. Martin's, 1991.

Lacouture, Jean. *Nasser: A Biography.* New York: Alfred A. Knopf, 1973.

Lake, David A., and Donald Rothchild. "Containing Fear: The Origins and Management of Ethnic Conflict," *International Security* 21, No. 2 (Fall 1996): 41–75.

Lall, Arthur. *The United Nations and the Middle East Crisis, 1967.* 2nd ed. New York: Columbia University Press, 1970.

Landau, Emily B. *Israel's Nuclear Image: Arab Perceptions of Israel's Nuclear Posture.* Tel-Aviv: Jaffe Center for Strategic Studies, 1994.

Lanir, Joseph. "A Confederative System as a Transitional and Permanent Solution to the Arab-Israeli Conflict," *International Problems, Society and Politics.* 28, Nos. 1–2 (1989): 28–37.

Lapid, Yosef, and Friedrich Kratochwil (eds.) *The Return of Culture and Identity in International Relations Theory.* Boulder: Lynne Rienner, 1996.

Lapidoth, Ruth. "Some Reflections on the Taba Award," *German Yearbook of International Law* 35 (1992): 224–248.

Lapidoth, Ruth. *The Red Sea and the Gulf of Aden.* The Hague: Martinus Nijhoff, 1982.

Lapidoth, Ruth, and Moshe Hirsch. *The Arab-Israel Conflict and its Resolution: Selected Documents.* Boston: M. Nijhoff, 1992.

Laqueur, Walter Z. *Confrontation: The Middle East and World Politics.* London: Wildwood House, 1974.

Laqueur, Walter Z. *The Road to Jerusalem.* New York: Macmillan, 1968.

Laqueur, Walter Z. *The Road to War, 1967: The Origins of the Arab-Israeli Conflict.* London: Weidenfeld and Nicolson, 1968.

Laqueur, Walter Z. *The Soviet Union and the Middle East.* New York: Fredrick A Preager Publishers, 1959.

Laqueur, Walter Z, and Barry Rubin. (eds.) *The Israel-Arab Reader.* New York: Penguin Books, 1991.

Lauterpacht, Elihu. "The Taba Case: Some Recollections and Reflections," *Israel Law Review* 23, No. 4 (Autumn 1989): 443–468.

Lauterpacht, Elihu. *The Suez Canal Settlement.* London: Stevens, 1960.

Lawson, Fred H. "Can U.S. Economic Assistance Alter Syria's Posture toward Israel?" *Middle East Policy* 4, No. 4 (October 1996): 102–109.

Lebow, Richard N. "Interdisciplinary Research and the Future of Peace and Security Studies," *Political Psychology* 9, No. 3 (1988): 507–525.

Lebow, Richard N. *Between Peace and War: The Nature of International Crisis.* Baltimore: Johns Hopkins University Press, 1981.

Lederman, Jim. "Economics of the Arab-Israeli Peace Process," *Orbis* 39, No. 4 (Fall 1995): 549–566.

Lederman, Jim. "Dateline West Bank: Interpreting the Intifada," *Foreign Policy* 72, (Fall 1988): 230–246.

Lefebvre, Jeffrey A. "Historical Analogies and the Israeli–Palestinian Peace Process: Munich, Camp David, and Algeria," *Middle East Policy* 3, No.1 (1994): 84–101.

Legro, Jeffrey W. "Which Norms Matter? Revisiting the "Failure" of Internationalism," *International Organization* 51, No. 1 (Winter 1997): 31–63.

Leiss, Amelia C., and Lincoln P. Bloomfield. *The Control of Local Conflict. A Design on Arms Control and Limited War in the Developing Areas,* 4 Vols. Cambridge: Center for

International Studies, Massachusetts Institute of Technology, 1967.

Lemke, Douglas, and William Reed. "Power is not Satisfaction," *Journal of Conflict Resolution* 42, No. 4 (August 1998): 511–516.

Lenczowski, George. *American Presidents and the Middle East*. Durham: Duke University Press, 1990.

Lenczowski, George. *The Middle East in World Affairs*, 3rd ed. Ithaca: Cornell University Press, 1962.

Leng, Russell J. "When Will They Ever Learn? Coercive Bargaining in Recurrent Crises," *Journal of Conflict Resolution* 27, No. 3 (1983): 379–419.

Leng, Russell J., and Stephen G. Walker. "Comparing Two Studies of Crisis Bargaining: Confrontation, Coercion, and Reciprocity," *Journal of Conflict Resolution* 26, No. 4 (1982): 571–591.

Leng, Russell J., and Hugh G. Wheeler. "Influence Strategies, Success, and War," *Journal of Conflict Resolution* 23, No. 4 (1979): 655–684.

Lesch, Ann. *Transition to Palestinian Self-Government*. Bloomington: Indiana University Press, 1992.

Lesch, Ann. "Prelude to the Uprising in the Gaza Strip," *Journal of Palestine Studies* 20, No. 1 (1990): 1–23.

Lesch, Ann. *Arab Politics in Palestine, 1917–1939*. Ithaca: Cornel University Press, 1979.

Lesch, Ann, and Mark A. Tessler. *Israel, Egypt, and the Palestinians: From Camp David to Intifada*. Bloomington: Indiana University Press, 1989.

LeVine, Victor T. "The African-Israeli Connection 40 Years Later," *Middle East Review* 21, No. 1 (1988): 12-17.

Levitte, Ariel. *Offense and Defense in Israeli Military Doctrine*. Jaffe Center for Strategic Studies Study No. 12. Boulder: Westview, 1989.

Levitte, Ariel, and Emily Landau. *Israel's Nuclear Image: Arab Perceptions of Israel's Nuclear Posture*. Tel-Aviv: Jaffe Center for Strategic Studies, 1994.

Levran, Aharon. "The Military Dangers of a Palestinian State," *Global Affairs* 4, No. 4 (Fall 1989): 133–150.

Levy, Jack S. "Declining Power and the Preventive Motivation for War," *World Politics* 40, No. 1 (October, 1987): 82–107.

Levy, Jack S. "The Polarity of the System and International Stability: An Empirical Analysis," In (ed.) Alan Ned Sabrosky. *Polarity and War*, Boulder: Westview, 1985.

Levy, Yagil. "After Rabin and Peres: the Personal Dimension of Israel's Turn to Peace," *Security Dialogue* 28, No. 4 (December 1997): 465–478.

Lewis, Bernard. "The Other Middle East Problems," *Middle Eastern Lectures* 1 (1995): 45–58.

Lewis, Bernard. "Rethinking the Middle East," *Foreign Affairs* 71, No. 1 (Fall 1992): 99–119.

Licklider, Roy. "The Consequences of Negotiated Settlements in Civil Wars, 1945–1993," *American Political Science Review* 89, No.3 (September 1995): 681–690.

Licklider, Roy. (ed.). *Stopping the Killing: How Civil Wars End*. New York: New York University Press, 1993.

Lipson, Charles. "American Support for Israel: History, Sources, Limits," *Israel Affairs* 2,

Nos. 3–4 (Spring–Summer 1996): 128–146.

Lipson, Charles. "Are Security Regimes Possible? Historical Cases and Modern Issues," In *Regional Security Regimes,* ed. Efraim Inbar. Albany: State University of New York Press, 1995.

Liska, George. *States in Evolution: Changing Societies and Traditional Systems in World Politics.* Baltimore: Johns Hopkins University Press, 1973.

Liska, George. *War and Order.* Baltimore: Johns Hopkins University Press, 1970.

Liska, George. *International Equilibrium.* Cambridge: Harvard University Press,1957.

Lloyd, Selwyn. *Suez 1956: A Personal Account.* New York: Mayflower Books, 1978.

Longrigg, Stephen H. *Syria and Lebanon Under French Mandate.* London: Oxford University Press, 1958.

Longrigg, Stephen H. *Iraq: 1900 to 1950: A Political, Social, and Economic History.* Beirut: Librairie du Liban, 1953.

Looney, Robert E. "The Economics of Middle East Military Expenditures: Implications for Arms Reduction in the Region," *Bulletin of Peace Proposals* 22, No. 4 (December 1991): 407–417.

Lorch, Netanel. *History of the War of Independence.* Tel-Aviv: Massada, 1966.

Louis, W. Roger. *The British Empire in the Middle East 1945–51: Arab Nationalism, the United States, and Postwar Imperialism.* Oxford: Clarendon Press, 1984.

Louis, W. Roger, and Roger Owen. (eds.) *Suez 1956: The Crisis and Its Consequences.* Oxford: Clarendon Press, 1989.

Louis, W. Roger, and Robert W. Stookey. (eds.) *The End of the Palestine Mandate.* London: I. B. Tauris, 1986.

Love, Kennett. *Suez—The Twice-Fought War: A History.* New York: McGraw-Hill, 1969.

Lowi, Miriam R. "Bridging the Divide: Transboundary Resource Disputes and the Case of West Bank Water," *International Security* 18, No. 1 (Summer 1993): 113–138.

Lucas, W. Scott. *Divided We Stand: Britain, The United States, and the Suez Crisis.* London: Hodder and Stoughton, 1991.

Lukacs, Yehuda. *The Israeli-Palestinian Conflict: A Documentary Record.* Cambridge: Cambridge University Press, 1992.

Lukacs, Yehuda. (ed.) *Documents on the Israel-Palestine Conflict, 1967–1983.* Cambridge: Cambridge University Press, 1984.

Lukacs, Yehuda, and Abdullah M. Battah. (eds.) *The Arab-Israeli Conflict: Two Decades of Change.* Boulder: Westview, 1998.

Lupsha, Peter A., and John Fullilove. "Beyond State Terror: The 'Grapes of Wrath,'" *Low Intensity Conflict and Law Enforcement* 5, No.3 (Winter 1996): 301–333.

Lustick, Ian S. "The Oslo Agreement as an Obstacle to Peace," *Journal of Palestine Studies* 27, No.1 (1997): 61–66.

Lustick, Ian S. "Writing the Intifada," *World Politics* 45, No. 4 (1993): 560–594.

Luttwak, Edward N. "Strategic Aspects of U.S-Israeli Relations," *Israel Affairs* 2, Nos. 3–4 (Spring-Summer 1996): 198–211.

MacDonald, Robert W. *The League of Arab States: A Study in the Dynamics of Regional Organization.* Princeton: Princeton University Press, 1965.

MacDowell, D. *Lebanon: A Conflict of Minorities.* London: Minority Rights Group, 1986.

Mackinlay, J. *The Peacemakers: An Assessment of Peacemaking Operations at the Arab-Israel Interface*. London: Unwin Hyman, 1989.

Macmillan, Harold. *At the End of the Day 1961–1963*. New York: Harper and Row, 1973.

Macmillan, Harold. *Pointing the Way 1959–1961*. New York: Harper and Row, 1972.

Macmillan, Harold. *Riding the Storm 1956–1959*. New York: Harper and Row, 1971.

Maddy-Weizman, Bruce. *The Crystallisation of the Arab State System*. Syracuse: Syracuse University Press, 1993.

Maimon, David. (Heb.) *The Terrorism That Was Beaten: The Suppression of the Terrorism in the Gaza Strip, 1971–1972*. Jerusalem: Steimatzky, 1993.

Makovsky, David. *Making Peace with the PLO*. Boulder: Westview, 1996.

Maksoud, Clovis. "From June 1967 to June 1997: Learning from Our Mistakes," *Arab Studies Quarterly* 19, No. 3 (Summer 1997): 99–112.

Maksoud, Clovis. "Peace Process (Israel-PLO) or Puppet Show?" *Foreign Policy* 100 (Fall 1995): 117–124.

Manam, Muhamad. "The Arab Deterrence and the Shattering of Israeli Strategy." In *The Arab Lessons from the October War,* ed. Emanuel Sivan. Tel-Aviv: Am Oved, 1974.

Mandelbaum, Michael. *The Nuclear Revolution*. Cambridge: Cambridge University Press, 1981.

Mandell, Brian S. "Getting to Peacemaking in Principal Rivalries—Anticipating an Israel-Syria Peace Treaty," *Journal of Conflict Resolution* 40, No. 2 (June 1996): 238–271.

Mandell, Brian S. "Rethinking the Mediator's Calculus: Challenges for American Peacemaking in the Arab-Israeli Conflict," *International Journal* 45, No. 3 (Summer 1990): 568–602.

Mandell, Brian S. "Anatomy of a Confidence Building Regime: Egyptian-Israeli Security Co-operation, 1973–1979," *International Journal* 45, No. 2 (1990): 202–223.

Mandel, Neville J. *The Arabs and Zionism Before World War I*. Berkeley: University of California Press, 1976.

Mansbach, Richard W. "Neo-This and Neo-That: Or, "Play It Sam" (Again and Again)," *Mershon International Studies Review* 40, No. 1 (1996): 90–95.

Mansbach, Richard W., and John Vasquez. *In Search of Theory: A New Paradigm for Global Politics*. New York: Columbia University Press, 1981.

Mansour, Camille. "The Palestinian-Israeli Peace Negotiations: An Overview and Assessment," *Journal of Palestine Studies* 22, No. 3 (Spring 1993): 5–31.

Ma'oz, Moshe. *Syria and Israel: From War to Peace Making*. Tel-Aviv: Ma'ariv Books, 1996.

Ma'oz, Moshe. "Syrian Israeli Relations and the Middle East Peace Process," *Jerusalem Journal of International Relations* 14, No. 3 (1992): 1–21.

Ma'oz, Moshe. (Heb.) *The Sphinx of Damascus*. Tel-Aviv: Dvir Publishing, 1988.

Maoz, Zeev. *Paths to Conflict: International Dispute Initiation 1816–1976*. Boulder: Westview, 1982.

Maoz, Zeev. "The Decision to Raid Entebbe: Decision Analysis Applied to Crisis Behavior," *Journal of Conflict Resolution* 25, No. 4 (December 1981): 677–707.

Maoz, Zeev, and Allison Astorino. "The Cognitive Structure of PeaceMaking: Egypt and Israel, 1970–1978," *Political Psychology* 13, No.4 (1992): 647–662.

Maoz, Zeev, and Allison Astorino. "Waging War, Waging Peace: Decision Making and Bargaining in the Arab-Israeli Conflict, 1970–1973," *International Studies Quarterly* 36, No. 4 (1992): 373–399.

Maoz, Zeev, and Ben D. Mor. "Enduring Rivalries: The Early Years," *International Political Science Review* 17, No. 2 (1996): 141–160.

Marcus, Jonathan. "Israel—What Now?" *The World Today* 45, No. 2 (February 1989): 22–25.

Marcus, Jonathan. "The Politics of Israel's Security," *International Affairs* 65, No. 2 (Spring 1989): 233–246.

Marcus, Yoel. (Heb.) *Camp David: Gateway to Peace.* Tel-Aviv: Shocken, 1979.

Margold, Peter. *Superpower Intervention in the Middle East.* New York: St. Martin's, 1978.

Marlowe, John. *Anglo-Egyptian Relations, 1800–1953.* London: Cresset, 1954.

Marschall, Christin. "Syria-Iran: A Strategic Alliance, 1979–1991," *Orient* 33, No. 3 (September 1992): 433–446.

Martin, David C., and John Walcott. *Best Laid Plans: The Inside Story of America's War Against Terrorism.* New York: Harper and Row, 1988.

Mattar, Philip. "The PLO and the Gulf Crisis," *Middle East Journal* 48, No. 1 (Winter 1994): 31–46.

Mattar, Philip. *The Mufti of Jerusalem—Al-Haj Amin Husseini and the Palestine National Movement.* New York: Columbia University Press, 1988.

Mattair, Thomas R. "The Breakthrough in Arab-Israeli Diplomacy," *Middle East Policy* 2, No. 3 (1993): 23–29.

Mattair, Thomas R. "The Arab-Israeli Conflict; from Shamir to Rabin to Peace?" *Middle East Policy* 1, No. 3 (1992): 118–154.

Mattair, Thomas R. "The Bush Administration and the Arab-Israeli Conflict," *American-Arab Affairs* 36 (Spring 1991): 52–72.

Mayer, Jochen, and Ralph Rotte. "Arms and Aggression in the Middle East, 1948–1991—A Reappraisal," *Journal of Conflict Resolution* 43, No. 1 (Feb 1999): 45–57.

McClelland, Charles A. "The Beginning, Duration, and Abatement of International Crises: Comparisons in Two Conflict Arenas," In *International Crises: Insights From Behavioral Research,* ed. Charles F. Hermann. New York: Free Press, 1972.

McClelland, Charles A. "Action Structures and Communication in Two International Crises: Quemoy and Berlin," *Background* 7 (1964): 201–215.

McClelland, Charles A. "Applications of General Systems Theory in International Relations," *Main Currents in Modern Thought* 12 (1955): 27–34.

McGeary, Johanna. "The Many Minds of Arafat," *Time* (23 October 2000): 43–54.

McGuinn, Bradford R. "The Perils of Conventional Wisdom: a Reassessment of Syrian Options," *Global Affairs* 8, No. 1 (Winter 1993): 148–160.

Mclellan, David S. *Dean Acheson: The State Department Years.* New York: Dodd, Mead, 1976.

Mearsheimer, John J. "A Realist Reply," *International Security* 20, No. 1 (Summer 1995) 82–93.

Mearsheimer, John J. "The False Promise of International Institutions," *International*

Security 19, No. 3 (1995): 5–49.

Mearsheimer, John J. "Back to the Future: Instability in Europe after the Cold War," *International Security* 15, No. 1 (1990): 5–56.

Mearsheimer, John J. *Conventional Deterrence.* Ithaca: Cornell University Press,1983.

Mehdi, Muhammad. "The Arab Summit," *Middle East Forum* 19, No. 4 (May 1964): 25–28.

Meir, Golda. *My Life.* Jerusalem: Steimatzky, 1975.

Meital, Yoram. *Continuity and Change: Egypt's Struggle for Peace 1967–1977.* Gainsville: University Press of Florida, 1998.

Melman, Yossi, and Dan Raviv. *Behind the Uprising: Israelis, Jordanians and the Palestinians.* New York: Greenwood Press, 1989.

Meo, Leila. "The War in Lebanon," In *Ethnic Conflict in International Relations*, eds. Astri Suhrke and Lela G. Noble. New York: Praeger, 1977.

Merari, Ariel and Shlomi Elad. (Heb.) *Sabotage Abroad: Palestinian Terrorism Abroad, 1968–1986.* Tel-Aviv: Kibbutz Hameuchad, 1986.

Merari, Ariel, Tamar Prat, and David Tal. "The Palestinian Intifada: An Analysis of a Popular Uprising after Seven Months," *Terrorism and Political Violence* 1, No. 2 (April 1989): 177–201.

Michels, Jeffrey. "National Vision and the Negotiation of Narratives: the Oslo Agreement between Israel and the PLO," *Journal of Palestine Studies* 24, No. 1 (Autumn 1994): 28–38.

Migdal, Joel, et al. *Palestinian Politics and Society.* Princeton: Princeton University Press, 1979.

Migdal, Joel. "State and Society in a Society Without a State." In *The Palestinians and the Middle East Conflict*, ed. Gabriel Ben-Dor. Princeton: Princeton University Press, 1979.

Milburn, Thomas W. "The Management of Crisis," In *International Crises: Insights from Behavioral Research*, ed. Charles F. Hermann. New York: Free Press, 1972.

Miller, Aaron David. "The Arab-Israeli Conflict: The Shape of Things to Come," *The Washington Quarterly* 11, No. 4 (Autumn 1988): 159–170.

Miller, Aaron David. "The Arab-Israeli Conflict, 1967–87: A Retrospective," *Middle East Journal* 41, No. 3 (Summer 1987): 348–360.

Miller, Aaron David. *The PLO and the Politics of Survival.* New York, Praeger, 1983.

Miller, Reuben. "The Golan Heights: An Obsolete Security Buffer," *Mediterranean Quarterly* 4, No. 2 (Spring 1993): 121–128.

Milner, Helen. "The Assumption of Anarchy in International Relations," In *Neorealism and Neoliberalism*, ed. David A. Baldwin. New York: Columbia University Press, 1993.

Milstein, Jeffrey. "American and Soviet Influence, Balance of Power and Arab-Israeli Violence," In *Peace, War, Numbers, and International Relations*, ed. Bruce Russett Beverly Hills: Sage Publications, 1972.

Mistry, Dinsha. "Ballistic Missile Proliferation and the MTCR, a Ten Year Review," *Contemporary Security Policy* 18, No. 3 (1997): 59–82.

Monroe, Elizabeth, and A. H. Farrar-Hockley. *The Arab-Israel War, October 1973— Background and Events.* Adelphi Papers 111, The International Institute for Strategic

Studies, London 1974–1975.

Monshipouri, Mahmood. "The PLO Rivalry with Hamas: the Challenge of Peace, Democratization and Islamic Radicalism," *Middle East Policy* 4, No. 3 (March 1996): 84–105.

Mor, Ben D. *Decision and Interaction in Crisis: A Model of International Crisis Behavior.* Westport, Connecticut: Praeger, 1993.

Morgenthau, Hans J. *Politics Among Nations.* 5th edition. New York: Knopf, 1948/1956/1973.

Morris, Benny. *Righteous Victims: A History of the Zionist-Arab Conflict 1881–1999.* New York: Alfred A. Knopf, 1999.

Morris, Benny. "Refabricating 1948," *Journal of Palestine Studies* 27, No. 2 (Winter 1998): 81–95.

Morris, Benny. "Israel's Elections and their Implications," *Journal of Palestine Studies* 26, No. 1 (Autumn 1996): 70–81.

Morris, Benny, *Israel's Border Wars, 1949–1956.* Oxford: Clarendon Press, 1993.

Morris, Benny. *The Birth of the Palestinian Refugee Problem, 1947–1949.* New York: Cambridge University Press, 1988.

Most, Benjamin A., and Harvey Starr. "Conceptualizing War": Consequences for Theory and Research," *Journal of Conflict Resolution* 27, No. 1 (March 1983): 137–159.

Moughrabi, Fouad M. "Public Opinion, Public Policy and the Israeli-Palestinian Conflict," *American-Arab Affairs* 30 (Fall 1989): 40–51.

Muslih, Muhammad. "The Golan, Israel, Syria and Strategic Calculations," *Middle East Journal* 47, No. 4 (Autumn 1993): 611–632.

Muslih, Muhammad. "Towards Coexistence: An Analysis of the Resolutions of the Palestine National Council," *Journal of Palestine Studies* 19, No. 4 (Summer 1990): 3–29.

Muslih, Muhammad. *The Origins of Palestinian Nationalism.* New York: Cambridge University Press, 1988.

Mutawi, S. *Jordan in the 1967 War.* Cambridge: Cambridge University Press, 1987.

Nakdimon, Shlomo. *First Strike: The Exclusive Story of How Israel Foiled Iraq's Attempt to Get the Bomb.* New York: Summit Books, 1987.

Nakhleh, Emile A. "Palestinians and Israelis: Options for Coexistence," *Journal of Palestine Studies* 22, No. 2 (Winter 1993): 5–16.

Nakhleh, Emile A. "The Palestinians and the Future: Peace through Realism," *Journal of Palestine Studies* 18, No. 2 (Winter 1989): 3–15.

Naor, Arye. (Heb.) *Cabinet at War, The Functioning of the Israeli Cabinet During the Lebanon War (1982).* Israel: Lahav, 1986.

Nassar, Jamal R. "The Culture of Resistance: The 1967 War in the Context of the Palestinian Struggle," *Arab Studies Quarterly* 19, No. 3 (Summer 1997): 77–96.

Nassar, Jamal R. *The PLO: From Armed Struggle to the Declaration of Independence.* New York: Praeger, 1991.

Naveh, Hanan and Michael Brecher. "Patterns of International Crises in the Middle East, 1938–1975: Preliminary Findings," in "Studies in Crisis Behavior," *The Jerusalem Journal of International Relations* (Special Issue) 3, Nos. 2–3 (1978): 277–315.

Neff, Donald. "Israel-Syria: Conflict at the Jordan River, 1949–1967," *Journal of Palestine Studies* 23, No. 4 (Summer 1994): 26–40.

Neff, Donald. "The U.S., Iraq, Israel and Iran: Backdrop to War," *Journal of Palestine Studies* 20, No. 4 (Summer 1991): 23–41.

Neff, Donald. *Warriors for Jerusalem: The Six Days That Changed the Middle East.* New York: Linden Press, 1984.

Newman, David. "Civilian and Military Presence as Strategies of Territorial Control: The Arab-Israel Conflict," *Political Geography Quarterly* 8, No. 3 (July 1989): 215–227.

Newman, David. *The Impact of Gush Emunim: Politics and Settlement in the West Bank.* London: Croom Helm, 1985.

Nimrod, Yoram. "Conflict over the Jordan—Last Stage," *New Outlook* 8, No. 6 (September 1965): 5–18.

Nimrod, Yoram. "The Jordan's Angry Waters," *New Outlook* 8, No. 5 (July–August 1965): 19–33.

Nimrod, Yoram. "The Unquiet Waters," *New Outlook* 8, No. 4 (June 1965): 38–51.

Nisan, Mordechai. "The Camp David Legacy," *Global Affairs* 5, No. 1 (Winter 1990): 96–115.

Nixon, Richard M. *The Memoirs of Richard Nixon.* New York: Grosset and Dunlop, 1978.

North, Robert C. "Research Pluralism and the International Elephant," *International Studies Quarterly* 11, No. 4 (1967): 394–416.

Nutting, Anthony. *No End of a Lesson: The Story of Suez.* London: Constable, 1967.

Nutting, Anthony. *I Saw for Myself: The Aftermath of Suez.* London: Hollins Carter, 1958.

Nye, Joseph S. Jr. "Neorealism and Neoliberalism," *World Politics* 40, No. 2 (1988): 235–251.

O'Ballance, Edgar. *The Gulf War.* London: Brassey's, 1988.

O'Ballance, Edgar. *The Kurdish Revolt: 1961–70.* Hamden, CT: Archon, 1973.

O'Ballance, Edgar. *Arab Guerrilla Power, 1967–1972.* London: Archon Books, 1973.

O'Ballance, Edgar. *The War in the Yemen.* Hamden, CT: Archon, 1971.

O'Ballance, Edgar. *The Sinai Campaign, 1956.* New York: Praeger, 1959.

O'Ballance, Edgar. *The Arab-Israeli War, 1948.* New York: Praeger, 1957.

O'Neill, Bard E. *Armed Struggle in Palestine: A Political-Military Analysis.* Boulder: Westview, 1978.

Oppenheimer, Peter. "Arab Oil Power: Permanent Eclipse or Temporary Fading?" *Middle East Review* 20, No. 3 (Spring 1988): 9–16.

Oren, Michael B. "Secret Egypt-Israel Peace Initiatives Prior to the Suez Campaign," *Middle Eastern Studies* 26, No. 3 (July 1990): 351–370.

Oren, Michael B. "Escalation to Suez: The Egyptian-Israeli Border War, 1949–56," *Journal of Contemporary History* 24, No. 2 (April 1989): 347–373.

Organski, Abrimo Fimo Kenneth. *World Politics.* New York: Knopf, 1968.

Organski, Abrimo Fimo Kenneth and Jack Kugler. *The War Ledger.* Chicago: University of Chicago Press, 1980.

Pappe, Ilan. *The Making of the Arab-Israeli Conflict, 1947–51.* London: I. B. Tauris, 1992.

Pappe, Ilan. *Britain and the Arab-Israeli Conflict, 1948–51.* New York: St. Martin's, 1988.

Parker, Richard Bordeaux. *The Politics of Miscalculation in the Middle East.* Bloomington: Indiana University Press, 1993.

Parker, Richard. "The June 1967 War: Some Mysteries Explored," *Middle East Journal* 46. No. 2 (1992): 177–198.

Parsons, Anthony. "Prospects for Peace and Stability in the Middle East," *Conflict Studies* 262 (June 1993): 1–29.

Paul, Thazha Varkey. *Asymmetric Conflicts: War Initiation by Weaker Powers.* Cambridge: Cambridge University Press, 1994.

Pentland, Charles. *International Theory and European Integration.* New York: The Free Press, 1973.

Peres, Shimon. *The New Middle East.* Tel-Aviv: Steimatzky, 1993.

Peres, Shimon. (Heb.) *Entebbe Diary.* Tel-Aviv: Idanim, 1991.

Peres, Shimon. "A Strategy for Peace in the Middle East," *Foreign Affairs* 58, No. 4 (Spring 1980): 887–901.

Peres, Shimon. *David's Sling.* London: Weidenfeld and Nicolson, 1970.

Peretz, Don. "The Intifada and Middle East Peace," *Survival* 32, No. 5 (Sept–Oct. 1990): 387–401.

Peretz, Don. *Intifada: The Palestinian Uprising.* Boulder: Westview, 1989.

Peretz, Don. "Intifadeh: The Palestinian Uprising," *Foreign Affairs* 66, No.5 (Summer 1988): 965–980.

Perlmutter, Amos. "Israel's Dilemma," *Foreign Affairs* 68, No. 5 (Winter 1989–1990): 119–132.

Perlmutter, Amos, Michael Handel, and Uri Bar-Joseph. *Two Minutes Over Baghdad.* London: Corgi, 1982.

Peters, Joan. *From Time Immemorial: The Origins of the Arab-Jewish Conflict over Palestine.* New York: Harper and Row, 1984.

Petran, Tabitha. *Syria.* New York: Praeger, 1972.

Pipes, Daniel. "Understanding Asad," *Middle East Quarterly* 1, No.4 (1994):49–60.

Pipes, Daniel. "Can the Palestinians Make Peace?" *Commentary* 89, No. 4 (April 1990): 26–30.

Pogany, Istvan S. *The Security Council and the Arab-Israeli Conflict.* New York: St. Martin's, 1984.

Polk, William R. *The Elusive Peace: The Middle East in the Twentieth Century.* London: Croom Helm, 1979.

Pollak, Allen, and Anne Sinai (eds.) *The Syrian Arab Republic: A Handbook.* New York: American Academic Association for Peace in the Middle East, 1976.

Porat, Yehoshua, *From Riots To Rebellion, The Palestinian Arab National Movement, 1929–1939.* Tel-Aviv: Am Oved, 1978

Porat, Yehoshua, *The Emergence of the Palestinian Arab National Movement.* Tel-Aviv: Am Oved, 1976.

Powell, Robert. "Absolute and Relative Gains in International Relations." In *Neorealism and Neoliberalism,* ed. David A. Baldwin. New York: Columbia University Press, 1993.

Power, Paul F. "Middle East Nuclear Issues in Global Perspective," *Middle East Policy* 1–2 (1995): 188–209.

Primakov, Yefgeni. "The Fourth Arab-Israeli War," *World Marxist Review* 16, No. 12 (December 1973): 52–60.

Pry, Peter. *Israel's Nuclear Arsenal.* Boulder: Westview, 1984.

Quandt, William B. *Peace Process: American Diplomacy and the Arab-Israeli Conflict since 1967.* Washington, D.C.: Brookings Institution; and Berkeley: University of California Press, 1993.

Quandt, William B. *Cold War Metaphors: Their Impact on the Arab-Israeli Conflict.* Paper presented at a conference sponsored by the Middle East Studies Association, Portland, Oregon, 28–31 October 1992.

Quandt, William B. "Lyndon Johnson and the June 1967 War: What Color Was the Light?" *Middle East Journal* 46, No. 2 (1992):198–229.

Quandt, William B. *The Middle East: Ten Years After Camp David.* Washington, D.C: Brookings Institution, 1988.

Quandt, William B. *Camp David: Peacemaking and Politics.* Washington, D.C.: Brookings Institution, 1986.

Quandt, William B. "Camp David and Peacemaking in the Middle East," *Political Science Quarterly* 101, No. 3 (Spring 1986): 357–377.

Quandt, William B. "Reagan's Lebanon Policy: Trial and Error," *Middle East Journal* 38, No. 2 (Spring 1984): 237–254.

Quandt, William B. "Lebanon, 1958, and Jordan, 1970." In *Force Without War: U.S. Armed Forces as a Political Instrument.* Barry M. Blechman and Stephen S. Kaplan, eds. Washington, D.C.: Brookings Institution, 1978.

Quandt, William B. *Decade of Decisions: American Policy Toward the Arab-Israeli Conflict, 1967–1976.* Berkeley: University of California Press, 1977.

Quandt, William B., Fuad Jabber, and Anne Mosley Lesch. *The Politics of Palestinian Nationalism.* Berkeley: University of California Press, 1973.

Qubain, Fahem Issa. *Crisis in Lebanon.* Washington, D.C.: Middle East Institute, 1961.

Rabie, Mohamed. "The U.S.-PLO Dialogue: The Swedish Connection," *Journal of Palestine Studies* 21, No. 4 (Summer 1992): 54–66.

Rabie, Mohamed. "Arab-Israeli Peace: A New Vision for a Transformed Middle East". *American-Arab Affairs* 36 (Spring 1991): 73–86.

Rabin, Yitzhak. "Israeli Strategic Thinking After Desert Storm." In *Thoughts on the Concept of National Security.* Ramat-Gan: Bar-Ilan Center for Strategic Studies, August 1991.

Rabin, Yitzhak. (Heb.) *The War in Lebanon.* Tel-Aviv: Am Oved, 1983.

Rabin, Yitzhak. *The Rabin Memoirs.* Boston: Little, Brown, 1979.

Rabinovich, Itamar. (Heb.) *The Brink of Peace: Israel and Syria, 1992–96.* Tel-Aviv: Yediot Ahronot Books, 1998.

Rabinovich, Itamar. *The Road Not Taken: Early Arab-Israeli Negotiations.* New York: Oxford University Press, 1991; and Jerusalem: Keter (Heb.).

Rabinovich, Itamar. "Israel, Syria, and Lebanon," *International Journal* 45, No. 3 (Summer 1990): 529–552.

Rabinovich, Itamar. "Controlled Conflict in the Middle East: The Syrian-Israeli Rivalry in Lebanon." In *Conflict Management in the Middle East,* ed. Gabriel Ben-Dor and

David De Witt. Lexington: Lexington Books, 1987.

Rabinovich, Itamar. *The War for Lebanon. 1970–1983.* Ithaca, New York: Cornell University Press, 1983.

Rabinovich, Itamar, and Hanna Zamir. (Heb.) *War and Crisis in Lebanon 1975–81.* Israel: Kibbutz Hameuchad, 1982.

Rafael, Gideon. *Destination Peace: Three Decades of Israeli Foreign Policy.* New York: Stein and Day, 1981.

Rafael, Gideon. "May 1967—A Personal Report," *Ma'ariv,* 21 April 1972.

Ramati, Yohanan. "Israel and Nuclear Deterrence," *Global Affairs* 3, No. 2 (Spring 1988): 175–185.

Rapkin, David P., William R. Thompson, with Jon A. Christopherson. "Bipolarity and Bipolarization in the Cold War Era," *Journal of Conflict Resolution* 23, No. 2 (1979): 261–295.

Reed, Stanley. "Jordan and the Gulf Crisis," *Foreign Affairs* 69, No. 5 (1990): 21–35.

Reeves, Richard. *President Kennedy: Profile of Power.* New York: Simon and Schuster, 1994.

Reguer, Sara. "Controversial Waters: Exploitation of the Jordan River, 1950–1980," *Middle Eastern Studies* 29, No. 1 (January 1993): 53–90.

Reich, Bernard. "The Art of the Impossible: Making Peace in the Middle East," *Mediterranean Quarterly* 7, No. 2 (Spring 1996): 60–86.

Riad, Mahmud. *The Struggle for Peace in the Middle East.* London: Quartet Books, 1981.

Richardson, James L. *Crisis Diplomacy: The Great Powers since the Mid-Nineteenth Century.* Cambridge: Cambridge University Press, 1994.

Richardson, Lewis F. *Statistics of Deadly Quarrels.* Pittsburgh: Boxwood; and Chicago: Quadrangle, 1960.

Richmond, Oliver. "Devious Objectives and the Disputants' View of International Mediation: A Theoretical Framework," *Journal of Peace Research* 35, No. 6 (1998): 707–722.

Robertson, Terence. *Crisis: The Inside Story of the Suez Conspiracy.* London: Hutchinson, 1964.

Robinson, Glenn E. "The Growing Authoritarianism of the Arafat Regime," *Survival* 39, No. 2 (Summer 1997): 42–56.

Robinson, James A. "Crisis: An Appraisal of Concepts and Theories." In *International Crises: Insights from Behavioral Research,* ed. Charles F. Hermann. New York: Free Press, 1972.

Rosecrance, Richard N. "Bipolarity, Multipolarity, and the Future," *Journal of Conflict Resolution* 10, No. 3 (1966): 314–327.

Rosecrance, Richard N. *Action and Reaction in World Politics.* Boston: Little, Brown, 1963.

Rosen, Steven J. *Military Geography and the Military Balance in the Arab-Israel Conflict.* Jerusalem Papers on Peace Problems No. 21. Jerusalem: Leonard Davis Institute for International Relations, Hebrew University of Jerusalem, 1977.

Rosenau, James N. *Turbulence in World Politics: A Theory of Change and Continuity.* Princeton: Princeton University Press, 1990.

Rosenau, James N. "Pre-Theories and Theories of Foreign Policy." In *Approaches to Comparative and International Politics,* ed. R. Barry Farrel. Evanston: Northwestern

University Press, 1966.

Rosenau, James N., and Mary Durfee. *Thinking Theory Thoroughly: Coherent Approaches to an Incoherent World*. Boulder: Westview, 1995.

Ross, Lauren G., and Izzat Sa'id Nader. "Palestinians: Yes to Negotiations, Yes to Violence," *Middle East Quarterly* 2, No.2 (1995): 15–23.

Roth, Stephen J. (ed.) *The Impact of the Six Day War: A Twenty Year Assessment*. Basingstoke (Hants), England: Macmillan, 1988.

Rothenberg, Gunther Erich. *The Anatomy of the Israeli Army: The Israel Defence Force, 1948–78*. New York: Hippocrene, 1979.

Rubin, Barry. "Reshaping the Middle East," *Foreign Affairs* 69, No. 3 (Summer 1990): 131–146.

Rubin, Jeffrey Z. *Dynamics of Third Party Intervention: Kissinger in the Middle East*. New York: Praeger, 1983.

Rubinstein, Alvin Z. *Red Star on the Nile*. Princeton: Princeton University Press, 1977.

Rubinstein, Elyakim, (Heb.) *The Peace Between Israel and Jordan: An Anatomy of a Negotiation*. Tel-Aviv: Jaffe Center for Strategic Studies, 1996.

Rubinstein, Elyakim. "From the Yishuv to the State: Institutions and Parties." In Benyamin Eliav, *The Jewish National Home: From the Balfour Declaration to Independence*. Jerusalem: Keter, 1976.

Ruggie, John Gerard. "The False Premise of Realism," *International Security* 20, No. 1 (Summer 1995): 62–70.

Rummel, Rudolf J. "Some Empirical Findings on Nations and Their Behavior," *World Politics* 16, No. 2 (January 1969): 226–241.

Rummel, Rudolf J. "The Relationship Between National Attributes and Foreign Conflict Behavior," In *Quantitative International Politics: Insights and Evidence*, ed. J. David Singer. New York: Free Press, 1968.

Sachar, Howard M. *A History of Israel: From the Rise of Zionism to Our Time*. New York: Knopf, 1976.

Sadat, Anwar el-. *In Search of Identity: An Autobiography*. New York: Harper and Row, 1977.

Sadat, Anwar el-. *Revolt on the Nile*, trans. Thomas Graham. London: A Wingate, 1957.

Safty, Adel. "The Arab-Israeli Balance of Power after the Storm," *International Relations*, 12, No. 3 (Dec. 1994): 51–74.

Safty, Adel. *From Camp David to the Gulf: Negotiations, Language, Propaganda, and War*. Montreal and New York: Black Rose Books, 1992.

Safty Adel. "Egyptian Negotiations and Decision Making from Sinai to Camp David: The Preponderance of the Psychological Perceptions of the Leader as Decision-maker," *International Studies* 28, No. 4 (October–December 1991): 409–442.

Safty Adel. "Sadat's Negotiations with the United States and Israel: From Sinai to Camp David," *American Journal of Economics and Sociology* 50, No. 3 (July 1991): 285–298.

Safran, Nadav. *Israel: The Embattled Ally*. Cambridge: Belknap Press, 1978.

Safran, Nadav. *From War to War: The Arab-Israeli Confrontation, 1948–1967*. New York: Pegasus, 1969.

Sagan, Scott D. "Nuclear Alerts and Crisis Management," *International Security* 9, No. 4 (1985): 99–139.

Sagan, Scott D. "Lessons of the Yom Kippur Alert," *Foreign Policy* 36 (Fall 1979): 160–177.

Sahliyeh, Emile. *In Search of Leadership: West Bank Politics since 1967,* Washington, D.C.: Brookings Institution, 1968.

Saideman, Stephen M. "Explaining the International Relations of Secessionist Conflicts: Vulnerability Versus Ethnic Ties," *International Organization* 51, No. 4 (Autumn 1997): 721–753.

Salem, Elie. *Violence and Diplomacy in Lebanon: The Troubled Years, 1982–1988.* London: I. B. Tauris, 1995.

Saliba, Samir N. *The Jordan River Dispute.* The Hague: Nijhoff, 1968.

Salibi, Kemal S. *Crossroads to Civil War, Lebanon 1858–1976.* New York: Caravan Books, 1976.

Sandler, Shmuel. "Ethnonationalism and the Foreign Policy of Nation States," *Nationalism and Ethnic Politics* 1, No. 2 (Summer, 1995): 250–269.

Sandler, Shmuel. *The State of Israel, the Land of Israel.* Westport: Greenwood Press, 1993.

Sandler, Shmuel. "The Protracted Arab Israeli Conflict: A Temporal Spatial Analysis," *The Jerusalem Journal of International Relations* 10, No. 4 (1988): 54–78.

Sandler, Shmuel. "Partition versus Sharing in the Arab-Israeli Conflict." In *Governing Peoples and Territories,* ed. Daniel Elazar. Philadelphia: Institute for Study of Human Issues, 1982.

Sandler, Shmuel, and Hillel Frisch. *Israel, the Palestinians and the West Bank.* Lexington, MA: Lexington, 1984.

Sandler, Shmuel, and Hillel Frisch. "Evaluating Shared Rule Arrangements on the West Bank: The Problem of Palestinian Communal Structure," *Middle East Focus* 7, No. 1 (May 1984): 8–13.

Satloff, R. B. *Troubles on the East Bank: Challenges to the Domestic Stability of Jordan.* New York: Praeger, 1986.

Sayegh, Fayez. *The Arab-Israeli Conflict.* New York: Arab Information Center, 1956.

Sayigh, Yezid, *Armed Struggle and the Search for a State: The Palestine National Movement 1949–1993.* Oxford: Clarendon Press, 1997.

Sayigh, Yezid. "Redefining the Basics: Sovereignty and Security of the Palestinian State," *Journal of Palestine Studies* 24, No. 4 (Summer 1995): 5–19.

Sayigh, Yezid. "The Intifada Continues: Legacy, Dynamics, and Challenges," *Third World Quarterly* 11, No. 3 (July 1989): 20–49.

Sayigh, Yezid. "Struggle Within, Struggle Without: The Transformation of PLO Politics since 1982," *International Affairs* 65, No. 2 (Spring 1989): 247–271.

Schelling, Thomas. *Arms and Influence.* New Haven: Yale University Press, 1966.

Schiff, Zeev. "The Green Light," *Foreign Policy* 50 (Spring 1983): 73–85.

Schiff, Zeev, and Eitan Haber (eds.) *Israel, Army and Defense, A Dictionary.* Tel-Aviv: Zmora, Bitan, 1976.

Schiff, Zeev, and Eitan Haber. "The Full Story of the Encirclement that Ended the Yom Kippur War," *Ha'aretz,* Sept. 14, 1975.

Schiff, Zeev, and Ehud Ya'ari. *Intifada.* Jerusalem: Shocken, 1990.

Schiff, Zeev, and Ehud Ya'ari. *Israel's Lebanon War.* London: Unwin, 1986.

Schlesinger, Arthur M., Jr. *Robert Kennedy and His Times.* Boston: Houghton Mifflin, 1978.

Schoenbaum, David. *The United States and the State of Israel.* New York: Oxford University Press, 1993.

Schonfield, Hugh Joseph. *The Suez Canal in Peace and War, 1869–1969.* Coral Gables: University of Miami Press, 1969.

Schonfield, Hugh Joseph. *The Suez Canal in World Affairs.* London: Constellation, 1952.

Schrodt, Philip A., and Deborah J. Gerner. "Empirical Indicators of Crisis Phase in the Middle East, 1979–1995," *Journal of Conflict Resolution* 41, No. 4 (August 1997): 529–552.

Schueftan, Dan. (Heb.) *Attrition: Egypt's Postwar Political Strategy, 1967–70.* Tel-Aviv: Ma'arachot/Israeli Defense Ministry, 1989.

Schueftan, Dan. *A Jordanian Option.* Tel-Aviv: Yad-Tabenkin, 1986.

Schueftan, Dan. "Nasser's 1967 Policy Reconsidered," *Jerusalem Quarterly* 3 (1977): 124–144.

Schwarzer, Gudrun. "The Peaceful Settlement of Interstate Conflict: Saar, Austria and Berlin," *Journal of Peace Research* 35, No. 6 (1998): 743–757.

Schweller, Randall L. *Deadly Imbalances.* New York: Columbia University Press, 1998.

Schweller, Randall L. "New Realist Research on Alliances: Refining, Not Refuting, Walt's Balancing Proposition," *American Political Science Review* 91, No. 4 (1997): 927–930.

Schweller, Randall L. "Bandwagoning for Profit: Bringing the Revisionist State Back." In *International Security* 19, No. 1 (Summer 1994): 72–107.

Scott, Bennett, D. "Measuring Rivalry Termination, 1816–1992," *Journal of Conflict Resolution* 41, No. 2 (April 1997): 227–254.

Seale, Patrick. "Assad's Regional Strategy and the Challenge from Netanyahu," *Journal of Palestine Studies* 26, No. 1 (Fall 1996): 27–41.

Seale, Patrick. "A Game of Masters and Proxies (in Lebanon)," *European Journal of International Affairs* 5, (Summer 1989): 108–120.

Seale, Patrick, *Assad: The Struggle for the Middle East.* London: Taurus, 1988.

Seale, Patrick. *The Struggle for Syria: A Study of Post War Arab Politics, 1945–1958.* 2nd Ed. New Haven: Yale University Press, 1987.

Seelye, Talcott. "Syria and the Peace Process," *Middle East Policy* 2, No. 2 (1993): 104–109.

Sela, Abraham. (Heb.) *Unity Within Conflict in the Inter-Arab System.* Jerusalem: Magnes Press, 1982.

Sela, Abraham. "The PLO, the West Bank, and Gaza Strip," *The Jerusalem Quarterly* 8 (Summer 1978): 66–77.

Shachan, Avigdor. (Heb.) *Operation Thunderball.* Tel-Aviv: Massada, 1993.

Shaked, Haim. "The Nuclearization of the Middle East: The Israeli Raid of Osirak," *The Middle East Contemporary Survey* 5 (1980–1981): 182–213.

Shaked, Haim, and Itamar Rabinovitch. (eds.) *The Middle East and the United States.* New Brunswick: Transaction Books, 1980.

Shalev, Ariyeh. *Cooperation under the Shadow of Conflict, the Israeli-Syrian Armistice Regime 1949–1955.* Boulder: Westview, 1994.

Shalev, Ariyeh. (Heb.) *The Intifada, Causes and Effects.* Tel-Aviv: The Jaffe Center for Strategic Studies, 1990.

Sharon, Ariel. *Warrior: An Autobiography.* New York: Simon and Schuster, 1989.

Sharett, Moshe. *At the Threshold of Statehood*. Tel-Aviv: Am Oved, 1966.

Shavit, Ya'acov. *"Self-Restraint" or "Reaction"*. Ramat Gan: Bar-Ilan University Press, 1983.

Shazli, Saad-al-Din. *The Crossing of Suez: The October War*. London: The Third World Centre for Research and Publishing, 1980.

Sheehan, Edward R.F. *The Arabs, Israelis and Kissinger—A Secret History of American Diplomacy in the Middle East*. New York: Reader's Digest Press, 1976.

Shehadi, Nadim A., and Dona Haffar Mills. (eds.) *Lebanon: A History of Conflict and Consensus*. London: I. B. Tauris, 1988.

Shehadi, Kemal. "Ethnic Self-determination and the Break-up of States," *Adelphi Paper* No. 283 (December 1993).

Shikaki, Khalil. "The Future of the Peace Process and Palestinian Strategies," *Journal of Palestine Studies*. 26, No. 1 (Fall 1996): 82–88.

Shimoni, Yaacov. (Heb.) *The Arab States: Their Contemporary History and Politics*. Tel-Aviv: Am Oved, 1977.

Shlaim, Avi. "The Protocol of Sevres, 1956: Anatomy of a War Plot," *International Affairs* 73, No. 3 (July 1997): 509–530.

Shlaim, Avi. "Prelude to the Accord: Likud, Labor, and the Palestinians," *Journal of Palestine Studies* 23, No. 2 (1994): 3–19.

Shlaim, Avi. *Collusion Across the Jordan. King Abdullah, the Zionist Movement and the Partition of Palestine*. New York: Columbia University Press, 1988.

Shuckburgh, Evelyn. *Descent to Suez: Diaries 1951–56*. London: Weidenfeld and Nicolson, 1986.

Shulman, Marshall. *Stalin's Foreign Policy Reappraised*. Cambridge: Belknap Press, 1963.

Shultz, George P. *Turmoil and Triumph: My Years as Secretary of State*. New York: Scribner's, 1993.

Shuval, Hillel. "Towards Resolving Conflicts over Water between Israel and Its Neighbours: The Israeli-Palestinian Shared Use of the Mountain Aquifer as a Case Study," *Israel Affairs* 2, No.1 (Autumn 1995): 215–238.

Shwadran, Benjamin. *The Middle East, Oil, and the Great Powers*. New York: John Wiley, 1973.

Singer, J. David. *A General Systems Taxonomy for Political Science*. New York: General Learning Press, 1971.

Singer, J. David. "The Level-of-Analysis Problem in International Relations," *World Politics* 14, No. 1 (1961): 77–92.

Singer, J. David, and Melvin Small. *Resort to Arms*, Beverly Hills: Sage, 1982.

Singer, J. David, and Melvin Small. *The Wages of War 1816–1965: A Statistical Handbook*. New York: John Wiley, 1972.

Singer, J. David, and Melvin Small. "Alliance Aggregation and the Onset of War 1815–1945." In J. David Singer, *Quantitative International Politics: Insights and Evidence*. New York: Free Press, 1968.

Singer, J. David, Stuart Bremer, and John Stuckey. "Capability Distribution, Uncertainty and Major Power War, 1820–1965." In *Peace, War, and Numbers*, ed. Bruce M. Russett. Beverly Hills: Sage, 1972.

Singer, Marshall R. *Weak States in a World of Powers.* New York: Free Press, 1972.

Singer, Max, and Aaron Wildawsky. *The Real World Order, Zones of Peace/Zones of Turmoil.* Chatham House,1993.

Sirriyeh, Hussein. "Is a Palestinian State Politically Possible?" *Israel Affairs* 2, No. 1 (1995): 46–58.

Sivan, Emmanuel. (ed) *The Arab Lessons from the October War.* Tel-Aviv: Am Oved, 1974.

Siverson, Randolph, and Paul Diehl. "Arms Races, the Conflict Spiral, and the Onset of War." In *Handbook of War Studies,* ed. Manus Mildarsky. Boston: Unwin Hyman, 1989.

Siverson, Randolph M., and Michael R. Tennefoss. "Interstate Conflicts: 1815–1965," *International Interactions* 9, No. 2 (1982): 147–78.

Small, Melvin, and J. David Singer. *Resort to Arms: International and Civil Wars, 1816–1980.* Beverly Hills: Sage, 1982.

Smith, Alastair. "International Crises and Domestic Politics," *American Political Science Review* 92, No. 3 (September 1998): 623–636.

Smith, Anthony D. "Ethnic Identity and World Order," *Millennium* 12, No. 2 (June 1982): 307–327.

Smith, Anthony D. *The Ethnic Revival.* Cambridge: Cambridge University Press, 1981.

Smith, Ron P. "Quantitative Methods in Peace Research," *Journal of Peace Research* 35, No. 4 (1998): 419–427.

Smooha, Sammy. "Arab-Jewish Relations in Israel in the Peace Era," *Israel Affairs* 1, No. 2 (Winter 1994): 227–244.

Snidal, Duncan. "Relative Gains and Pattern of International Cooperation" In *Neorealism and Neoliberalism,* ed. David A. Baldwin. New York: Columbia University Press, 1993.

Snyder, Glenn H., and Paul Diesing. *Conflict Among Nations: Bargaining, Decision Making, and System Structure in International Crises.* Princeton: Princeton University Press, 1977.

Snyder, Glenn H. "Crisis Bargaining." In *International Crises: Insights from Behavioral Research,* ed. Charles F. Hermann. New York: Free Press, 1972.

Sobel, Lester A. (ed.) *Israel and the Arabs: The October 1973 War.* New York: Facts on File, 1974.

Sofer, Sasson. *Begin: An Anatomy of Leadership.* Oxford: Basil Blackwell, 1988.

Solingen, Etel. "Domestic Aspects of Strategic Postures: The Past and Future in a Middle East Nuclear Regime." In *Middle Eastern Security,* ed. Efraim Inbar and Shmuel Sandler. London: Frank Cass,1995.

Sorokin, Gerald L. "Patrons, Clients, and Allies in the Arab-Israeli Conflict," *Journal of Strategic Studies* 20, No. 1 (March 1997): 46–71.

Sorokin, Gerald L. "Alliance Formation and General Deterrence: A Game-Theoretic Model and the Case of Israel," *Journal of Conflict Resolution* 38, No. 2 (June 1994): 298–235

Specter, Leonard S. *The Undeclared Bomb.* Cambridge: Ballinger,1988.

Spiegel, Steven L. *Conflict Management in the Middle East.* Boulder: Westview, 1992.

Spiegel, Steven L. *The Other Arab-Israeli Conflict: Making America's Middle East Policy from Truman to Reagan.* Chicago: University of Chicago Press, 1985.

Starr, Joyce R. "Water Wars," *Foreign Policy* 82 (Spring 1991): 17–36.

Stein, Arthur. "Coordination and Collaboration: Regimes in an Anarchic World." In *Neorealism and Neoliberalism,* ed. David A. Baldwin. New York: Columbia University Press, 1993.

Stein, Janice Gross. "Deterrence and Learning in an Enduring Rivalry: Egypt and Israel, 1948–1973, *Security Studies* 6, No. 1 (Autumn 1996): 104–152.

Stein, Janice Gross. "The Arab-Israeli War of 1967: Inadvertent War Through Miscalculated Escalation." In *Avoiding War: Problems of Crisis Management,* ed. Alexander L. George. Boulder: Westview, 1991.

Stein, Janice Gross. "Pre-negotiation in the Arab-Israeli Conflict: The Paradoxes of Success and Failure," *International Journal* 44, No. 2 (Spring 1989): 410–441.

Stein, Janice Gross. "Extended Deterrence in the Middle East: American Strategy Reconsidered," *World Politics* 39, No. 3 (April 1987): 326–352.

Stein, Janice Gross. "Detection and Defection: Security 'Regimes' and the Management of International Conflict," *International Journal* 40, No. 4 (1985): 599–627.

Stein, Janice Gross, and Raymond Tanter. *Rational Decision-Making: Israel's Security Choices, 1967.* Columbus: Ohio State University Press, 1980.

Stein, Kenneth W. "Continuity and Change in Egyptian-Israeli Relations, 1973–97," *Israel Affairs* 3, Nos. 3–4 (Spring–Summer 1997): 296–320.

Steinberg, Gerald. "Israeli Security and the Peace Process," *Security Dialogue* 25, No. 1 (March 1994): 51–62.

Steinberg, Gerald. "Israeli Arms Control Policy: Cautious Realism," *Journal of Strategic Studies* 17, No. 2 (June 1994): 1–16.

Steinberg, Gerald. "Israel among the Nations: Foreign Policy and the Peace Process." In *Who Is the Boss in Israel; Israel at the Polls, 1988–1989,* ed. Daniel J. Elazar and Shmuel Sandler. Detroit: Wayne State University Press, 1992.

Stephens, Robert. *Nasser.* New York: Simon and Schuster, 1971.

Stevens, Georgiana. *Jordan River Partition.* Hoover Institution Studies, No. 6. Stanford: Stanford University Press, 1965.

Stevenson, William. *90 Minutes at Entebbe.* New York: Bantam Books, 1976.

Stock, Ernest. *Israel on the Road to Sinai, 1949–1956.* Ithaca: Cornel University Press, 1967.

Stoll, Richard J. "Nice States Finish . . . Pretty Well: Collective Security Behavior in Militarized Interstate Disputes, 1816–1992," *International Interactions* 24, No. 3 (1998): 287–313.

St. John, Robert. *The Boss: The Story of Gamal Abdel Nasser.* New York: McGraw-Hill, 1960.

Suzuki, Motoshi. "Economic Interdependence, Relative Gains, and International Cooperation: The Case of Monetary Policy Coordination," *International Studies Quarterly* 38, No. 3 (1994): 475–498.

Sykes, Christopher. *Crossroads to Israel, 1917–1948.* Bloomington: Indiana University Press, 1973.

Sykes, Christopher. *Crossroads to Palestine: Palestine from Balfour to Bevin.* London. First published by Collins, 1965, Mentor, 1967.

Tamari, Salim. "The Palestinian Movement in Transition: Historical Reversals and the Uprising," *Journal of Palestine Studies* 20, No. 2 (Winter 1992): 57–70.

Tamir, Avraham. "The Use of Military Force: An Israeli Analysis." In *The Middle East in Global Perspective*, ed. Judith Kipper, and Harold H. Saunders. Boulder: Westview, 1991.

Tanter, Raymond. "International Crisis Behavior: An Appraisal of the Literature," *The Jerusalem Journal of International Relations* (Special Issue) 3, Nos. 2–3 (1978): 340–374.

Taylor, Alan. *The Superpowers and the Middle East.* Syracuse: Syracuse University Press, 1991.

Taylor, Alan. *The Arab Balance of Power.* Syracuse: Syracuse University Press, 1982.

Taylor, Rupert. "Political Science Encounters 'Race' and 'Ethnicity,'" *Ethnic and Racial Studies* 19, No. 4 (October 1996): 884–895.

Telhami, Shibley. "The United States and the Middle East Peace: The Case for Arbitrating Israeli-Palestinian Disputes," *Brookings Review* 13, No. 44 (Fall 1995): 32–35.

Telhami, Shibley. "Israeli Foreign Policy after the Gulf War," *Middle East Policy* No. 2 (1992): 85–95.

Tessler, Mark, and Jodi Nachtwey. "Islam and Attitudes toward International Conflict," *Journal of Conflict Resolution* 42, No. 5 (October 1998): 619–636.

Tessler, Mark. *A History of the Israeli-Palestinian Conflict.* Bloomington: Indiana University Press, 1994.

Teveth, Shabtai. (Heb.) *Moshe Dayan: A Biography.* Tel-Aviv: Shocken, 1972.

Thomas, Hugh S. *The Suez Affair.* (rev. ed.) London: Penguin, 1970.

Thucydides. *The Peloponnesian War,* translated by Rex Warner. Baltimore: Penguin, 1972.

Tibawi, Abdul L. *A Modern History of Syria Including Lebanon and Palestine.* London: Macmillan, 1969.

Tibi, Bassam. *Conflict and War in the Middle East, 1967–91: Regional Dynamic and the Superpowers.* New York: St. Martin's, 1993.

Tillman, Seth P. *The United States in the Middle East.* Bloomington: Indiana University Press, 1982.

Tilly, Charles. *From Mobilization to Revolution.* Reading: Addison Wesley, 1978.

Tlass, Mustafa. (ed.) (Heb.) *The Israeli Invasion of Lebanon.* Tel-Aviv: Ma'archot/Israeli Ministry of Defense, 1988.

Torrey, Gordon H. *Syrian Politics and the Military, 1945–1958.* Columbus: Ohio State University Press, 1964.

Touval, Saadia. *The Peace-Brokers: Mediators in the Arab-Israeli Conflict, 1948–79.* Princeton: Princeton University Press, 1982.

Treverton, Gregory. *Crisis Management and the Superpowers in the Middle East.* Farnborough: Gower, 1981.

Tripp, Charles. "Timing Is Everything: The Making of the Israel-PLO Deal," *Israel Affairs* 1 No.1 (Autumn 1994): 164–170.

Triska, Jan F., and David D. Finley. *Soviet Foreign Policy.* New York: Macmillan, 1968.

Troen, Selwyn I., and Moshe Shemesh (eds.) *The Suez Sinai Crisis 1956: Retrospective and Reappraisal.* London: Frank Cass, 1990.

Truman, Harry S. *Years of Trial and Hope.* The Memoirs of Harry Truman, Volume 2. New York: Doubleday, 1956.

Truman, Harry S. *Year of Decisions: 1945.* The Memoirs of Harry Truman, Volume 1. New

York: Doubleday, 1955.

Truman, Margaret. *Harry S. Truman.* New York: W. Morrow, 1973.

Tucker, Robert W. "Origins of the New World Order." In *The Gulf Crisis and its Global Aftermath,* ed. G. Barzilai, A. Klieman, and G. Shidlo. London: Routledge, 1993.

Ulam, Adam B. *Expansion and Coexistence: A History of Soviet Foreign Policy, 1917–73.* New York: Praeger, 1973.

Usher, Graham. "The Politics of Internal Security: The PA's New Intelligence Services," *Journal of Palestine Studies* 25, No.2 (Winter 1996): 21–34.

Van Creveld, Martin L. *Military Lessons of the Yom Kippur War: Historical Perspectives.* Beverly Hills: Sage, 1975.

Vance, Cyrus. *Hard Choices: Critical Years in America's Foreign Policy.* New York: Simon and Schuster, 1983.

Vasquez, John A. "The Realist Paradigm and Degenerative versus Progressive Research Programs: An Appraisal of Neotraditional Research on Walt's Balancing Proposition," *American Political Science Review* 91, No. 4 (1997): 899–911.

Vasquez, John, A. "Distinguishing Rivals That Go to War from Those That Do Not: A Quantitative Comparative Case Study of Two Paths to War," *International Studies Quarterly* 40, No. 4 (1996): 531–558.

Vasquez, John, A. "Why Do Neighbors Fight? Proximity, Interaction, or Territoriality," *Journal of Peace Research* 32, No. 3 (1995): 277–293.

Vasquez, John, A. "Why Global Conflict Resolution Is Possible." In *Beyond Confrontation: Learning Conflict Resolution in the Post Cold War Era,* ed. Vasquez et al. Ann Arbor: University of Michigan Press, 1995.

Vasquez, John, A. *The War Puzzle.* Cambridge: Cambridge University Press, 1993.

Vasquez, John A. "The Steps to War: Towards a Scientific Explanation of Correlates of War Findings," *World Politics* 40, No. 1 (October 1987): 108–145.

Vatikiotis, Panayiotis Jerasimof. *Arab and Regional Politics in the Middle East.* London: Croom Helm, 1984.

Vertzberger, Yaacov Y. I. *The World In Their Minds: Information Processing, Cognition, and Perception in Foreign Policy Decisionmaking.* Stanford: Stanford University Press, 1990.

Vertzberger, Yaacov Y. I. *Misperceptions in Foreign Policymaking: The Sino-Indian Conflict, 1959–1962.* Boulder: Westview, 1984.

Vocke, Harold. *The Lebanese War.* London: Hurst, 1978.

Vogele, William B. "Learning and Nonviolent Struggles in the Intifada," *Peace and Change* 17, No.3 (1992): 312–340.

Wagner, Abraham R. *Crisis Decision-Making: Israel's Experience in 1967 and 1973.* New York: Praeger, 1974.

Wagner, Robert. "Peace, War and the Balance of Power," *American Political Science Review* 88, No. 3 (September 1994): 593–607.

Wagner, Robert. "The Causes of Peace." In *Stopping the Killing,* ed. Roy Licklider. New York: New York University Press, 1993.

Wallace, Michael D. "Polarization: Towards a Scientific Conception." In *Polarity and War,* ed. Alan Ned Sabrosky. Boulder: Westview, 1985.

Wallace, Michael D. "Alliance Polarization, Cross-Cutting, and International War,

1815–1964: A Measurement Procedure and Some Preliminary Evidence," *Journal of Conflict Resolution* 27, No. 4 (1973): 575–604.

Wallensteen, Peter, and Margareta Sollenberg. "Armed Conflict and Regional Conflict Complexes," *Journal of Peace Research* 35, No. 5 (1998): 621–634.

Wallensteen, Peter, and Margareta Sollenberg. "After the Cold War: Emerging Patterns of Armed Conflict 1989–94," *Journal of Peace Research* 32, No. 3 (1995): 345–360.

Walt, Stephen, M. "The Progressive Power of Realism," *American Political Science Review* 91, No. 4 (1997): 931–935.

Walt, Stephen, M. *The Origins of Alliances*. Ithaca: Cornell University Press, 1987.

Walter, Barbara F. "The Critical Barrier to Civil War Settlement," *International Organization* 51, No. 3 (Summer 1997): 335–364.

Waltz, Kenneth N. "Evaluating Theories," *American Political Science Review* 91, No. 4 (1997): 913–917.

Waltz, Kenneth N. *Theory of International Politics*. Reading: Addison-Wesley, 1979.

Waltz, Kenneth N. "International Structure, National Force, and the Balance of World Power," *Journal of International Affairs* 21, No. 2 (1967): 215–231.

Ward, Michael D., and Ulrich Widmaier. "The Domestic-International Conflict Nexus: New Evidence and Old Hypotheses," *International Interactions* 9, No. 1 (1982): 75–101.

Waterbury, John. *The Egypt of Nasser and Sadat: The Political Economy of Two Regimes*. Princeton: Princeton University Press, 1983.

Watt, Donald C. *Documents on the Suez Crisis, 26 July to 6 November 1956*. London: Royal Institute of International Affairs, 1983.

Watt, Donald C. *Britain and the Suez Canal*. London: Oxford University Press, 1957.

Wayman, Frank W. "Bipolarity and War: The Role of Capability Concentration and Alliance Patterns Among Major Powers, 1816–1965," *Journal of Peace Research* 21, No. 1 (1984): 61–78.

Weissbrod, Lily. "Gush Emunim and the Israeli-Palestinian Peace Process: Modern Religious Fundamentalism in Crisis," *Israel Affairs* 3, No. 1 (Autumn 1996): 86–103.

Weissbrod, Lily. "Israeli Identity in Transition," *Israel Affairs* 3, Nos. 3–4 (Spring–Summer 1997): 47–65.

Weissman, Steve, and Herbert Krosney. *The Islamic Bomb: The Nuclear Threat to Israel and the Middle East*. New York: Times Books, 1981.

Weizmann, Chaim. *Trial and Error*. New York: Harper, 1949.

Welch, David. "Crisis Decisionmaking Reconsidered," *Journal of Conflict Resolution* 33, No. 3 (September 1989): 430–445.

Wendt, Alexander. "Constructing International Politics," *International Security* 20, No. 1 (Summer 1995): 71–81.

Wendt, Alexander. "Anarchy Is What States Make of It," *International Organization* 46, No. 2 (Spring 1992): 391–425.

Whetten, Lawrence. *The Canal War: Four-Power Confrontation in the Middle East*. Cambridge: MIT Press, 1974.

Wilkenfeld, Jonathan, and Michael Brecher. *Crises in the Twentieth Century: Vol. 2. Handbook of Foreign Policy Crises*. Oxford: Pergamon Press, 1988.

Wilkenfeld, Jonathan, and Michael Brecher. "International Crises, 1945–1975: The UN Dimension," *International Studies Quarterly* 28, No. 1 (1984): 37–59.

Wilkenfeld, Jonathan, and Michael Brecher. "Superpower Crisis Management Behavior." In *Foreign Policy: US/USSR, Sage International Yearbook of Foreign Policy Studies* 7, ed. Charles W. Kegley, Jr., and Pat J. McGowan. Beverly Hills: Sage, 1982.

Wilson, Keith M. (ed.) *Imperialism and Nationalism in the Middle East: The Anglo-Egyptian Experience, 1882–1982.* London: Mansell, 1983.

Wolfers, Arnold. *Discord and Collaboration.* Baltimore: Johns Hopkins University Press, 1962.

Wolfsfeld, Gadi. "Fair Weather Friends: The Varying Role of the News Media in the Arab-Israeli Peace Process," *Political Communication* 14, No. 1 (Jan–Mar 1997): 29–48.

Wood, David. *Conflict in the Twentieth Century.* Aldelphi Papers No. 48. London: Institute for Strategic Studies, June 1968.

Wright, Quincy. *A Study of War,* 2 Vols. Chicago: University of Chicago Press, 1942; rev. ed., 1965.

Wrightson, Patricia Stein. "Morality, Realism, and Foreign Affairs." In *Roots of Realism,* ed. Benjamin Frankel. London: Frank Cass, 1996.

Ya'ari, Ehud. (Heb.) *Egypt and the Fedayeen 1953–1956.* Givat Haviva: Center for Arab and Afro-Asian Studies, 1975.

Yaniv, Avner. "Non-Conventional Weapons and the Future of Arab-Israeli Deterrence," *Israel Affairs* 2, No.1 (Autumn 1995): 135–149.

Yaniv, Avner. *Deterrence without the Bomb.* Lexington: Lexington Books, 1987.

Yaniv, Avner. *PLO—a Profile.* Haifa: Israel Universities Study Group for Middle Eastern Affairs, 1974.

Yorke, Valerie. *Domestic Politics and Regional Security: Jordan, Syria, and Israel: The End of an Era?* Aldershot: Gower, 1988.

Young, Oran R. *The Politics of Force: Bargaining During International Crises.* Princeton: Princeton University Press, 1968.

Young, Oran R. *The Intermediaries: Third Parties in International Crises.* Princeton: Princeton University Press, 1967.

Zacher, Mark W. *International Conflicts and Collective Security, 1946–77.* New York: Praeger, 1979.

Zak, Moshe. "Israel and Jordan: Strategically Bound," *Israel Affairs* 3, No. 1 (Autumn 1996): 39–60.

Zartman, William I. "Explaining Oslo," *International Negotiation* 2, No. 2 (1997): 195–215.

Zartman, William I. (ed.) *Collapsed States: The Disintegration and Restoration of Legitimate Authority.* Boulder: Lynne Rienner, 1995.

Zartman, William I. "The Unfinished Agenda: Negotiating Internal Conflicts." In *Stopping the Killing,* ed. Roy Licklider. New York. New York University Press, 1993.

Ze'ira, Eli. (Heb.) *The Yom Kippur War.* Tel-Aviv: Idanim, 1993.

Zinnes, Dina A., Robert C. North, and Howard E. Koch, Jr. "Capability, Threat, and the Outbreak of War." In *International Politics and Foreign Policy,* ed. James N. Rosenau. New York: Free Press, 1961.

Zisser, Eyal. "Hizbullah in Lebanon: At the Crossroads," *Terrorism and Political Violence* 8, No. 2 (1996): 90–110.

Zisser, Eyal. "Syria and Israel: From War to Peace," *Orient* 36, No. 3 (September 1995): 487–498

Zisser, Eyal. "Assad of Syria—the Leader and the Image," *Orient* 35, No. 2 (June 1994): 247–260.

Zisser, Eyal. "Assad Inches toward Peace with Israel," *Middle East Quarterly* 1, No. 3 (September 1994): 37–44.

Zunes, Stephen. "The Israeli-Jordanian Agreement: Peace or Pax Americana?" *Middle East Policy* 3, No. 4 (April 1995): 57–68.

Zviagelskaia, Irina. "Steps versus Solutions in the Arab-Israeli Conflict," *Annals of the American Academy of Political and Social Science* 518 (November 1991): 109–117.

INDEX

SUNY SERIES IN GLOBAL POLITICS

James N. Rosenau, Editor

List of Titles

Hierarchy Amidst Anarchy: Transaction Costs and Institutional Choice — Katja Weber

Counter-Hegemony and Foreign Policy: The Dialectics of Marginalized and Global Forces in Jamaica — Randolph B. Persaud

Global Limits: Immanuel Kant, International Relations, and Critique of World Politics — Mark F. N. Franke

Power and Ideas: North-South Politics of Intellectual Property and Antitrust — Susan K. Sell

Money and Power in Europe: The Political Economy of European Monetary Cooperation — Matthias Kaelberer

Agency and Ethics: The Politics of Military Intervention — Anthony F. Lang, Jr.

Life After the Soviet Union: The Newly Independent Republics of the Transcaucasus and Central Asia — Nozar Alaolmolki

Theories of International Cooperation and the Primacy of Anarchy: Explaining U. S. International Monetary Policy-Making After Bretton Woods — Jennifer Sterling-Folker

Information Technologies and Global Politics: The Changing Scope of Power and Governance — James N. Rosenau and J. P. Singh (eds.)

Technology, Democracy, and Development: International Conflict and Cooperation in the Information Age — Juliann Emmons Allison (ed.)

The Arab-Israeli Conflict Transformed: Fifty Years of Interstate and Ethnic Crises — Hemda Ben-Yehuda and Shmuel Sandler

Systems of Violence: The Political Economy of War and Peace in Colombia — Nazih Richani

Debating the Global Financial Architecture — Leslie Elliot Armijo

Political Space: Frontiers of Change and Governance in a Globalizing World — Yale Ferguson and R. J. Barry Jones (eds.)

Crisis Theory and World Order: Heideggerian Reflections — Norman K. Swazo

Political Identity and Social Change: The Remaking of the South African Social Order — Jamie Frueh

Social Construction and the Logic of Money: Financial Predominance and International Economic Leadership — J. Samuel Barkin